Intimate Lies

Also by Robert Westbrook

The Magic Garden of Stanley Sweetheart
Rich Kids
The Left-Handed Policeman
Nostalgia Kills
Lady Left
Journey Behind the Iron Curtain

Intimate Lies

F. Scott Fitzgerald
and Sheilah Graham
Her Son's Story

ROBERT WESTBROOK

 HarperCollins*Publishers*

HarperCollins books may be purchased for educational, business, or sales promotional use. For information, please write: Special Markets Department, HarperCollins Publishers, Inc., 10 East 53rd Street, New York, NY 10022.

FIRST EDITION

Designed by Gloria Adelson/Lulu Graphics

Library of Congress Cataloging-in-Publication Data

Westbrook, Robert.
    Intimate lies : F. Scott Fitzgerald and Sheilah Graham : her son's story / Robert Westbrook.—1st ed.
      p. cm.
    Includes bibliographical references and index.
    ISBN 0-06-018343-8
    1. Fitzgerald, F. Scott (Francis Scott), 1896–1940—Relations with women. 2. Authors, American—20th century,Biography.   3. Graham, Sheilah—Relations with men.   4. Women journalists—United States—Biography.   5. Los Angeles (Calif.)— Biography.   1. Title.
PS3511.I9Z92   1995
813'.52—dc20
[B]   95-19277

95 96 97 98 99 ❖/HC 10 9 8 7 6 5 4 3 2 1

for my wife, Gail,
many miles of love

CONTENTS

Photographs follow page 182.

ACKNOWLEDGMENTS

I HAD A GREAT DEAL OF HELP WITH THE WRITING OF THIS BOOK AND would like to express my gratitude to the following people:

Prof. John Kuehl, an old family friend and Fitzgerald scholar, a constant inspiration who pointed me in the right direction and made suggestions after reading an early draft; my sister, Prof. Wendy Fairey, who offered invaluable advice, support, and criticism after reading the manuscript; and most of all, my wife, Gail Westbrook, who often guided me through the emotional quagmire of the past and patiently went through this book several times with a pencil in search of faulty grammar and fuzzy thinking.

A warm thanks also to Prof. Alan Margolies, Prof. Ruth Prigozy, and Prof. Jackson R. Bryer of the F. Scott Fitzgerald Society; Prof. Nicholas Beck; Prof. Matthew J. Bruccoli; Dr. Alexander Clark, the retired curator of the rare books collection at Princeton; Alice Clark, Margaret Sherry, Charles Green, and Don Skammer, currently at Princeton University Library; Peter Shepherd of Harold Ober Associates; Mike Kaplan; Budd Schulberg; Frances Kroll Ring; Carol Ardman; Tony Buttitta; Gerold Frank; and Henri Requin who put us up in Paris during the 1994 International Hemingway/Fitzgerald Conference. A special thanks to Monica Hannasch who gave us a quiet place to live in southern Italy for three months to do the final editing.

I am greatly indebted to my Tuesday night Writers Group in

Taos, New Mexico, who over the period of a year and a half made many suggestions as they listened to the first draft of this book: Phyllis Hotch, Debbie McCann, Virginia Black, Erik Konnshaug, Patti Davis, and Alan Ferguson.

Inexpressible gratitude to my agent, Ted Chichak, who performed miracle after miracle and without whom this book could never have happened; my editors at HarperCollins, Gladys Justin Carr and Elissa Altman; and to Eleanor Lanahan, Scott's granddaughter, and the Trustees of the F. Scott Fitzgerald Estate for permission to quote from his published and unpublished writings.

PROLOGUE

A HOLLYWOOD ENDING

"... because all I love is imperfect"—Li-Young Lee

THIS IS A FAMILY STORY, one I heard often throughout my child-hood. It left a lasting impression because it had all of the elements of grand opera. There was love and ambition, a tragic author, a beautiful but mysterious young woman, poetry, drink, wild debauch, and untimely death. Like most childhood stories, the adult version turned out to be more complicated than I supposed.

The first time I ever heard the name Scott Fitzgerald, I was five or six years old, sitting in my mother's lap in her downstairs library at our California home. She was very beautiful then, older than she pretended to be, but youth was one of her many illusions. She radiated a kind of breathless vitality and as a child I loved to be physically close to her. The library was her office, generally busy with the sound of ringing telephones and a huge manual typewriter going clickety-clack, tapping out the latest Hollywood gossip.

Everything about my mother's library seemed green to me: green stucco walls, and the drowsy shade of trees outside the window. On the day I remember, my mother and I were cuddled together on a green leather armchair, next to a wall of green bound books—books with titles I could not then decipher, but which I would get to know in a few years' time as *Flappers and Philosophers, Tales of the Jazz Age, The Great Gatsby, The Beautiful and Damned*. Written into these books, often on the title page, were inscriptions in an impulsive and flowing hand:

> To the Beautiful from the almost damned.
> "What struggle to escape - !"
> With love from
> Scott Fitzgerald
> to Sheilah Graham

And:

> For my darling Shielah
> —after *such* a bad time
> from
> Scott

And also:

> For Sheilah
> the Beloved Infidel
> with eternal devotion
> Scott Fitzg -
> 1938

There were more, approximately three hundred volumes— novels, poetry, biographies, history books, and philosophies—all marked at various places either in pen or pencil by the same flowing hand. As often as not, Fitzgerald reversed the *i* and the *e* in my mother's name—"Shielah"—for his spelling was child- ishly bad. In 1959 these volumes, full of their misspelled refer- ences to such figures as "Hemmingway" and "Bethoven," would be given to the Princeton University Library, but when I was a child they were simply on the shelves in the green library. Occasionally my older sister took them down to add her own writings and doodles, to the consternation of later scholars. As I snuggled in my mother's lap, she pulled out her thick *Columbia Encyclopedia* from a nearby shelf, thumbed through the dense pages to the letter *F*, and stopped at Fitzgerald, Francis Scott Key.

She read to me the paragraphs about this man she had once known, more than I could then understand. I learned it was an honor to have your name in such a large encyclopedia, and that Fitzgerald, Francis Scott Key, was a very famous person, although when my mother knew him, he was not famous at all. Scott died nearly penniless, she told me, his books out of print, out of fashion, a forgotten man. And now people called him a Great Writer. His books were taught in universities, and his estate brought in millions every year.

Wouldn't Scott be pleased? All the money and acclaim he had so desperately wished for in life had finally arrived after death. It was bitter and wonderful, all at the same time. I was to grow up on this tale, never certain if this were a happy ending or a bad joke; a success story or an American tragedy. Over the years my mother told me more, that I was named Robert after the humorist Robert Benchley, who had first brought her and Scott together in his Hollywood bungalow on Bastille Day, July 14, 1937. She said that Robert Benchley was to have been my godfather, but he died shortly before my birth of a peculiar nose bleed that would not stop. Sudden death seemed connected with my birth. I was born on Christmas Eve 1945; five years earlier, a few days before Christmas, Scott Fitzgerald stood up unexpectedly from a green leather armchair in my mother's apartment, clutched briefly at a marble mantelpiece, and fell down dead upon her floor.

When I grew older, I often heard my mother say that the best and the worst things in her life had always happened to her around Christmas. My birth, she assured me, was of the best; Scott's death, the worst. We encompassed together her Christmas joy and wintry grief. In 1941 she married an Englishman named Trevor Westbrook because, as she put it, she could not bear to face alone the first anniversary of Scott Fitzgerald's death. It was not a foundation for a lasting marriage, and Trevor divorced my mother when I was only a few months old. In the absence (except for the briefest periods) of any other man around the house, the ghost of my mother's dead lover filled the void, an all-purpose father figure. It wasn't so much his eventual success which came to influence me—it was more the cautionary tale of his great suffering and worldly failure. In an improbable way that has often been difficult to describe, I grew up in the light, and very deep shadows, of F. Scott Fitzgerald. It is from these old things—old stories, lingering phantoms of pain and joy—that this book was born.

In the late fifties, my mother began what may best be described as a controlled experiment in truth—her autobiography, a task, constantly revised, which would occupy her on and off for the rest of her life. In the second half of her life, she became transfixed by the events of the first half, her years of struggle and deceit.

The first attempt to tell her story was the 1958 bestseller, *Beloved Infidel*, written in collaboration with Gerold Frank, a popular biographer of the time. I was thirteen years old when the book came out, left alone with my mother in Beverly Hills when my older sister Wendy was sent east to boarding school. My mother and I were as close as we were ever to be, constant companions. Each week we eagerly awaited *Time* magazine to see at what exact spot *Beloved Infidel* hovered on their bestseller list. The book climbed gradually to number five, lingered in this middle range for a number of weeks, and then began its gradual slide into oblivion.

Beloved Infidel was a commercial success for a very good reason: It told an appealing story, and created, as good books must do, a consistent and tangible world which the reader might enter—a sentimental world, in this case, which skillfully removed any awkward detours and ambiguities from the tale. Gerold Frank was a brilliant engineer of other people's lives; he had coauthored a number of best-selling autobiographies of the moment, books with titles like *I'll Cry Tomorrow* and *Too Much Too Soon*, and he knew almost too well how to transform the flimsy stuff of human experience into page-turning readability.

My mother was of two minds about her autobiography. She enjoyed having a bestseller and remained grateful for Gerold Frank's extremely professional help; she had little faith at the time in her own ability to tell her story. Nevertheless, the weepy tone of the book bothered her and she was the first to admit, privately to close friends, that *Beloved Infidel* was only a pale shadow of what had really happened in her life. There was a certain irony in this, for the story was about a young woman with a secret past who had a penchant for telling enormous fibs to everyone about her. The reader of *Beloved Infidel*, of course, was led to believe that to them, at least, the privileged few, she was admitting the truth, a confession of everything. This candor was artfully employed to mask the book's many omissions, inaccuracies, and in certain important places, deliberate lies. Chapter One, in fact, began with a lie which was to cause my mother a great deal of trouble: She pretended to be a woeful English orphan with no family, no one to call her own, and this claim was used as a cornerstone of the story to justify and explain much of her subsequent behavior. To further this fiction, a character was created from thin air, Aunt Mary, who is first seen in the opening pages of *Beloved Infidel* accompanying the six-year-old Sheilah on the top of a double-decker bus to an orphanage in the East End of London. Aunt Mary with her wonderfully genteel name had done service before in my mother's fabricated past, helping to explain away a number of events she very much wished to leave in the dark, as well as a large family of whom she was bitterly ashamed. Unfortunately, Sheilah's real family refused to be consigned to oblivion so easily; one neglected brother came forward to the British press to denounce my mother's book as a fraud. In fact, despite its confessional tone, *Beloved Infidel* managed to conceal nearly as much information as it revealed. My mother, quite simply, was not yet willing to tell her full and (she believed) shocking story.

The book suffered in a more generic way from the era in which it was written, the 1950s, a decade which favored sentimentality over sex and sanitized popular love stories behind an impenetrable curtain of petticoats and euphemisms. In 1958 my mother felt she was risking her reputation simply to admit publicly to an affair with a married man; beyond this she was not prepared to go. Even the frankly left-wing politics of Hollywood in the late thirties were carefully bled from the story, for at the time her autobiography was written the House Un-American Activities Committee was still in session and liberal politics were considered even more taboo than sex. Unfortunately for the readers of *Beloved Infidel*, sex and left-wing ideology was a great deal of what Hollywood in the thirties was all about.

In all, the fifties were the worst possible vantage point from which to look back twenty years to the 1930s, a more ironic, cosmopolitan, and fast-moving time. With the very background of the story surgically removed, the characters in my mother's autobiography bore only passing resemblance to what they had been in life: Scott Fitzgerald was presented as a kind of wounded romantic genius, and Sheilah was his ever-loving nurse, who may have told some fibs in the beginning, but redeemed herself through selfless love. To glue everything together, Gerold Frank added a sense of violins trembling near the surface of every sentence. He began, in fact, by skillfully exploiting her children—me and my sister, that is—portraying Sheilah as a loving and patriotic mother in an imaginary letter from Sheilah in Hollywood to Scott in the pink clouds:

Dear Scott,

. . . Only the other day Wendy, coming upon your name, asked, "Would he have liked me, Mother?" I tried to explain to her why we were never married. I said, "I could not marry him because his wife was very ill in a sanitarium and there was a daughter he loved very much, and he could not abandon them." I told her of your relationship to Francis Scott Key and once when she sang "The Star-Spangled Banner" she turned to me and said, quite proudly, "I'm kind of related to F. Scott Fitzgerald, aren't I?" And then Robbie asked, "I'm related to him too, aren't I, Mom?" I said, "Yes, you are, both of you—in a kind of a way." I told them that you would have liked them. Very much.

As the "Robbie" of this entirely fictitious exchange, I was enormously embarrassed and appeared somewhat furtively at school for a number of months. My mother had the good sense to be embarrassed as well and she came to regard her autobiography with distaste. The book had gotten away from her somehow.

Then came a further misfortune: a movie, in 1959—a glossy Technicolor 20th Century-Fox production of Beloved Infidel in which Gerold Frank's implied violins became manifest, soaring to tearful heights behind every scene. A stiff and patriarchal Gregory Peck was absurdly miscast as Scott Fitzgerald. Peck had recently completed Moby Dick and seemed unwilling to change roles; his Fitzgerald bore an uncanny resemblance to Captain Ahab seeking the White Whale in all the wrong places. Deborah Kerr was more subtly miscast as Sheilah Graham. My mother often demurred that Miss Kerr was "too lady like" for the role. Her own choice for the part, among actresses then available, was her friend Marilyn Monroe—a woman more like herself, more vulnerable, insecure, and sexual than the too spinsterish and aristocratic Deborah Kerr.

For my mother, the movie of *Beloved Infidel* served as a wake-up call. She became determined to tell her story in a more accurate manner and without quite the throb of violins. It was not destined to be an easy task for a woman who had created her life from daydreams. In the end, her story—as much as she was willing to reveal in public—came out coyly over the long years. *Beloved Infidel* was only a first elegant glove removed in what would be a long striptease. The books, the revisions which followed, included *The Rest of the Story* (1964), *College of One* (1966), *The Garden of Allah* (1970), *A State of Heat* (1972), *The Real F. Scott Fitzgerald* (1976), *The Late Lily Shiel* (1978), and *My Hollywood* (1984). Unfortunately, from a publisher's point of view she had told her life story already in *Beloved Infidel*, and she could not very well start from scratch and tell it once again. As a result the ensuing books came out as disjointed footnotes which one needed constantly to compare against the original, *Beloved Infidel*, to put the story into a whole. It was a task most readers declined to perform. Unlike *Beloved Infidel*, none of the later books received much of an audience, and they quickly drifted out of print.

And so at last, she enlisted my help, suggesting that after her death I take on the family tradition of retelling her tale. The idea was repeated during long-distance phone calls and in person when I saw her—now a small and eccentric old lady with faded blue-green eyes, white hair, but still an optimistic smile. The older she grew, the more my mother became transfixed by her own stories of the past. She was convinced that none of her books had ever quite gotten it right. It was self-evident to her that I should inherit the seemingly endless task of appending her autobiography: I was a writer, I was her son, I had grown up on her anecdotes, and best of all, I could throw *Beloved Infidel* out the window and begin anew.

I was not enthusiastic. As a child I had found my mother's adventures fascinating; she was a woman with physical presence and a lovely speaking voice, who told her stories, in fact, far better around a dinner table than she would ever write them down. But as an adult these same tales had worn thin for me. Most of all I had my own life to live, my own stories to tell; I was hungrily seeking answers to my life, not hers. She was my mother, and I loved her, but I didn't want any part of her dangling autobiography. Or so I thought when she was alive.

I was far from home, on a Greek island, when my mother died in 1988 at the age of eighty-four. I learned the details from my sister on a bad telephone connection, and the next day I read an obituary in an international edition of *Time* magazine. The short paragraph seemed unreal to me and strangely distant. Sheilah Graham, Hollywood gossip columnist, dead at eighty-four— "writer of catty prose," they said. It wasn't so much an obituary as a bad review. I had to smile, for my mother had had an ongoing feud with *Time* for decades; they had blasted *Beloved Infidel* back in 1958 and continued to take a swipe at her from time to time, finding her an easy target. Sometimes my mother wrote nasty letters in return which she spent hours composing and reading to me on the telephone, but these letters as far as I know were never published. For Sheilah, *Time* remained a symbol of something from which she seemed forever excluded, the voice of the establishment, the thumbs-down of those who had gone to the right schools and knew, almost in some mystical way, that she was not their kind. These same insiders had enjoyed taking potshots at Scott Fitzgerald too when he was alive, though not of course after he won his posthumous glory.

When I returned to America, I saw that the *New York Times* had done my mother more justice in a longer obituary which remembered her association with Scott Fitzgerald. But still she was not there. Sheilah Graham, Hollywood gossip columnist, writer of catty prose, beloved of Scott Fitzgerald . . . none of these things began to capture the warm, difficult, vulnerable, and entirely alive person I knew.

Seven years have now gone by since my mother's death, and I

have spent much of that time trying to make sense of her life—to understand what really happened, and why. I knew almost from the moment I stood on a dusty Greek street with her obituary in hand that I would write about her. Among other things, she was the best story I knew, and I had learned long ago from Scott Fitzgerald that a writer never turns his back on a good story, not ever. There seemed to me a painfulness about her tale that lingered and sought a resolution. And so I set out with high hopes to play detective with the past.

I was lucky to find a long written record left behind. I began with my mother's battered copy of *Beloved Infidel* which I discovered among her belongings, a book whose spine was bent and whose pages were coming unglued. I had not read *Beloved Infidel* since I was thirteen and in my mother's copy I immediately came upon unexpected gold: At some time in her life she had gone through and annotated her story, writing scrawled notes in the margins as to what was true, and what was not. In some cases she provided the dialogue she and Scott had spoken to one another; in other places there were only cryptic comments, such as "the treaty we had" concerning Zelda, though the exact nature of this treaty between Scott and Sheilah is nowhere explained. "Dreadful How could I forgive him" is written on the top of page 300—a good question since at this moment in the tale Fitzgerald had just kicked his nurse in the shins and was busy rampaging through the kitchen drawers trying to find his gun to kill her.

She corrected small matters. One scene in *Beloved Infidel* showed Sheilah driving Scott to the beach, but she wrote in the margin that this was wrong: When he was sober, Scott would never let her drive, believing speeds above twenty miles per hour a hideous folly and that only his own white-knuckled efforts at the wheel might guide them safely along the perils of California roads. Some of my mother's notes revealed a lingering bitterness which was never expressed in any of her published writings: "He would never have done this to Zelda her family was better than his. He was a desperate snob," she wrote without the aid of much punctuation on page 299. Other comments were painful laments: "when he died I was shattered I had nothing whatever he had grafted on me he took with him," she set down in stream-of-consciousness on page 195.

I went on to reread each of her books in which over the years she had detailed and revised her autobiography. I soon discovered that in different books she often described the same events in contradictory ways. I drew up elaborate charts and chronologies hoping to bring together the many loose ends, keeping in mind that my mother was not always to be trusted as the narrator of her tale. Whenever possible, I checked her version of the facts against other sources.

Before long, I turned to the other main participant of her story—Scott Fitzgerald. Here again I was lucky to have a paper trail to guide me. All of Fitzgerald's last writings are autobiographical, some obliquely so, but more often to the dismay of close friends he lifted events directly from real life, down to the very words which were spoken. Such was the case with my mother; he found her a fascinating subject, he jotted down in his notebook her more astonishing remarks, and he used her as a kind of natural resource from which he might draw literary material: She became the model for several short stories as well as the heroine of his unfinished novel, *The Last Tycoon*. Not only did Scott write of significant moments in their relationship, but he explored his own emotional response—what he really thought about Sheilah Graham, his ambiguous feelings as well as his love.

From Scott and Sheilah's writings I gradually branched outward to the many biographies and studies written about Fitzgerald over the years, and then I continued in concentric circles to such figures as Robert Benchley, Dorothy Parker, Ernest Hemingway, Donald Ogden Stewart, and others—the crowd in which Sheilah and Scott lived and worked. Like every Fitzgerald-seeker before me, I have made my pilgrimage to the rare books collection at Princeton University, where all the Fitzgerald manuscripts and letters and memorabilia reside. Here I had the distinctly odd experience to sit in a vaultlike room and have an attendant bring to me boxes for which I signed, finding inside writings in my mother's unmistakable hand—such things as old shopping lists, postcards and telegrams, and even a short story she once attempted with Scott's editorial corrections in the margins. In the Princeton collection there are the shed remains of a lifetime, everything from scrawled reminders of dental appointments to love scenes never published: the sublime and the everyday collected indiscriminately in folders side by side.

The book that came out of this research is not quite what my mother had in mind when she used to speak to me about it on the long-distance telephone. This is not in fact a biography of either Scott or Sheilah, for I have left out huge portions of both their lives; rather I have attempted the anatomy of a love affair. What interested me was that two such unlikely characters might come together against astonishing odds in the briefly literate (and yes, glamorous) Hollywood that existed before the Second World War: a great but failed author at the end of his life, and a beautiful though false young woman with little education escaping her past. I became convinced that for all its telling, this story had never been told either accurately or well.

From the Fitzgerald side, the final years he spent in Hollywood from 1937 to 1940 are generally treated in a last thin chapter at the end of long books, a coda to his tale. The biographers of Scott Fitzgerald quite rightly center their interest upon his years of astonishing creativity in which he wrote such novels as *The Great Gatsby* and *Tender is the Night*, as well as his tumultuous marriage to Zelda Sayre—they are concerned, that is, with Scott's youth, rather than what is usually depicted as an unfortunate and premature end. Scott himself, of course, was one of the great advocates of youth; he led the charge of America's first youth generation of the 1920s. Nevertheless, it is my opinion that Fitzgerald's "old age"—he lived to be forty-four—is of great interest. He suffered greatly, but he never became cynical. He kept faith with himself and with his art, and despite his Hollywood crucifixion in a decade he did not much like, he arrived at a hard-won maturity and a dignity that is worthy of note.

I do not, of course, pretend to be objective but I have done my best to be accurate. My primary source for these pages is a lifetime of knowing my mother. However, I have put this book together after a great deal of research, and the curious reader will find the sources listed for all quotations in the notes. I always tried to get back to the feeling of the spoken stories I heard as a child, but I was careful not to trust my own memory, particularly in the matter of dialogue. Several people who were witness to some of the events have been helpful in reconstructing the tale: Budd Schulberg, and particularly Scott's personal secretary during the last year and a half of his life, Frances Kroll Ring. This is not an all-inclusive book: I have left out many anecdotes and have concentrated rather on what strikes me as the emotional core. My goal was simply to fill in some gaps, put the pieces of the puzzle in place, and bring this story alive in a modern way. I sensed this tale needed to be transcribed from the past so that it might endure into the future.

There is only a thin line that separates daydreams, lies, and the creation of great art. This is the story of those who did not acknowledge the limits of truth as most of us learn to do, and therefore were left unfettered—to seek fairy tales of glory and immortality, to come to grief perhaps, or find a Hollywood ending.

1

A WALKING DOOM

I sit worrying about next week's $35.00 hotel bill! . . . And the dullest dogs making $1000 a week in Hollywood. Something has got to be done. . . .

> —F. Scott Fitzgerald in a letter to his agent,
> Harold Ober, March 23, 1937

Oh come, my love, and join with me
The oldest infant industry.
Come seek the bourne of palm and pearl,
The lovely land of Boy-Meets-Girl,
Come grace this lotus-lade shore,
This Isle of Do-What's-Done-Before.
Come, curb the new, and watch the old win,
Out where the streets are paved with Goldwyn. . . .

> —Dorothy Parker, from
> *The Passionate Screen Writer to His Love*

I

THE TRAIN CUT A PATH ACROSS THE CONTINENT, rolling past the small towns of America, carrying Scott Fitzgerald westward to

California and to his last chance to put together the broken pieces of his life. He was forty years old and starting all over again.

It was early July 1937 and the heat of deep summer would have been heavy upon the land, oppressive in a Pullman car of a pre-air-conditioned era passing through the dusty plains of the Great Depression. Oklahoma drifted by. Texas. There are some things we can only imagine: the gritty windows cracked open at the top, the shriek of the whistle, clatter of wheels; the colored porters walking heavily down the aisles calling out the names of towns; the salesmen, grifters, mothers in gingham dresses, restless children—an enclosed world in motion, a gleaming silver shell speeding toward the promise of the West.

"These Texas lands are like crossing a sea—spiritually, I mean, with a fat contract at the end," Scott wrote a friend from the train, musing upon his predicament. He could only hope the fat contract worked out for him. This was not Fitzgerald's decade of choice, nor was this his land, the brown dustbowl plains of Oklahoma and Texas. He must have appeared an eccentric figure to the other passengers in his ever-impeccable Brooks Brothers suit and close at hand a wrinkled raincoat, a battered hat, and wool scarf, in case from this blazing summer day there come a sudden chill. He chain-smoked cigarettes and drank Coca-Colas one after another. There is a photograph of him taken shortly before he left New York: a man with a wounded, gentle smile, his necktie just a little askew, his fingertips touching together at his stomach in an oddly hesitant manner, as though he didn't quite know what to do with his hands.

By 1937 Scott had seen his early fame slip away. He had invented the Jazz Age, the phrase itself, giving words and expression to his time, the youthful, rebellious, fanciful 1920s. But he had lived long enough to watch helplessly as his writing fell out of style, passed-over in the new proletarian mood of the thirties. "Nothing is as old as last year's new," Scott observed moodily toward the end of his life. Everything had gone wrong for him. His beautiful wife Zelda was mad, shut up in a mental institution in North Carolina; he was more than broke, he was hugely in debt—nearly forty thousand dollars—to his agent and publisher. The long madcap party of the twenties had come to a end, leaving him stranded in an unfriendly decade to wage an epic battle with alcoholism.

As a young man, Scott had been very handsome, famous almost as much for his profile on the dust covers of his books as for the prose within. In those days he had yellow hair, a finely sculptured nose, a delicate mouth and piercing sad blue eyes that were touched with a hint of calculating green—eyes that were the color of the Irish Sea, someone once said. It had been a feminine sort of beauty, angelic, almost too pretty for a young man. Now in 1937 at the age of forty, he was prematurely aged. Alcohol had caused his features to widen. He was still good-looking, but like an aging matinee idol who preferred to be glimpsed from the rear of the theater rather than the first row. He did not appear to be in good health. His face was of an almost blue paleness and seemed to dissolve into many small wrinkles as you looked at him more closely. It was a face, as he described it, "that was aging from within, so that there were no casual furrows of worry and vexation but a drawn asceticism as if from a silent self-set struggle—or a long illness." To salvage what he could of his appearance, he combed his faded yellow hair carefully to hide where it was thinning on top. He was self-conscious of the growing bulge of his stomach, mournful of what time had changed.

He had always been a small man, less than five feet eight inches tall. Ernest Hemingway, oddly obsessed with Fitzgerald's measurements, had found Scott's legs too short for his upper body. Fitzgerald's size had kept him from college football, his first love, where a ninety-yard run might win the heart of every man and woman in a cheering stadium. . . . Scott knew what glory was, and he had always aimed high, to be the very best, beloved by the world. Even as an author—a career appropriate only for someone too short for football—writing was more than mere literature, but a matter of catching the ball gloriously before a wild adoring crowd and running with all your might ahead of the trailing pack clear off the field into immortality—arriving in no stuffy paradise for English teachers, but a heaven where the most beautiful girl waited to place the garland upon your head.

In these matters of football, fiction, and beautiful girls, Scott Fitzgerald was unashamedly a romantic; unfortunately, romanticism was no longer the fashion in these hard days of the Depression. Down on his luck, riding a train across America, Scott had the look about him of a prince in exile. His young admirer, Arnold Gingrich, editor of *Esquire*, was moved to write: "Both the first and the last time he left for Hollywood [Scott] set out with a sad proud air of resignation, like a young Russian nobleman being banished to Siberia."

The trip west signaled a major change of life. Sitting by himself in his Pullman chair, staring through the window at the passing continent, Scott replayed the reels of his failed career; he pondered his spoiled chances, and in true Fitzgerald fashion, he made specific plans to conquer Hollywood. He was an optimist, a man who believed in fresh starts and last-minute reprieves. This time he would not drink and pull the crazy stunts which had ruined him in the past. He would be a success yet again. This was Scott's third trip to the Coast seeking money, always money, the hard currency so necessary to keep his dreams afloat. In his notes, Scott jotted down the weekly pay scale for Hollywood writers: "Junior writers $300; Minor poets—$500 a week; Broken novelists—$850–1000; One play dramatists—$1500; Sucks—$2000. Wits—$2500." Scott had a six-month contract with Metro-Goldwyn-Mayer for a thousand dollars per week, which put him at the top of the broken novelist category; he would be one of a team of writers assigned to the movie, *A Yank at Oxford*, starring Robert Taylor and Maureen O'Sullivan.

As the train pulled out of El Prado, Texas, Scott began a letter to his teenage daughter Scottie:

Dearest Pie:

I feel a certain excitement. The third Hollywood venture. Two failures behind me though one no fault of mine. The first one was just ten years ago. At that time I had been generally acknowledged for several years as the top American writer both seriously and, as far as prices went, popularly. I had been loafing for six months for the first time in my life and was confident to the point of conciet [*sic*]. Hollywood made a big fuss over us and the ladies all looked very beautiful to a man of thirty. I honestly believed that with *no*

effort on my part I was a sort of magician with words—an odd delu-
sion on my part when I had worked so desperately hard to develop
a hard, colorful prose style.

> Total result—a great time and no work. I was to be paid only a
> small amount unless they made my picture—they didn't.

Scott and Zelda made this first foray to the Coast in January
1927, at the height of their wild years. In those days they were
more than a famous author and his wife, they were living symbols of the Roaring Twenties. "A more irresponsible pair than
we'll be will be hard to imagine," he had boasted at the start of
the decade, and it was a pledge he meant to keep. In 1920, flush
with success, Scott undressed in a Broadway theater; Zelda,
without bothering to undress, dived into the fountain at Union
Square. They rode on top of taxis, they lived in hotels, drank
bootleg champagne as though it would flow forever, and when
they moved from the Biltmore to the Commodore Hotel, they
spun around and around in the revolving front door for more
than a half an hour out of sheer exuberance. A few months later,
attempting briefly to live a more quiet and work-filled existence
in Westport, Connecticut, Zelda set off a fire alarm just out of
boredom and a general desire to stir things up.

For Scott and Zelda's generation, which had seen millions
slaughtered in the trenches of Flanders and France, all authority
was open to question. It was, as Scott reported to his avid readers, "a new generation dedicated more than the last to the fear of
poverty and the worship of success; grown up to find all Gods
dead, all wars fought, all faiths in man shaken." The final nail in
the coffin of prewar sensibilities was the passage of the Volstead
Act in 1919, the Eighteenth Amendment which banned the sale
and consumption of alcohol. This meant that without question
every progressive, youthful, and madly stylish person in
America must rush to their nearest bootlegger or speakeasy to
get their forbidden fill of euphoria. Alcohol was to the twenties
what marijuana would be to the sixties—more than a mere substance, it became the very elixir of revolt whose illegal use was a
grand way to thumb one's nose at authority. In this revolt, Scott
and Zelda led the way; they were the prophets of intoxication,
the gorgeous young brats of the decade.

As a couple Scott and Zelda were "really unbelievably hand-some. They were the flawless people," remembered Gerald Murphy, the charismatic heir to the Mark Cross fortune who became the model for Dick Diver in *Tender is the Night*. And yet the flaws of this handsome couple were becoming daily more apparent. In the early twenties, Scott met a lovely actress, Laurette Taylor, and to pay extravagant homage he dropped upon his knees and repeated again and again, "My God! You beautiful egg! You beautiful egg!" But the actress returned in tears to her husband that night and declared with passionate clarity: "I have just seen the doom of youth. Understand? The doom of youth itself. A walking doom."

Her words were to prove prophetic. For Scott and Zelda, the first sign of the disaster ahead was money, which was hemor-rhaging out at an alarming rate. There never seemed enough cash to keep their extravagant lifestyle afloat. Even in the early years of success, Scott managed to be constantly in debt to Charles Scribner, his most obliging publisher, drawing royalties far in advance of actual sales. Out of this constant need for money, Hollywood presented itself as the miraculous answer to their prayers. In Hollywood there was all the money in the world, and the promise of a lifestyle to match their carefree mood. So in 1927 it was westward-ho for the Fitzgeralds; there really wasn't any other choice. Scott landed an assignment to write a collegiate comedy, *Lipstick,* which would star Constance Talmadge, a story about a girl who had a magic lipstick that made every man want to kiss her. The setting was Princeton, Scott's own alma mater, and so this seemed a natural assignment. Unfortunately, the "great time and no work" which he described to his daughter ten years later got in the way of any serious moviemaking.

On this first visit west, Scott and Zelda stayed two months in Hollywood, sharing a four-apartment bungalow at the fashion-able Ambassador Hotel with John Barrymore, the actress Carmel Myers, and author Carl Van Vechten. Hollywood in 1927 was leg-endary for its wild ways, but the Fitzgeralds were determined to outdo everyone else around them. Zelda took Black Bottom lessons and consulted psychics in Santa Monica. They went to a fashionable party dressed only in their pajamas. At another party, a costume party given by Samuel Goldwyn to which they had not been invited, they showed up at the front door on their hands and knees pleading to be admitted as puppies. At still another party at the Ambassador Hotel, the Fitzgeralds went around to each guest asking for watches and jewelry pretending they were about to do a magic trick. Then they took the gathered loot into the kitchen and boiled everything in a big pot of tomato sauce, giggling happily over their strange stew. But the guests were not so amused. Scott and Zelda had failed to understand that Hollywood, despite its reputation, was a working town. There were limits to behavior, for one must look good before the cameras the next morning, or make a presentable appearance at the studio office.

Zelda was soon disenchanted with California. "There's nothing on earth to do here but look at the view and eat," she wrote. "You can imagine the result since I do not like to look at views." Scott took a more romantic view; Hollywood both fascinated and repelled him. He described the movie capital as "a tragic city of beautiful girls,—the girls who mop the floor are beautiful, the shop ladies. You never want to see any more beauty." But of these beautiful girls, there was one who caught his eye: the young movie actress Lois Moran, seventeen years old, blond, blue-eyed, fresh and unspoiled by her success as the star of the 1925 movie *Stella Dallas*. Lois Moran had just returned from an extended European tour with her mother; not only was she beautiful, she was cultured as well: She spoke fluent French, kept a chapbook full of poetic quotations, and she was utterly taken with Scott Fitzgerald, the famous thirty-one-year-old author. Scott for his part could not resist a young woman who seemed to embody so many qualities of romance. Eventually he would immortalize her as Rosemary Hoyt, the young actress traveling with her mother in *Tender is the Night*.

The affair with Lois Moran was passionate but unconsummated; the girl's mother was generally in attendance as chaperon, and Fitzgerald was a bit of a prude where sex was concerned. Nevertheless, Lois was Scott's revenge for Zelda's real affair three years earlier with a glamorous French aviator,

Edouard Jozan, in the south of France in the summer of 1924. (Jozan, like Lois Moran, would also end up in *Tender is the Night*, fictionalized as Tommy Barban.) Zelda may have been the one who opened this door to marital chaos, but now she was not at all amused to find herself on the wrong end of the romantic equation—to be twenty-seven years old and discover there existed a new crop of flirtatious girls, younger and more vivacious than herself—to be usurped in fact in a role that she herself had once played for all it was worth. Zelda dismissed Lois Moran as "a young actress like a breakfast food that many men identified with whatever they missed from life." This breakfast food, however, was not so easy to digest.

To make matters worse, Lois had a remarkable idea: She wanted Scott to become an actor, the leading man of her next movie, and to this end she arranged for him to have a screen test. Zelda's jealousy soared to an extreme which hinted at future madness. One night when Scott was having dinner with his ingenue, Zelda set fire to some of her dresses in the bathtub of their hotel suite. Later, on the train leaving Hollywood, she grew angry at the very mention of Lois Moran and threw out the window a platinum wristwatch which Scott had given her as an engagement present. Fortunately for the Fitzgerald marriage, Scott's screen test was rejected by the director of the movie: The verdict came back that his thirty-one-year-old face was too old for the merciless scrutiny of the camera. How Zelda must have chortled with delight! *Too old!* She was not the only one to wake and discover golden youth had passed her by—they who had lived for youth, who had put all their eggs in that particular basket, the fleeting romantic years when all impressions were fresh and new.

Despite the flattering conquest of a young actress, Fitzgerald decided he did not much like Hollywood people, and what he described as their "almost hysterical egotism and excitability hidden under an extremely thin veil of elaborate good-fellowship." The script for *Lipstick* was rejected by the studio and so the trip was a bust; as usual, the Fitzgeralds with their wild ways managed to spend vastly more money than Scott had earned. As a final spectacular gesture, Scott and Zelda piled up all the furniture in the middle of their hotel room and placed their unpaid bills on top as a sort of offering to the gods of excess. Then they escaped to the train, sneaking through the lobby and crawling on their hands and knees to their compartment to avoid detection.

Lois Moran sent them a telegram: . . . BOOTLEGGERS GONE OUT OF BUSINESS COTTON CLUB CLOSED ALL FLAGS AT HALF MAST . . . BOTTLES OF LOVE TO YOU BOTH.

So ended the first Hollywood venture of 1927.

The second trip to California came in November 1931. Scott was invited west by Irving Thalberg, the boy genius of Metro-Goldwyn-Mayer, to help make a star out of Jean Harlow in *Red-Headed Woman*, a film based upon a successful novel by Katherine Brush. By this time, the great stock market crash of October 24, 1929, had come and gone, putting an end to the high-flying twenties, and the Fitzgeralds' decade-long party had crashed along with it. Zelda, always a great "original," had skirted the edges of insanity for some years, but in 1930 she broke down; she began her lifetime journey through a series of asylums first in Europe and then later in the United States. For both Scott and Zelda, the magic of youth was lost forever—as Scott put it, "the good gone times when we still believed in summer hotels and the philosophies of popular songs."

Zelda's sanitariums were expensive and created a new urgent need for money. Out of this darkness, Irving Thalberg seemed to step forward like some gorgeous all-powerful god, offering Scott a five-week contract at twelve hundred dollars per week; once again Hollywood appeared to be the answer to a writer's prayers. And so in November 1931 Scott journeyed to California alone, leaving Zelda behind at her parents' house in Montgomery, Alabama.

Scott summed up this second attempt to conquer Hollywood in his letter to his daughter while riding the train en route to his third venture:

> The second time I went was five years ago. Life had gotten in some hard socks and while all was serene on top, with your mother apparently recovered in Montgomery, I was jittery underneath and

beginning to drink more than I ought to. Far from approaching it
too confidently I was far too humble. I ran afoul of a bastard named
de Sano, since a suicide, and let myself be gypped out of command.
I wrote the picture and he changed as I wrote. I tried to get at
Thalberg but was erroneously warned against it as "bad taste."
Result—a bad script. I left with the money, for this was a contract
for weekly payments, but disillusioned and disgusted, vowing
never to go back, tho they said it wasn't my fault and asked me to
stay. I wanted to get East when the contract expired to see how
your mother was. This was later interpreted as "running out on
them" and held against me.

Despite his apparent candor, Scott was not telling his daughter
everything. On this second journey west, Scott was drinking
hard—quite a lot more than he ought to, as he so delicately put
it. He was met in Hollywood by the press and with some fanfare;
in 1931, his literary reputation, though fading, was still intact,
and Metro had a stake in publicizing the arrival of their new
man. All this went to his head, along with the gin, and Scott was
soon up to his old antics.

One night he went to a party at the house of his old friend
Carmel Myers, where he escaped upstairs and held court merrily
for the rest of the evening from a bathtub. This was the old pixie,
the daring, improbable Scott of the twenties trying for a comeback, but the era had passed him by and his actions now seemed
only a little embarrassing and strange. At Metro, his screenplay
for *Red-Headed Woman* was also a failure. He had a collaborator
whom he considered a studio hack—the future suicide, Marcel de
Sano—and together they struggled to write a comedy about a red-
headed siren who works her way up the social ladder by passing
from bed to bed. After hiring Scott, Irving Thalberg made himself
mostly unavailable for comment or direction. The boy genius, in
fact, was a notoriously hard man to see; the humorist S. J.
Perelman had such trouble gaining an audience that he "seriously
began to question whether Thalberg existed, whether he might
not be a solar myth or a deity concocted by the front office to garner prestige." Once Harpo, Groucho, and Chico Marx were kept
waiting so long for the great man that they built a small fire outside his office, forcing Thalberg to rush out and see them when he

smelled smoke. The Marx Brothers presumably had some clout at MGM. It was far more difficult for Scott Fitzgerald, a mere writer, to gain access. When Scott finally did see Thalberg, it was at a tea party where he managed to make a very great fool of himself.

This 1931 tea party was held on a Sunday afternoon and hosted by Norma Shearer, Thalberg's movie star wife, at their Santa Monica home—a house which "was built for great emotional moments—there was an air of listening, as if the far silences of its vistas hid an audience, but this afternoon it was thronged, as though people had been bidden rather than asked." This was what was known in Hollywood as an "A" event, a gathering of the movie industry's crème de la crème. "It would be a party of the top drawer," Scott wrote. "The Marion Davies crowd, the high-hats, the big currency numbers, perhaps even Dietrich and Garbo . . . people who were not seen everywhere." Only a few writers had been invited to this rarefied event, including Dwight Taylor, who in his memoirs remembers entering the huge living room: "I could see at once that we had landed on our feet. Everybody who *was* anybody in the picture colony was there. . . . The room was restless and exciting, with all the glamor of a fair."

Scott was in his element, but there was a problem: Irving Thalberg, the man he must impress, was known to despise drunks. "I won't have anything to drink," Scott promised himself. But someone put a cocktail into his hand and soon "he felt happy and friendly toward all the people gathered there, people of bravery and industry . . . he liked them—he loved them. Great waves of good feeling flowed through him." He talked with his lovely hostess, Norma Shearer, and she seemed to gaze upon him with special favor. Then "he took another cocktail—not because he needed confidence but because she had given him so much of it." In his euphoria, he saw "it was good here—the American Riviera and all that, if there were ever time to enjoy it. The handsome, well dressed people in the room, the lovely girls. . . ." A few more cocktails and he felt he could do anything.

The trouble began with the actor Robert Montgomery, who came up to Scott wishing to meet the famous author. Montgomery had arrived at this tea party dressed in white riding breeches and black boots, looking like some celluloid fantasy of an English gentleman. "Why didn't you bring your horse in?" Scott asked facetiously. His tongue was loosened with liquor, his confidence bolstered, but Robert Montgomery was an important actor, much more important than Scott Fitzgerald, and he turned curtly and walked away from the perceived insult.

Scott was just warming up. He decided he would do a parlor trick; he must sing for the gathered Hollywood professionals a silly song he and Edmund Wilson had composed years ago at Princeton. With "his blood throbbing with the scarlet corpuscles of exhibitionism" he approached Norma Shearer with his request for a small dog and a piano accompaniment. A maid was sent to fetch a poodle from upstairs, and Ramon Novarro—the star of *Ben-Hur*—was enlisted to improvise at the piano. The party had been about to break up, but now the guests wandered back and gathered in a half-circle around the piano—"but not too near," Dwight Taylor recalls, "their faces devoid of expression, like people gathered at the scene of an accident."

Scott cradled the poodle in his arms and began to sing a ditty about dogs:

> In Sunny Africa they have the elephant
> And in India they have the zebera [*sic*]—
> Up in Canada the Rocky Mountain goat
> And in Idaho the shoat
>   (You've heard about!)
> But of all these animals
> You will find the best of pals—
>   Is!
>
> Dog, dog—I like a good dog—
> Towser or Bowser or Star—
> Clean sort of pleasure—
> A four-footed treasure—
> And faithful as few humans are!
> Here, Pup: put your paw up—
> Roll over dead like a log!
> Larger than a rat!
> More faithful than a cat!
>   Dog! Dog! Dog!

The gathered professionals, the best-paid entertainers in the world, waited for the obviously drunk author to deliver the punch line, but unfortunately this was it. There were more verses about other animals, and every verse ended with the refrain: "Dog! Dog! Dog!," which summed up the general mood in which the song was received.

Scott knew he was making a spectacle of himself, but it was too late to stop. Near the piano, John Gilbert, "the Great Lover of the screen glared at him with an eye as keen as the eye of a potato." Scott was able to observe himself with a terrible clarity:

> . . . as he finished he had the sickening realization that he had made a fool of himself in view of an important section of the picture world, upon whose favor depended his career. For a moment he existed in the midst of a confused silence, broken by a general trek for the door. He felt the undercurrent of derision. . . [then] the Great Lover, his eye hard and empty as the eye of a needle, shouted "Boo! Boo!" voicing an overtone what he felt was the mood of the crowd. It was the resentment of the professional toward the amateur, of the community toward the stranger, the thumbs-down of the clan.

The rejection was bad enough, but to make it worse, Scott's boss, Irving Thalberg, was watching this drunken episode with a disapproving eye from across the room. Thalberg asked the writer Charles MacArthur to take Scott home. Charlie MacArthur had seen Scott's antics before. A few years earlier, drunk together in the south of France, Scott and Charlie had attempted to saw a waiter in half, speculating together on what waiters might be made of; they had been stopped only by the poor man's desperate shouts for the police. Two Americans might have fun and games in the south of France, but Hollywood meant business. Charlie MacArthur did as Thalberg told him.

Scott was appalled by his own behavior. It seemed that time after time he had managed to turn success into failure. As he described himself in the third person in his *Notebooks:* "Just when somebody's taken him up and is making a big fuss over him he pours the soup down his hostess' back, kisses the serving maid and passes out in the dog kennel. But he's done it too often. He's run through about everybody, until there's no one left."

The next day Norma Shearer sent Scott a charming telegram: I THOUGHT YOU WERE ONE OF THE MOST AGREEABLE PERSONS AT OUR TEA. Scott was relieved, but as was often the case, he had managed to charm the wife but alienate the husband. At the end of five weeks' work, when his contract was up, Irving Thalberg rejected Scott's script and handed over the project to Anita Loos. Fitzgerald returned to his wife and daughter in Alabama.

Such was the end of the 1931 venture, Scott's second attempt to conquer Hollywood, a jewel which remained for him out of his reach. He hated not to come out on top—more than most, he was a man who wished to be extravagantly loved and admired; he wished to hear sweet applause ringing forever in his ears. And when he failed, time and time again, he turned to writing as a last resort. "If you weren't able to function in action," he admitted, "you might at least be able to tell about it . . . it was a back door way of facing reality."

So Scott wrote. The humiliating tea party at Norma Shearer's house was transformed into "Crazy Sunday," one of his best short stories, and Irving Thalberg, the studio boss who had rejected him in 1931, would become the romantic hero for his final novel, *The Last Tycoon*.

He would have preferred to be a man who dominated life with sheer animal magnetism: a football player, a movie star, a general or king. To be a great writer was a good thing, of course. But for someone with a taste for heroics, it was decidedly second best.

II

After 1931, Zelda drifted in and out of various mental institutions in Maryland and North Carolina. When she was released briefly from one of her hospitals, Zelda set fire to the Fitzgeralds' rented home outside of Baltimore, destroying most of the second floor. Scott asked the landlord not to make immediate repairs, since it would interfere with his work, and he continued writing in the smoke-blackened house with the roof partially caved in. Some of their friends hardly knew who was the most mad, Zelda or Scott.

Scott was drinking furiously. After he was arrested for drunk driving, a New York doctor told him he was killing himself. The doctor gave Scott a small glass and told him that this must be his daily limit of alcohol, no more. Scott took the measured glass and on his way home stopped in Wilmington to visit his old college friend, John Biggs. He told Biggs about the doctor's order, and then carefully filled his allotted glass with gin. He drank the portion in a single gulp, and then measured the glass full once more . . . and then again and again, until the bottle of gin was empty. With a combination of insouciance and despair, Scott courted his self-destruction.

He put all his remaining hopes into his long-awaited novel about insanity and alcoholism and glamorous lives gone sour. In 1934, after nine years of sporadic work, seventeen separate versions, and an entire smorgasbord of titles—including *The Boy Who Killed His Mother, The Melarkey Case, The World Fair, The Drunkard's Holiday, Dr. Diver's Holiday,* and *Richard Diver—Tender is the Night* was finally published by Scribner's, taking its title at last from Scott's favorite poem, Keats's "Ode to a Nightingale." Scott hoped his new novel would restore his tarnished reputation and fill his empty coffers, but he was to be gravely disappointed. *Tender is the Night* came out to mixed reviews and modest sales. America of 1934 had its own problems, and was decidedly not interested in the dissolute ways of the boom years, nor the rarefied lives of a graceful though tragic couple on the French Riviera. The Depression Thirties shunned any reminder of the Roaring Twenties, and assigned Scott Fitzgerald to a literary grave.

This was a tremendous blow, and Scott entered his bleakest years. With Zelda in an institution, and Scottie in boarding school, he crept away into obscurity, finding refuge in the small towns of the South, where no one knew him. "The conjuror's hat was empty," he wrote about this time. "One harassed and despairing night I packed a brief case and went off a thousand miles to think it over. I took a dollar room in a drab little town where I knew no one and sunk all the money I had with me in a stock of potted meat, crackers and apples."

Tender is the Night ends with the image of the once-charismatic Dick Diver disappearing into the small country towns of America, finding some fading comfort in the women he still could charm. Dick Diver does not die, he simply becomes second-rate—for Scott Fitzgerald, the worst fate of all, and for a time this fictitious ending seemed to become a self-fulfilling prophesy. He drifted; he had a number of dissolute affairs with women who provided a brief audience for his antics, but generally became quickly disillusioned with his drink and despair. At the Grove Park Inn in Asheville, North Carolina, he broke his shoulder doing a high dive into the pool, showing off for a young lady. His adolescent dreams of glory refused to die, but it was doubtful if she was impressed.

He suffered greatly, he drank himself into oblivion, and it appeared that his life had arrived at an obscure and sordid end. But he kept writing. Finally, Scott became a connoisseur of his own despair in a series of essays analyzing his fall from grace. The essays were suggested by Arnold Gingrich, the editor of *Esquire*, which remained Scott's last literary outlet. The results were three startling and most autobiographical confessions—"The Crack-Up," "Pasting It Together," and "Handle With Care"—which were published in the February, March, and April 1936 issues of *Esquire*. In these pieces, Scott described his condition as "an over-extension of the flank, a burning of the candle at both ends; a call upon physical resources that I did not command, like a man over-drawing at his bank." With clinical detachment, he searched for "the leak through which, unknown to myself, my enthusiasm and my vitality had been steadily and prematurely trickling away." In sparse and precise prose, Scott forged a new style and examined the truth of his life without the usual camouflage of fiction. He was proud of his work and suspected his three essays were as good as any nonfiction ever written by an American. Yet the *Esquire* articles were received badly; they were regarded as an embarrassing confession of personal weakness. Ironically he had described his desperate condition so well that the remaining threads of his reputation quickly fell apart.

Scott's friends were particularly aghast. Ernest Hemingway, whose career Scott had advanced in the mid-twenties, thought of the articles as disgraceful whining in public. Hemingway had been advising Scott for some years now to keep up a more manly facade about personal troubles. In a 1934 letter he wrote:

> Forget your personal tragedy. We are all bitched from the start and you especially have to be hurt like hell before you can write seriously . . . You see, Bo, you're not a tragic character. Neither am I. All we are is writers and what we should do is write. Of all people on earth you needed discipline in your work and instead you marry someone who is jealous of your work, wants to compete with you and ruins you . . . I thought Zelda was crazy the first time I met her and you complicated it even more by being in love with her and, of course you're a rummy. But you're no more of a rummy than Joyce is and most good writers are. But Scott good writers always come back. Always. You are twice as good now as you were at the time you thought you were so marvelous.

Six months after Scott's *Esquire* articles, Ernest used the same magazine to publish a story, "The Snows of Kilimanjaro" in which he could not resist taking a swipe at "poor Scott Fitzgerald and his romantic awe of [the rich] and how he had started a story once that began 'The very rich are different from you and me.' And how someone had said to Scott, 'Yes they have more money.' But that was not humorous to Scott. He thought they were a special glamorous race and when he found they weren't it wrecked him just as much as any other thing that wrecked him." Scott was extremely hurt by Hemingway's public attack, and when the story was published in a collection by Scribner's, he persuaded Max Perkins to change his real name to a fictitious "Julian."

Other friends tried to be more supportive. John Dos Passos wrote a letter that was gruff and encouraging: "Christ, man, how do you find time in the middle of the general conflagrations to worry about all that stuff?. . . We're living in one of the damndest tragic moments in history—if you want to go to pieces I think it's absolutely O.K. But I think you ought to write a first-rate novel about it (and you probably will) instead of spilling it in little pieces for Arnold Gingrich." The novelist John O'Hara commiserated by telling Scott about his own troubles—how he had just been jilted by his girl and gotten a dose of the clap. All in all, for the public at large—and for any future editors and publishers who might buy his work—Scott had admitted he was damaged goods, no longer viable merchandise.

Then came the finishing blow. On September 25, 1936, the *New York Post* published a damning front-page interview to commemorate Scott's fortieth birthday which had come and gone one day earlier. The interview was conducted by Michael Mok on September 24 in Asheville, North Carolina. It began: "Long ago, when he was young, cock-sure, drunk with sudden success, F. Scott Fitzgerald told a newspaper man that no one should live beyond thirty." The article continued to describe how Scott, who had clearly lived ten years too long, spent his fortieth birthday "as he spends all his days—trying to come back from the other side of Paradise, the hell of despondency in which he has agonized for the last couple of years." Michael Mok carefully noted Scott's "jittery jumping off and onto his bed, his restless pacing, his trembling hands, his twitching face with its pitiful expression of a cruelly beaten child." During the interview, Scott made "frequent trips to a highboy, in a drawer of which lay a bottle. Each time he poured a drink into the measuring glass on his bedside table, he would look appealing at the nurse and ask, 'Just one ounce?'"

What the article failed to note was that Scott Fitzgerald was a born dramatist who to some extent was leading the journalist on. When Michael Mok asked him what he thought now about "the jazz-mad, gin-mad generation" that he once wrote about, Fitzgerald declaimed with theatrical abandon:

"You know as well as I do what has happened to them. Some became brokers and threw themselves out of windows. Others became bankers and shot themselves. Still others became newspaper reporters. And a few became successful authors."

His face twitched.

"Successful authors!" he cried. "Oh, my God, successful authors!"

He stumbled over to the highboy and poured himself another drink.

All this made sensational copy and when the *New York Post* interview was picked up and reprinted by *Time* magazine, Scott believed himself a ruined man. He made a desperate stab at suicide, swallowing a phial of morphine—"four grains enough to kill a horse," he wrote later to his agent, Harold Ober. "It happened to be an overdose and almost before I could get to the bed I vomited the whole thing and the nurse came in + saw the empty phial + there was hell to pay awhile + afterwards I felt like a fool. And if I ever see Mr. Mock what will happen will be very swift and sudden."

But there was to be a silver lining in all this, a strange twist of fate. For out in the world, among the wide public who read Michael Mok's article with a clicking tongue and shake of the head, there was a writer who in his youth had admired Scott Fitzgerald greatly. This man, Edwin Knopf, had once wished to be a great novelist himself, but without quite the pain and misery that being any sort of true artist seemed to entail. Fantasizing himself as Scott Fitzgerald, Edwin Knopf wrote a screenplay which combined Scott's experiences with his own; the characters originally were called Scott and Zelda but Samuel Goldwyn eventually fictionalized the names and released the film as *The Wedding Night*, starring Gary Cooper as an imitation Scott, and a new sex goddess, Anna Sten, as a look-alike Zelda.

Edwin Knopf had made some money from his Scott Fitzgerald fantasy. Perhaps he felt guilty, or he was saddened to read of Scott's dire straits. Whatever the reason, Knopf himself had risen in the world—he was now the story editor at Metro-Goldwyn-Mayer—and he was moved to offer Scott his final Hollywood chance, the third trip west in the early summer of 1937.

Scott was fully aware that this was a miraculous reprieve. He had failed twice now in Hollywood: in 1927 with *Lipstick,* and in 1931 working for Irving Thalberg on *Red-Headed Woman*. His private life had fallen into even worse repair than his professional reputation; in 1935, at his lowest ebb, he had come very close to a complete physical and mental collapse. Nevertheless, by 1936 Scott had found the energy and coherence to write eloquently and with wry humor about his wretchedness in the "Crack-Up" articles. This was no small feat, and despite the poor public reception these *Esquire* pieces had received, he had a stubborn pride and knew they were good. Most incredible of all, by the winter and spring of 1937, Scott had managed at last to stop drinking. And so his friends despaired of him, the literary establishment put him down as a has-been and a failure—yet had anyone looked closely, they would have noticed that Scott Fitzgerald was showing definite signs of life. Though he was battered, he still had his old optimism intact as well as his restless talent. By his July trip west he was determined to do well, remain sober, and avoid the mistakes of his first two misadventures. "The train has left El Paso since I began this letter—hence the writing—Rocky Mountain writing," he joked to his daughter in his letter en route to California. Then he coldly analyzed his situation:

> I want to profit by these two experiences [the 1927 and 1931 trips]—I must be very tactful but keep my hand on the wheel from the start—find out the key man among the bosses and the most malleable among the collaborators—then fight the rest tooth and nail until, in fact or in effect, I'm alone on the picture. That's the only way I can do my best work. Given a break I can make them double this contract in less [than] two years.

These were fighting words. Even as it stood, Scott's 1937 contract with MGM was incredibly lucrative—six months at $1,000 per week, with an option for an additional year at $1,250. There was no place on the planet but Hollywood where one could make this kind of money simply by dreaming up clever bits of dialogue. And Scott needed the money desperately. By the time of the third trip west, he was in debt $9,000 to Scribner's alone in loans and advances, nearly another $13,000 to his agent Harold Ober, and another $1,150 to his editor Max Perkins; he owed income tax, he was behind in his payments to Zelda's expensive sanitarium in North Carolina, behind on Scottie's tuition at the Ethel Walker School in Connecticut . . . behind everywhere, seemingly drowning in a sea of debt.

In order to get out of this black hole, Scott set himself a Spartan schedule. In a July 6, 1937, letter, he asked his agent to withhold the greater part of his thousand-dollar-a-week paycheck to pay off his debts as follows:

100 to you—commission
150 "   "   on debt
50 "   Scribners on debt, as follows
        1st to be paid against Perkins loan
        2nd to be paid against insurance assignment
        held by Charles Scribner
        3rd to be paid against their movie loan on *Tender*
        4th to be paid against my retail bill there
200 to be banked by you against taxes somewhere where I can
    get compound interest. Perhaps you can make a suggestion
    where
100 to be banked at 1st National Baltimore for "vacation
    money" for I will be taking six to 8 weeks off a year.
400 to be put to my account out here for which I will pay
    expenses + $100 insurance. For the present we will call this
    one the expense check + when I find a bank in California
    will deposit it there.

1000

Out of Scott's four-hundred-dollar allowance, he needed to pay both Zelda's sanitarium and Scottie's tuition, as well as his own hotel bills, which left him very little. Still in his methodical way he was preparing to settle with the past and make a comeback. Edwin Knopf had arranged for Scott to stay at a quiet residential hotel near the beach in Santa Monica, believing the sea air would be good for an ailing author. But Scott had different ideas: He had been out of sight too long and now wished to be in the thick of things. He moved into The Garden of Allah Hotel on Sunset Boulevard, on a block bordered by Havenhurst to one side and North Crescent Heights to the other. Across the road was The Players Club owned by playwright Preston Sturges—one of the most popular hangouts in town. Nearby on Sunset were the Mocambo, the Trocadero, all the hot spots within walking distance; across North Crescent Heights was Schwab's drugstore, the legendary meeting place for all of Hollywood.

The Garden of Allah had been built by the eccentric silent movie star, Alla Nazimova, and was popular with a flamboyant crowd of East Coast writers and actors—exiles who generally declared Hollywood a terrible place, resented that they had been forced to prostitute their talent and come there, but who were meanwhile making tons of money and living to the hilt. Scott could not have picked a spot which would more sorely test his new resolve not to drink. The hotel consisted of a main house and twenty-five white Spanish bungalows with red tile roofs that were connected by a maze of narrow paths. The grounds were overgrown and the buildings not entirely in good repair, giving an impression of an exotically seedy jungle outpost. The paths were treacherous and uneven, and many a fashionable woman turned an ankle in her high-heeled shoes as she attempted to make her way from bungalow to bungalow among the chaotic growth of lush vegetation: orange trees, grapefruit trees, loquat, bamboo, palm, and strange banana trees that never bore fruit.

In the center of this peculiar Hollywood jungle there was a swimming pool shaped like the Black Sea—this was said to remind Alla Nazimova of her childhood home in Odessa. For reasons of sobriety, many of the hotel guests ended up in this Black Sea at odd moments fully clothed, or with no clothes on at all—but rarely in the appropriate attire. The mood here was more like that of an artists' colony than a proper hotel. For the sake of discretion, there was no house detective and one could come and go by numerous side entrances to the grounds which were never locked, day or night.

Scott moved into an upstairs bungalow apartment at the top of a flight of red-tiled steps; he entered his new home through an arched Spanish doorway and by passing a large ceramic Moorish pot. The bungalow, like many dwellings in Hollywood, seemed more like a movie set, as if built to provide a certain cinematic mood rather than actual shelter. Inside Scott's apartment, the furniture was heavy pseudo-Spanish, with dark wood and faded carpets. Everything could have used a new coat of paint. The double bed sagged in the middle. There was a heavy maple-framed mirror on the wall and the Moorish-Spanish-Hollywood motif dictated depressing heavy grillwork around the windows. The Garden of Allah was a paradise which had seen better days.

Scott set about making himself at home; he bought a rattling secondhand 1934 Ford coupé, and now considered himself a true Californian. He reported to work in Culver City, probably on

Saturday, July 10, and found an office waiting for him on the
third floor of the Writers and Producers' Building—now offi-
cially renamed the Thalberg Building, after Irving Thalberg's
death in 1936. The building lay just outside the main gate at
MGM; it was a long, ugly rectangular block with bare and
depressing corridors—the writers generally referred to their
workplace as "the Iron Lung." Scott's office had only a small
square of paper on the door to announce his name. There were
various symbols of status at MGM, and the paper title on the
door revealed Scott's lack of importance. The producers, who
inhabited a higher world on the fourth floor of the building—literally walking on the writers' heads—had their names engraved
more permanently on plaques of fourteen-karat gold. These men
of the fourth floor were ironically referred to as the College of
Cardinals, though they were mostly Jewish. They included
Eddie Manix, Sam Katz, and the father of the studio himself,
Louis B. Mayer, who had begun life as a junk dealer, but had
dreamed himself upward in a very big way.

Scott set upon his desk the sharpened pencils and yellow legal
pads of his trade. From his briefcase he pulled his daily supply of
Coca-Cola and when the bottles were empty he lined them
around his office. He joked to his agent, H. N. Swanson—Swanie,
who was Harold Ober's California associate—that he would celebrate when the Coke bottles completely encircled the room by
going off the wagon. Finally he reported to the story editor,
Edwin Knopf. "Here comes this completely crushed and frightened man," Knopf remembers. "The features were there, the
drawing, but not the face. He had that almost blue paleness. Not
big wrinkles but little wrinkles all over because he was sick."

Despite his determination in 1937 to do well in his new
Hollywood venture, Scott's confidence was gone. He had been
out of sight for too many years. It was painful to remeet old
friends both at Metro and The Garden of Allah—friends such as
Anita Loos, Dorothy Parker, Robert Benchley, and John O'Hara
whom he had known in better days when he was young, brash,
and on top of the world. At that time, Scott had been the important one, but now his position was reversed and he was deeply
humbled. Timidly, he walked down the hall and knocked on old

friends' doors. "Scott had that unhealthy humility of the reformed alcoholic," Anita Loos said later.

Lunch at the MGM commissary was a major event, of both social and professional importance. The commissary was humorously called the Lions Den, and it was here that ambitious young men and women were thrown, to eat or be eaten. There were several tables of consequence: "the Big Table" in the center of the room where the important producers sat, and "the Left Table," where the writers sat—left because it stood against the left side of the room, and because of its general politics. At the Left Table every afternoon there was a loud gathering which included at various times such writers and actors as Anita Loos, Ogden Nash, Groucho Marx, Aldous Huxley, Spencer Tracy, and Clark Gable—an imposing group by any standards. The price of admittance to this gathering was that one had to be as irreverent and funny as possible.

At first Scott chose to sit by himself, not certain of his welcome among any group. Frances Goodrich, who with her husband, Albert Hackett, wrote the screenplays for *Ah, Wilderness* and The Thin Man series, was struck by his appearance: "The first time I saw Scott he was . . . sitting alone at a table. He just sat there but he didn't order. What I noticed were his eyes. Never in my life will I forget his eyes. He looked as if he were seeing hell opening before him. He was hugging his briefcase and he had a Coke. Then suddenly he got up to go out. I said to Albert, 'I just saw the strangest man.' He said, 'That's Scott Fitzgerald.'"

The Hacketts soon persuaded Scott to join them at the writers' table. Amidst much noise and laughter, Scott sat with a sad smile, saying little. "We accepted [Scott] because we respected him," Anita Loos remarked. "He wasn't a phony and there were a lot of phonies at Metro in those days . . . people treated [Scott] like an invalid."

Fitzgerald inspired a mixed response at the table. Groucho Marx remembered "a sick old man—not very funny stuff." But Ogden Nash noticed something quite different: Scott, sitting with his Coca-Cola surrounded by the general hilarity as though a thousand miles away, "very quiet but extremely attractive with a sweet nature that came through." For Scott, all these meetings were difficult and he did his best to avoid social engagements. He hated being the object of curiosity, and even worse—pity. On Monday, July 12, Scott's first full day of work at the studio, he was forced to confront an old friend who meant a great deal more to him than the celebrities at the writers' table. Ernest Hemingway had come to town, rushing about like an important dignitary, raising money for the Spanish Loyalists. In 1925 Scott had brought the young Hemingway to the attention of Max Perkins at Scribner's, and then had watched in awe as his one-time protégé became the most celebrated author of his time. Ernest had won all the fame and glory Scott had sought for himself, but had seen slip through his fingers.

Scott attended a screening of Hemingway's fund-raising documentary, *The Spanish Earth*, at the home of Frederic March. After the screening, Scott drove Lillian Hellman to Dorothy Parker's house, where a party was planned for Hemingway. But at Dorothy Parker's house, Scott decided he simply could not go inside to face his old protégé-made-good. "I'm riding low now. . . I'm scared of Ernest, I guess . . . It's a long story. Ernest and me," he told Lillian Hellman. She talked him into going inside, but Scott soon crept away. The next day, he sent Hemingway an ambiguous telegram: THE PICTURE WAS BEYOND PRAISE AND SO WAS YOUR ATTITUDE. Always one to analyze every social situation, Scott wrote in his notes, "I talk with the authority of failure—Ernest with the authority of success. We could never sit across the table again."

Two days later, on Wednesday evening, July 14, 1937—Bastille Day—Scott received an invitation that would change his life.

The night arrived to find Scott by himself in his bungalow apartment with no plans. The Garden of Allah, quiet as a hangover during the day, woke as the sun went down. On an evening in mid-July, there would be the sweet fragrance of many flowering trees and shrubs deepening in the air—a perfume to stir memories. The walls were thin; you could hear laughter from other bungalows, the clinking of glasses, the indistinct voices of people having fun. For Scott these drifting scents and sounds were tangible reminders of his aloneness.

Then the phone rang. It was the humorist Robert Benchley inviting him down to his bungalow for an impromptu party. Bob was often called the patron saint of The Garden of Allah; there was always a party gathered around him. This invitation tonight seemed the usual nonsense: They were celebrating the engagement of some English marquess to a pretty girl. Scott should come over right away. The party had begun at a house up the road, but neighbors had complained of the noise and so the whole crowd had just spilled back to Bob's bungalow where they could carry on as they pleased.

Scott must have hesitated; he would wonder what such a party had to do with him. People would be drinking and he knew he must not even be tempted to join in. Also he was well aware that he would be served up at this gathering as an object of curiosity, a kind of living museum piece, the once-great author who had fallen so hard. Yet to go seemed preferable to remaining alone on such a fine summer evening. Scott dressed carefully in a blue suit with a jaunty bow tie and walked down the steps from his second-floor apartment and along the winding jungle path to Benchley's bungalow.

As Scott entered the living room, he could not help but notice the most prominent feature there—a makeshift bar of two upended cartons which had been built for Benchley by the restaurateur, Dave Chasen. It seemed a typical party, loud and boisterous and liquid. Scott saw people he knew: Dorothy Parker, with whom he had had a brief affair in 1934; her new husband, Alan Campbell; Lew Ayres; Frank Morgan, who would play the wizard in *The Wizard of Oz*; the actor Charlie Butterworth; and others, including playwright Eddie Mayer, who lived in the apartment below Scott. Back east, Eddie had written a play, *The Firebrand*, about the life of Cellini. When the play was a hit on Broadway, Eddie came west to cash in. This was the breed of writer Scott detested most: the one-play-playwright or the one-book-novelist who headed to California on the heels of their first success, and never did anything serious again.

Everyone was drinking champagne, laughing and talking seemingly all at once. In earlier years, Scott would have managed quickly to become the life of such a party. Now he sat down qui-

etly in an armchair beneath a lamp, with a Coca-Cola in one
hand, and lit a cigarette. And then he saw her: the pretty girl
who was marrying the marquess. She was blond and had high
cheekbones and lovely skin. Her eyes were a complex color of
emerald green, gold, and blue. But what he noticed above all
was her radiance. She appeared lit up from inside with sheer
animal vitality and youth. Scott, who was aware of every alcoholic drink in every hand, saw that she was the only other person besides himself who was not drinking. And yet she glowed
with a private intoxication all her own. Was it happiness for her
coming marriage? The girl was laughing at a joke someone was
telling her; her laughter seemed to ring with all the youthful
magic of the world which he himself had lost. He could not help
but stare at her. She reminded him of Zelda. Not Zelda as she
was today in her sanitarium in North Carolina, but the way
Zelda had been at the beginning—lovely and sure of herself, and
brimming over with life.

For the briefest moment, the girl looked his way. Perhaps she
felt the intense energy of his stare. Their eyes met quickly, she
smiled, and then she turned away. Scott wrote later: "Smiling
faintly at him from not four feet away was the face of his . . . wife,
identical even to the expression. . . . the eyes he knew looked back
at him, a curl blew a little on a familiar forehead; the smile lingered, changed a little according to pattern; the lips parted—the
same. An awful fear went over him, and he wanted to cry aloud."
He had not come here tonight expecting such a jolt from the past.

Scott rose from the armchair and fled, leaving behind only the
smoke of his cigarette circling upward in the light of the lamp. He
returned shakily to his own bungalow apartment, fleeing as he
had run two nights before from the golden aura of Ernest
Hemingway's great success. It was intolerable that these things
should go on without him: success, beauty, youth, vitality . . . those
things he had once claimed as his own, and recognized still, but
were now so mysteriously departed from his life. Before long his
telephone rang. It was Bob Benchley asking Scott to come back to
the party.

"Who is still there?" Scott asked cautiously.

Bob rattled off a list of names, and one name, Tala Birel, struck

Scott as the sort which might belong to the young woman who had struck him so forcefully. He asked Bob to describe her; Tala was blond and pretty, Bob said, though in Hollywood this wasn't much to go on.

"Is she wearing a silver belt with cut-out stars?" Scott asked.

"Yes, she is, come back and meet her," Bob insisted.

Scott decided he should get a second look. He made his way back to the party, past the Moorish pot by his front door, down the red-tiled steps, along the overgrown winding pathway, and back to Benchley's bungalow, a living room that was filled with smoke and laughter. Scott was not a young man anymore and it must have been unsettling that a pretty girl should be able to do this to him still—drive him away, then bring him back. But he searched among the crowd and she was not there.

Scott had made a mistake. He had put the right belt on the wrong girl. Benchley introduced him to Tala Birel, who wore the belt with the cut-out stars; she was a pretty actress newly arrived from Europe, but she was not the one he sought.

Scott must have been disappointed, and yet relieved. He had been through too much. Why stir the finally peaceful ashes of a fire which had burned too bright and hard?

He left the party a second time almost immediately upon discovering his mistake, and this time he did not return. Dear God, why start everything all again?

THE ENGLISH GIRL

English people don't commit suicide when they don't get what
they want . . . they come to America.

—F. Scott Fitzgerald, notes for *The Last Tycoon*

I

AT THE TIME OF HER ENGAGEMENT PARTY on Bastille Day of 1937,
the English girl had been in California for two and a half years.
She arrived in Hollywood on Christmas Day 1935, fleeing an
affair with a married man in New York. It was typical for her to
be escaping one situation and hoping for salvation in another.
She flew into California in a nonpressurized TWA DC2, a plane
with a seating capacity of twenty-one passengers which took
nineteen hours to cross the country, setting down four times on
its long journey from Newark to the Los Angeles airport—at that
time little more than a few runways and sheds in the open fields
of Burbank.

She called herself Sheilah Graham—Sheila with an *h* because
somehow it seemed more elegant. The name was entirely self-
invented, so why not tinker with the spelling? Friends back east

41

had given her plenty of last-minute advice as to the dos and don'ts of Hollywood. "Be sure you don't accept mink coats from directors," her boss John Wheeler had warned gruffly, but he was in fact the married man she was escaping and had a stake in her virtue. A younger man who was taking over her New York apartment cautioned against going to bed with actors. "Ninety percent of them have clap or syphilis," he confided knowingly. Armed with such dire warnings, Sheilah was prepared for nearly anything as her foot set down for the first time upon California soil. Whatever happened, she had a sense that her wheel of fortune was spinning. She was young and pretty and eager to conquer. She had faith she could move mountains with her smile, and that there was a God in heaven who had special plans for her.

The Los Angeles in which Sheilah arrived was a town of low buildings and great distances. Not yet a full-fledged metropolis, it stood poised for growth but remained at heart a small and provincial place, an outpost in which people from the East Coast tended to band together with a sense of common exile. On Christmas Day 1935, Los Angeles had not yet even dreamed the word *smog;* the air was so clear that the mountains in the background seemed too perfectly etched, unreal, as though—as Robert Benchley used to say—they were only a painted set for a movie, and at any moment some Director-God might call out, "It's a wrap, boys! Strike the set!" And Los Angeles, with its fat sun and palm trees, might disappear into the darkness of the studio rafters. Occasionally, on cold winter mornings, black smoke rose into this pure air from the smudge pots protecting the nearby orange groves, and only then did the brown mountains lose their knifelike edge.

Hollywood at the end of 1935 was a brash and busy place, as if in a hurry to invent itself all at once. One week after Sheilah's arrival, on New Year's Day, the headlines screamed the elopement of Claudette Colbert, who had run off with her doctor, Joel Pressman, a nose-and-throat man who cured the star of her sinus problems and won her heart. As the new year of 1936 began, Shirley Temple was the top box-office attraction in the world, treated like a fairy princess with her own personal bungalow on the 20th Century-Fox lot. The studios ruled with absolute power and they were turning out movies in quantities as they had never done before, and would never do again. Every soundstage from one end of town to the other was busy with the clamor of moviemaking: electricians setting lights and cables, extras in exotic costumes, actors and actresses, directors and producers— and writers too, dreaming up plots and characters as fast as they could. *Mary of Scotland* was before the cameras at RKO, starring Katharine Hepburn and directed by John Ford; at Warner Brothers, Leslie Howard, Bette Davis, and Humphrey Bogart were filming *The Petrified Forest*; Greta Garbo and Robert Taylor were making *Camille* at MGM; and Charlie Chaplin was busy with *Modern Times*, costarring Paulette Goddard, an actress to whom no one knew for certain whether he was married or not.

The land itself seemed exotic to a young woman from England. There was a smell of eucalyptus in the air, sharp and strange, and steep hillsides dotted with Tudor mansions, Spanish haciendas, gingerbread castles, Swiss chalets, flowering bougainvillea, and palm trees—a fantasy array of architectural styles and vegetation to dazzle the eye. Sheilah loved the Pacific Ocean with its dramatic surf and wide beaches, and the sunsets which set the western sky ablaze each evening. Yet nothing seemed quite solid in Los Angeles; earthquakes or great scandals might at any moment rock the ground.

In 1936, Willie Bioff, the labor union leader of IATSE, was convicted of receiving thousands of dollars in cash from Joseph Schenck, the studio boss of 20th Century-Fox, in return for a guarantee that there would be no labor troubles at his studio. But the most sensational scandal during Sheilah's first year in Hollywood concerned sex: the courtroom drama of the aristocratic actress Mary Astor, who had a torrid love affair with the playwright George S. Kaufman, and was sued for divorce by her husband, Dr. Frank Nolan. During the divorce proceedings, Dr. Nolan produced Mary Astor's diary in court, in which the actress declared after a night with her lover: "thrilling ecstasy. He fits perfectly . . . Many thrilling moments . . . Twenty, count 'em diary, twenty—I don't see how he does it. He's perfect!" George S. Kaufman, naturally, became instantly one of the most sought-after playwrights in America.

This was the Hollywood to which Sheilah had come: a scandalous, incestuous industry town—a boomtown, in fact, that was vulgar, energetic, and carried on its shoulders a sense of limitless possibilities. The movies had triumphed, and in a few short decades had become the world's most popular form of entertainment. There was money to be made, empires to conquer, and each day from around the globe eager new faces arrived seeking their fortune.

Sheilah counted among her assets a quick mind, long legs, a lovely smile, good teeth for an English girl, a radiant complexion, and alarmingly bright gold-green eyes. In appearance she was often taken for an aspiring actress, though she was in fact a journalist—a writer of sensational paragraphs, the more sensational the better. She had come from England to New York in 1933, lingered in Manhattan for several years, and then like many before her, found herself drawn ever westward in search of her American dream. In California there was a new job waiting for her. She was to be the Hollywood gossip columnist for the North American Newspaper Alliance (NANA), a newspaper syndicate which would distribute her daily column throughout the country. It was a job which had the potential to confer enormous power, or she could strike out and get nowhere at all.

No one quite knew what to make of the new arrival, Sheilah Graham, who was deceptively pretty, spoke with a soft British accent, but wrote with a bite which soon made people wary of her. She did not fit in. There was a freshness about her; she seemed more at home on a tennis court than in a smoky nightclub. Some thought her naive, others as ruthless as any woman who ever came to Hollywood with conquering on her mind. She replaced NANA's previous Hollywood columnist, Molly Merrick, who bitterly complained to anyone who would listen that this English upstart had stolen her job by sleeping with the boss in New York. As for the studios, stars, and press agents—they soon were wishing Sheilah might return to wherever it was she came from. The English girl was an outsider, and would not play the game their way. Indeed she hardly seemed to know the rules.

*   *   *

Sheilah's first crisis in Hollywood was not knowing anyone, for this was a town where the right contacts were nearly everything. Working as a reporter back east she had met a few stray California celebrities, such as Carole Lombard and Merle Oberon, who all said she must look them up if ever she came west. Sheilah took them at their word, unaware that in California this was simply the way one talked; it meant nothing at all. Soon after she arrived she dialed information to inquire the phone numbers of Misses Lombard and Oberon, and was surprised to discover these stars had unlisted numbers and were not so easily to be found. In London she had once had a memorable dinner with Charlie Chaplin, but he proved even more difficult to reach—perhaps the most unreachable celebrity in all of Hollywood after Greta Garbo. Sheilah realized she was hopelessly on the outside, and this was a problem for her new job. How could she report the latest gossip if she hardly knew a soul?

Her second week in town, she heard that Marion Davies and William Randolph Hearst were about to give an important party, the biggest bash of the year. All of Hollywood would be there, but not the press, who were deliberately excluded. Sheilah tried her best to wrangle an invitation, but had no luck. The door was shut firmly in her face. No Cinderella ever longed to attend a ball as much as Sheilah did this party. She decided it was essential for her budding career that she somehow get inside Marion Davies's Santa Monica beach cottage, scoop the other columnists and make a name for herself.

Out of desperation she came up with a sly idea. She heard that Raoul Fleischman, the owner of *The New Yorker,* was in town and in the same predicament as herself: He wanted to go to the party but could not finagle an invitation. Like herself, Raoul Fleischman was a nobody by Hollywood standards, but he was a rich East Coast nobody, someone Hearst and Marion Davies would know by reputation.

She telephoned Marion Davies's secretary. "My name is Sheilah Graham, and I'm calling for Raoul Fleischman," she lied pleasantly. "He's in town and would love to go to the party." The secretary said they would be happy to send her an invitation for the New York publisher. Sheilah now phoned the unsuspecting Mr. Fleischman, a man she had never met, and told him that she had two invitations to Miss Davies's party, and would he care to go? He seemed surprised but said yes, he certainly would. Sheilah put down the phone with a sense of relief. In fact, she was extremely shy and self-conscious. It was difficult for her to make brazen telephone calls to people she did not know. For Sheilah it was like taking a deep breath and jumping off a cliff into water far below. She forced herself because there was no one to help her, and these acts of deception must be done if she were to get anywhere at all.

And so she managed to beguile herself inside the door of Marion Davies's 110-room beach "cottage"—a cottage so enormous and bejeweled with hanging crystal chandeliers that it was eventually turned into a hotel. Once inside the door, however, Raoul Fleischman quickly went off by himself, his object obtained, leaving Sheilah awkwardly on her own. She felt particularly self-conscious standing alone in this glittering crowd, a fixed smile on her face—the anxious smile of a gate-crasher. She saw Charlie Chaplin drift past accompanied by Paulette Goddard; impulsively she tried to talk with him—didn't he remember their dinner in London a few years back? But Chaplin decidedly did not remember and continued quickly past. Then there were Ronald Colman, Joan Crawford, Gary Cooper, Leslie Howard, David Niven, and others . . . beautiful people, all of them so comfortably at home with one another, enjoying their common success with an easy camaraderie. Throughout the long evening Sheilah felt a knot in her stomach from knowing she was an imposter in this glittering crowd, and feared a butler might appear at any moment, tap her on the shoulder, and say she must leave at once.

At home she cried herself to sleep. Fortunately, a writer has the last word, a brief consolation of words—and it has always been the revenge of the gate-crashing author to strike back. Sheilah wrote about Marion Davies's party in her first column, "Hollywood Today," on January 6, 1936. She enumerated all the glamorous names who had attended, and then added a barbed comment to prove herself unimpressed by such a crowd. With all

the magnificent paintings in the dining room, Gainsboroughs
and other eighteenth-century masterpieces, why must Miss
Davies hang hideous pictures in her entrance hall? Sheilah wondered aloud to her readers. What Sheilah did not know was that
these awful paintings were of Marion Davies herself, dressed in
the costumes of various roles she had played; it was unfortunate
that Sheilah had recognized a Gainsborough when she saw it,
but not her hostess. As a result, she was never to be invited to
another party given by either Marion Davies or William
Randolph Hearst.

The remark about the paintings was a blind faux pas, just a
reckless striking out in return for her discomfort. But it set a
precedent. As "Hollywood Today" embarked upon its stormy
career, Sheilah continued to write as if determined to attack
everyone, the stars, the movies, the Hollywood establishment
itself. Not long after the party, she was introduced to MGM's
biggest star, Clark Gable, on the set of his new movie, *Love on the
Run*. She wrote in her column, "Clark Gable threw back his
handsome head and exposed a neckline on which a thin ridge of
fat is beginning to collect." After a screening of *Suzy* starring
Jean Harlow and Cary Grant, Sheilah wrote: "I can't understand
why MGM, which has the best stars, the best writers, the best
directors, could make a film like *Suzy* which has the worst acting, the worst dialogue and the worst direction."

Remarks like these guaranteed that her column would be
read, but it was a dangerous road to success. She wrote her
unflattering paragraphs and then waited apprehensively for the
dust to clear, never knowing if she would be sued, or cut dead,
or grossly insulted by the powerful celebrities she had berated.
The studios were soon up in arms against her. Howard Dietz, the
New York publicity head of MGM, wrote to all of Sheilah's
newspapers asking why his studio should bother to advertise
Suzy in their paper when Sheilah Graham had ruined the picture
in advance. Sheilah's boss, John Wheeler, phoned her to take it
easy. When she did not take it easy, he sent her an urgent
telegram: "You are *not* Walter Winchell," he warned.

But Sheilah seemed out of control, unable to stop. She hardly
knew herself why she did it. She even took on the Trocadero, the

most fashionable restaurant in town: "Not even the doubtful pleasure of rubbing elbows with Louis B. Mayer can compensate for the high prices charged for rather inferior food." Sheilah had not been aware that Billy Wilkerson, the owner of the Trocadero, also owned *The Hollywood Reporter,* an important trade paper. In a single sentence she had alienated Louis B. Mayer, the most powerful man in Hollywood, and *The Hollywood Reporter,* which now declared war on Sheilah Graham and from that moment rarely missed an opportunity to attack her.

When John Wheeler sent Sheilah west to be his new columnist in Hollywood, he gave her a letter of introduction to Robert Benchley, the one-time managing editor of *Vanity Fair* and drama critic for *The New Yorker*—a writer who had made the unusual career move to become a comic actor in the movies. Bob was considered a very funny man, though he modestly maintained that his reputation for wit came mostly from laughing at other people's jokes. He arrived west to star in a number of shorts, beginning with *The Treasurer's Report* in 1928—the first all-talking motion picture—and he continued his hybrid career with such short films as *The Sex Life of the Polyp, Stewed, Fried and Boiled* (not about cooking), *How to Become a Detective,* and many more. On film, as in life, he was a sophisticated bumbler with a round kindly face who seemed utterly incapable of the most everyday household act without it becoming some wild absurdity; he could barely drop an ice cube into his drink without it causing a slapstick disaster. Nevertheless, John Wheeler hoped he would take Sheilah under his wing and show her around.

Bob was friendly on the phone. He invited Sheilah to his bungalow and when she arrived he pressed a cocktail in her hand, a gin concoction which he served in a very tall glass. Sheilah did not smoke and she hardly ever drank. She took the cocktail only to be polite, and soon she felt giddy and vague, not her normal self at all. Benchley smiled grandly. He was a large man of oblong shape who had a horror of physical exercise of any kind. Sheilah thought he looked rather like a walrus with his sleek mustache and his black hair slicked back, though she found him far too intimidating to tell him this. He was extremely urbane, a great boulevardier, dressed always in an elegantly cut dark suit, pearl gray spats, silk shirt, conservative tie, and derby hat, though with his walrus figure, Benchley made the wearing of this uniform a vaguely comic event. Bob enjoyed having pretty young women gathered around him, and generally took on the chivalrous role of their favorite uncle. From his bungalow, he ushered Sheilah with some fanfare to dinner at the Hollywood Brown Derby. The moment they sat down he ordered for her a whiskey straight up in a tall glass. Sheilah tried to say no; she was already reeling from her cocktail at The Garden of Allah, and she had heard the common wisdom that one should never mix drinks. Bob assured her this was nonsense; gin and whiskey mixed just fine. "Take my word for it—best mixture you could possibly have." He was such a charming man that it was hard to refuse him. "Don't worry," he coaxed, "God takes care of drunks and children." Sheilah was dubious, but Robert Benchley was her first important contact in Hollywood and she did not want to appear out of step. Within a few minutes she was retchingly ill. Bob drove her home from the restaurant laughing at her predicament; when he laughed his blue eyes became thin slits, which gave him the appearance of some improbable jolly Mandarin. He was clearly enjoying showing this freshly recruited Hollywood columnist around town.

The next day Sheilah woke with an unaccustomed hangover and she was furious; she felt she had been the victim of a practical joke. But Bob phoned and apologized; he invited her to dinner as a peace offering, and from that time the ice was broken between them and they became friends. Benchley was curious about her. He wondered how such an unlikely person might come to be a Hollywood gossip columnist. She told him that she was an English debutante who had grown up with private tutors, attending the best French finishing schools. At the age of eighteen she had been presented at Buckingham Palace in full court dress, obligatory feathers and train, to King George V and Queen Mary—one of those social hurdles an English girl from good society must endure. It was all quite boring of course and so she had become a journalist to see the world and embark upon a more adventurous life. Benchley thought it extravagantly funny that a young woman from such a genteel past should make her way to Hollywood and boldly take on in her column the very biggest names in town, from Gable to Louis B. Mayer. "Little Sheilah, the Giant-Killer," he called her.

He was a nice man and Sheilah liked him. But nearly everything she told him about herself was a lie—the French finishing schools, the private tutors, the aristocratic background, none of it was anything more than a puff of wishful thinking. Only the story of her coming-out at Buckingham Palace had been true, but in this instance she had managed to fool the king of England.

Sheilah soon became friendly with the group of screenwriters and actors who revolved around Bob Benchley and The Garden of Allah. There was the sharp-tongued Dorothy Parker, a small brunette woman, deceptively meek in appearance; her handsome playwright husband, Alan Campbell; the screenwriter Eddie Mayer, overweight, blind in one eye, very flirtatious; John O'Hara, morose and quiet, a big uncomfortable bull of a man who had made a hit with his first novel, *Appointment in Samarra*, and had just written *Butterfield 8*; Ogden Nash, who wrote funny limericks when he was wasn't doing screenplays; and Marc Connelly, author of the hit Broadway play *The Green Pastures*, a spry, balding leprechaun of a man who flew back and forth from New York and would stay in Hollywood, as he put it, "until my stomach revolted."

It was a merry crowd in all. There were Frances and Albert Hackett, and the actor Frank Morgan and his wife—the Morgans had a house in Beverly Hills which was a central watering hole. Frank had been in Eddie Mayer's play, *The Firebrand*, on Broadway. Sometimes Ernest Hemingway flew into town, and was grandly received. Humphrey Bogart, not yet a star, often could be found in Bob Benchley's bungalow hiding out from his tempestuous wife of the moment, Mayo Methot, who would attack Bogey with her handbag as they walked down the street, or throw plates and bottles at him in restaurants when she was angry. There were others too: Lillian Hellman, Dashiell Hammett, the humorist Sid Perelman and his brother-in-law, Nathanael West, who wrote strange books no one much read.

The group contracted and expanded depending on who was in town, and who had fled east. Sid and Laura Perelman, who worked as a screenwriting team, bought a farm in Bucks County, Pennsylvania, looking for a more civilized place to live than despised California, and this convinced Dottie Parker and her husband Alan to do likewise and become the Perelmans' Pennsylvania neighbors. But they were all back in Hollywood when they needed money, or found themselves simply bored in the idyllic woods without enough nervous action to create the irony and good times upon which they fed.

The group was the thing. Most of them had known each other from lunches at the famous Algonquin Round Table in New York a decade earlier. They had glommed together first on the East Coast and now on the West; they hung out at the same bars, lived in the same hotels, often had incestuous affairs among themselves, and even worked on the same movies, taking over projects from which someone in their group had just been fired or had left in disgust. To Sheilah they all seemed extremely clever. They spoke about books and made references to things to which she did not have a clue. She had never been part of any group before, certainly not an intellectual one, and she did her best to smile very brightly so she might fit in. Often she pretended to have read books she had never heard of so that people would not think she was stupid. When anyone asked, she told them her rehearsed lines about her aristocratic English childhood and expensive French finishing schools.

"Sometimes hearing them bounce from topic to topic, I did not realize, until I saw the deep marks, that I had been pressing my nails hard into the palms of my clenched fists in my lap. The tension was exhausting," she later recalled. The only part of herself she was entirely certain about was her sexuality. Men turned her way when she walked into a room. Often it was subtle, a guarded glance, a change of posture, but Sheilah knew what it meant. She had discovered that she could transmit invisible currents of sexual enticement to whichever man she chose—quite tangible currents she could visualize as she sent them to do their work through any room, bypassing tables and chairs, climbing up ankles and legs, entangling her chosen victim in a delicious silver web. She was a tremendous flirt and often soothed her sense of inadequacy with a quick conquest. However, she had not been in Hollywood long before she herself was conquered.

She fell to the successful movie director King Vidor, with whom she had an affair throughout much of 1936. Vidor won her heart, despite remembered warnings about directors, because he was gentle and poetic and refined—a smooth operator with fine aristocratic manners. Even his name had a certain panache that set Sheilah dreaming. He invited Sheilah to his home where he plied her with delicious fried shrimp served by his Filipino servant. Then the servant withdrew and played a guitar accompaniment in the next room while King sang to her a seductive rendition of Gershwin's "Summertime" from *Porgy and Bess.* It was overwhelming, a romantic scene straight out of one of his movies. For Sheilah it was impossible to say whether it was the shrimp, the man, or the music, but she soon believed she was in love. Before long King began to mention marriage and a beautiful house he would build in the hills where they would live. He showed her the blueprints and wanted her approval for each detail of the design. But a few days before Christmas in 1936— the anniversary of her first year in Hollywood—King Vidor eloped with another woman and Sheilah spent the holidays miserably by herself. Several years earlier she had undergone an operation over Christmas and she was beginning to have a lifelong superstition about this winter holiday.

The incident with King Vidor was a difficult blow; she cried, her pride was hurt, but she picked herself up and kept going because she had no life to return to and there wasn't any other choice. She saw that Hollywood was not easy. This was a town for the very tough of spirit; despite the sunshine, there was a chill in the air. No matter—romantic, frightened, and brash, Little Sheilah, the Giant-Killer, was determined to succeed.

II

The girl from England who called herself Sheilah Graham had been migrating westward all her life. The first step of the way, however, was a distance much greater than from England to California; she had to cross from one world to another, from the East End of London to the West End, where her dreams lay.

In 1920, the year in which F. Scott Fitzgerald was busy proclaiming a new decade with his successful first novel, *This Side of Paradise*, a sixteen-year-old girl named Lily Shiel hoarded her money whenever possible to ride the top of the red double-decker bus from Stepney Green to the bright lights of Piccadilly and W.1. This was the theater district, the posh and glamorous London she longed for. From her seat high above the street, she gazed at the proud buildings on stately avenues: Lloyds, the Midland Bank, the great shipping companies, Cunard and the United States and French Lines. She passed wonderful gaudy signs that lit up, erased themselves, then spelled out their beckoning messages once again. Lily envied the elegant people who drifted in and out of these fine places; they seemed to be part of some enchanted world. Her ambition was to become a "typewriter," as she thought of it, in a West End office. She imagined a handsome, poetic, young employer, someone who would be gentle and rich and kind, whose eyes might twinkle when he looked at her. There was no doubt in her mind that he would fall madly in love with her and take care of her forever.

At the age of sixteen, Lily was already pretty though not as pretty as she would later become. She had thick ash blond hair which fell in luxuriant waves to her shoulders, and a figure which caused her intense embarrassment in public; her breasts were large and had developed early, making her often the object of unwanted remarks and whistles. (Fortunately in the West End gentlemen were polite.) She had a round, moonish face that was slightly pudgy due to her astonishing appetite for sweets and every kind of food to which she could lay siege. She had been hungry as long as she could remember. She dressed badly since she had no money for clothes and she spoke with a Cockney accent, dropping her *h*'s and adding expressions such as "Oo-er!" and "lum-me" to nearly every sentence. She had a misty, soft English complexion, and she positively glowed with energy. Even in the West End, men often gave her a second look.

The top of the bus was her place for dreaming. Sometimes Lily took the long bus ride to the West End for no other reason than to use the magnificent bathroom at the Savoy Hotel. She knew it was bold to walk into the great lobby of the hotel as though she belonged in such a place. She avoided the eyes of the doorman and the concierge and her heart beat quickly at the thought that one of these imposing figures might bear down upon her, pick her up, and toss her back out into the street. Yet danger was part of the excitement of such a brazen act.

She drifted along the thick, muted carpets of the corridor toward the ladies' room to sequester herself in a lovely private stall. She had never known such a bathroom before. The cool toilet seat against her naked rear was the very kiss of luxury. She lingered as long as possible. Then finally, reluctantly, she pulled up her knickers, smiled grandly at the bathroom attendant, and left the Savoy Hotel, hoping that some girl—some dreamy girl like her—might perhaps be watching enviously from the top of a passing bus.

Throughout 1920 Lily carried the image of the Savoy Hotel in her heart, a secret talisman that helped her through the misery of her real life. She was bitterly unhappy except in her daydreams.

A year later, at the age of seventeen, Lily made her escape. She moved to the West End and left her old life behind. It wasn't so much a journey from one part of London to another as a total exorcism of the past. From that day on, whenever anyone asked about her childhood, she told them lies. She wiped clean her personal history as completely as a damp cloth moving across a blackboard.

Lily found a job and a room to live in on the same fateful day. The job appeared through an advertisement in the newspaper: "Wanted: Girls with Good Teeth. No Experience Necessary." This seemed to fit her miraculously well on both counts. Lily took a bus to an office in Holborn, a district which lay between the City and the West End, and applied for the job. A man told her to smile; in fact, she was so breathlessly excited by the interview she could barely stop smiling. Because she was pretty she was hired without any further need to prove her qualifications and told to report on Monday morning at Gamages department store. Her assignment: to demonstrate and sell a radically new kind of toothbrush.

Lily left the employment office feeling as if she were a conquering character in an epic poem. From Holborn she made her way to a boardinghouse in Sussex Square which had advertised a small room at the rear of the building for ten shillings a week. Sussex Square was in W.2 rather than W.1, where she wished to be—W.1 being, as far as Lily was concerned, the heart of the universe. Nevertheless, her new room was within walking distance of the theater district and Lily was euphoric to be on her own. Money of course would be very tight. The salary at Gamages was one pound a week plus ten percent commission on whatever she sold; she could only count on ten shillings with which to live after she paid her rent. To economize she decided she would rise early and walk each morning to the department store in Holborn. This was a distance of several miles but everything was possible for a girl so energized at the prospects of a new life.

Lily moved into the boardinghouse, unpacked her few belongings, and when night fell she set out walking toward Piccadilly Circus, Leicester Square, Coventry Street, and Shaftesbury Avenue, where the gaudy lights of the theater district flashed invitingly. In 1921 this part of London was alive with the jazzy rhythms of the new decade. For Lily it all seemed like a wonderful party staged for her alone. She watched from the sidewalk as stately Rolls-Royce automobiles drifted up the wide avenues distributing elegant men and women in their evening finery into the crowded theaters and restaurants. She had no money to go into these places herself. She could only watch from the street and imagine the delights within, but this did not in any way dampen her spirits.

The streets were a carnival show and they drew her night after night back to W.1. Each evening after work she left her boardinghouse and headed back to Piccadilly and Leicester Square, to walk and dream and breathe in all the people and sights. Often men smiled and spoke to her; she thought it must be because she was glowing with destiny and they could not resist her. She was extremely naive and a virgin. She did not suspect that the area in which she walked was well known for prostitutes. "Hello, darling!" the men accosted, and she was pleased to be noticed. Sometimes heavily made-up women on street corners told her to shove off, but this was only a small unpleasantness. She decided she liked men ever so much more than women, and she began to play a game to see how many gentlemen she might lure each night to smile at her and say hello. She had only been pretty a short time, since about the age of fourteen; before that, she had been extremely gawky and plain, and so it was gratifying to test out her new power over men.

She knew of course that it was a dangerous game to walk the streets of London at night. She wasn't as naive as all that; she read *The News of the World* and knew about white slavery, that there were sinister men with swarthy complexions and foreign accents who were lurking in shadows hoping to abduct good English girls like her into some Arabian sheikh's harem where she would be forced to commit unspeakable sexual acts. Lily shuddered to think about these things—and she thought about them frequently.

One night she heard footsteps behind her as she walked near Piccadilly Circus. She had a fish on the line and she played him expertly for several blocks. As she approached a streetlight she half-turned her face and gave a thoughtful smile toward a distant building, just a small maneuver so the man might see her profile. Then she turned all the way to get a glimpse of him and her heart nearly stopped beating. He was a black man! He was dressed in elegant clothes, but his face was black as coal, the blackest black she'd ever seen. All of Lily's wildest fears of white slavery rushed into her mind. Would he try to inject her with some drug to make her do whatever he wished? She was about to run when he grabbed hold of her arm.

"Here, you shouldn't be on the streets like this," he said sternly. "How old are you?"

"Nineteen," she lied.

The black man hailed a taxi and put her inside. He gave her a ten-shilling note for the fare, enough money to pay her rent for a week. "Now you go home, you hear me?" Lily had been scared witless, and now she felt rather silly. Still it was a treat to find herself seated in a taxi for the first time in her life and she drifted in great luxury back to her boardinghouse on Sussex Square. She never knew what to expect on her nocturnal walks; adventure was always in the air. One night, however, she had an encounter that put an end to her walking. A dapper middle-aged man wearing a gray homburg came up to her on the street and said unexpectedly, "I'm about to have dinner. Would you like to join me?"

They were standing near an elegant restaurant where a framed menu with French writing beckoned from a curtained window. Exotic aromas drifted into the street. Lily had only fantasized about such places and she could not resist. "I don't mind if I do," she replied. The dapper middle-aged man opened the door and ushered her into a new world. There were fabulously dressed gentlemen in long black tails and stiff white shirts gliding among tables set with white linen and silver. It took Lily a moment to understand they were only waiters. Her eye was caught by the dessert cart with its extravagant array of glazed pastries, tarts, and cakes such as she had never seen before. She was inclined to go no further than this lovely cart but the man took her arm and led her upstairs to a private dining room, a small but well-appointed room with a table set for two and a settee at one side. To Lily this seemed like a scene from a book. A waiter appeared with menus written in an incomprehensible French. Her escort smoothly took the lead. "Shall we start with soup?" he asked. Lily said yes indeed. "And, after soup would you care for roast chicken, or perhaps lamb chops?" Lily chose the lamb chops because she had never eaten them before—they were something for rich people because there was so little meat on the bone.

The food arrived and she ate with a ravenous appetite, slurping up the soup, inhaling baskets of bread, gnawing at the lamb chop bones to yield every possible morsel of meat. She ate as fast as she could, as if afraid this magical feast might disappear from the table if she paused for a single moment. The middle-aged man attempted rudimentary conversation, asking about her life. She fibbed happily. She told him she was a companion to a rich old lady who lived in a great mansion in Brighton, but of course it was very quiet by the sea and sometimes she simply had to come into town for the theater and other amusements. When the dinner was finished, he asked if she would care to move to the settee for coffee. Lily said she would; it seemed quite elegant to arrange herself on such a settee. But when the waiter left, the man drew Lily close and kissed her on the lips. She did not like this very much, for he seemed awfully old to her. But he had bought her an expensive dinner and she knew she must be nice. "You're a very pretty girl," he told her—and this was gratifying. But when he kissed her again, she pushed him away.

"What's the matter?" he asked. He tried to pull her to him by force but she broke free and stood up from the settee.

"You let me go!" she cried. "You let me out of here!"

The man remained seated on the settee and studied her with curiosity. "Why did you come with me?" he asked finally.

Lily was so thoroughly ashamed that she told him the truth: "I thought how nice it would be to have a dinner."

"Then go," he said coldly. "You've had your dinner."

Lily escaped down the stairs; she fled though the crowded dining room, past well-dressed patrons and waiters in black tie and tails until she was outside the door and standing once again in the freedom of the street. She knew she had skirted something unspeakable; she vowed she would never tell anyone about this episode. But meanwhile an entirely inappropriate smile came to her lips. She had gotten away with it, the most marvelous meal of her life!

These were the nights. Lily's days were spent more prosaically on the ground floor of Gamages department store, where she stood near the perfume counter amid a display of tooth-brushes—an entirely new sort of toothbrush that was scientifi-cally designed to clean the backs of teeth. No one had ever seen such a toothbrush before. It was shaped oddly like a pair of false teeth with a handle attached to the middle. Lily's job was to demonstrate how to move the handle from side to side until the backs of your teeth were miraculously clean. Unfortunately, a second conventional toothbrush was needed for the front of your teeth and this made the invention a hard sell. The seventeen-year-old girl did her best. Hour after hour she delivered a memo-rized speech to whoever might rest a moment from shopping to listen to her; she warned of unseen tooth decay lurking behind the bright facade of every smile—yes, the small device she held in her hand at two shillings sixpence was more expensive than a regular toothbrush, but it would save a fortune in dental bills, not to mention the anguish of the drill. Most busy shoppers quickly passed her by, but sometimes men lingered, smiled at her, and bought her goods. Lily soon discovered that she had significantly more success with male customers than female. Women, she sensed, did not care about hygiene as much as they should.

One day a man literally blew into her life, swept into the department store by wind and rain to escape the weather. He stood shaking off the water from his belted raincoat near the corner where Lily was delivering her sales pitch. His name was Major John Graham Gillam, an army officer from the Great War; he was a handsome man with dark hair growing low on his forehead and deep blue eyes that twinkled with amusement. When he noticed the young salesgirl struggling to sell her impossible item, he stopped to listen to her pitch with the expression on his face of a true believer. When she finished, he reached into his pocket and produced his two shillings sixpence for a toothbrush. "By Jove," he laughed, "if you can sell this toothbrush, you can sell anything. You're just the girl I need to handle my fancy-goods department."

There was something dashing about Major Gillam. He had been awarded the Distinguished Service Order for his part in the disastrous battle of Gallipoli, and even as a civilian there lingered about him the romantic aura of a war hero. His favorite expression seemed to be "By Jove!," which he said often with great gusto and with a wonderfully upper-class accent. Major Gillam left the girl his business card, just in case she should ever seek a change of employment—and she did, within a matter of days, when the company which manufactured the toothbrush for the backs of teeth went out of business for lack of sales. Lily found herself without warning unemployed, her first crisis as an independent woman. She remembered the nice gentleman who had left his card and it seemed worth a try to call him. She gave her name to a secretary and was startled when the woman cried out that the Major had been trying to find her all week and she should please hold on. In a moment, Major Gillam himself was on the phone. "Where have you been?" he demanded. He said he had returned to Gamages only to find her gone. He seemed almost angry that she should disappear so inconsiderately from his life. "Why didn't you leave an address?" he complained.

She had rarely felt so wanted. "By Jove, I thought I'd never find you," he exclaimed happily a few hours later when she was seated across from him in his office. The Major hired her on the spot to be the newest employee of the John Graham Company, John Graham Gillam, Managing Director, in charge of his "fancy-goods" department. Lily would receive two pounds a week plus a twenty percent commission on what she sold—a significant raise from her toothbrush enterprise. He assured her the job was easy. She was to travel the streets of London from store to store with a bag of samples and take orders for the Major's line of goods. Lily felt herself wonderfully saved. Unfortunately, "fancy-goods" was a euphemism for items of an even more dubious nature than the toothbrush designed for the backs of teeth—goods which were entirely too fanciful for the conservative needs of British life. There was, for instance, the Lift-to-Lite lamp, a cordless lamp with a small battery in the base which one turned on simply by lifting the device in one easy motion from the table. And Suji Muji car polish, a miracle product designed to make any automobile shine with oriental splendor. But these items paled in comparison to the fiendishly clever cigarette with which the Major hoped to make a fortune—a cigarette which lit without the need for a match simply by striking one end against a rough surface.

Simply put, John Gillam was one of the world's impractical men. He was befuddled with an optimism so charming and unfounded in reality that he could not have survived in business for a week had it not been for the financial support of a rich older sister who adored him. He bought absurd items at the wrong time and for the wrong price. Someone convinced him there was a fortune to be made in Turkish Delight. The Major impulsively rented an entire factory to make the sticky candy believing he had found at last a product which could not possibly fail. But he had not bothered to investigate whether he could compete effectively against the candy factories which were already well established. He could not.

Johnny—as he soon became known in Lily's life—was positive he would be a millionaire any day soon, but meanwhile he was generally in need of a loan. Sometimes when they worked late in the evening, he took Lily to a small Greek restaurant nearby in Soho, the Mars, where she ate everything in sight with an astonishing appetite, as though she hadn't eaten for a week, and might never have a chance to eat again. Johnny tactfully suggested she might not actually need to eat the bones of the fish and which knife and fork were appropriate for different courses. "You're always sniffling, Lily—*do* blow your nose," he told her gently. It seemed natural that he should become her teacher, guiding her through the protocol of restaurant manners, convincing her above all things of the need to simply slow down. He told her that it was correct to say "What?" when she did not understand something rather than the more convoluted "Pardon," and that young ladies in society were called debutantes rather than de*bun*tees as Lily had previously thought. Johnny had to tell her everything. He advised her to remove her coat at dinner so that her sleeve would not fall sloppily into the gravy of her plate; he told her the proper pronunciation of the French perfume was "Sha-nell" not "Channel." Lily knew none of these things. She was a wild creature, ignorant of the most elemental rules of society. Johnny was endlessly amused by her; he laughed at the odd things she did and said, but always in a gentle way and never at her expense. Where could such a creature have come from? And why was such a pretty girl so utterly on her own? There was a mystery about her certainly, but Johnny was tactful enough not to inquire too closely.

He bought her clothes; he said it was a business investment since a representative of the John Graham Company must look the part. He was twenty-five years her senior, but Lily found him utterly romantic. Before long, she thought she was in love with her sweet and optimistic employer. If he did not happen to have a practical bent in business, Lily believed this a fine thing— lesser beings such as herself might concern themselves with sur-

vival. She took Johnny's dreamy nature as a sure sign of aristocracy. She had always fantasized an upper-class employer who
would save her. Johnny was simply two decades older than the
figure in her dreams. However, there was to be a complication in
this matter of the heart—a man named Monty Collins, who
chanced to be a millionaire.

Lily met Monty Collins on a double date arranged by a
sandy-haired young man, George, who had the next booth to
hers at the *Daily Mail*'s Ideal Home Exhibition. Lily was at the
exhibit trying to peddle the Major's battery-powered Lift-to-Lite
lamp, but business was slow and George sometimes ambled
over to talk. He confided that his sister Helen was being courted
by a millionaire, though she had not quite managed to dredge
forth a definite proposal of marriage. The millionaire had suggested a night at the theater in his private box, asking George to
find a date for himself to make it a foursome. Would Lily care to
come along?

Lily would. For the seventeen-year-old salesgirl, the word *millionaire* had a magical glow. It wasn't anything definite, just a
general feeling of miraculous possibilities. So she borrowed an
evening gown from a friend and waited at an upper window of
her boardinghouse until she saw a long sleek black Rolls-Royce
pull up her street. It was a magnificent automobile that was open
in the front for the chauffeur and enclosed at the rear for the
lucky passengers within. Lily had fervent hopes that every person in her boardinghouse was watching with envy as she drifted
downstairs into the luxury of this fabulous machine. Inside the
car, George, his sister Helen, and Mr. Monty Collins made room
for her; she sat down upon the softest gray upholstery she had
ever known, enclosed in a floating world of quiet leather and
polished wood. Monty Collins was unfortunately not as splendid
as his car. He was a short squat man, thirty-eight years old—
younger than Johnny, but he appeared in fact much older. There
was an unhealthy puffiness about his eyes, his hair was thin and
sparse, and he did not speak with an upper-class accent. Monty
Collins was a self-made man who owned a chain of grocery
stores throughout London. He inspected Lily in the same way a

greengrocer might examine a particularly fine and attractive peach in the last days of summer.

At the theater, the women sat in the front of the box and the men settled into chairs behind them. As Lily sat watching the play, she became aware that Mr. Collins was staring at her back. She could feel the heat of his breath upon her neck. It would be most curious, she thought, if she could make this man fall in love with her. Would he shower her with money and jewels? All these possibilities fairly danced in her head as she imagined a life for herself of great wealth. A millionaire, a Rolls-Royce, a large house in the country, an endless banquet of food—four meals a day if she wanted, not counting high tea. In all these dreamy pleasures, Lily never once stopped to consider that the man was already spoken for by George's sister, Helen.

During the intermission, a waitress appeared with a bottle of champagne and four glasses. Lily had never tasted champagne before; it seemed to her wonderfully fizzy and a bit like lemonade. After the theater, they once again loaded themselves into the Rolls-Royce and were whisked off to the Café de Paris where Monty had reserved a table. Here there was more champagne and a dinner such as Lily had never seen: Scottish smoked salmon, Dover sole in a cream sauce, and for dessert crêpes suzettes served in flaming brandy by the waiter at the table.

"A penny for your thoughts," Monty asked her flirtatiously, filling her glass with champagne.

Feeling giddy and bold, Lily raised her glass in a toast: "Here's to our friendship," she declared. George and Helen watched with sickened expressions, but Monty and Lily were hardly aware they were even at the same table. After dinner, George tried one last strategy to get his sister's romance back on course: He suggested they drop Lily off first—get rid of her at any cost—since she lived quite nearby on Sussex Square while they were all the way in Hampstead, a middle-class suburb on the edge of town. But the millionaire knew what he wanted. "No, we'll take *you* home first," he said in a tone which did not invite discussion.

Lily had triumphed. She had a millionaire in tow, and she would have enjoyed her triumph greatly had it not been for a

simple fact of nature brought on by the unaccustomed champagne. As soon as the group left the Café de Paris she became
aware that she must go to the bathroom. Unfortunately, she did
not quite know how to broach this delicate subject while riding
in a splendid limousine through the dark streets of London. It
seemed uncouth even to mention such a thing. But the trip to
Hampstead was a long one. When they arrived, Lily thought to
ask George and Helen if she could use their bathroom, but Helen
shot her such a look of undisguised malice that this did not seem
a wise request.

The Rolls turned and began its long trip back to the West End.
Lily was now alone with her millionaire and he proceeded to
focus his full attention upon her, asking many personal questions
about her life. Did she have a boyfriend? Would she like to see
him again? She answered in staccato bursts of discomfort, "no,
no . . . yes, yes," crossing her legs in tight dismay, feeling her
bladder expand at every slight bounce in the road. It was sheer
torture, an impossible situation—and yet it seemed equally
impossible simply to say that they must stop somewhere, anywhere, immediately, so she could pee.

Not even a Rolls-Royce could keep nature from its tumultuous
course. To Lily's horror she felt a warm gush of liquid release
from between her legs and spread on the seat beneath her. She
wanted to die. When they arrived at her boardinghouse in W.2,
she rose miserably from her seat and dared steal a quick glance
behind her to see her worst fears confirmed—there were two
dark half moons of dampness on the light gray upholstery. It was
unthinkable what she had done—she had desecrated this fabulously expensive car! Monty Collins walked her to the door and
kissed her briefly on the cheek; he seemed to take her agitation as
a romantic sign. But she could not even look at him. She ran
upstairs, flung herself on her bed, and wept for many hours as
though her soul had burst apart.

She believed she was disgraced forever. She was certain she
would never see her millionaire again—but in this matter she
was wrong. Two days later Monty Collins called to invite her to
lunch at Skindles, a restaurant in the country at Maidenhead-on-
Thames. When the lunch was over, before they might step into

his Rolls, he pointedly informed her where the ladies' room might be found.

Life, as Lily was quick to learn, was a twisty course of accidents and ironies. As it happened, Monty Collins was shopping for a virgin, a young innocent girl to be his wife—that rare being who would be demure to the point of subservience and accept without question the rules he laid down for her. A girl who was too shy to ask for the bathroom was precisely what he had in mind. She could not have won his millionaire heart more completely in any other way than by peeing so disgracefully upon the upholstery of his splendid automobile.

Lily began to lead a double life, courted by two men who were each ignorant of the other's existence. Monty gave her clothing and jewels; Johnny his laughter and charm. Monty was a graceless dancer, treading heavily across the floor; Johnny took her gliding to music so smoothly in his arms that she felt weightless and free.

There was no question which man she preferred, but Monty was the millionaire and in her internal debate she always returned to this unequivocal fact. Moreover, despite many lovely evenings with Johnny, he had never mentioned the word *love*. He had hinted at it obliquely with fine aristocratic reserve, but had never come out and said simply, "I love you, Lily, I want to marry you." This left Lily open to the lure of the million banknotes she sometimes imagined fluttering down about her head, all those intriguing pounds sterling. One night Monty settled the matter. He literally showered her with diamonds. He gave her a diamond bracelet, then a diamond brooch, and, almost as an afterthought, he presented her with a glittering diamond engagement ring. He did not ask, but rather simply informed her that they would be married. It was a superfluous pleasure when she said yes.

And so it was settled, she was engaged to Monty Collins—or rather it would be settled if she could only bear to tell the news to Johnny. But she could not. She had many chances for there were frequent dinners with Johnny at the Mars, and often she went to his flat on Oxford Street to bathe in his luxurious marble tub while he went off to regimental dinners. Sometimes she allowed Johnny to kiss her—it seemed innocent enough, though often his kisses were placed strategically upon her legs as he buried his head passionately beneath her dress. Lily understood that this triangular situation could not last; eventually she must either tell Johnny about Monty Collins, or Monty Collins about Johnny, but she hoped to put off the day of reckoning as long as possible. If she was lucky perhaps she could fool everyone forever, and they would all love her and give her nice things. But the truth came out on a long bank holiday.

It was the Easter weekend of 1923 and Monty suggested they spend the vacation at Brighton, where he had reserved separate rooms at the Metropole Hotel, determined that his fiancée remain a virgin until their wedding night. But Johnny had finally begun to suspect something was amiss, and it spurred him into action. He managed to follow Lily and showed up at the Metropole Hotel just as she and Monty were sitting down for dinner. The Major was astonished to find his fancy-goods sales-girl at the restaurant table bedecked in jewels and wearing an expensive gown.

"I know this lady," Johnny said curtly as he interrupted their meal. "Would you mind very much if I had the next dance with her?" On the dance floor, Johnny demanded, "Who is that man? And these clothes? Have you gone wrong or something?"

"I'll explain later," she said weakly. For Lily it was a nightmare to have the two men in her life come together at the same time and place. It meant she was found out, all her lies were exposed. But Johnny was wise enough not to criticize her; he knew this was his last chance to declare himself if he ever was to have her. "Can you leave that man now so that we can talk? I love you. I want to marry you," he said as they were dancing.

Lily was aware that Monty was watching angrily from the table. She whispered to Johnny that she loved him too. "Are you sure you want to marry me?"

"Yes," he said. "That's why I came here."

"Then let's do it quickly," she told him. They arranged to meet at six in the morning and take the first train for London. Then Johnny escorted Lily back to her table, executed a curt military bow in the general direction of Monty Collins, and left Lily to do the hard part.

"That man's in love with you. I want an explanation," Monty exploded the moment they were alone. In reply Lily took off her diamonds—the brooch, the bracelet, and the engagement ring— and threw them at him across the table. "Good-bye," she said. Her voice was unnatural and loud; she stood and walked fatefully from the room, leaving the table strewn with jewels. It seemed to Lily a very grand gesture. The next morning she found a note from Monty in her mailbox as she was leaving the hotel: "I am prepared to forgive you if you have an explanation." But she tore the note into little pieces. Her decision was made; she would be the wife of Major John Graham Gillam, wholesaler of dreams. She did not quite understand that she had come to an important intersection in her life, and of the two paths open to her had taken the one toward romance and adventure, rather than financial security and, if she was lucky, a mild domestic peace. The wedding ceremony took place the following Friday afternoon at the Caxton Hall registry office in Westminster with two charwomen acting as witnesses. Lily was nineteen years old but lied on her marriage certificate, pretending to be twenty-one, which in 1923 was the legal age of consent.

As for Monty Collins, he committed suicide soon after Lily's marriage. He telephoned her on the evening before his death to say good-bye. He was not a romantic man, he could not dance well, and his conversation was heavy. Yet apparently he had been mortally lonely, and when Lily with her youth and wide-eyed wonder passed from his life, she left a prospect of unbearable emptiness in her wake. It seemed he too was capable of a grand gesture on demand.

Lily was stunned. It had never occurred to her that her web of ambitions and fantasies might affect anyone else. She was somber for a few days, and then added the memory to all the others in her past, a bank vault of accumulating guilt. She had always believed herself a terrible person, but at the moment there was no time to look backward or dwell upon her sins. Her life was moving too quickly to new crises and even more complicated lies, and she needed all her wits to survive.

3

THE MYSTERIOUS
MRS. GILLAM

She would be a runaway all her life, running away from the consequences of her actions. She would run away from her country,
from her background, from poverty, from her religion, from
people and places, from situations. To the end of her life she
would be running, sometimes beyond the limits of her grasp and
often running scared.

—Sheilah, describing her life in 1978

LILY'S MARRIAGE IN THE SPRING of 1923 to Major John Gillam was
beset immediately by twin problems that would greatly alter the
course of her life. The first of these problems became obvious on
her wedding night. The Major was impotent, could not maintain
an erection, and despite a great deal of huffing and puffing on
his part, he was unable to take his young wife's virginity.

"Ah, if only you were Spanish," he told her with a sigh.
"Spanish women excite me tremendously." But Lily was not

even remotely Spanish, and after a second failed attempt, Johnny never tried sex again. For Lily this was a bitter disappointment. She was a very physical young woman and had saved her virginity for this breathless moment, her wedding night, only to have her husband ejaculate limply upon her leg and fall asleep.

The second problem came quickly on the heels of the first. Johnny's business went bankrupt when his rich older sister learned of his marriage to a Cockney girl and became so enraged that she cut off her charming younger brother without a further cent. For years Johnny's sister had been paying the red ink of failed schemes, and no amount of fancy-goods could save the John Gillam Company without her support. Life was harsh in London without money. The electricity in the Gillam flat was turned off when the bills remained unpaid, and Johnny sent his young wife to deal with the problem, hoping her lovely smile would inspire some credit. A day soon came when they had sixpence to their name—and rather typically, Johnny lost it. Walking to the store to buy bananas for their supper, the coin slipped through his fingers and fell down a crack in the sidewalk. That evening they went hungry.

In the absence of any other means of support, Johnny soon began to regard his pretty wife with the same entrepreneurial eye with which he had once contemplated his stock of trick cigarettes that lit without the need for a match. She could save them both; he was sure of it. She must be an actress, he decided—by Jove, it was just the thing! She would be smashing on the London stage. "You're so pretty all of London will be at your feet," he assured her. He borrowed from the Jewish moneylenders for his wife to enroll at the Royal Academy of Dramatic Arts, where she performed Shakespeare with a Cockney accent that sent both her teachers and fellow students into paroxysms of laughter. In speech class, Lily worked endlessly on simple words such as "moon," which had a way of coming out of her mouth as a bleating "mee-yoon." Gradually her Cockney mannerisms lessened and nearly disappeared, though they might return at any moment when she was nervous. Eventually Johnny decided that Shakespeare was the wrong path for a girl with her looks but uncertain accent. Clearly she would fare better in musical comedy, and he borrowed more money (he was always willing to borrow money on a sure thing) so that she might have private lessons in singing and dance. Lily suspected these lessons were a lost cause, but bankruptcy and impotency were not a young girl's dream of a perfect marriage and she was willing to give anything a try.

Fortunately the passing years had done a great deal for her appearance. The pudginess was gone. Her round, moonish face had thinned to reveal the classic lines of the beautiful woman waiting underneath. Her legs seemed longer, her skin more perfectly smooth, her eyes more green and catlike than before. There was also a new aura of sophistication in the way she dressed and carried herself. She certainly knew the proper spoon to use now in restaurants. Johnny decided she must have a new name; Lily Gillam was not glamorous enough by far. And so she usurped his middle name, Graham, and dreamed up Sheilah with the elegant *h*.

Now she was ready. Through a friend, Johnny was able to arrange for the newly created Sheilah Graham to audition before the famous impresario Charles B. Cochran. She sang a nervous rendition of "Rosemary, I Love You" into a darkened theater and to her astonishment was hired to be a chorus girl in the revue, *One Damn Thing After Another*. She would be a Cochran Young Lady, who were famous throughout England for their beauty and sex appeal.

Sheilah looked the part, at least. She was soon voted "The Most Beautiful Chorus Girl in London" and received a trophy upon which were inscribed the words, "Be Faithful, Brave and O Be Fortunate." It was the faithful part that was to prove so difficult. Before long she was besieged by an endless array of rogue males—fashionable bachelors and married men who seemed to have a very good idea what chorus girls were for. Johnny encouraged her to befriend these wealthy men. At the start of Sheilah's new career, he had made a staggering suggestion: Why not pretend that she was single? Clearly she would do better in the theater if people believed she was unmarried. And she *must* succeed, he stressed, in order to save them both.

Sheilah was not at all certain she could pull it off; it seemed to her an enormous lie. How, for instance, was she to explain his presence? Nothing was easier, he replied. When he came to the theater, she would introduce him as her uncle Johnny—quite an easy deception due to their twenty-five-year difference in age. And perhaps while sitting with her new friends at elegant midnight suppers, she could use the intimacy of the moment to convince her rich suitors to invest their money in her uncle Johnny's clever business schemes—schemes which needed only a small outlay of capital to get off the ground. Any moment soon they would be fabulously rich; then they could tell the world the truth and laugh about the whole thing. Meanwhile, for desperate people, truth was a luxury they could not afford.

And so Sheilah Graham, the creature recently evolved from Lily Shiel, began to live a complicated life, slipping into the platonic bed of her husband at two or three in the morning after a romantic rendezvous with Sir This, or Lord That, or other gay blade about town. One night as she danced at The Embassy Club the Prince of Wales passed within inches and smiled at her. The Prince of Wales!—Pragger-Wagger to his friends. Her date was a captain in the Irish Coldstream Guards and later he told Sheilah, "Pragger-Wagger wanted to know who was the beautiful blonde I was dancing with." All this was very exciting to a girl who had recently been selling toothbrushes. Johnny was greatly pleased at her social success and refrained from asking indelicate questions. Sheilah was glad to lose her virginity at last but sensed this was not what marriage was supposed to be. She was a romantic, after all, and had not married Johnny for practical reasons. But what could she do? It was inevitable that the combined pressures of a sexless marriage, Johnny's tolerance, and the odd life of the theater should send her seeking satisfaction into other arms. As with the case of Monty Collins, she felt a persistent guilt, a sense that she must be a very wicked person. But meanwhile the glittering nightlife of London in the 1920s was a delicious adventure for someone so newly arrived, and she refused to be denied. She was young, so much younger than Johnny, and most of all she just wanted to have fun.

However, the complications grew steadily more ornate, compounded by the lies she was forced to tell, and she soon discovered it was not so easy to live a double life. Eventually one of Sheilah's lovers began to pay the rent on Johnny and Sheilah's flat at 128 Wigmore Street, ignorant of the fact that she was married. Johnny was pleased with the arrangement since now he could concentrate more fully on his various investment schemes. But for Sheilah there were many awkward moments due to this complex ménage. Occasionally Johnny was forced to sneak out quickly when the lover came to call, and once he hid himself in the closet until the man was gone. Such incidents left Sheilah a nervous wreck. But it was all temporary, Johnny assured her. Any day now his ship was bound to come in.

Her professional life caused even more anxiety. For Sheilah it was easier to fool wealthy men into believing she was single than to pretend that she could sing, act, and dance. She was so pretty that Cochran gave her every chance to prove herself, but she knocked her dance partners to the ground, crashed into scenery, and one performance she nearly brought the entire set down when a hat she wore became attached to a backdrop curtain. She lived in a state of constant tension. One night she was invited with the other Young Ladies to a private midnight supper where they were asked to do high kicks for a group of rich men, who laughingly put their heads close to the floor and hoped to gain a revealing glimpse of legs and thighs. Sheilah could not care less about the legs and the thighs; what she was terrified to reveal was that she could not in fact do a high kick. She feigned a sudden headache to escape the midnight performance.

She lived with a continual sense that she was a fraud, a grand imposter. She could barely sleep at night; she suffered chronic indigestion. Then Cochran gave her a lead part in a new show, Noel Coward's *This Year of Grace*, and even more was expected of her than before. To get the part, she said she could do ballet, a wild claim based on three or four lessons. But in the rehearsals she was not able to stay up on her points and the choreographer had to simplify her part again and again. Eventually she faked her ballet number by using her arms and hands more than necessary and wearing a long costume to hide her feet.

On the opening night in Manchester, Sheilah and her partner received loud applause after singing a number, "Mad About

You." The applause was so thrilling that Sheilah became carried away and attempted a genuine high kick. This was a mistake; she fell down on stage, landing painfully on her rear. She stood up and tried to get back into step with the other dancers, but she could not find the right rhythm. The audience began to shout derisively. Sheilah was so unnerved that as she made her exit from the stage, she fell headlong into a papier-mâché prop, a huge painted wooden rock. The crash from backstage echoed through the entire theater and made the audience howl with laughter. Sheilah ran into her dressing room unable to stop weeping.

The stress was too much, on stage and off. In 1929 it all came to an end when an aging millionaire, Sir Richard North, made a positively indecent proposal. Sir Richard was retired from the Indian Civil Service and he liked his women young. He thought of Sheilah as the daughter he had never had and proposed that he legally adopt her so that his incestuous fantasies might have more meat to them; she could become for him forever his sexy and playful little girl. Sheilah had already discovered that the upper classes had their eccentricities. Not long before, she had been on a yacht off the south of France alone with a lord of the realm, a member of Parliament, when this personage quite without warning pulled off his bathing costume and begged for her to whip him. When she refused, he simply masturbated in front of her. Somehow Sir Richard's proposal was the last straw in an already impossible situation. Sheilah simply broke down. Crying hysterically, she told Sir Richard that he could not possibly adopt her for she was secretly married. In a gush of honesty, she admitted nearly everything: She was a fraud, she could not dance or sing, and she was at the end of her wits trying to fool the world into thinking that she could.

Sir Richard blanched momentarily at the confession of her marriage, but he was a broad-minded man. He would adopt her still—he certainly didn't care if she could not sing or dance. As for her marriage, he chivalrously volunteered to act as corespondent so she might obtain a divorce. But when Sheilah wouldn't stop crying, he became alarmed and called in his Harley Street doctor to examine her. The doctor decreed the obvious, that Sheilah was

on the verge of a serious nervous breakdown. Sir Richard paid for
her to enter an expensive nursing home for a complete rest and
recuperation, and afterward he funded a vacation for both Johnny
and Sheilah in the south of France. Johnny had a splendid time on
Sir Richard's money, a fact which Sheilah found vaguely unsettling. She began to suspect that her husband—dear, sweet
Johnny—did not possess a very strong character.

Major Gillam was not content to be simply, any day now, a
fabulously wealthy entrepreneur. He wished for success in something of an even more speculative nature than fancy-goods: John
Gillam wanted to be a writer.

After the Great War, the Major had published his memoirs of
the Gallipoli campaign in a book he called *A Gallipoli Diary*. The
crux of this work was a defense of Winston Churchill, who had
been much criticized as the First Lord of the Admiralty for his
handling of the Gallipoli campaign. Johnny's thesis was that
Churchill had a splendid plan which would have worked wonderfully well in the best of possible worlds had it been followed
immediately, rather than after a disastrous delay. The fact that
life did not often accommodate itself to the best-made plans did
not matter in the least to Major Gillam. He was a man with a platonic vision of the world, an idealist. Winston Churchill, at the
moment out of public favor, was grateful to have at least one
supporter, and he wrote Johnny a brief note of thanks—just a few
words but they acted like the pouring of gasoline upon the
flames of John Gillam's ambitions to be a writer. Johnny was
stimulated to make an entire career out of the Gallipoli campaign, writing book after book on the subject, though only one
effort after the initial diary was ever published, a novel he titled
Gallipoli Adventure.

Shortly before Sheilah's nervous breakdown, while she was
still a Cochran Young Lady, Johnny came up with an idea for an
article on the historical origins of the Easter egg, a subject that
fascinated him, which he was certain he could easily sell to a
magazine. But Sheilah had long ago lost her belief in Johnny's
schemes. "Oh, Johnny, you're wasting your time," she told him.
"People aren't interested in Easter eggs."

Johnny threw his pencil down. "Well, what *are* they interested in, if you know?"

Although she had no experience in writing, Sheilah quickly came up with an idea. She told Johnny about her first night on the London stage, and how after the show was over she had left by the stage door expecting the alley to be thronged with handsome men wearing top hats and evening clothes—the mythical stage-door Johnnies she had read about in novels, their arms full of flowers and jewelry for the beautiful actresses whose favors they wished to win. What Sheilah found in the alley instead were two ill-dressed girls seeking autographs. She thought something might be written on this. The article could be called "'The Stage-Door Johnny,' by a Chorus Girl."

Johnny smelled money. "By Jove!" he cried, suddenly enthusiastic. "You have something there. Why don't *you* write it?"

Sheilah had never considered journalism before this moment, but she thought she might give it a try. She wrote a breezy piece full of a chorus girl's anecdotes of life inside the theater and when if was finished she mailed it to the *Daily Express*, aiming ambitiously for one of the most widely circulated newspapers in England. To her delight, the article was accepted and she was paid the grand sum of two guineas for her trouble. On the night before publication, Johnny and Sheilah went to the newspaper's printing plant and watched as her piece was set into type. The next day her words were all over London. Cochran congratulated her, and the writer A. P. Herbert, a friend of Cochran's, gave her some pointers on grammar and composition. Sheilah's career as a journalist was launched. When she had her nervous breakdown a few months later in 1929 and was forced to leave the stage, she turned her full attention to writing.

She suffered the usual ups and downs of the novice author. After the easy acceptance of her first piece, she was disappointed as the next five articles she wrote were turned down. It took some thought to discover what she was doing wrong; the problem, she decided, was A. P. Herbert and his rules of grammar and composition—they were strangling her. So she promptly unlearned the pointers of this learned man, and soon she was on a hot streak once again. She sold "'I Married a Man 25 Years

Older,' by a Young Wife" to the *Sunday Pictorial* for eight guineas. After this came the tantalizing question, "'Baby or a Car' by a New Bride," which she sold to the *Daily Mail*. Sheilah favored the car over the baby for no other reason than the fact that this would cause more controversy. The challenge now was to come up with sizzling new themes, such as "My Screen Test—by a Film-Struck Girl." The screen test in question had been an embarrassing failure, but with a bit of exaggeration and rearranging of facts it made an entertaining tale for the *Daily Mail*.

She was ambitious. She made contact with the *Saturday Evening Post* in far-off America, which gave her a tentative assignment to interview Lord Beaverbrook, the British newspaper tycoon. Sheilah telephoned Beaverbrook's office but was told the great man was not available to the press. Undeterred, she tracked him down and went to Beaverbrook's country estate, Cherkley Court. Two times she was turned away by a forbidding butler, but Sheilah did not give up. The second time the butler opened the door, she was on the verge of tears. "He simply *has* to see me," she pleaded. And on the third try, like a fairy tale, the butler let her in. "Lord Beaverbrook says that such persistence should be rewarded," he pronounced grandly as he ushered her into the mansion.

And so she got her interview, and she learned an important lesson as well, that she could brave any humiliation to get what she wanted, stand outside of any door and keep on knocking until someone let her in.

When she wasn't busy writing her scandalous journalism, Mrs. Gillam (as she now let herself be known) entered what she later referred to as her "society period."

The path into Britain's upper classes opened almost by accident. An attractive young woman, Judith Hurt, moved with her mother into the third-floor flat directly above Johnny and Sheilah's at 128 Wigmore Street. The Hurts were down from Scotland for the London season and they seemed to know everyone. Fashionable young men from Oxford and Cambridge were constantly tramping up and down the stairs to the third floor. Sheilah and Judith were the same age and when they met in the hallway they sometimes had friendly chats. One afternoon Sheilah was walking in Hyde Park when she heard Judith call to her. "Oh, Mrs. Gillam . . . We're going to Grosvenor House to skate—would you like to come?"

Such was Sheilah's introduction into what seemed to her an enchanted world: the indoor ice rink at Grosvenor House in Mayfair off Hyde Park where she learned to glide, to laugh, and fall on the smooth hard white surface as a small orchestra played. Ice-skating soon became a regular event in her life. It did not seem to matter that her accent was not quite as refined as Judith's for they were all young and it was a very modern time. It was enough simply to be pretty and full of laughter.

She met an interesting crowd, old families of country wealth who often kept a flat in London for the winter season. One afternoon a tall blond man of military bearing came up to her, introduced himself as Jack Mitford, and asked for a waltz. Jack Mitford appeared to Sheilah the very definition of aristocracy: He and his wife had eight children, seven daughters and one handsome son, Tom; they were related to Winston Churchill and were one of the very oldest families in England.

The Mitfords were glad to open their hearts to a stray—a pretty young woman with a vivid smile who had been so dashing as to act in musical comedies in the West End, and whose husband, the Major, was seldom in evidence. Like many old British families, the Mitfords had close ancestral ties with Germany, and they often talked about a charming man they had met recently in Munich, Adolf Hitler, who was having a romance with Unity, one of their seven daughters. Young Tom was an ardent fascist. Jack Mitford more cautiously suggested that this fellow Hitler had some fairly radical ideas, it was true, but Europe was in a mess and strong measures were required, particularly in dealing with the Jews.

Sheilah's bright smile never faltered. She did not understand the fine points of fascism, but she knew very well about the Jews. Everyone hated the Jews. All her life she had heard the taunting words of hatred, the disparaging remarks about kikes and Jew-boys. Sometimes on sleepless nights an old voice whispered to her from the distant past: *"Lilyanna!"* it called.

"Lilyanna!" A name that was warm and golden as the Russian steppes from which it came. But she refused to listen.

As she advanced in the world, her shame of the past grew more acute. Each step of the way was like passing through a door which closed behind her and could never be opened again. Johnny, always trying to improve her, had managed through one of his relatives to have Sheilah presented at court to King George. But where did this leave her? . . . in an impossible situation, in neither one world nor the other, and increasingly fearful that she might be exposed as a fraud. When one of her new friends from the ice rink asked about her past, she answered quickly that she was the daughter of John Lawrence and Veronica Roslyn Graham. She pretended that she had grown up in Chelsea, a Bohemian part of London, hoping this might explain any lapse of behavior. Once told, these stories took on a life of their own. She could not go back.

She found it remarkable that the Mitfords and all the others seemed to accept her at her word. Sometimes they invited Sheilah to come along with them on ski vacations to Switzerland and Germany. Johnny encouraged her to go on these trips: Make contacts, he said. Better yourself. On the ice rink outside the Palace Hotel in St. Moritz, Sheilah had a bad moment one afternoon as a shrewd older woman skated her way, took her arm, and suggested they go once around the rink together. When they were in step, the woman smiled ruthlessly, and said, "You're an adventuress, aren't you?"

Sheilah was stunned. She thought frantically of some reply, but she could not think of a thing. So she answered finally, "Yes, I am."

It was apparently the right answer, for the shrewd older woman kept Sheilah's secret and did not expose her to her hosts, the Mitford family. It was a narrow escape and Sheilah knew she must be more careful. In Germany later that same winter she rode a bobsled and danced one romantic evening with a handsome blond ski instructor who called himself Eustace the Nazi. He flirted marvelously and shared with her his ecstatic vision of a Europe undefiled by Jews.

Did she stiffen in his arms? Not at all. With her blond hair and high cheekbones she was the very definition of a Nordic beauty.

She was happy to be among the beautiful people. There were no Jew-boys here, no moneylenders, no squalor, no strange foreign words, no cloying smells. No past at all, except what you invented it to be.

Tom Mitford introduced her to his cousin, Randolph Churchill, the arrogant and brilliant son of Winston Churchill. Randolph was tall and handsome; he had brown hair and a fine ruddy complexion, and his superb bearing would have placed him squarely in Britain's upper class had he never so much as opened his aristocratic mouth—a mouth which was, however, open much of the time. The young man believed he had the correct opinion about nearly everything, and he had a sense of *droit de seigneur* that there should be beautiful women in attendance around him. He began inviting Sheilah for frequent lunches and dinners at Quaglino's, a fashionable restaurant, where she was expected to sit without uttering a word while Randolph and Tom passionately discussed politics.

It was to one of these dinners at Quaglino's that Sheilah arrived one evening to discover that Charlie Chaplin, the famous Little Tramp, was a guest at Randolph Churchill's table. Sheilah was thrilled; she had never met a movie star before. But the thrill turned to dismay as she witnessed the supreme condescension with which young Churchill treated the world's greatest comedian.

"Of course, you've always had the advantages," Charlie told Randolph with admiration. "I haven't. I've had to fight for everything I have." Charlie spoke apologetically of his poor childhood in England, and his early days of struggle as a music-hall entertainer. "How lucky you are to have been born with the name Churchill. To be born to wealth and position," Charlie said enviously.

Randolph Churchill accepted this homage as his due. "Oh, well, you've worked hard to get where you are," he said dismissively.

Chaplin began to talk about politics, but Randolph loudly interrupted. "Oh, Charlie, for Heaven's sake shut up! You don't know what you're talking about. Let's talk about things you know. Tell us about Hollywood, Charlie." As if to accentuate his rudeness, young Churchill reached across the table and stubbed out his cigarette in an ashtray which was nearly in Chaplin's face.

From her spot across the table, unobserved—merely a decorative item at the table, of no more importance than the celery dish—Sheilah was dumbfounded to watch this exchange. It wasn't only Randolph Churchill's rudeness that bothered her—she was used to that—but the astonishing fact that the great Charlie Chaplin accepted this behavior without a word of protest, simply because he had been born low and Churchill high. Sheilah felt a wave of cold anger rise up within her. After all, the Little Tramp was a genius, he had made something of his life through enormous talent and energy. How dare he humble himself before an arrogant young man who had no other claim to respect than an old name? But this was Britain, and no matter what talent Charlie Chaplin might possess, he would always be the underdog, restrained by a rigid social hierarchy which made Randolph Churchill the better man. Sheilah had grown up with this caste system; she had accepted it from birth. But to witness the social drama played out between the most talented comedian in the world and the mere son of somebody suddenly made the entire thing seem absurd and incredibly unfair.

Sheilah listened intently as Charlie did as he was bidden, and spoke amusingly about the Hollywood film colony. She thought it must be wonderful to live in a place where the old rules did not count—where you could be judged for what you accomplished, rather than the circumstances of your birth. These things had never appeared to her quite so clearly; her eyes were open, and from this moment, Britain began to feel to her like a prison. She longed to break out, try her own talents, and be something new.

From the time of this dinner, Hollywood began to whisper to her, a place of sun and opportunity. A fantasy of liberation calling hither. Perhaps she too could do well there.

Sheilah's life in England seemed ever more intolerable and false. The only time she could be herself was when she was playing squash rackets at the International Sportsman's Club in Grosvenor Square, a club founded by some of her society friends who had put her up as a member. Here at last there was no need for pretense. She could run about the court with all her youthful energy, smash the ball, and release the pent-up frustration of elegant dinners where she dared not say a word, and the meaningless marriage in which she felt trapped, and the lies she told to be accepted. She played squash furiously day after day. Her friends did not understand. They sometimes said, "Sheilah, why do you play so hard? It's only a game." But her friends knew nothing about her—how could they?

While playing squash racquets in the winter of 1932, Sheilah began to take notice of an attractive young man in his mid-twenties who was practicing with the same fury and abandon as herself. She learned this was the Marquess of Donegall, captain of the men's team, and a member of an old and distinguished family. He had seemingly dozens of titles, an extravagance Sheilah found intriguing. He was the Marquess and Earl of Donegall, the Earl of Belfast, Viscount Chichester of Ireland, Baron Fisherwick of Fisherwick, Hereditary Lord High Admiral of Lough Neagh, just to name a few. Though he certainly did not need to work, Lord Donegall had taken a fancy to journalism and he wrote a weekly society column for the *Sunday Dispatch*. Sheilah read the column religiously to keep up with the fabulous doings of the titled rich—a world of dinners and balls and trips to France and Italy. She had occasionally seen Lord Donegall come into Quaglino's with groups of his friends and watched how the waiters fawned on him as he made his way to his table.

His lordship was a slender and delicate young man with large brown eyes that seemed gentle and kind. She had noticed his hands: They were small and soft and entirely aristocratic, as if after so many generations of leisure, the genes themselves had forgotten how to produce brutish instruments of work. One afternoon Sheilah contrived to finish her game of squash at the same time as Lord Donegall. He came up to her smiling. "Well, I've been watching you," he said. "You play a good game." He wanted to know why he had never seen her before. Where had she been hiding herself? Sheilah smiled back with every watt of concentrated energy she possessed. She was full of pep, glowing from exercise, she knew she looked good. She said she had been traveling.

Donegall invited her for a cocktail and Sheilah made a conscious decision to have this attractive young lord fall in love with her. Before long, they were going to dinners in town, boating parties on the Thames, and long drives in the country. As always, Johnny encouraged her, happy that she was spending her time in such fine company, and stoutly willing to maintain the fiction that it was all very innocent. Donegall owned an airplane, a Gypsy Moth, and one afternoon he took Sheilah high into the clouds hoping to impress her with spectacular loop-the-loops and other acts of derring-do. Sheilah was merely terrified. As she hung upside down in the open cockpit, held from death by only a few leather straps, she watched the English countryside spin beneath her head and wondered briefly if this upper-class conquest was really worth the dangers.

Except for the Gypsy Moth, Donegall was a great deal of fun—handsome, rich, and full of boyish laughter—a thoroughly twentieth-century lord who had a great enthusiasm for jazz music and new things. She told him her usual story about John Lawrence, Veronica Roslyn Graham, and her elegant but Bohemian childhood in Chelsea. She was prepared to back this story up, extemporize, spin further webs if she had to, but Donegall took her at face value—a very pretty face—and did not need to know more. She liked him as much as you can ever like someone to whom you tell nothing but lies. He knew nothing about her, and about him there was not much to know. It was a love affair of attractive surfaces, of sex and laughter and charm.

A few months after they met, Donegall gazed into her eyes and said, "I'm in love with you, Sheilah. I want to marry you."

"Oh, Don! . . . I already have a husband, you know."

"You have heard of divorce—"

Sheilah laughed and stopped him from going any further; she was not in love with him and perhaps this had already gone too far. "Don, you don't really mean it. Besides, your mother wouldn't approve."

Don had to admit that Sheilah might be right about his

mother, who was known to be an old-fashioned woman. "But don't forget I asked you," he said gently.

Sheilah would not forget. It was good practice to conquer a lord of the realm. But despite his augmented titles, he was just a nice boy, a friendly puppy, and not in her league at all. She did not suspect that this 1932 love affair was to have some consequence in her life, and follow her clear to California.

Sheilah made her first brief trip to America in 1931, shortly before she met Lord Donegall. Johnny suggested she go, pleased with her success in England, but certain she required a larger stage. Sheilah had heard about a wonderful American invention—newspaper syndication: She could write a single article and have it printed in hundreds of papers throughout the country. It seemed just the thing for a girl anxious to make a name for herself.

Soon after she arrived, Sheilah marched into the Manhattan office of the North American Newspaper Alliance, which she had been told was the best of these syndicates. She always aimed for the best—this was her motto—and she smiled so brightly hardly anyone could tell how nervous she was inside. She had copies in hand of her English clippings, and she was able to get an interview with the publisher, John Wheeler, a tough, pink-faced man with a cigar in the corner of his mouth and a green eyeshade perched on his forehead. He reminded her of every newspaperman she had ever seen in American movies. There was an unruly shock of brown hair sticking up from his visor, and he had the complexion of a drinking man. He was bullishly sure of himself and Sheilah found this attractive. She made certain that as she sat down she crossed her legs to show as much shapeliness as possible. A girl in need had to use whatever weapons were available.

John Wheeler was a New Yorker who had seen everything and was impressed by nothing. He grunted a skeptical hello and then frowned as he read Sheilah's letter of introduction. She handed him the first of her articles on stage-door Johnnies. "Not what we want," he barked and gave it back to her. She proceeded to feed him her clippings one by one, which he glanced at briefly and returned without comment. Finally he came to something which caught his interest and he muttered a grudging, "Not bad." But perhaps he had only noticed Sheilah's leg that was dangling as bait. To her surprise, he smiled; it was an odd facial movement for such a brusque man and for a second he looked almost boyish. He suggested that perhaps they might continue this conversation over a drink at a nearby bar. Sheilah felt the knot in her stomach relax; she believed she was on the road to success in America.

But it was an arduous road. Wheeler might be flirtatious, but he was also extremely cagey where business was concerned. He committed himself to nothing, suggesting only that he and Sheilah sign a letter of agreement that they would split the money from any of her writings that he was able to sell. But during this 1931 foray to America, John Wheeler sold nothing. New York remained indifferent to her eager smile and urgent dreams. It was a city which had seen too many smiles and dreams before, and she got nowhere. Despite her lack of success, Sheilah liked New York and hoped vaguely to meet some fabulous millionaire who might rescue her, but in 1931 millionaires were in short supply and none was forthcoming. So she returned to England, sailing on the *Aquitania*, lying in her cabin and weeping at the unaccustomed outrage of failure.

But Sheilah refused to accept defeat as anything more than a temporary setback. She sailed into New York Harbor a second time in June 1933 on the *Aquitania*, the very ship which had returned her to England after her first visit. She arrived in a sweltering heat wave of ninety-six degrees, dressed inappropriately in a dark green velvet suit and an orange silk blouse, with less than a hundred dollars in her pocket and a bagful of letters of introduction. The heat was the least of her worries: This time she was determined to succeed, and to do so quickly, before her money ran out.

Sheilah had spent the winter in London writing a mystery novel and in America she planned to present herself rather grandly as a British authoress. Her novel, *Gentleman Crook*, told the adventures of an aristocratic thief who committed daring crimes with stunning savoir faire and courtly manners—a stock character of the commercial fiction of the day. She had managed to sell the book to the publishing firm of Rich and Cowan for a twenty-five-pound advance, and *Gentleman Crook* was due to come out in August. It was Johnny who dreamed up the strategy that this was the perfect moment for Sheilah to give America another try. As an authoress, she was not such a nobody as before. Johnny was sad to be left behind in England, but he urged her to go as soon as possible. If she sailed to New York before the publication date, she could present herself as an author who was about to hit the bestseller lists, rather than one whose first book had been a flop. The Major had recently lost yet another job, and he was hoping his wife would do well enough in America to bail him out of a difficult situation.

In 1933, at the moment of her second trip to America, Sheilah was twenty-nine years old but appeared to be much younger; only Johnny knew her true age, or any other truth about her. It was not only her complexion and features which were so young, but her blind egotism, the sense that she was the star of her own ongoing movie. She could not imagine how anyone might resist her. And indeed this time New York yielded to her, as the city sometimes will to those who are very persistent and lucky. Just as her money was running out, John Wheeler was able to help her get a job as a reporter on the *New York Mirror*; a few weeks later she took a second job as well on the *New York Journal* before someone told her that these were not the rules people played by, and she could not be employed simultaneously by two opposing newspapers.

Sheilah succeeded in New York, as she said later, by a "combination of daring, brazenness and desperation." She interviewed murderers and climbed in bedroom windows to get exclusive photographs; she was terrified of airplanes after flying in Donegall's Gypsy Moth, but she went up anyway in an open two-seater to cover Lindbergh's triumphant return from Europe. She reveled in shock tactics and stopped at nothing. There was one story she called "Who Cheats the Most in Marriage?" in which she examined infidelity among the French, English, Germans, and Americans: She claimed that in England the ménage à trois was a common domestic arrangement, with the wife, the husband, and the lover living under the same roof and the lover paying the bills. She went on to say that all Frenchmen had mistresses for the afternoon, that Germans were too stodgy to care about sex one way or the other, and in the summer in New York every husband had an affair while his wife was out of town in the country. It was all wild exaggeration, but who cared? The *New York Journal* was so impressed with the article that they sent a photographer to capture Sheilah in a dozen poses, and they publicized her as their find of the year. Not long afterward, John Wheeler suggested she write a piece saying that all dogs should be kicked out of New York City. This was the way to get the eye of an indifferent public, and Sheilah unleashed a storm of angry letters and gained a notoriety which was to guarantee that everyone would read her column for the next scandalous install-ment.

At the heart of such tactics was her profound belief that she did not possess either the legitimate talent or education to suc-ceed as a real writer. She could only bluff her way along, finagle jobs by showing as much leg as possible to anyone who might hire her, and then let loose such a hailstorm of controversy that no one would notice she could barely put together a proper sen-tence. With so many self-doubts, Sheilah began to think that California might be the place for her. The ignorance of Hollywood people was legendary as far away as London. It was said that tycoons like Samuel Goldwyn and Louis B. Mayer could barely speak English. In Hollywood no one would notice her own lack of education. Over a number of months she worked on John Wheeler to give her a chance on the West Coast. He was skeptical, but she kept at him. When the contract expired for NANA's Hollywood columnist, Molly Merrick, Sheilah saw her chance: She convinced Wheeler that she would do a better job for less money. It was this last fact, money, which eventually con-vinced John Wheeler to grunt a reluctant yes.

And so after two and a half years in New York, Sheilah Graham made her way to Hollywood, arriving on Christmas Day 1935, to set up house in a small apartment on a side street off Sunset Boulevard. Ironically it was in Hollywood that she felt her lack of education most keenly and was least able to pass herself off as just a pretty face. It was her own fault. Among all the cliques in the movie industry she might have befriended—producers, agents, actors, publicists, showgirls—Sheilah courted the one group whose members were superbly well educated and against whom she might judge herself most lacking—the writers at The Garden of Allah, the group she met through Robert Benchley.

During these early years in America, Sheilah maintained a long-distance correspondence with Johnny, her platonic husband back in England. She sent him money every month, sometimes fifty or a hundred dollars—whatever she could spare. Once while she was still in New York and feeling flush, she had brought him to America for a short vacation. It had never been any sort of marriage but she felt responsible for him. She knew Johnny was awfully weak, but he was a fixed point in her life and she loved him as a daughter might love a slightly exasperating and doddering father. She was certain he would be unable to survive without her. Occasionally she contemplated divorce, but she kept putting it off for a future time. She liked having someone to take care of; it gave a purpose to her own hard-won success.

Throughout these passing years, Sheilah also stayed in touch with Lord Donegall, the boyish aristocrat with the gentle brown eyes, who did not give up his romantic pursuit. He continued to court her long distance with a barrage of love letters to California, once even sending a phonograph recording asking again for her hand: "My darling Sheilah," came his voice, sounding thin on the phonograph, "I have thought of so many ways to phrase this, and the simplest is the best. I want to marry you when you are free. I am hopeful that I can bring Mother on our side. Do think about this and consider it. And please don't send me an answer you don't mean."

Sheilah replied with ambivalence to keep Donegall's offer of marriage on hold, a final card she might play. She did not believe she loved him except in odd moments—generally moments of temporary defeat—when the lure of his wealth and title and the security he offered cast a certain romantic glow. By 1937, after several years of tossing the question about in her mind, Sheilah at last decided to divorce Johnny. She wrote to a lawyer she knew in London and then in June she made a brief trip from Hollywood to England to complete the formalities. It was a sad but inevitable occasion. She and Johnny had been married now for fourteen years; he was family in his way, and her last connection with the past. But the marriage had always been an absurdity. In America she had been in love and out of love several times: There had been her affair with her boss in New York, King Vidor in 1936, and most recently in Hollywood the millionaire Jock Whitney, who liked to take Sheilah to the racetrack and give her money to bet.

Early in 1937 Jock Whitney had asked Sheilah to be his mistress—he used the actual word *mistress*—offering to set her up in style. But this gave Sheilah pause and in fact led to her decision to divorce Johnny. She didn't like the word *mistress*, decided she did not want to be one, and sensed it was time to get her life on a more conventional footing so that if the right man came along she would be free to marry. Johnny was dejected about the divorce, but he too bowed to the inevitable. Fortunately, he did not lose her completely; she continued to support him after their divorce in June 1937 with regular monthly checks until he died in 1965.

Sheilah saw Donegall for lunch on her final day in London. She hesitated to mention her divorce for fear Donegall might go to the registry office and discover her vital statistics—all of which she had reason to hide. It was only as the lunch was ending that she finally said, "It may interest you to know that I got my divorce this morning."

"What!" he cried, nearly dropping his knife and fork. "How could you have sat through the whole meal without telling me. Sheilah, darling, now the way is clear!" He took her hand fervently, reaching over the remnants of his steak-and-kidney pie. "I'm coming to Hollywood myself to make up your mind for you," he told her. "You'll see I mean this. I'll be there in two weeks."

Donegall was as good as his word. Two weeks later he appeared in Hollywood to conclude his long courtship and also to cover for his London newspaper the funeral of George Gershwin, who had died unexpectedly of a brain tumor a few months before his thirty-ninth birthday. Much to her own surprise, Sheilah finally said yes. She was fond of Donegall, certainly; she had convinced herself it might even be love. But most of all, it was an alluring dream to become Her Grace, the Marchioness of Donegall, and never again be obliged to talk her way onto a movie set or into a party where she wasn't wanted. Donegall was determined that she not have a chance to change her mind. He rushed her off to a fashionable jewelers on Hollywood Boulevard and bought an engagement ring. He gazed lovingly into her eyes as he slipped the ring on her finger. "This will do until I have one made up in London for you," he said. He was awfully sweet and Sheilah was sure she would be happy.

And so her life appeared a settled thing. For a honeymoon, they would take a slow sea cruise around the world; Don had heard that the swaying motion of ships was conducive for the production of heirs, and heirs were very much on his mind. Sheilah would have children of noble birth; her son would be the Earl of Belfast, her daughter Lady Wendy Chichester. All these long and enumerated titles meant something to Sheilah as she fantasized an end to "Hollywood Today" and a brand new life.

While Donegall was in Hollywood, Sheilah introduced him to her circle of friends. Donegall found Bob Benchley a particularly fabulous fellow; he called him "the most civilized American I have ever met," and failed to notice that Benchley found this remark condescending. "Bob will be our best man," Don urged, carried away by his own enthusiasm. When Bob learned Donegall was returning to England tomorrow, he decided they had better have a party tonight. He reminded them that it was Bastille Day—July 14, 1937—and they had a double cause for celebration.

The party began at the house Sheilah had rented only a few weeks before at 1530 North Kings Road, high on a treacherous road in the Hollywood Hills above Sunset Boulevard. The house was a large pink Mediterranean villa with a red-tiled roof set down precariously on a steep hill among languid oak trees and a single towering palm—that distinctive Hollywood landmark which Dorothy Parker once labeled as "the ugliest vegetable God created." The engagement party was held outside on Sheilah's second-floor terrace among the treetops, a terrace from which all the lights of Los Angeles spread out like a carpet at her feet. From this vantage point it was possible to see a sliver of The Garden of Allah complex on Sunset Boulevard far below.

Bob loaned Sheilah the use of his German butler, Albin, and the party was a roaring success. Albin was not a good butler; he had a strange way of saying "Here is Albin" whenever he appeared—and often he did not appear at all when Bob wanted him—but tonight he was on a romantic mission and did his best with the drinks and hors d'oeuvres. There were dozens of actors and writers on the terrace, and much drinking of champagne and endless toasts to the happy couple. Sheilah felt it was a night of magic; she clung happily to Donegall's arm. "Be quiet!" a neighbor finally shouted when things became too loud.

"Let's all go to my place!" Bob called above the din. "Remember the Bastille!"

The group piled noisily into a half dozen cars and made their way down the winding road to Benchley's bungalow at The Garden of Allah. Here Bob used his telephone to invite a whole new crew of guests, including Dorothy Parker and her husband Alan Campbell. Sheilah was the center of it all. She basked in the glow of attention with the tall, slim Lord Donegall by her side. For the girl who had once been Lily Shiel, this seemed a happy ending to a precarious tale.

Tonight she felt at last on the inside of things, standing in the warm embrace of the group, laughing with the smart, successful people. She listened as Frank Morgan told a hilarious story to a group gathered around him, everyone with a drink in hand, crowded all together into Benchley's bungalow with cigarette smoke hanging in the air. Sheilah knew this was her night of nights; she was beautiful, she belonged to the hilarity.

And this was when she saw him, an outsider in their midst, a man who clearly did not belong here. She was not quite certain what drew her eye across the room beyond the circle in which she stood. The man was looking at her. He was extraordinarily pale and he sat quietly by himself in an armchair beneath the glow of a lamp. There was a Coca-Cola in one hand and a cigarette in the other; the smoke from his cigarette curled upward into the lamp and seemed to envelope him in a swirling mist of unreality. Sheilah was struck by his appearance. She said later that this strange figure "appeared to be all shades of the palest, most delicate blue: his hair was pale, his face was pale, like a Marie Laurencin pastel, his suit was blue, his eyes, his lips were blue, behind the veil of blue smoke he seemed an apparition that might vanish at any moment."

Surrounded by laughter and conversation, this unusual man sat alone as if marooned on his own separate island, an armchair set adrift in the glow of the lamp. There was an inexpressible sadness about him; he appeared solemn and tired. And yet Sheilah found him most attractive; the sadness and suffering she saw in his face lent him an air of quiet dignity. She noticed that he was the only person at the party besides herself who was not drinking alcohol, and she liked this small fact.

He made an odd impression. Sheilah graced him with her smile and then turned to laugh with Frank Morgan—but when she looked again the man was gone, leaving behind only the curling wisp of his cigarette smoke still rising into the glow of the lamp. Had she really seen him at all?

She turned to Robert Benchley. "Who was that man sitting under the lamp? He was so quiet."

"That was F. Scott Fitzgerald—the writer. I asked him to drop in," Bob told her. He peered about the room for his missing guest. "I guess he's left—he hates parties when he's not drinking. I'll get him back."

"No, don't bother," she said. Sheilah had only a vague notion of who F. Scott Fitzgerald was; the name stirred memories of an earlier era, girls with bobbed hair dancing wildly in Prohibition speakeasies. The whole thing now was utterly passé. Without having read a word he had written, Sheilah had occasionally used his name in her column, describing a certain sort of old-fashioned heroine as "a Scott Fitzgerald type." Somehow she had assumed the author was dead, along with his era. Gazing now at the empty armchair shrouded in smoke, she thought it was a pity he had left so abruptly—he might have provided a line or two for her column. Then Bob Benchley launched forth upon an absurd speech in which every sentence—Eddie Mayer told her later—was the punch line of a dirty joke. Sheilah didn't get a word of it, but she had long ago learned to fake her way, smiling and laughing as if she understood it all.

She quickly forgot the pale man in the armchair. She and Don left early and returned to her pink house high on the hill. The next day she drove him to the airport where he would begin the long air and sea voyage back to London. When he arrived home he would begin his campaign to bring his mother around to approve of the marriage. It would not be easy, but he assured Sheilah he would not take no for an answer. He might be a modern sort of lord who liked jazz and would follow a pretty girl clear to California, but it did not occur to him that he could marry without his mother's blessings.

And so the fairy tale ending to Lily Shiel's life must be put temporarily on hold while permission was obtained. Don kissed her good-bye and left his fiancée to make her own way in Hollywood a few months more.

She had only to be patient and she would glide into a safe harbor at last.

4

POLITICS AND DANCING

The mood should be two people—free—He has an overwhelming
urge toward the girl who promises to give life back to him . . .
she is the heart of hope and freshness.

—F. Scott Fitzgerald, notes for *The Last Tycoon*

HOLLYWOOD POLITICS OF A LEFTWARD KIND brought Scott and
Sheilah together for the second time—a meeting orchestrated by
a most unlikely Cupid, that great cynic of love, Dorothy Parker.

By the summer of 1937, the diminutive figure of Dorothy
Parker was often seen darting about town with holy zeal, making her way purposefully from script conference to political
meeting. She was barely five feet tall, deceptively meek in
appearance for a writer who had the reputation of being the wit-
tiest woman in America. Generally she had a dog or two somewhere close to her person; her dogs were notoriously undisci-
plined and tended to create a sense of chaos around her. In Los
Angeles Dottie wore her politics by dressing like a Soviet farm
woman, showing up for work at the studio in a ruffled peasant

blouse, flat-heeled shoes, a baggy skirt, and a babushka tied about her head. The scarf allowed her dark bangs to fall upon her forehead, accenting brown eyes that were generally huge and helpless. She was almost adorably cute, until she opened her mouth and in her quiet patrician tones unleashed a torrent of insults and obscenities that would make a sailor take note. People enjoyed her the way Romans once liked an afternoon at the Coliseum.

By 1937 Dottie and her husband Alan Campbell were doing very well, earning more than five thousand dollars a week writing screenplays for Samuel Goldwyn. Despite the money (or perhaps because of it), she despised Hollywood even more than she despised everywhere else. But a curious thing happened to her in Los Angeles: Her sarcasm metamorphosed into an evangelical urge for political activity. Like most great cynics, Dottie was an idealist at heart, wounded with longing for a more perfect world. In Hollywood she set about to make this perfect world come to pass. She led the fight for nearly every left-wing cause in sight. She agitated for the release of "the Scottsboro Boys"—eight young Negro men in Alabama accused of raping two white girls. She raised money to fight Franco in Spain. She took on Hitler, and even the tyrants she found closer to home: Louis B. Mayer, Samuel Goldwyn, Darryl Zanuck, and the assorted Warner brothers.

The most divisive issue in the movie industry in the 1930s was the creation of the Screen Writers Guild, the first union to come to Hollywood and attempt to wrestle some degree of power from the mighty studio bosses. The writers were nearly uniformly of the left, and pro-union, while the producers were of the right and believed they might as well all move to Russia if unions were allowed to be. For three years, from 1935 to 1938, the union issue raged in Hollywood until at last—after a series of votes, an act of Congress, and a Supreme Court ruling—the Screen Writers Guild became a reality. Throughout these three years, the bitterness between opposing camps was profound and created a right-left divide in the movie industry which has not entirely healed to this day. "You writers are being misled by your leaders who are a bunch of radical bastards and soap box sons of bitches," Jack

Warner once screamed at a group of his writers—or "schmucks with Underwoods," as he was wont to call the men and women who wrote his films. Even Irving Thalberg, the boy genius at MGM, had believed before his death in 1936 that "laborers" should be allowed to unionize, but not "artists," and he attacked the leaders of the Screen Writers Guild as "sons of bitches, bastards and Goddamn reds."

Such was the adversarial mood and Dorothy Parker gladly led the charge for the other side. She was elected to the board of the fledgling Screen Writers Guild and told everyone who would listen that "the bravest, proudest word in all the dictionaries" was *organize.* She held endless meetings to recruit new members in her North Roxbury Drive home in Beverly Hills and she spent much of her time proselytizing to friends and colleagues. Then in July 1937 an old friend showed up in town, a new body to convert to her holy cause—Scott Fitzgerald.

Dottie hoped to lure Scott into her politics by invitations to various social occasions. It was she who invited Scott to the private screening at Frederic March's house of *The Spanish Earth,* the film Ernest Hemingway had made with the Dutch director Joris Ivens showing the horrors of Franco and the Spanish Civil War. And it was Dottie who invited Scott to a fateful dinner dance, a benefit she organized to raise money for the Screen Writers Guild on July 22 in the Fiesta Room at the Ambassador Hotel.

Scott sat in his tuxedo, black coat and white tie, in the hotel ballroom at one of the many long white tables, each table set for twelve. The orchestra played jazzy tunes in upbeat tempos and the room was crowded with Hollywood people in elegant clothes—writers mostly, but actors as well who had come to show their support of the Screen Writers Guild. Dorothy Parker had taken an entire table, an expensive gesture, and Scott sat in her group as her guest. He was not very fond of Dottie, despite their brief affair in New York three years ago—a time when Zelda was in a mental institution and he was drinking heavily. Scott was repelled by her cynicism. He believed her shrill conversion to communism was merely a facade to hide her basic indifference to anyone's suffering except her own, and a clever way to justify her well-known reluctance to actually sit at her typewriter and write. When Scott arrived in Hollywood at the beginning of July, Dottie warned him that screenwriting was an exhausting business and he would have no energy for serious work. Scott scoffed at her laziness. He told her he planned to rise very early in the morning to do his own work before reporting to MGM.

Scott had accepted Dottie's invitation tonight partly to show that he was politically aware, in tune with the new thinking. More than any other single cause, it was the changing politics of the thirties that had rendered him out of fashion as a writer. This was frustrating because Scott considered himself a liberal, quite far to the left, and he could not understand why the public insisted on labeling him as someone concerned only with the affairs of the rich. People refused to remember that he had declared himself a socialist from the start, in *This Side of Paradise*, written in 1919, in a scene where his young hero, Amory Blaine, does a creditable job arguing the radical cause to a rich industrialist who has picked him up hitchhiking. In later novels, *The Great Gatsby* and *Tender is the Night*, his heroes Jay Gatsby and Dick Diver were in fact destroyed by the rich—destroyed as completely as one-dimensional characters might perish in any didactic capitalist-versus-worker tale someone might write in Soviet Russia. But again, no one seemed to take notice of this fact. A new generation come to age in the Depression insisted on regarding Fitzgerald as a bourgeois reactionary, if they thought of him at all. It was a ruinous perception and Scott was truly baffled. He seemed to fit nowhere, at home with neither the conservative right nor the doctrinaire left.

Hollywood politics, he thought, were really very funny. During his second trip to California in 1931, Scott had a memorable conversation with King Vidor, the movie director with refined manners and aristocratic tastes who five years later would seduce Sheilah by singing "Summertime" over a delicate feast of fried shrimp. In 1931 King Vidor was more concerned with revolution than romance; as a rich man he was terrified he might end up before a firing squad. He confided to Scott in great seriousness that he kept a pair of workman's clothes and old

shoes in his closet in case he needed to make a quick change of
identity. When the revolution came, he planned to head to the
mountains and claim to be a common laborer—King Vidor no
longer, just Comrade Vidor, simple workingman.

"They'll look at your hands," Scott told the director slyly.
"They are not the hands of a workman."

Vidor stared at his hands in horror, fearing it was true—his
delicate hands would betray him. Scott had smiled, enjoying his
little joke. He was a man who seldom laughed out loud, but
more often smiled deeply, a mischievous and knowing smile that
set his cold green eyes twinkling with impish delight. Now in
the midsummer of 1937, he was greatly amused to watch
Dorothy Parker dress up as though she were a Soviet farm
worker, and his old friend from St. Paul, Donald Ogden
Stewart—a graduate of Exeter and Yale, as well as the best-paid
screenwriter in town—who waved at every carpenter and elec-
trician he passed on the studio lot in order to show his solidarity
with the common man. It seemed to Scott that any sane person
must smile at these things. Unfortunately, no one smiled with
him and he felt increasingly isolated in a decade of humorless
political ideology. Apparently any self-serious revolutionary
would rather face bullets than be mocked, however gently.

Sitting quietly with his thoughts in the Fiesta Room at the
Ambassador Hotel, Scott watched the dancing couples and overheard the earnest conversation around him. He was deeply sympathetic with the union struggle in steel mills back east, but
found it difficult to take seriously the labor problems of workers
who lived in mansions in Beverly Hills. Above all he was not a
joiner and he found it aesthetically displeasing to hear people
parroting slogans. Nevertheless, despite its political pretensions,
this was really just a party like many others he had attended in
his life. The Hollywood proletariat appeared to him almost
childishly eager to put on their tuxedos and gowns, flirt and
drink, and have a good time. It all seemed flat to Scott with a
Coca-Cola in his hand rather than a glass of champagne. He felt
old and out of step and he was not much fun tonight.

There came a moment when all the others at his table went off to dance while he sat by himself, alone among eleven empty chairs, ashtrays, the debris of dinner, and half-finished drinks. His eyes traveled across the room and he was surprised to see sitting at Marc Connelly's table—the table next to his—the girl he had observed briefly at Robert Benchley's bungalow eight nights before. It was the English girl who was marrying the lord. It seemed odd that she also was alone, deserted temporarily by her group, resting at an empty table. They faced each other across a smoky divide. "The white table," he wrote, "lengthened and became an altar where the priestess sat alone. Vitality welled up in him." A young woman, after all, was life itself and much more fun than politics; suddenly he no longer felt so old and out of step. The girl was dressed in an evening gown of soft light-gray checkered silk, tied at the waist with a belt of crimson velvet. He smiled at her across their separate tables.

"I like you," he said.

She smiled vividly in return, a smile that animated her face. "I like *you*," she replied, stressing the pronoun. It seemed very flirtatious for a woman with an engagement ring on her finger; Scott found her lovely but perhaps a little too forward.

Three years later, Fitzgerald struggled through many drafts of Chapter Two of his final novel to express his first ambiguous reaction to this girl whose name he did not yet know:

> She was shy and bold, though which quality predominated it was hard to say. She looked, for a split second, like the brazen image that boys pick out of the front row of the chorus one time when they are young—and who afterwards possibly influence the marrow of their souls. For that second as I say, she was as "common" as they come, ready for anything—a wench, a freebooter, an outsider. And then Stahr saw that she was a great beauty . . . she gave an impression of living half way between heaven and earth.

In this unpublished draft, Scott called himself Stahr, and the girl he named at first Thalia, and later Kathleen—he was to call her many things before he was done. The split between what was brazen in her and what was sublime was to leave Fitzgerald endlessly groping. In various drafts of Chapter Two, he played with the description of Thalia/Kathleen:

She looked, for a split second [he revised] like an out-and-out adventuress . . . ready for anything male—a wench. . . .

And then again:

She looked, for a split second, like an out-and-out pushover . . . ready for anything in trousers. . . . And then Stahr saw that she was a raving beauty. She was hapless and lost, but radiant and shocking . . . piteous, not at all happy . . . something about her made you clutch your breath, made you choke back any last thought of your own, "knocked your eye out," as they say.

Scott rewrote line after line, working away at this strange dichotomy. "Oh, she was beautiful". . . "he remarked it only casually in a city where beauty was almost an enemy, an abundant counterfeit coin." But in the negative column: "She came up to him, right like a tart"—this because she dared smile at him. And: "That was the night he found his . . . wretched trollop—like a puppy, a tailless tyke washed into his backyard by a flood."

Then she spoke. "Shall we dance?"

Scott's smile saddened as he decided against her. "I promised the next dance to Dottie," he regretted. And that was that. She nodded and looked away. He might have easily broken his promise to dance with Dottie—gladly, under the right circumstances. But the flirtatious offer to dance led him to believe that the girl was common after all, ready for anything in trousers. When it came to woman, Fitzgerald was a puritan and rather old-fashioned. And besides, if she was too easy, there could be no joy in what he liked best—a carefully planned seduction until at last, unable to resist him any longer, her will bent to his and she said yes.

This was the first time Sheilah had been out on her own since Donegall had returned to England. She felt special and very beautiful in her best evening gown with Donegall's diamond ring glittering on her finger. She could hardly sit still, flushed with the egotism of finding herself young and lovely in a room where music played.

The politics of the evening were beyond her comprehension.

Ever since she had arrived in Hollywood a year and a half earlier, she had listened to endless talk about the Screen Writers Guild. She pretended to agree with everything that was said—oh, yes, it was shocking that screenwriters earned only three, four, sometimes eight or nine thousand dollars a week! They were surely the downtrodden of the earth, hardly able to support their legions of ex-wives. But in fact, Sheilah herself earned only $160 for her five weekly newspaper columns plus an additional Saturday feature, and she was not greatly sympathetic. What puzzled her most was how badly the writers spoke about the producers who paid them such extravagant sums. Dorothy Parker was particularly virulent in her sarcasm, holding up Samuel Goldwyn, Louis B. Mayer, and the other producers to a constant flood of ridicule. Sheilah had little education and she was humbled by the great intellects around her. Probably you had to be a graduate of Harvard, like Bob Benchley, or Yale, like Don Stewart, to completely understand how terribly the Hollywood writers were exploited. Nevertheless, she told herself that should anyone pay her several thousand dollars a week, she would be very grateful; she would not say a bad word about such a person ever.

She was well aware, of course, that she was a shallow person. She was here at this benefit dinner dance simply to flirt, dance, and have fun. She had no political agenda beyond the ongoing saga of Lily Shiel—and at the moment Lily Shiel was doing very well. The engagement to Lord Donegall left her with a deep glow of satisfaction and a sense of finally belonging somewhere. The engagement was particularly pleasant now that Donegall was many thousands of miles away. He was such a tactful man. Sheilah felt so content that she did not even mind when the others at her table left her momentarily alone. Then she glanced up from her empty table and was surprised to see once again the man she now recognized as F. Scott Fitzgerald. He was at the next table over, regarding her intently, his head tilted thoughtfully to one side, a quizzical and rather poetic half-smile on his lips. She found him strangely appealing, pale in his black tuxedo. He looked tired, but he was still a handsome man. She liked his mouth and the gentle melancholy of his smile, and the finely chiseled features of his face. "He appeared to be in his forties," she said later, "but it was difficult to know; he looked half-young, half-old: the thought flashed through my mind, he should get out into the sun, he needs light and air and warmth."

She didn't mean to flirt with him exactly, and yet it was hard not to, particularly after he leaned forward and said, with such grave charm, "I like you." Her reply, "I like *you*," with its unconscious emphasis, rather slipped out, nothing more than a discarded jewel of her own excitement. Once it was out, they smiled at each other in silence with everything between them hanging on a delicate balance. "Why aren't I dancing?" she thought. "Why am I wasting my excitement?" It seemed natural to ask this charming man to dance, but as soon as the words were out of her mouth, she felt his manner change. He turned her down. She did not know why but it made him more interesting to her.

It was a lost moment. Sheilah continued to smile but she felt the keen edge of rejection; she hated to be turned down. And then the band ended its tune, and the dancers from both tables came back with a great commotion, settling into their chairs. Where there had been two people on the verge of something, now there was just a crowd.

Sheilah left the party soon afterward, careful not to glance at the man at the next table. Her life had became an enchantment of parties and possibilities, and she soon almost forgot the dance that had not happened. It was nothing, she told herself. Nothing at all.

Scott's bungalow at The Garden of Allah stood just to the right of the swimming pool that was shaped like the Black Sea—a pool that had a telephone with what was said to be the longest extension cord in Hollywood. Scott's bungalow contained two separate apartments, upper and lower. He was on the second floor among the palm fronds; below him lived the screenwriter Edwin Justus Mayer.

Eddie Mayer was a sweet man— everyone said so—but he had a problem with women. Here he was in Hollywood, land of beautiful women, and all the girls turned him down. Women often liked him as a friend but found him physically unattractive as a lover. He was overweight and blind in one eye, which gave him a strange look, like a car with headlights pointed off in different directions. He had diabetes and would sometimes become very ill when he drank too much; at a party he might suddenly disappear into a bedroom to give himself a shot of insulin. He ended every sentence by adding, "You know what I mean?" None of this was very romantic.

Even when occasionally he succeeded in a seduction, for Eddie it always seemed to turn out wrong. He once told Sheilah about a night he spent with the great silent star Norma Talmadge, who was married at the time to Joe Schenck, the studio boss at 20th Century-Fox. In the morning, Norma Talmadge slipped out of bed and her passion turned cold. "If you tell anyone, I'll ruin you," she threatened. "My husband is more important than you are." Eddie laughed bitterly when he told Sheilah this story. It said everything about Hollywood: *My husband is more important than you are!*

One night about a year before Scott Fitzgerald arrived in Hollywood, Eddie watched Sheilah as she stood on the black and white squares of Frank Morgan's foyer in Beverly Hills; when she thought no one was looking, Sheilah broke out into a spontaneous tap dance on the squares. She had always been a fool for dancing. She whirled around and around in her impromptu dance, and when she saw Eddie Mayer watching her she gave out a little cry. She almost fell into his arms. They laughed together and Eddie thought she was wonderful. He asked Sheilah to wait while he got his car; he said he would drive her home. Like the other women in town, Sheilah did not find him attractive, but she liked him as a friend. He seemed gentle and very nice. But when they arrived at Sheilah's front door, the gentle writer turned into a wolf. He begged his way into the house and then forced Sheilah into the bedroom, where he began tearing at her clothes. Sheilah did not want to go to bed with him. She struggled but he threw her onto the bed and ripped off her dress and underpants. She cried for him to stop, but he was determined to have her and refused to listen.

She fought him off as best she could, but his frustration had been building to this moment and he was like a crazed man. She managed at least to keep her legs locked together and try as he

might, Eddie could not pry her knees apart. Finally her resistance made him angry and he slapped her hard. Sheilah fell back
dazed onto the bed. Her ears were ringing from the slap, but
suddenly—and most unexpectedly—she was aroused. She
stopped struggling and he raped her, her clothes half-torn and
his pants at half-mast. When it was over, he was deflated and
apologetic. He promised sheepishly that he would never do such
a terrible thing again. He was gentle Eddie once more, a very
civilized ex-playwright; and Sheilah's brief moment of passion
died accordingly. He was mystified by her sudden reversal. "You
wouldn't yield until I smacked you. Why?" he asked. But she
did not tell him—it was a complicated matter and Sheilah was
inclined to keep her secrets.

In the wake of such mysteries, Eddie Mayer believed for some
months that he was in love with Sheilah Graham, though she
refused to go to bed with him after the first time and Eddie kept
his vow and never tried again to take her by force. Strange as it
may seem, Sheilah did not hold the rape against him—in truth,
as a single young woman without protection, she had suffered
worse in her life. She had a realistic idea of what to expect from
men and was shocked at very little. In Eddie's case, he really was
rather nice except for that one moment, and she was certain she
could keep him under control. In general, she was not inclined to
be moralistic about the sins of others, having committed some
sins of her own. And so she became good friends with Eddie and
rather enjoyed his courtship, and they never spoke about the
incident again. He often took her to dinner at Romanoff's, an
expensive and fashionable restaurant, where he was amazed at
her ravenous appetite. "If you would only look at me the way
you were looking at that steak!" he said regretfully one time.
Dorothy Parker, who did not know the full story, told people
that Sheilah was treating Eddie Mayer very badly. Sheilah found
it difficult to explain that for a brief moment he had appeared
masterful, and this had excited her, but then he turned out to be
only a puppy like all the others. In all her life she had never met
a man she had been unable to dominate.

Scott knew nothing about Eddie's rape of Sheilah Graham,
and he never would. But he suspected there was something sex-

ually wrong with the screenwriter who lived downstairs from him at The Garden of Allah. "Eddie Mayer hates women. Like Tom Wolfe. But for different reasons," Scott wrote in his notes. "He goes to them for sexual satisfaction, but he likes men emotionally more. I certainly don't know how far back it reaches but certainly women play a very mean and unstable role in his plays. He admired his father excessively, I gather. He sticks with the gang. You feel that he values his conquests so that he can brag about them. Talking is his vice. He would rather confide in men though than in women . . . His talent is not exactly thin, like Dotty's and so many Jewish and Irish talents—it is simply infrequent. He needs years to dream."

On Saturday evening, July 24, two days after the dinner dance for the Screen Writers Guild, Scott walked downstairs to this man who hated women and asked to get fixed up with a date. "Do you know a girl here I might like?" he asked Eddie. He added—"nothing serious, of course."

Eddie immediately thought of Sheilah. "She's engaged to an earl, he's in London, and I'm sure she doesn't want anything serious either."

Scott sensed this must be the girl he had seen at Benchley's and at the Screen Writers Guild benefit. He described Sheilah in detail: "Blond hair, green eyes, a complexion like smooth notepaper, a marvelous mouth, a great smile, and a great flirt."

Eddie agreed that this was without question Sheilah Graham, and Scott begged him to give her a call and try to set up something. Scott sat close as Eddie picked up the telephone. It was nearly seven-thirty in the evening; Sheilah was about to walk out the door of her hillside home when her phone rang. "What are you doing tonight?" Eddie asked her.

She told him she was about to go to a concert at the Hollywood Bowl with Jonah Ruddy, the Hollywood correspondent for the London *Daily Mail.*

"Oh, what a pity," Eddie said. "Scott Fitzgerald is here, and he wants to meet you."

Sheilah wavered. "I'd love to, Eddie, but it's really too late to cancel Mr. Ruddy."

"Why don't you bring him along?" he suggested. For Sheilah,

the fleeting image of the pale author with the melancholy smile
exerted a strange fascination. It was awkward to change plans so
late on a Saturday night, but she said yes. Somehow she would
work it out. Scott had been standing close to the receiver and
had overheard everything. He was triumphant as Eddie hung up
the phone, for he was a man who took an almost military delight
at a successful romantic campaign; indeed the siege was generally more interesting to him than the conquest.

Sheilah for her part put down the receiver more thoughtfully.
She was engaged to be married—she had to keep reminding herself of this. Now she had the delicate task on her hands of dealing with Jonah Ruddy when he arrived a few minutes later
expecting to take her to a concert. Jonah was a fellow
Englishman, part of the small but very visible British colony in
Hollywood—a wiry little man with bushy eyebrows and flamboyantly curly dark hair who liked to steal small things, ashtrays
and such, from people's homes. Once Sheilah discovered him in
her garage loading his car with her firewood; after that she was
more careful not to let him out of her sight. Despite this odd
inclination for kleptomania, he was often useful in feeding
Sheilah items for her column, and she sometimes paid Jonah to
cover premieres and parties she was unable to attend. He had
managed tonight to get the Hollywood Bowl tickets with some
trouble. When he arrived, she told him coquettishly that she had
"half-promised" Eddie Mayer they would go to The Garden of
Allah instead of the concert; she coaxed ever so nicely. Jonah
grumbled at the waste of the tickets, but there was not much
choice for him but to agree. He too was curious to meet the legendary Scott Fitzgerald, and they drove together down the hill
from Sheilah's house to Sunset, where they dropped off the concert tickets at a friend's house and made their way to The
Garden of Allah.

Eddie greeted them at his bungalow and Scott and Sheilah
were formally introduced at last. Then Eddie suggested they all
pile into his big Buick and drive to the Clover Club for dinner, a
place nearby on Sunset where there was gambling on the ground
floor and dining and dancing upstairs. Sheilah had the leisure
for the first time to examine Scott closely. He was dressed in a

pepper-and-salt suit with a bow tie, and, oddly enough, for this was late July in Southern California, he wore a wrinkled gray raincoat, a scarf around his neck, and a battered, gray homburg. It seemed to her a remarkable outfit. He was dressed as if to face the winter rains of some eastern city rather than midsummer in Los Angeles, apparently determined not change his habits due to a mere accident of weather and geography. Scott Fitzgerald seemed to her not only out of keeping with California, but also misplaced in time. He was very polite, gravely courteous. There was a reticence about him that she found attractive, and that seemed to belong to some earlier and more gentle age. In dress and manner he was like a college boy from before the Great War, strangely young in all his movements. She had never met anyone like him before.

At the bar downstairs in the Clover Club, Sheilah and her three escorts ran into Humphrey Bogart and Mary Phillips. Sheilah was impressed when Bogart said hello to Scott in a deferential way, for she had always assumed that when you were a failure in America, no one remembered you.

"Won't you have a drink with us?" Bogart asked Scott. But Scott shook his head with a pleasant smile and said he wasn't drinking these days. Bogart seemed surprised but let the matter drop.

Jonah, Eddie, Scott, and Sheilah continued upstairs and sat at a table not far from the band. Sheilah enjoyed being the only woman among three attentive men. Jonah was the first to ask her to dance. When they returned to the table, they ordered dinner and while they were waiting for the first course to arrive Scott stood up, offered his arm, and guided her back to the dance floor. She found him delightful. He danced in the collegiate style of the twenties: their heads touching, cheek to cheek, and their rears jutted outward at a thirty-degree angle. Sheilah hadn't danced like this in a decade. Soon she lost consciousness of everything but him. They danced for more than half an hour, tune after tune, completely forgetting Eddie Mayer and Jonah Ruddy and the food that was waiting back at their table.

"I *love* dancing!" she cried.

"I do, too."

"When I was a girl in England, I lived to dance—it gave me such a feeling of freedom."

The band struck up a tango and Scott and Sheilah took over a corner of the dance floor. Scott broke free and began spontaneously to experiment with the most amazing steps—the silliest tango Sheilah had ever seen. Laughing happily, Sheilah did her best to follow along. She could not believe he was forty years old, a man with a supposedly tragic past; he seemed young to her, full of wild fun.

"How old are you?" he asked as they danced.

"Twenty-seven," she lied, cheerfully erasing five years. Scott Fitzgerald had long ago perfected the art of being charming to women. When he was younger, one of his favorite strategies was to look at a woman in his special romantic way, as though nothing existed but her, and say that he had just come up with the perfect adjective to describe her. Scott cunningly understood that a writer did not have the animal magnetism of a great football player or movie star, and if he were to get the most beautiful women he had to use to advantage his one special field of expertise: words. There were few women who could resist his spider's trap of prying their own personal adjective from his lips—this from a writer who in every other instance of his craft professed to despise adjectives, preferring instead the more active immediacy of verbs.

In this case, it would take Scott another month to find the perfect word for Sheilah, for she was a complicated case. Nevertheless, Sheilah had met her match in the open field of flirtation; she was up against a professional.

"How did a girl as beautiful as you come to be a columnist?" he asked. As they danced she found it thrilling to feed fragments of her story—a sublimely edited version of her story—to this man who listened so well. She mentioned her elegant childhood in Chelsea. She said she had been on the stage, a dancer. She told him how she had tried Shakespeare at the Royal Academy of Dramatic Arts, but she had been so terrible that Kenneth Barnes, the director, had sent her a note: "It is imperative that you improve."

Scott laughed at just the right places. He seemed to believe this was the most entrancing story he had ever heard. He was so marvelously sincere that Sheilah nearly felt guilty for telling him so many fibs. Later when Sheilah said something clever, he told her he would write down what she said the moment they returned to their table so he could use her phrase in a novel somewhere. This was very flattering. What more could a girl want than a great writer to make her immortal? A few years later, Scott would indeed put her into his novel and he wrote about this first dance: ". . . she was deep in it with him, no matter what the words were. Her eyes invited him to a romantic communion of unbelievable intensity . . . Then she dropped her arms, stopped dancing, and looked at him, a laughing wanton. 'When I'm with you, I don't breathe quite right,' she said."

Sheilah also was to write about this dance:

> It is hard to put into words how Scott Fitzgerald worked this magic, but he made me feel that to dance with me was the most extraordinary privilege for him. He did it by his words, which seemed directed to me alone; he did it by the way he tilted his head back, a little to one side, as though he were mentally measuring, and then took complete possession of my eyes, my hair, my lips, all with a kind of delighted amazement at his good fortune to be dancing with me. He gave me the delightful feeling that hundreds of attractive men were just waiting for the chance to cut in on him and to snatch me away because I was so irresistible—and the feeling, too, that he would not let me out of his arms if he had to fight every one of them. He did it, too, by the rapt attention he gave to what I said.

There was more: Many men had flirted with her convincingly in the past, and she knew what it was they wanted. But Scott Fitzgerald did not grope or leer; he seemed to be impressed by her intelligence and fanciful imagination, rather than simply the curves of her body. For Sheilah this was amazing and new. She felt instinctively that she could talk to this man, and he would understand. She was the one to make it physical. They danced so closely that a strand of her dark gold hair fell into his mouth. She knew this was more than flirting—this was sexual intimacy.

"Is it getting in your mouth?" she said—not a question but pure seduction.

"I like your nose," he told her. And then a bit sadly he added: "When are you getting married?"

"In about three months." The reply, as she wrote two years later in 1939, "had a sobering effect on her. Why did [Donegall] leave her exposed to attractive men like this? She must watch her step. A working girl didn't have a chance to be a Countess everyday."

As they continued to dance, Scott barely spoke of himself, but instead asked Sheilah a stream of personal questions. This was more than an effort to be charming and bring her out: He sensed something not quite right about her story and like Robert Benchley before him, Scott was puzzled by this girl from British society becoming a Hollywood gossip columnist. Scott wrote later that Sheilah made him think of a story conference at the studio where someone might say, "We know nothing about the girl. We don't have to know much—but we have to know something."

At the end of all her answers lay an essential mystery, an enormous tantalizing blank. "Eddie tells me that you're engaged to a Duke," he prodded. "Is that higher than a Marquess?"

She laughed; he had gotten it all wrong. Gazing into his eyes, flirting for all she was worth, Sheilah explained that her future husband *was* a marquess. She gave Scott a rundown of British titles, from duke, marquess, earl, viscount, all the way to plain ordinary lord. Scott found this fascinating. Everything about her was surprising and fresh. Most of all he loved her childlike laughter which seemed to dismiss all the dukes and earls and viscounts to something incalculably less important than this dance. "[Her] weapon was her laughter," he wrote later. "First being ready to laugh at all times and then—never disappointing you when it came. Perhaps that's beauty . . . laughter waiting around the corner, and then—an everlasting reserve of more laughter."

Back at the table, Eddie Mayer and Jonah Ruddy watched the two dancers with amazement. They knew Sheilah was a flirt, but this seemingly endless dance was a surprise to them both. Sheilah finally became aware of their appraising eyes.

"We must get back to Eddie and Jonah," she told Scott regretfully at last. Scott too was disappointed. Being with a pretty young woman who was so full of life made him briefly forget his many troubles. It was good to dance again, and more amazing still at this late stage of his life to make a conquest. Before he let her out of his arms, he asked if he could see her again. She told him yes.

Scott and Sheilah made a dinner date for Tuesday night, in three days' time. Then they returned to Eddie Mayer and Jonah Ruddy and the cold dinner that was waiting for them on the table.

Over the next few days Sheilah often found herself fingering the diamond engagement ring Donegall had bought for her less than two weeks earlier on Hollywood Boulevard. The ring represented confusion in her life, choices that had to be made.

Could she really marry Donegall? It wasn't just a matter of deciding whether she loved him, but the graver question still: *Could she get away with it?* What if Donegall discovered the truth about her, that her supposed parents, John Lawrence and Veronica Rosyln Graham, were nothing but a figment of her imagination, along with the bohemian Chelsea childhood and the French finishing schools? He would hate her for it, and quite rightly she believed. A decade earlier she had not hesitated to pass herself off as a ballet dancer to the impresario Charles B. Cochran and step out upon the London stage with no training, but the approaching marriage seemed a more dangerous act still; it would be like trying to stay up on her toes for years without end.

Yet marriage to Donegall was a great temptation. Sheilah was accustomed to taking what she wanted and this marriage presented itself as a veritable deus ex machina to deliver her from Hollywood and a job she had begun to hate. She disliked gossip as a rule, and hated to intrude into other people's lives; however, such qualms didn't in the least prevent her from saying the most outrageous things about any celebrity who presented a tempting target. A girl had to make a living, after all. But it had become increasingly difficult to steel herself to the task, as well as to endure the inevitable snubs of the stars she had massacred in her column. By the summer of 1937, a number of movie sets were closed to her, and she always experienced a tremulous feeling on entering a room where she might encounter some recent victim of her typewriter.

Even before Donegall's latest proposal, Sheilah had toyed with the idea of escaping California. When she made her short trip to London earlier in the summer to divorce Johnny, she had seriously considered remaining in England. But to complicate the matter, a new temptation had presented itself. Just before she set out on her trip, an East Coast advertising executive had come to see her with a job offer in the United States that was hard to refuse: a five-minute spot on a weekly radio variety show that would be broadcast live from Chicago. Sheilah would do her segment of the show from Hollywood, joining the coast-to-coast broadcast with the latest gossip about the stars. The advertising man offered her a hundred dollars a week.

"Oh no," she told him. "I'm leaving Hollywood for good. My life will be in England from now on." The executive leaned closer, smiled with snakelike charm, and raised his offer to two hundred dollars. Sheilah's heart beat faster with sugar-plum visions of so much lovely money. As someone who had spent her entire life preoccupied with survival, this was hard to turn down: Added to the $160 a week she was already making from her column, she would be earning much more money than she had ever made before, a good deal for a single woman in 1937 with no responsibilities and a steady line of men eager to take her to the finest restaurants and clubs. So she said yes to the radio show, and yes to Donegall, knowing the two possibilities pulled in opposite directions and eventually she would have to choose between them: a career in Hollywood, or a fine fraudulent marriage in England. Somehow she always got herself into these jams; deep in her heart she wanted everything and it seemed unfair that life always called for choices. Meanwhile, she must wait six months before her divorce from Johnny was final, so there was some breathing room. Six months was an eternity for a girl who believed in miracles.

Scott Fitzgerald did not figure in any of these plans. After her Saturday evening at the Clover Club, the memory of Scott glowed pleasantly in her mind. She had never met anyone who made her feel quite the same way—so amusing, so interesting as a person, almost as if she were a character in a novel. She did not at all intend the involvement to be serious but when she ran into Eddie Mayer she couldn't help but ask all sorts of questions about Fitzgerald. Who was he really, and why did everyone speak about him in such tragic tones? Eddie smiled wickedly for he had been at Sheilah's engagement party to Donegall on Bastille Day and it shocked him how fickle a girl could be. But he told her about Scott's early fame, and Zelda, and the wild pranks they played, and how it had all turned bad. Eddie spoke almost as if he were glad it had turned bad, for writers are often a jealous breed.

Eddie remembered a time sitting in the outer office of a publishing company in the early 1920s, watching Scott Fitzgerald literally dance in the door—impossibly handsome, full of high spirits, absolutely on top of the world. It was hard not to feel envious when you were overweight and blind in one eye and the editor you had come to see kept you waiting in the reception room. Sheilah was surprised at Eddie's cutting tone. And surprised also that he spoke of Scott Fitzgerald grudgingly not just as a good writer, but as a great writer. Why then, she wondered, didn't people read him anymore?

She pondered these questions as she waited for their Tuesday date for dinner. Then on Tuesday afternoon the floor seemed to fall out from under her feet: She received a telegram from Fitzgerald saying that regretfully he could not make dinner that evening after all; his daughter had come into town unexpectedly and he must spend the evening with her. There was nothing in the telegram to suggest another date.

Sheilah was surprised at the intensity of her disappointment. What had been a pleasant glow of expectation changed into a dark oppression. Suddenly her life felt stale without his presence to look forward to. She pondered her canceled date obsessively, reliving their short history. "The man's lying," she decided at last. There had to be more to it than his daughter's visit. She could not bear it when people told her no. All her life she had felt a blind urge to do something, anything at all rather than accept rejection. Without further thought, she proceeded to break her own code of how to deal with men—she picked up the telephone and called The Garden of Allah.

Scott was clearly embarrassed when he answered her call, but Sheilah pressed relentlessly. "Why don't I have dinner with you and your daughter?" she persisted.

He hesitated. And then with obvious reluctance he agreed, granting at last a not-very-enthusiastic, "All right."

And so the date was on again. Barely.

Scott was sexually flattered but morally repelled to have a woman act like this over him. Obviously she was a tart, he said to himself distastefully. It was a pity because he had enjoyed dancing with her. Like Sheilah, he was a person who came alive when he was flirting. He loved the rush of adrenaline, the strange magic the game cast over everything in its early stages of will-she, won't-she. He had not experienced this for quite some time and it was a boost to his desperately cracked ego to have an overtly pretty young woman respond to him. But ever since Saturday night he had been debating the pros and cons of proceeding with the relationship, and in the end he decided he simply had too many responsibilities to launch forward on what seemed to him, on calmer reflection, a dubious affair.

There was another reason as well for his reluctance to have Sheilah join him for dinner: His fifteen-year-old daughter Scottie might get the idea he was chasing women in Hollywood; in this case a woman who was either "as common as they come" or "a raving beauty"—he couldn't quite decide which, but if his daughter should believe the former it would be appalling to his self-image. Where Scottie was concerned, Scott was a stern old-fashioned moralist, as conservative as they come.

When Scottie was born on October 26, 1921, Zelda had uttered, "I hope it's beautiful and a fool . . . a beautiful little fool." But after such a grand pronouncement, Zelda had lost interest in "it," her child, forever more. When Scottie was eight years old, a doctor in a French hospital asked Zelda what role her child played in her life. She replied without apparent concern, "That is done now. I want to do something else." This left

Scott holding the parental bag and he stepped into the vacuum of his wife's disinterest determined that Scottie should grow up without the terrible faults of her parents—his alcoholism and Zelda's insanity. As Scottie entered adolescence, all of Scott's fears for his daughter crystallized; he knew the perils of adolescence too well. Trying to provide some stability, in 1936 he sent Scottie to boarding school—the Ethel Walker School in Simsbury, Connecticut—asking his agent, Harold Ober, and Ober's wife, Anne, to act as unofficial foster parents from their home in Scarsdale, New York. Scott bombarded his daughter long distance several times a week with letters of advice and impossibly dire warnings of the dangers before her should she make a single wrong turn on life's unforgiving path. Only a few weeks earlier he had written a typical paragraph:

> . . . I don't want you to do anything inappropriate to your age. For premature adventure one pays an atrocious price. As I told you once, every boy I know who drank at eighteen or nineteen is now safe in his grave. The girls who were what we called "speeds" (in our stone-age slang) at sixteen were reduced to anything they could get at the marrying time. It's in the logic of life that no young person ever "gets away with anything."

Scottie put up with these lectures with remarkable patience for a fifteen-year-old girl. She came west late in July in the chaperoned care of the actress Helen Hayes and her husband, Charlie MacArthur—an ex-reporter turned playwright. Charlie MacArthur and Helen Hayes were part of the sprawling Algonquin Round Table crowd and knew the Fitzgeralds well. There were many old connections. Charlie had had a brief but emotional affair with Dorothy Parker in 1922 and later became Robert Benchley's roommate in New York. Dottie had an abortion as a result of her affair with MacArthur and was quoted as saying it served her right for having "put all her eggs in one bastard."

When Scottie arrived in California, Scott and his daughter and Charlie and Helen made the rounds together to see old friends: a call on the Stephen Vincent Benéts in Pasadena, a visit to Zoë Akins, a playwright, and one strained evening with Norma

Shearer (Scott never quite forgot the disgrace he had made of himself singing his song about dogs at her tea party in 1931). Scottie stayed at the Beverly Hills Hotel with the MacArthurs since there was no room for her in The Garden of Allah bungalow. This arrangement suited Scott fine since he needed to work and he did not quite possess the nerves required to deal with a teenage daughter on a round-the-clock basis.

Scott was clearly nervous about having his daughter meet Sheilah Graham. Two boys, friends of Scottie's from back east, called at the last minute, and Scott invited them along Tuesday night to make for a larger, less intimate group. They had dinner, a party of five, at the Trocadero, the fashionable restaurant on Sunset Boulevard which Sheilah had savaged in one of her early columns. Sheilah was nervous as well, but she liked Fitzgerald's daughter immediately. Scottie—as Sheilah was to put it in a writing exercise two years later—had "golden hair with a flame behind it. Wide apart blue eyes, the blue of a summer day with a hint of thunder . . . A little mouth that when she is cross looks like a short 'u' upside down . . . perfect teeth . . . She is *vivacious* and *so busy*—can't sit still." The young girl was chubby and somehow missed the startling physical beauty of either her mother or father. Scott told Sheilah later that he was glad his daughter was overweight; it would hold off the boys longer and keep her to her studies.

But although Sheilah liked the daughter, the father was another matter: Tonight he was an irritable, prissy middle-aged man she could barely recognize. It was inconceivable that this was the same Scott Fitzgerald she had danced with so wonderfully on Saturday night, the free spirit who had made up such comical new steps for the tango. At dinner he corrected his daughter over every little thing, embarrassing her before her friends. "Scottie, finish your meat," he scolded. "Scottie, don't touch your hair." "Scottie, sit up straight." It was unbearable to watch. The teenage girl endured all this as best she could. "Yes, Daddy . . . Yes, Daddy," she replied again and again. But every now and then, an "Oh, Daddy, please" escaped her lips. Sheilah's sympathies were entirely with the girl. Scott nervously drummed on the table, lit one cigarette after another, and drank a river of Coca-Cola. Occasionally Scottie and the two boys laughed among themselves and began to speak of their East Coast friends, but Scott interrupted heavily and told self-conscious anecdotes which were supposed to be funny but left an embarrassed silence in their wake.

Sheilah could not imagine how she had found this man attractive. There was no romance in him at all tonight, and not the slightest charm. He was nothing more than an anxious middle-aged father and she wondered what she was doing with such a boring, commonplace man. Scott dutifully asked her to dance and then proceeded to guide her about the floor in morose silence. She tried to speak amusingly about the young people left behind at the table. "They make me feel old," she said with a smile. "Me too," he responded glumly. But neither of them had felt the slightest bit old the previous Saturday night. Sheilah was relieved when they returned to the table and he said at last, "Scottie, don't you think it's time for you to be in bed? I ought to take you back to the hotel."

They left the restaurant and Scott drove his daughter and Sheilah in his rattling 1934 Ford coupé at the agonizing speed of twenty miles per hour along Sunset Boulevard to the Beverly Hills Hotel. Fitzgerald crouched anxiously over the wheel, as if he were guiding a huge battleship into harbor. Sheilah had never seen anyone drive so obsessively slow. They dropped Scottie at the hotel and then turned around and drove in silence at the same torturous speed back toward Sheilah's house in the hills. It had been a terrible evening and she wanted only to get home as quickly as possible—though quick was apparently not what Fitzgerald had in mind.

From Scott's point of view, they were racing along Sunset Boulevard. They were alone, he wrote, in "the intimacy of the car, its four walls whisking them along toward a new adventure." He was sensitive to the damage he had done. Scott was no fool, he knew his behavior all evening had been the opposite of romantic. When he came to write about this evening, he underlined in his notes the importance of his hero's motivation for what he would do next: *He seduces her because she is slipping away.* Perhaps it was too late and she was already gone.

Suddenly this made her much dearer to him than before.

They drove up Kings Road, Sheilah's treacherous hill, where Scott parked and walked her to her door. Scott said good-bye and Sheilah felt such a unexpected stab of loneliness that she was close to tears. It seemed to her that she had lost something, a fantasy perhaps—charm and laughter, someone gentle who might understand her. She took the key from her bag but then hesitated, torn between her warm memory of the man at the Clover Club and the horrid stuffiness of him tonight.

As Scott described it:

That was the moment to go in, but she wanted to see him once more and she leaned her head to the left, then to the right, trying to catch his face against the last twilight. She leaned too far and too long, and it was natural when his hand touched the back of her upper arm and shoulder and pressed her forward into the darkness of his throat. She shut her eyes, feeling the bevel of the key in her tight-clutched hand. She said "Oh" in an expiring sigh, and then "Oh" again.

From Sheilah's memory, as she stood at her front door she "felt inexpressibly sad that something that had been so enormously exciting and warming had gone. I thought, oh, what a pity to lose this. In the half light, as he stood there, his face was beautiful. You could not see the tiredness, the grayness, you saw only his eyes, set so beautifully in his head, and the marvelous line from cheekbone to chin."

"You look like a blue rose," he said softly, as their faces drifted closer in the night shadows.

"Please don't go, come in," she said.

She pulled him close and they kissed on the doorstep, and the stale mood of a disappointing evening magically departed. She took his hand and led him across the threshold upstairs to her room.

5

THE BRAVE LIE

He saw she was lying, but it was a brave lie. They talked from
their hearts—with the half-truths and evasions peculiar to that
organ, which has never been famed as an instrument of precision.

—F. Scott Fitzgerald, notes for *The Last Tycoon*

IN EARLY AUGUST 1937 Sheilah received a telegram from Lord
Donegall in London:

BEST NEWS ON EARTH DARLING STOP MOTHER IS ON OUR SIDE STOP THIS
MAKES THINGS SO MUCH EASIER STOP WIRE ME SWEETHEART MY LOVE

DON

Sheilah was at home, sitting at her desk with her typewriter
and clutter of papers by a window overlooking the steep hillside
at the rear of her house. She read the cable several times. *Mother
is on our side!* The words were ludicrous to her. What did this
horribly proper mother have to do with her?—too much, it

seemed. Now there existed no further obstacle to her marriage with Donegall—except for the small matter of her ecstatic love affair with Scott Fitzgerald.

Sheilah knew she was in a fix. It was a predicament strangely reminiscent of the time nearly fifteen years earlier when she had simultaneously dated two men, the millionaire with the lovely Rolls Royce, Monty Collins, and the quixotic dreamer, Major John Gillam. Once again a choice was demanded between money on one hand and romance on the other; once again Sheilah did her best to avoid a decision and keep all options open. She wrote Lord Donegall a chatty and evasive letter saying she was awfully pleased his mother approved of her; meanwhile she was extremely busy and would write again soon when there was more time.

Then she sat gazing out her window at the scorched golden hills of California in August, wondering what in the world she was going to do.

"Early August is for imprudent loves and impulsive and unmotivated crimes," Scott wrote afterward, thinking back on this time. For Sheilah certainly it was most imprudent to fall in love with Scott Fitzgerald. It made no sense at all in her life. Yet it was a struggle to resist.

Their first night together had been wonderfully tender. They made love gently in the darkness of her upstairs bedroom and then lay in each other's arms for many hours until she finally let him return to his bungalow at two in the morning. "She was very ready and it was right," Scott wrote. "It would have been good any time, but for the first time it was much more than he had hoped or expected. Not like very young people, but wise and fond and chokingly sweet."

The memory of this unexpected sweetness carried over into their busy lives. Each day Scott went off to MGM while Sheilah drove her secondhand Ford to different movie studios in search of items for her column. Usually she had lunch with a star, sometimes a director, producer, or press agent, and afterward she visited the sets with her pencil and notepad in hand. Scott often joked about the color of her car, a bright gaudy blue, but she laughed and said at least she could always find it in a parking lot. Scott's beat-up 1934 Ford coupé was also a source of humor between them, particularly its wheezy horn which he would honk merrily coming up Sheilah's hill in the evening after work. For Sheilah, the sound of this absurd horn coming up her hill was the true beginning of her day.

When she was with Scott, it seemed she was always laughing. She loved the silly way he played Ping-Pong. It was unfair really. In the middle of a difficult point he might cross his eyes ferociously, look off to the left, slice the ball to the right, then perform a ridiculous pirouette while waiting for her to return his shot— leaving Sheilah so helpless with laughter that she could barely play. She had never known such a childlike man. Sometimes he turned on her radio, bowed formally, asked her to dance, and then proceeded to make up the kind of absurd steps which had delighted her so much during their first evening at the Clover Club. If they weren't playing Ping-Pong or dancing, he might suddenly start shadowboxing about the living room, acting like some pug from the movies, putting on a James Cagney voice and telling her she'd better put up her guard or he would slug her one.

Finally when they finished with all these antics, they talked. Sheilah could never remember talking so much before—about books, friends, politics, movies, the differences between England and America, everything and anything at all. Fitzgerald spoke always in a theatrical manner, lowering his voice to a hush, then raising it to dramatic crescendos. He told stories as vividly in person as he did on the written page, and he had a passionate opinion about nearly everything. Sheilah was awed by the breadth of his knowledge and yet she was not in the least intimidated by him, as she had been by the arrogant and opinionated Randolph Churchill. The difference between the two men was simple: Churchill had made her feel stupid and inadequate, while Fitzgerald managed just the opposite, imparting by some special insinuation that she was the only one who could understand him so well, and that it was wonderful to share such insights and conversation together. Scott had "a gift for intimacy," as his biographer Andrew Turnbull would write. But another observer, an old friend, put this gift in a slightly different light: "As far as I know, everyone who was really exposed to him loved him. He simply couldn't bear it if they didn't."

His charm was all-pervasive. He called her by many pet names: Sheilo, dear heart, dear face, sometimes Presh, short for precious. If they were reading quietly, each in their different chairs, he might look up at her suddenly and exclaim, as if struck by her beauty for the first time, "Where did that gorgeous face come from?" Sheilah had never in her life been as thoroughly besieged by a man as she was by Scott Fitzgerald. He sent her flowers several times a week accompanied by funny little notes: from "F. Scott Fitzdillinger" after they had talked about gangsters one night; "From Dmitri to Grushenka," after an evening urging her to read *The Brothers Karamazov*; once a card with a silly drawing he had made showing a stork carrying a baby Scott, a caricature of himself complete with battered hat. Sheilah basked in the warm rays of this attention. It was impossible to resist.

During the week she often met Scott for lunch at the Metro commissary, where she encountered a person who bore no resemblance to the Fitzgerald of a month earlier, the "sick old man—not very funny stuff," whom Groucho Marx described after a lunch with Fitzgerald in this very room. Scott's new romance had brought him back to life and he was such funny stuff that he could barely contain himself. For weeks at a time, sitting with Sheilah in the commissary, he carried on a running joke with their waiter, claiming he had a twin brother, Irish Fitzgerald, who ate there as well. Whenever the waiter tried to resume their conversation from the day before, Scott appeared perplexed. "You must have been talking to my twin brother, Irish," he would say. The following day, when the waiter spoke to him in a friendly tone, he would reply with a straight face, "Are you sure you're not confusing me with my twin brother Scott?" Having succeeded in thoroughly confusing the waiter, Scott's face beamed with boyish mischief. Sheilah began to discount the stories she had heard of Scott's tragic past; this simply could not be the cracked plate of which people spoke.

*   *   *

Scott's daughter remained in Los Angeles through much of August. Scott insisted she take tap dancing lessons, believing idle feet might lead a young girl into trouble. But in general his new love affair had transformed him into a surprisingly mellow father. In mid-August he was able to write to Max Perkins, "All goes beautifully here. So far Scottie is having the time of her young life, dining with Crawford, Shearer, etc. talking to Fred Astaire and her other heroes. I am very proud of her." Sheilah managed to make a small anecdote of Scottie's meeting with Fred Astaire for her column, and she was often present at the various dinners. One night she was part of a foursome with Scott, Scottie, and Jimmy Stewart, who like Scott had gone to Princeton. Scottie liked Jimmy Stewart but she was puzzled after her tea with Joan Crawford. The actress spent the entire visit showing Scottie a huge album full of photographs of herself, with not an unflattering pose in the lot. "Wouldn't you think she was tired of seeing her own face?" Scottie asked Sheilah afterward. "Actresses never tire of that," Sheilah assured her. Sheilah liked the teenage girl and Scottie responded in kind, sensing that her father's new relationship took some of the heat off herself, and that Sheilah would prove an ally against his unreasonable demands.

When Scottie returned to her boarding school in Connecticut, Scott and Sheilah continued to go out several times a week. In the early days of their relationship, they often went to dinner with friends such as Dorothy Parker and Alan Campbell, the Ira Gershwins, the Ogden Nashes, or the Nathanael Wests. The restaurant of choice was generally Romanoff's on Rodeo Drive north of Wilshire, a restaurant in which Robert Benchley, John O'Hara, Dorothy Parker, and the millionaire Jock Whitney were partners along with Prince Mike Romanoff. Prince Mike, everyone knew, was a shameless fraud: He was no more a Romanoff than the extras strolling the narrow alleys of MGM were gladiators or cowboys. He had been born Harry Geguzunoff in Lithuania but had become inspired to pose as a member of the Russian imperial family while working as a tailor in New York. Despite the fact that Prince Mike was imprisoned briefly for fraud, the Hollywood intelligentsia and film stars were amused by his pretensions and made his restaurant the place to go. When Scott and Sheilah wanted to get off by themselves someplace more quiet, they generally went to the Brown Derby, often the Beverly Hills branch: "a languid restaurant," Scott wrote, "patronized for its food by clients who always look as if they'd like to lie down."

"It was so easy to fall in love with the boyish, collegiate-looking man who seemed so much less than his 40 years in the dim lights of the restaurants we frequented," Sheilah later remarked. "The sad lines on his face when I saw him in the daylight simply made him more interesting."

Such was the start of their affair, a seductively easy summer love that was full of laughter, Ping-Pong, and endless conversation. And at night, with the lights dimmed, sex was a slow, gentle, and courtly act between them. She was never to see Scott naked, for he was old-fashioned in these matters. She knew he was no longer the Adonis he had been in his youth. He had a belly now and his hair was thinning on top, and because she sensed he was self-conscious of these signs of age, she pretended not to notice. His imperfections only endeared him to her further. Most of all she loved his gentleness. She was a woman of experience, but love had never been like this before, a thing of infinite kindness—a balm and consolation for many deep old wounds.

Sheilah enjoyed being in love but she knew she could not allow herself to relax. There were dangers all around her. Five days a week she must bluff her way through the insecurities of a Hollywood career, knowing very well that there were bright and ambitious girls in the wings gunning for her job—just as she had usurped the NANA column by stealth and seduction from Molly Merrick. By the summer of 1937, Little Sheilah, the Giant-Killer, often felt as if she had taken on the entire industry. The scintillating paragraphs she wrote had brought her success as a gossip columnist, but they had also left her increasingly isolated in the town where she must work.

Not long after the start of her affair with Scott, she found herself in one of her typical jams. She had a date to visit the set of

Topper Takes a Trip, the latest of a series of successful *Topper* movies, and was terrified to encounter the leading lady, Constance Bennett, about whom she had recently written several unflattering paragraphs. It was one thing to dream up her catty remarks in the privacy of her office, and quite another to greet her victim face-to-face. It always surprised her when the great stars proved to be so thin-skinned. After all, they were so successful. Couldn't they see that she was just a working girl struggling to get by?

When she arrived on the soundstage, Sheilah kept to the shadows as much as possible. She spoke to other actors and hoped to escape without an introduction to the star. Then the producer, Milton Bren, came her way and asked if she had met Connie Bennett yet.

"No," she admitted, "but I must rush away."

"Oh, come on, she's on the set, I'll introduce you."

Sheilah wished she could turn and run, but it was impossible. To make matters worse, she knew very well that what she had written about Constance Bennett had been unfair; the actress had simply presented a tempting target for a clever line. As she followed Milton Bren across the soundstage, walking past great hissing lights and electric cables, she felt a growing sense of dread. She did her best to pretend a haughty nonchalance, but her heart was pounding.

"Connie, I want you to meet one of our good columnists, Sheilah Graham," the producer said in smiling innocence.

Constance Bennett was seated on a canvas chair. She raised her cool insolent eyes and stared at Sheilah for a long appraising moment. When she finally spoke her words were loud enough to carry to every corner of the soundstage. "It's hard to believe," she said, "that a girl as pretty as you is the biggest bitch in Hollywood!"

A hush fell upon the stage. Sheilah was miserably aware that the entire cast and crew had stopped work to watch her humiliation. The blood rushed to her head and she felt an animal urge to defend herself. She opened her mouth and said blindly the first words that came to her: "Not the biggest bitch, Connie, the *second* biggest bitch!"

Constance Bennett was momentarily taken aback. Sheilah at this point was nearly dizzy with adrenaline. When the actress continued to sit in stunned silence, she took the chair next to her and attempted to ask in a more natural voice what it was exactly in her column that had upset her. But before she could finish, the star rose grandly to her feet and turned to her producer with a scornful smile. "Oh, Milt," she said, "why do you let these strays clutter up the set?" She took the producer's arm and led him away so that Sheilah sat alone, left by herself on the field of battle, trying very hard not to cry. She felt utterly defeated, but she refused to run off the set in tears. Before long Milton Bren rushed back to Sheilah full of embarrassment.

"Do you think if I go now it will still look as if she threw me off the set?" she asked.

"Oh, Sheilah, of course you can go. I'm so sorry—"

Sheilah left the soundstage with as much dignity as she could muster, but she broke down the moment she was safely in her car. She cried all the way home, hardly able to see through her tears and anger, repeating over and over again the pale consolation of her reply: "Not the biggest bitch, Connie, the *second* biggest bitch!" Now that she had the time, she thought of all the devastating remarks she might have made.

She was still crying when Scott arrived that evening for dinner. His face darkened as she wept a new torrent of tears and told him what happened. "This must be avenged," he said with quiet rage. Scott took matters of personal honor very seriously. At different times in his life, he had written three separate lists to record various snubs he had himself endured; the longest of these lists enumerated sixty-six people who had snubbed him from 1925 to 1929. With such a crisis at hand, dinner was forgotten; Scott and Sheilah spent the rest of the evening discussing their revenge. Casting about for ammunition, Scott wanted to know the details of Connie Bennett's current role as a ghost in the *Topper* series. As it happened, he knew the actress casually; she had been a flapper in the twenties and had attended several dances at Princeton. Sheilah watched Scott with some astonishment as he sat at her table, a cigarette in one hand and a pencil in the other, frowning with concentration as he struggled to think up a perfectly devastating remark to put the actress in her place. In all her life, no one had ever helped her fight a battle before; Johnny was the closest ally she had ever had, but Johnny was so weak he was generally in need of help himself.

Together Scott and Sheilah wrote and rewrote a murderous paragraph for her column. "It's lucky no children happened to be on Constance Bennett's set yesterday. Her language was absolutely shocking"—this was Sheilah's contribution, hypocritical since she had used the same language herself. But the rest of the paragraph was pure Scott: "Poor Connie. Faded flapper of 1919 and now, symbolically, cast as a ghost in her latest production."

It was Scott Fitzgerald's first and final contribution to syndicated Hollywood gossip.

Despite the laughter and chivalry of Scott, and pirouettes at Ping-Pong, Sheilah soon discovered there was a dark side to him as well—an occasional chilling moment, as if a cloud had appeared from nowhere. One evening Sheilah invited him to the premiere of a movie for which she had been given tickets. She knew that Scott loved going to movies. But as they approached the theater by car, he noticed the waiting crowds and searchlights scanning the Los Angeles sky and he became sullen. It was the usual hysteria of a Hollywood premiere as far as Sheilah could see; there were flashbulbs exploding everywhere, and fans pushing against the barricades, screaming and frantic, hoping to get a better glimpse of their favorite star. Sheilah had seen all this before, and so had Scott. The eyes of the crowd moved hungrily to each arriving limousine, then clouded with impatience when someone who was not a celebrity, a mere mortal, dared to emerge.

Scott told Sheilah brusquely that they would avoid the crowds and go in a side entrance to the theater. As it happened the side entrance was inconvenient for Sheilah since she was here partly on business—to greet celebrities in the lobby and fish for any gossip, news, or passing scandals which might come her way. But Scott was adamant and there seemed nothing to do but humor him. They made a discreet entrance and slipped almost

furtively into seats in the rear, far from where the important people would be found. Scott slouched down into his seat and
buried his head in his program until the houselights dimmed.
Sheilah wondered if he was ashamed to be seen with her.
Perhaps he was ashamed for himself, his fallen position as an
unsuccessful author in this room where only celebrities counted.
Whatever the reason, it was clear that Scott did not want to be
recognized and for Sheilah this left an odd and unsettling
impression.

Another time, they had a small and unexpected quarrel at a
party, an industry event to which she had been invited and knew
many people, but Scott knew no one at all. She became worried
he was having a bad time, for people at a Hollywood party
could be cruel when they did not know you. At one point she
noticed Scott wandering about the room looking lost and alone.
All her protective instincts went out to him. She caught his eye
and patted the empty space next to her on the settee where she
was sitting. "Scott, come and sit here next to me," she called. But
his eyes turned cold with anger; he glared at her briefly and
turned away.

Later when they were leaving the party he said sharply,
"Don't ever do that."

"But Scott," she protested, "you looked so uncomfortable."

"I can perfectly well take care of myself," he told her. He had
never spoken to her so sharply before and Sheilah was hurt. It
was a lesson for her. She saw that Scott was a man of grave dignity and that she must never, under any circumstances, patron-
ize him again.

Throughout the imprudent month of August, Scott often ques-
tioned Sheilah about her early life. He was not only personally
curious, but professionally curious as well. A novel about
Hollywood was turning over in his mind. California seemed fer-
tile soil for an author, a land stranger than fiction, and he was
considering Sheilah as a character. But he simply must know
something more about her.

His questions came not all at once, but sporadically over time
as they sat in restaurants, or drove in a car, or stood on Sheilah's

hillside terrace gazing at Hollywood far below—a view, Scott said, which was like contemplating the Hanging Gardens of Babylon. Sheilah was alarmed. No one had ever wanted to know so much about her before. What sort of name was Graham? he wondered. Was it Scotch? German? Who were her ancestors? Where had she attended school? Did she have brothers? Sisters? What was her childhood like? Would she describe for him please the fine house where she grew up in London?

Sheilah answered one question only to have a dozen more rain down upon her. It was as if Scott wanted to possess her very memories, see the sights she had seen, relive the smells and sensations of her childhood. Sheilah was an old hand at improvisation, but such well-focused curiosity was a strain. Fortunately, she had some props—faked ancestral photographs she had made up in England and brought with her across the ocean. She showed Scott a picture of her brother David, who had died before her birth—actually a photograph of Johnny as an angelic child with long blond curls in a sailor suit with a big blue bow. Next in this family gallery came Sheilah's elegant sister, Alicia—in fact a snapshot of Sheilah herself surgically altered by an artist's brush, which had added a fluffy white dress, a new hairstyle, and a pretty flower in her hand where once there had been a wooden spoon. Last of all came the photograph of her "grandfather," an aristocratic fellow sitting on a fine horse wearing a top hat and pink coat; this in fact was Sir Richard North, the would-be pedophile who had once hoped to adopt her.

Using these photographs, Sheilah spun for Scott her well-rehearsed tale of a bored society girl who had taken to the musical comedy stage as something to do—and when the stage proved too stressful became a writer. Her mother, she said, had died when she was seventeen, her father shortly after her birth; she made up a rich Aunt Mary, a lovely fairy godmother sort of aunt, who had looked after her and presented her at court. Sheilah threw odd fragments of truth into the tale and clung to these tidbits as a victim of a shipwreck might reach for a floating plank of wood. Her career on stage in Cochran's chorus always made a series of amusing anecdotes, as did the true event of being presented at Buckingham Palace, though her sponsor had been a relative of Johnny's rather than the benevolent Aunt Mary of her dreams.

She had told all these stories before, but never to a listener as keen as Scott Fitzgerald. He kept probing without end, leaving off his inquiry one day only to take up his line of questioning at some new moment when she was caught off guard. Where was Alicia now? he wondered. Alicia? she stumbled . . . oh, her *sister* Alicia! Well, that was very tragic, she was afraid. Her sister Alicia was dead. The whole family was wiped out, alas. Aunt Mary as well, God rest her soul.

For Sheilah the questions became daily more stressful; she felt as if she were a criminal on trial for her life, defending herself against a sly prosecutor who was always trying to find a chink in her armor. She misunderstood Scott's motives, unaware that this was his usual method of gathering material for his books. Throughout his professional life, Scott had often made a pest of himself by questioning everyone around him, often with a pad and pencil in hand. Robert Benchley found it particularly invasive when Scott wrote down some clever line which had just been said at a party. Fitzgerald was omnivorously hungry for new characters, dialogue, and most of all, stories. In the past he had even paid strangers to tell him their anecdotes. Sheilah knew none of this and took Scott's questions in a paranoid and most personal way. At first she was flattered, believing this marvelous man was so smitten that he must know everything about her; then she became alarmed at his persistence and interest in every small detail.

The lies she told him were increasingly difficult to keep afloat. And yet she believed she must. She lied at first in order to be found worthy of love. And then later so that he would never discover that the woman he loved was a liar.

Throughout August, and for several months into the fall, Sheilah continued to accept occasional dates from other men: Eddie Mayer, Robert Benchley, John O'Hara, and Arthur Kober, a writer who had been married to Lillian Hellman and had come west to work on Marx Brothers movies. These men were considerate enough to ask few questions and provided Sheilah with the opportunity to flirt in her accustomed manner. They were her old gang and they formed a line of protection against the dangerously strong emotions she felt for Scott Fitzgerald. After all, she still might marry Donegall; it was important not to make too much of her love affair with Scott.

But none of the other men was much fun after Scott. The novelist John O'Hara was a particularly dreary dinner companion. He drank a great deal but each cocktail only made him more morose, until Sheilah almost felt like crying. As Scott put it: "John O'Hara is in a perpetual state of just having discovered it's a lousy world." One evening after taking Sheilah to dinner, he left his car engine running while he walked her to her front door. "Does he think I'm going to rape him or something?" Sheilah wondered. A few days later she heard mention that O'Hara was telling everyone in town that he had a terrible dose of the clap and she was glad she had not invited him in. All this was far from romantic, but it served to keep Scott at a certain distance.

Scott was not happy that she went out with other men, but he also was uncertain of how far he wanted his relationship with Sheilah to go. He admitted to himself that he had "moral doubts about her." Yet the fact that she was so greatly in demand by other men made her seem very desirable to him. He liked it also that Sheilah knew nothing of his past. He could be brand-new for her, admirable, uncategorized by the public infamy of his crack-up.

"I don't have the right to monopolize you," he told her disingenuously, for indeed he hoped he might. He added sadly: "You know I can never abandon my poor lost Zelda." Zelda, particularly "my poor lost Zelda," was always the last card in Scott's romantic arsenal; a tragic wife in an insane asylum provided at once an intriguing come-on, fascinating to a certain sort of Gothic young woman, as well as a foolproof way to extricate himself from these women whenever he pleased. In truth by 1937 he was entirely certain he would never live with Zelda again even if by some miracle her illness was cured. For a number of years he had contemplated divorce. But he was no more prepared to tell Sheilah the truth of this matter than she was willing to tell him the real story of her past.

Scott's charm worked magic but it was not as spontaneous as it seemed. Everything about him, his art and his personality, was carefully planned. Years ago he had totaled up his assets and liabilities and worked out for himself a grand strategy for success in love. "I didn't have the top two things: great animal magnetism or money," he analyzed with cold precision in his notebooks. "I had the two second things, though: good looks and intelligence. So I always got the top girl."

Sheilah Graham was currently the "top girl" in his circle at The Garden of Allah, and Scott went about wooing her with as much calculation as some men waged war. And she for her part continued her many lies and flirtations, understanding how well this kept him on the hook. As two strategists vying for advantage, they were well matched.

It was only meant to be a summer love affair, warm and beguiling, the recreation of ambitious people pursuing Hollywood careers. Like all summer romance, there was an element of calculation behind sunny smiles, and some doubt as to whether it would survive the colder truth of fall.

6

LILYANNA

I was prepared to suffer any ordeal rather than reveal the truth about myself. I thought, he has chosen me. I want him to be proud of the woman he has chosen. He must never feel that his girl is in reality a grubby little waif who has gotten to him by a series of deceptions.

—Sheilah, writing in 1958

ONE WEEKEND AFTERNOON at the end of the summer of 1937, Scott drove Sheilah to lunch in Malibu, some twenty miles up the winding Pacific Coast Highway. At that time, Santa Monica comprised the outer limits of the fashionable coastline and Malibu was hardly more than a cluster of ramshackle cottages in the northern wilds of the county. "Malibu: A bunch of dressing cabins for people who can't swim," Scott observed with sarcasm. There was a small restaurant Scott and Sheilah liked to go where the owner kept a sea lion in a raised concrete pool in the parking lot, attracting stray tourists and romantically inclined couples.

Scott drove the Coast Highway at his usual twenty miles per hour, tightly clutching the wheel and peering at the pavement ahead with desperate concentration. Several times Sheilah had tactfully offered to drive, but Scott would not hear of it. Riding at this torturous speed, Sheilah was unprepared for a new round of questions regarding her past. He wanted to know more about the previous men in her life, a touchy subject at best. They had covered this ground before but Scott would not leave it alone; he seemed anxious to confirm his worst fears about Sheilah—that she was, as he wrote in his notes, "a lady whose past was booked solid with men."

She had already told him about Johnny. Scott found Major Gillam a wonderfully British character who might have stepped straight out of Dickens with his gentle optimism and financial woes. Sheilah carefully omitted the more disturbing aspects of her youthful marriage, such as Johnny's eagerness to fix her up with rich men, and Scott accepted the existence of this husband with a smile. He believed Sheilah to be twenty-seven years old and at that age clearly everyone had a past. Beyond marriage, however, there was a moral abyss which he knew too well, having trod there himself from time to time—but not often, and never happily. This was the area which concerned him.

Driving toward Malibu, Scott asked if she had been in love with Johnny. Yes, very much, she replied—at least in the beginning. Then in a teasing voice he added, "And any others?"

"Oh, I've had romances," she told him. His teasing manner had put her off guard and she thought this a flirtatious game. "You know, I'm an English girl and we're quite straightforward about such things. If we love a man, we love him."

"I know all about love among the British upper classes," Scott assured her. His words still seemed teasing, but if Sheilah had listened more carefully she would have heard the strain. "And as one of Cochran's Young Ladies I imagine you must have been quite popular," he prodded. "More than one romance?"

"Why, of course. Eight, if I remember," she said flippantly. Sheilah made up the number eight on the spur of the moment; it seemed a respectable figure for a modern woman who had come to sexual awareness in the London of the 1920s rather than—as

Scott had—in the St. Paul, Minnesota, of the teens. At the age of thirty-two, Sheilah would have been hard-pressed to recall the actual number of her past lovers, but it was certainly a figure many times the number eight. For Scott's benefit, knowing how he liked anecdotes, she began cheerfully to recount a few of the more interesting conquests from her abbreviated list. She was not looking at Scott and became only gradually aware of his ominous silence.

When she glanced his way she saw that there was a terrible sick smile fixed on his lips. She realized too late that he was shocked. Could this really be the Scott Fitzgerald who had rocked the sensibilities of postwar America with his tales of girls who kissed and petted in the backseats of cars? Sheilah said she was sorry, very sorry, they had got onto this subject. "You're angry," she observed.

"Oh, no, no, no, no," he insisted. But he added tensely: "Tell me, who were they?"

She backtracked skillfully, hoping to repair the damage she had done. She told Scott the men were unimportant, mere phantoms of a pre-Fitzgerald past. When this tactic failed to work, she claimed (quite truthfully) that she had lied about the number eight—she had been only teasing him.

Scott knew very well that his voyeuristic jealousy was not attractive. It was an old weakness that had haunted him before. In *Tender Is the Night*, Dick Diver made love to Rosemary Hoyt, the young actress modeled upon Lois Moran, and afterward was driven to this same sort of obsessive inquisition into her amorous past. In the novel, Rosemary finally exploded: "I've slept with six hundred and forty men—if that's the answer you want." With Sheilah, Scott managed to take refuge behind a grand pronouncement. He said unhappily, "When a man falls in love it is a completely new experience. But for a woman it is an additional experience to those she has already had."

Sheilah had only the vaguest idea what he was talking about. Could this mean that Scott had forgotten Zelda in favor of herself—that, as someone new, she had managed to wipe clean the slate of Scott's romantic memory? Somehow this didn't seem possible. Meanwhile she worked hard to erase the harm her false confession had done. She did her best to assure him that there had never been anyone in her life remotely like him.

Scott struggled with himself. He had always suspected the worst about her and yet she moved him in some inexplicable way. A voice kept whispering in his ear: "This is your chance . . . Better take it now. This is your girl. She can save you, she can worry you back to life. She will take looking after and you will grow strong to do it."

Eventually he managed a more natural smile. "It's all right, Sheilo," he said. He assured her that the lovers in her past really didn't matter. Then he wisely changed the subject.

Sheilah had known Scott barely six weeks and yet she found it increasingly difficult to lie to him. Sometimes, in odd giddy moments, she wondered what it would be like to tell him the truth—not the stories she had been making up all her life, but what had actually happened in her childhood and who she truly was. This temptation surprised and frightened her, for she had never had the least inclination to open any real doors to herself before. But Scott was different from any person she had known. His gentleness and warmth penetrated to some guarded place that she had always kept inviolate from prying eyes. He was so incredibly understanding . . . but could he understand her?

No, she decided; he could not. It was crazy even to think it and she quickly put the idea from her head. Scott would hate her because he was a person with integrity, and she knew very well that she was not. The very qualities she found so attractive in him—his gentle, old-fashioned, and somewhat proper ways— would cause him to revolt in horror should he ever find out about her. Because she did not want to lose him, she resigned herself to keeping up her old facade, the pep girl with her pretty smile and expensive past who was always ready to have fun. She was determined to lie so well that he could not help but love her. Nevertheless, for the first time in her life she felt consciously lonely to have so many secrets, and to love someone she knew would despise her if he discovered the truth.

She prayed he would become bored and stop asking questions. Most men she had known preferred to talk about themselves: Why couldn't Scott? But he would not leave it alone. Driving back after lunch from Malibu he began his relentless questioning once again. He wanted to know what she was like as a child, and then later as a young woman before going on stage. His interest seemed almost carnivorous, as if he wanted to eat her alive. Sheilah was exhausted by the whole matter; she said she had told him these things before. Why go over and over it? But Scott was gently insistent, probing deeper: He still didn't have her fully in his mind; if he were to write her into a novel the character wouldn't yet add up.

He asked again about her father: What was his full name? John Lawrence Graham, she told him. And her mother? Veronica Roslyn Graham. Tell him again in what section of London had they lived? And what about her sister Alicia? How had she died? In what year? The questions came one after another in a nonstop barrage of curiosity. Sheilah felt as if she were drowning. She could not remember what she had told him already about Alicia's death. She could barely breathe. And why was she telling these lies to someone she loved? It seemed almost a form of suicide. She was strong, but not so strong she could keep this up any longer.

They were driving back along Sunset Boulevard, almost in Beverly Hills. Sheilah was talking about her mother and father and her brother David and sister Alicia, a jumble of names and false information, when quite without warning she began to sob hysterically. Scott was greatly surprised and he pulled his car to the side of the road to find out what was wrong.

"What is it, what is it?" he asked. He put his arm around her as she continued to weep. "What have I said to hurt you? . . . I'm sorry, Sheilo, I had no idea—is there something you don't want to tell me? You needn't—"

Even now she knew she could stop; a new lie might explain everything, that she was sobbing about Alicia's tragic death . . . and yet it was hopeless, there never had been any Alicia and this moment of reckoning had been building for years with a momentum that was unbearable. Scott was only the catalyst, the first sympathetic person, a kind touch, a gentleness to him that made her relax. Though she had barely known this man for six weeks, she was urgently ready to yield to him the secrets she had been guarding all her life. All the suppressed memories of her childhood came as a flood of water pressing against a dam. One moment she was determined to resist, to tell her lies until her dying breath; and the next, to her own surprise, she allowed the dam to break loose and she blurted out everything—that she was a fraud, that hardly anything she had told him was true, that even her family photographs were fake. Scott was astonished. He held her closely while she cried. "I'm sorry," he said many times over. "I'm always so curious about everything. Don't cry."

He was very tender. Sheilah's tears gradually subsided and they sat in his car at the side of the road for a long time while she told him everything, the horrible truth, a story she had never told to anyone before. He listened intently and with great sympathy. "She was absorbed in herself," he wrote later, "stung into excitement by telling of her own adventures." When she came at last to the end, he was simply bowled over. "His moralities somehow collapsed—she had managed to top him."

After subtracting two decades of imagination, the facts were these:

Lily Shiel was born on September 15, 1904, the youngest of six children in a Jewish family which had emigrated from Kiev to England at the end of the nineteenth century to avoid the persecution of the cossacks. Lily's father had been a tailor, an educated man who owned his own business, but he died when she was ten months old of tuberculosis during an unexplained trip to Germany, leaving his large family destitute. Lily's mother was forced to take a job as a washerwoman to bring in what money she could, working in a public bathhouse in the East End of London cleaning the tubs and laundering by hand the huge piles of soiled towels at the end of the day. As poor Jews and foreigners, the Shiel family existed at the very lowest strata of English society. Nevertheless, the neighbors referred to Lily's mother ironically as "the Duchess" because she had airs and kept herself aloof. If there was ever another name for her mother, Lily never told it in later years to her children or to any living soul. Poverty, she came to believe, was an anonymous grave that robbed you of a name.

Lily's mother could neither read nor write. She was a solemn square-jawed woman of peasant stock, her mouth set in a permanent scowl. Her face reflected the hardness of life, a bad diet, and one sickness after another in the damp gray cold of England—a country hardly more hospitable to Jews than the Ukraine they had fled. She often called her youngest daughter Lilyanna, a warm nickname from the old land, but this was nearly the only sign of affection she would ever show. "Lilyanna!" she cried, when the little girl wandered off. "Lilyanna!" The girl was not an attractive child. Her nose seemed to be forever running, her skin was blotched with eczema, and she had painful chilblains in her fingers from the perpetual damp; she was as skinny, awkward, and unappealing as any child might ever be.

Lily's earliest memory was of hunger. She was four years old, standing on a London sidewalk waiting for an older child to take her to the neighborhood soup kitchen. When the older child did not appear, Lily simply set off on her own down the street to where she remembered from previous visits food might be found. The journey frightened her, for the London street was immense and dangerous, but she went off anyway determined to eat. Later the adults punished her for giving them such a scare. They told her she was a very bad girl.

Her second memory was of sex. There was a bearded middle-aged man who lived with them; Lily did not know if he was a boarder or a relative. Once when there was no one else around, the man sat her on his lap and he put his hand under her dress and touched her private parts. Then he began to breathe in sharp gasps, wiggling uncomfortably beneath her until at last he gave a great sigh of relief. When it was over, he warned the little girl never to tell a soul what happened or she would get into a great deal of trouble. As it happened Lily enjoyed the experience and was inclined to keep their secret. She liked the pleasurable sensation of the man's hand between her legs, and most of all she enjoyed the attention he gave her. No adult before had ever sat down with her and given her such an undivided few moments of his time. She rather hoped it would happen again, but soon after-

ward the bearded man disappeared from their home and she
never saw him again.

There was one other memory from her early childhood. One
evening her older brother Myer, took her to a great dark house.
Lily had no idea what they were doing in such a place, but suddenly she and her brother were running from a large dog, hoping to reach a high wall before the dog caught them. Lily was
terrified. She ran with all her strength and it seemed the snarling
dog would eat her up alive. But then at the last moment she was
on the wall and her brother's hand pulled her over to the other
side.

She never forgot these three primal things: hunger, sex, and
running from danger. They were the images that formed her and
they stayed with her for the rest of her life.

In 1910 when she was six and a half years old, Lily's life
changed drastically. Her mother could no longer afford to take
care of her. They were simply too poor to survive and she
arranged for her daughter to enter an orphanage—the Jews
Hospital and Orphan Asylum in Norwood, a southeastern section of London.

Lily's oldest brother Henry took her to the orphanage on the
top of a double-decker bus, and then he waited somewhere on
the grounds while Lily and a group of other newcomers were
led into a bathroom and ordered to undress. The girls stood in
one line, and the boys in another. Lily had never been naked in
front of a boy before and she was embarrassed when they giggled and pointed at her. Then adult hands took her forcibly, sat
her upon a hard chair, and cut off all her hair. The cold heavy
clippers moving across her scalp frightened her. Lily sat very
still as she watched her ash-blond hair fall all about her to the
floor. When it was finished, she touched her hand experimen-
tally against her scalp: It was a curious sensation, particularly
when she rubbed the bristles the wrong way. Then the boys and
girls were lowered three at a time into a tub of steaming hot
water. They were bathed and dried and given identical faded
blue rompers to wear. With their newly shorn heads it was no
longer possible to tell the boys from the girls. At last Lily was

taken to say good-bye to her brother, who kissed her awkwardly and seemed anxious to depart.

She did not cry when Henry turned his back and abandoned her. She did not cry until several weeks had passed and the adult hands took her a second time, forced her to sit on a hard chair, and she felt once again the cold clippers moving upon her scalp. She managed to hold back the tears until it was finished. Then she touched herself reluctantly, her bald and naked scalp, and young as she was she understood that everything she had ever possessed had been taken from her—her past, her family, her small vanities, and all her self-esteem.

She was no one now, only an empty page, and she wept bitterly for what she had lost. Lily lived in the orphanage for the next eight years and her hair was cut to the scalp once a month, every month, until she was twelve. There were occasional outings to parks and pantomimes on Boxing Day where people would point and stare at her, and wonder aloud if she were a boy or girl. Lily knew she was very unappealing; why else should her mother abandon her? At the orphanage, the teachers and trustees occasionally touched and petted the cute children, but no one touched or petted her. It was not only her blotchy skin and runny nose that made the adults avoid her; there was a look in her green eyes of guilt, cunning, and pathetic unhappiness which made people turn away.

Because she had left home so young, she soon forgot her old life, her mother and brothers and sisters, except as a distant memory. She did not particularly miss them because they had never had much to do with her. Her mother had always been busy or sick, and her brothers and sisters were much older than herself and preoccupied with their own affairs; it was a family in which the sullen hardships of poverty had left little room for kindness. The orphanage was a self-enclosed world with its own rules and realities and Lily quickly set about to adjust to her new life and survive. She was always hungry for there never seemed to be enough to eat. Breakfast consisted of two pieces of bread with rancid margarine and watery cocoa served from large vats into chipped enamel mugs. Lunch was the main meal of the day, usually a heavy suet pudding, or a watery soup with some vegetables and an occasional floating piece of gristle.

Food became an obsession, an endless longing. Lily's least favorite meal was mash covered with a single soft boiled egg that was open and runny and always made her gag. There was "wet fish" which she hated and "dry fish" which she could tolerate a little more. Before long she made an important discovery: The staff, the teachers and headmaster, ate far better than the orphans entrusted to their care. Lily could smell the warm aroma of their meat pies drifting from the kitchen down long corridors into her waiting nostrils. The smell was irresistible and a clever girl knew what to do. When Lily was nine or ten years old, she taught herself to steal. She knew this was a bad thing to do, and that the punishment would be terrible if she were caught. But she refused to be helpless.

Cunningly she watched the kitchen and discovered the odd times of the day when it might be deserted. Then she crept into the forbidden room with its huge ovens and vats and counters to find the lovely meat pies cooling on large wire racks. She cast a guilty eye in every direction, then quick as her hand could move, she stuffed the hot pies down into her bloomers. At last, walking a little strangely, she made her way stealthily out from the kitchen back to her dormitory to hide the pies for a secret late-night feast in bed.

It was exciting to steal, a great heart-pounding adventure, and her success encouraged her to try again. Her bloomers had a drawstring at each knee and seemed ideally designed to carry any number of things. In the kitchen one afternoon she discovered large vats filled with cocoa and sugar. She thought this might be a tasty combination and she shook the mixture into a kind of candy as she walked with her bulging bloomers back to her dormitory. She had a friend with whom she sometimes shared her treats; they sat together in the dark munching on stolen meat pies, sweet buns, and cocoa long after everyone else was asleep, making up stories, pretending they were at a fancy boarding school instead of their orphanage—Lily had read of such places in books.

She grew bolder in her endless foraging for food. Sometimes she pretended to be sick to gain admittance to the infirmary, where she knew there was a large jar of apricot jam. As soon as the nurse left the room, she reached into the jar to eat handfuls of jam as fast as she could, then licked herself clean before the nurse could return. Once on the religious holiday of Sukkoth Lily dared to steal food from an arbor which had been set up as part of the traditional festivities; she took a banana she believed was meant for God. She knew it was a great sin. Unfortunately, she was caught and severely beaten for this sacrilege. It was the price she must occasionally pay for her willingness to take chances. Lily bore her punishments in silence. She believed that to show pain would be to admit defeat.

The headmaster of the orphanage took a particular delight in beating the children. Often he hid in various places along paths and corridors so that he might sneak up on the orphans and smack them hard on their bottoms. He regarded childhood as a tumultuous anarchy which must be repressed by any means possible. For a minor offense, the children were made to hold their hands outstretched while a teacher hit them hard with a ruler first on one palm and then the other. For a major offense, they were forced to stand with their pants down, bare bottoms exposed to the entire orphanage, and then they were beaten with a cane. Lily found this stirring in a way she could hardly explain; once when a matron beat her bottom with a hairbrush, she felt a disconcerting pleasure between her legs. Another time she witnessed the public caning of a boy who had run away from the orphanage. At the end of the beating, the boy was forced to stand before the gathered community dressed only in girls' underpants. Humiliation was always the final weapon to crush rebellious spirits.

Lily spent a great deal of her time figuring out ways to avoid punishment. This was particularly necessary in her case because, to her great sorrow, she often peed in her pants and at night she wet her bed. She didn't know why she did these things and it took all her cleverness to escape being caught. She volunteered to sort through the bags of laundry before they were washed, and she would hold up the soiled underwear to the adult in charge. "Look what somebody did!" she declared with outrage. "Oh, we must show Miss Green!" The ploy was a brilliant one and no one ever suspected that she herself was the culprit. As for wetting her bed, she managed to conceal this fact for nearly five years, often by exchanging her wet mattress for a dry one from a spare bed. One day when she was eleven years old, a teacher unexpectedly came into the dormitory and Lily was caught redhanded in the midst of dragging her mattress from one bed to another. "*What* are you doing?" the teacher cried, and for once Lily could not come up with a quick excuse. She was exiled to a special bed wetters' dorm where the girls had to sleep on mattresses of straw. The humiliation of being in this dormitory was enormous, for now everyone at the orphanage knew she wet her bed. Each morning a leather-faced matron appeared, placed her nose close to each straw mattress, and sniffed twice. The guilty offenders were beaten unmercifully with a hair brush. Lily was beaten twice before she decided that no matter what, she must never wet her bed again.

The effort made her ill: She prayed at night to the God who made bananas that when she woke in the morning her mattress might be dry. When this had no effect, she refused to drink water for days at a time; she tried to never sleep, to be always on her guard against the warm soothing gush between her legs. Finally she was successful, and after two months the matron allowed her to move back to her old dormitory. Life, it seemed, required an inordinate amount of determination. But you could do anything if you tried.

Occasionally there were unexpected gifts which came out of the blue. World War I arrived and brought air raids, a spectacle of light and sound never before experienced by mankind. Lily thought they were wonderful. During the day, huge enemy zeppelins lumbered over the outlying districts of London dropping bombs; she remembered once being on a swing, her feet arching into the sky, watching upside down the bright distant explosions from somewhere on the edge of the city. Later in the war, airplanes came at night from the coast of northern France. The German ace Baron Von Richthofen ruled the sky and all the children spoke of him with awe. Often the air-raid sirens woke the children from their sleep, and the teachers led them downstairs to a stone corridor that was considered as safe as any place at the orphanage. On these occasions, the children were given extra food, delicious sweet buns, as well as an extra hour of sleep in the morning. Lily prayed that the air raids would go on forever.

Once a year the rich trustees of the orphanage arrived for a visit, driving through the main gate in their magnificent automobiles. One year Lily watched as a young girl with long golden curls stepped from one of the automobiles, a princess, the daughter of a trustee. She was dressed all in white. Her coat, hat, shoes, even her gloves were white. Lily stared at her, bewitched. The girl looked so wonderfully loved and cared for as she walked by the side of her rich father, her little hand in his. She was nearly the same age as Lily, but the gulf between them was so enormous it could be crossed only by an act of imagination. From this moment, Lily began to daydream. She fantasized a world where girls in white dresses were possible—a place where mothers and fathers loved wonderfully pretty daughters who had long golden hair that was never cut to the scalp.

Often she carried a fantasy adventure running in her head as she went about the business of her day; each day there was a new installment, and at night when she closed her eyes she fell into the embrace of her fairy-tale world. In Lily's dream world, she was happy and well fed: *She* was the trustee's daughter, living in a splendid house with loving parents. Marvelous things happened to her all the time. There was always a rich young man who was charming and handsome and close at hand to rescue her whenever she was in trouble. Everyone adored her, they indulged her every wish; sometimes crowds of smiling well-dressed people applauded when she entered a room simply because of the many heroic things she had done. She was no ordinary girl.

Lily's natural flair for fantasy was fueled by the many romantic stories she read in the penny press, weekly publications such as *Peg's Paper* which told tales of handsome mill owners' sons who saved pure maidens from evil foremen. Poetry was also a source of inspiration. The headmaster occasionally offered a sixpence prize to whoever in the school was the first to memorize a poem he assigned, and this dangling sum encouraged Lily to action. She

found she could memorize the poems almost instantly after reading them on the bulletin board and while walking to the headmaster's office. She nearly always beat out the few other children
who bothered to compete with her, and she used her sixpence to
buy sweet buns at a small bakery near the orphanage. Lily loved
grand epic poetry, the grander and more epic the better. Many of
the poems she memorized for the headmaster had a patriotic
theme, and Lily found this thrilling. She too was willing to sacrifice her life for the glory of England, should anyone ask her.
There was one epic poem, *Boadicea*, whose verses she remembered long past childhood. It told a glorious tale of a British war-
rior queen who threw off the yoke of ancient Rome. Under
Boadicea's command, the Britons:

> Went to battle, fought and died
> Dying hurled them at the foe,
> Ruffians, pitiless as proud,
> Heaven awards the vengeance due:
> Empire is on *us* bestowed,
> Shame and ruin wait for you.

The sweep of such grandiose language carried her far away
from her life of urine-soaked mattresses and mash covered with
runny eggs. She found she could memorize nearly anything with
little effort—verses of songs as well as poetry. There was one
soothing lullaby she loved particularly that was nostalgic of all
the love she had never received, and the mother who had never
sung to her. Many years later she would sing this orphanage
song to her own children:

> Buddha made the harvest and made the
>   wyndes to blow
> Sitting at the doorway of a day of long ago
> Gave to each his harvest, food and toil and
>   mate
> And mother's heart for sleepy head
> Oh, little son of mine.

Of course life in the orphanage never allowed her to become
too dreamy, for in the end a girl in her situation must be practi
cal. She developed the ability to switch instantly between her

daydream world, and the one of stolen meat pies and possible punishments in which she must always be on guard. She knew she was homely, but it soon became obvious that she was clever. Even more important, she possessed a driving energy that set her apart from the others around her. Lily wished to be admired and win applause—a counterfeit of love, at least, if not the real thing—and she decided she must outshine all the other children at Norwood. Her marks were so good at school that she skipped a grade, and even then she soon became the top student of her new class.

In her last year Lily outdistanced all the others and became the only student in a special Sixth Standard which was created for her alone, working in a separate row by herself in the classroom. Her essays were read aloud to the entire school. In 1917 when Arthur Balfour promised in the House of Commons that after the war Palestine would be given as a homeland to the Jews, Lily was chosen to write this great man a letter of gratitude. At the age of thirteen, she was named the Head Prefect and she sat at a special table during meals. She also became captain of the girls' cricket team and under Lily's command, the girls beat the boys' team for the first time in orphanage history. The younger children looked up to her. When she reached the age of twelve, the adults had at last allowed her hair to grow out in thick ash blond luxury, falling nearly to her shoulders by the time she was thirteen and a half. Now she looked almost human when she walked to the bakery for her sweet buns; people no longer stared at her as if she were a freak.

Unfortunately, her beautiful new hair became a problem. It was soon so thick she could not get a comb through it. She had no practice in combing hair; she didn't really know how. Each day her ash blond curls became more tangled, a hopeless rat's nest, until finally one of her teachers noticed it in class and was appalled. She ordered Lily to leave the room at once and not return until she had combed her hair.

Lily was sensitive about her tangled curls and she spoke back, most unwisely. She told the teacher quite haughtily that she had not come to this orphanage to be ordered about like a slave—as if Lily, a ward of charity, had any choice in the matter. The teacher was furious and slapped Lily across the face with her open hand. And this is when Lily did a truly momentous thing: Without thinking, she slapped the teacher back. The classroom was in an uproar and there was hell to pay. As the other students looked on, Lily was hauled down the hall to the infirmary where the teacher ordered the nurse to cut off all her hair—every inch of it—to teach her a lesson.

Lily screamed hysterically as the scissors moved across her scalp. She watched her new hair fall tragically to the floor one final time. She begged, she pleaded, she said she would rather die. Finally the nurse became afraid the girl would do herself some injury and she took pity. She told Lily to calm down; she would cut no more except to tidy it up and make it even. When it was done Lily looked comically like a lamb who had received half a shearing. She was as ugly as she had ever been in her life and for many weeks could not look into the mirror without bursting into tears. Her other honors and privileges were shorn away as well. Because of her crime, she was no longer allowed to be the Head Prefect nor the captain of girls' cricket team, and she could not eat at the special table during meals. The entire orphanage knew of her disgrace.

The same willful pride which had raised her up, now had cast her down. Lily wondered why she was different from other people, marked and set apart. All she really wanted was to fit in.

The Great War ended when she was fourteen years old. Six months later Lily was legally of age to leave the orphanage. Because she was so bright, one of her teachers, Miss Goodman, was able to arrange a scholarship that would pay her way through high school and college. Lily was delighted and believed she was on her way to great things. Twice a year she had been taken to see a dentist in the West End of London and from the top of the bus she had eagerly observed the existence of an elegant world of stores, offices, and stately boulevards. With an education perhaps she could be part of this world. But the dream depended on further schooling, and this was not to be. Without warning, Lily's mother came back into her life and put an end to all her ambitions.

Over the years, Lily's mother had appeared occasionally on visiting days bearing sandwiches and small treats. Lily enjoyed the status of being among a small group at the orphanage who had a parent still alive, but the visits were awkward. Her mother could only stare at her sadly, sigh a great deal, and never seemed to know what to say. Lily had left home too young for there to be any real relationship. They were strangers to each other. And then just as Lily was set to leave the orphanage her mother became ill with cancer and requested that she return home to cook and clean and take care of her. It caught Lily by surprise but she knew there was nothing she could do but obey the summons.

And so at the age of fourteen and a half, gravely disappointed at the abrupt end to her education, she returned to the Cockney squalor of the East End and a mother she barely knew.

Her family now lived in Stepney, a poor district of London, in a small two-room flat that was kept spotlessly clean. Lily's oldest brother Henry was at home as well. Henry had deserted from the army and hidden himself throughout the last years of the war with a second cousin in Newcastle in the north of England. When it seemed safe to emerge, he returned to his mother in London to sleep on a horsehair sofa he made up each night in the living room. Lily shared the small bedroom with her sick mother. As for the rest of Lily's older brothers and sisters—Myer, Morris, Sarah, and Esther—they had grown up and left home during the time she had been in the orphanage, and she was never to have anything more than the vaguest sense of them.

At first she was excited to be home. She tried to summon an image of heroic sacrifice, to care for her sick mother with all the noble purpose of a figure in a book. Nearly all of Lily's images of the outside world were culled from books, or sheer imagination. But the truth required some adjustment and she found the East End an alien place. She hated the streets themselves. There was a brewery nearby on Stepney Green which saturated the surrounding neighborhood with the smell of beer. Lily found the smell loathsome; this was not the elegant world of her dreams.

Another cause of unhappiness came unexpectedly from her appearance. At nearly fifteen years old she was no longer the plain and gawky child she once had been. To her astonishment she saw that she was almost pretty. Most striking of all, she had a figure beyond her years, and large breasts which caused an agony of embarrassment as she walked in the East End. A simple matter of going to the store for groceries became an ordeal for her. The end of the war meant that there were men everywhere, young and old, loafing on every corner. They whistled and called out lurid remarks and sometimes they even gathered around her and created excuses to brush against her breasts. Each time Lily stepped out from her mother's flat, she had to face this obstacle course of loutish men. The drunks were worst of all.

Lily was afraid of these rude men and despised them with all her heart. On the streets she walked quickly with the haughtiest expression she could manage, but this made the men believe she was putting on airs and they set upon her with an even greater predatory delight. She did indeed believe herself superior to her surroundings, and had received a far better education at her Jewish orphanage than she would have had she remained in her neighborhood council school. It was true that she spoke with a Cockney accent, but still she spoke better English than those around her. Lily had made herself important at Norwood as Head Prefect and captain of the cricket team: She was the girl who could memorize a poem faster than anyone else. Now it was a great blow to be treated as if she had no importance at all.

Life was no easier at home. A surgeon had saved her mother's life by performing a colostomy for colon cancer, cutting away a section of malignant intestine. In 1919 this was a painful and messy medical procedure that left her with an aperture in her stomach from which to evacuate her bowels; one of Lily's daily chores was to clean this dreadful hole and then launder her mother's soiled bandages. It always made Lily gag. Then she was to clean the flat each day, scrubbing the floor on her hands and knees, as well as do all the shopping and cooking for her mother and Henry. For a girl with romantic dreams, this seemed a wretched end.

Her brother Henry was a sullen and unhappy man, unpopular at the factory where he worked. He had been married before the war, but his wife had divorced him due to the disgrace of his desertion from the army. All these things made Henry moody and he was inclined to take out his frustrations on Lily, ordering her about as though she were his personal servant. When he came home from work, he often gave her an empty jug and ordered her to go to a nearby pub to fetch his beer. For Lily this was a nightmare journey. The pub frightened her even more than the open streets. She hated the dense smoke and the men with red leering faces who lurched her way with loud coarse remarks. Walking home with her brother's beer, she often had to pass around drunks who were vomiting or lying on the sidewalk. She could not imagine how people could let themselves fall so low. One evening she simply refused to fetch her brother's beer when he asked her. She was not his servant, she said; let him do it himself. Henry was furious. He raised his hand to slap her, but when he saw the look of defiance in his sister's eyes he was the one to back down.

Lily was a terrible housekeeper. She often fell to daydreaming when she was supposed to be scrubbing a floor. She refused to bargain with the fishmongers for good prices and she was obviously so unhappy that her mother soon decided it was best that she find a job outside of the home. With the money Lily earned, someone more appropriate could be hired to do the housework. A few months short of her fifteenth birthday, she answered an ad in the newspaper and was hired by the Addressograph factory at one pound a week to stamp metal name plates for businesses to use in addressing envelopes. Her hours were from 8 A.M. to 6 P.M. five days a week with a half-day on Saturday.

But Lily did not last long at her new employment. Dancing was her downfall. All the girls at the Addressograph factory were wild about dancing. Those who knew the new dance steps taught those who did not, and during their breaks for lunch and tea they often practiced with one another. Lily thought dancing a marvelous thing, much more fun than the endless repetition of stamping out metal plates. Before long she began to leave her machine for the privacy of the restroom, where she closed the door and danced with great abandon with imaginary partners, watching herself in the mirror. One afternoon the supervisor, a middle-aged woman, opened the restroom door to discover Lily in the midst of her solitary dance. "What's going on, what do you think you're doing?" the supervisor cried. "You'd better come with me. Dancing! What do think this is, the Pally de Dance?"

Lily followed the supervisor to the office where she was fired on the spot. She did not greatly mind losing her job; what she minded was the need to explain her disgrace to her mother and Henry. At first she tried to lie. She said she was sacked with a number of girls because the factory was doing badly and there weren't enough orders. But Henry went to the factory himself the next morning and he learned the truth. He stormed back to the flat, confronting Lily with her lies. He and Lily's mother could only shake their heads in dismay and mutter dire warnings. Whatever would happen to a girl who told such fibs and danced in the washroom when she should be doing her job?

It was at this time that Lily began to escape on the bus to the West End whenever possible, to use the bathroom at the Savoy Hotel and gaze with longing upon a more splendid world. These excursions made it even more painful to return home and find she was nothing but the family servant. She hated cleaning house, the boredom of it as well as the indignity. There was a stone courtyard she had to clean each day on her hands and knees with a pumice stone: She disliked this task above all others because the neighbors could look down from their windows and see how low she had fallen. One Friday afternoon, Lily rebelled. She had just sat down to rest and daydream when her mother appeared with a pail and the hated pumice stone and ordered her to clean the courtyard.

"No, I won't do it," Lily sulked. "I'm tired."

"Yes, you will," insisted her mother.

"I won't," Lily said. Her mother raised her hand and smacked Lily across her face to beat some sense into the girl. But then, just as she did with the teacher who slapped her at the orphanage, without even thinking, Lily slapped her mother back. She knew immediately that it was a monstrous thing to do, to strike her poor mother who was dying of cancer. It was simply a quick uncensored reaction, a wild urge to fight back. Lily was almost more startled than her mother at what she had done. She wept and apologized but her mother only pushed her away and sank into a chair crying to herself.

Unfortunately, Henry walked in the door at just this moment. In a dangerous voice he demanded to know why his mother was crying. When he heard the unbelievable story, he lunged at his sister in a rage and began to beat her. Lily ran into the bedroom and closed the door between them. But Henry burst through the door, even more furious that she should try to hide. He hit Lily again and again with his fists. At first it hurt, and then she felt herself becoming vague. From a distance, she heard her mother begging for Henry to stop, but he kept hitting her until she was lying on the floor with blood in her mouth. Even then he did not stop. He beat Lily until she was unconscious.

Her mother thought it best for Lily to go away. Two days after the beating, she found herself on a train bound for the fashionable seaside resort of Hove, a suburb of Brighton. A teacher at Lily's orphanage had found her a job as a maid in a four-story Regency mansion which belonged to two aging sisters. Lily was given a uniform, but she refused to wear the cap, believing this would brand her a servant forever. The two sisters were outraged at this small act of rebellion, but they were getting her cheap and they agreed eventually that she could do without the cap as long as she kept her hair in a tidy bun. Lily was the only servant in the huge house and it was exhausting going up and down the endless stairs; at least the sisters fed her well, wanting to keep up her strength. She had every Thursday afternoon off, from three to seven—four glorious hours a week to do whatever she pleased. For a girl like Lily, anything might happen in four hours.

One afternoon, Lily was walking on the boardwalk by the beach when a young man pulled up alongside her on a motorcycle and offered a ride. He seemed such a nice young man with a smiling pleasant manner that she agreed to get on the back. It was exhilarating to have the wind on her face as he drove her to a nearby park. He asked how old she was, and she lied—she said that she was eighteen. Then she lied some more—she said she lived in a great mansion nearby, which was true, but she omitted to mention that she was the maid. It was the first time in her life that she ever dared to make her daydreams real by speaking them aloud. She found it strangely easy to fool the young man and it seemed a wonderful freedom. She didn't have to be a poor skivvy if she didn't want to; suddenly the only boundaries were the limits of her imagination. Lily continued to spin fantasies of a life of ease and wealth until the young man stopped her with a kiss. Lily enjoyed being kissed, but when he tried to put his hand inside her dress, she pushed him away. Her mother had warned her that she must never let boys do such things or no one would ever marry her and she would suffer a terrible life.

Eventually the boy drove her back to the sisters' house on his motorcycle and he watched from across the street as Lily walked with some trepidation up the front steps of the mansion. She wished he would drive away for she had strict orders to use only the servants' entrance at the rear of the house. The boy grinned at her, straddling his motorcycle, and Lily realized with a shock that he had not believed a word of her tall tales. Now there was no choice but to go through with it. She waved at him as haughtily as a princess, then turned toward the house and boldly rang the doorbell. A niece who lived with the two sisters answered the bell and Lily swept inside before there could be a scene. She apologized and said she had lost her key for the back door; the niece gave her a good scolding, but let her get away with it this one time.

For Lily it was an instructive episode. She had tried her wings for the first time, just a short flight but it left an impression. She knew now that she could defy gravity if she wished; it was only a matter of fooling people. Reluctantly she returned to her servant's room in the basement of the big house and dreamed of making all her fibs come true.

Lily remained in Hove for only a few months, and then Henry wrote to the two sisters to say that Lily's mother was gravely ill and urgently needed the girl at home. The sisters were furious to lose their maid so inconveniently and they pointedly refused to say good-bye to her when she packed her bags and left.

Back in London, Lily found her mother very sick. Cancer was spreading quickly throughout her body and at night she often cried out in pain. Only a few feet away in the next bed, Lily grimaced but was unmoved. She resented her mother's illness which had forced her to become a servant instead of continuing her education with the scholarship she had earned. To Lily it seemed as if her mother had been ill as long as she could remember. She felt guilty to be so cold-hearted, but she could not help herself; her mother's cancer had robbed her own youth. Then one afternoon when she was in the living room, Lily heard a sound from the bedroom. "Lily . . . Lilyanna!" It was her mother's voice, hardly more than a whisper. She saw that her mother had half-fallen from the bed and was vomiting some black liquid onto the floor. Lily ran to her in horror and disgust. She tried to lift her back onto the bed but she was too heavy. Then a deep convulsing rattle came from her mother's throat, and in a moment the sick woman died in her arms.

Lily had never seen death before. She thought it odd how the room filled with neighbors and soon Henry was there as well. Where did they all came from? she wondered. Death seemed to crave an audience, attracting curious faces from up and down the hall. People began comforting her, saying incomprehensible words. She wanted very much to cry; the neighbors were crying and they had hardly known Lily's mother. But for the daughter no tears would come. She felt only a curious numbness and also a sense that she must be an awful person to remain so dry-eyed in a room full of weeping people.

She wondered what would happen to her now. Where would she live? Henry was planning to be married again soon, this time to an overweight and pathetically homely woman. "You cannot live here by yourself," he said gruffly to Lily. "You will live with me and my wife."

But she was seventeen years old and free for the first time in her life and she would not do what Henry told her. Lily refused even to go to the funeral. She knew this was one more terrible act to add to all the others that would set her forever apart. But she was an orphan now truly, and she thought she might go mad if she saw her mother put into the ground.

*   *   *

And so in the year 1921 at the age of seventeen, Lily cast herself forth in motion outward to the world—to the West End of London, to Johnny, the theater, a complicated life of sexual duplicity, and finally to America. Lily Shiel became Sheilah Graham, but she never forgot the misery of her early years. The lessons she learned young stayed with her always: Guile was necessary in order to survive, and lies must be told to become what she wished to be. She was successful beyond her dreams, but forever anxious that her bluff might be called. It was as if she were dancing in some eternal chorus line where she did not truly know the steps, and at any moment might tumble off stage into a papier-mâché rock.

Such was the secret past which she confessed at last to Scott Fitzgerald as she sat in his car by the side of the road. She began with what was hardest—her very shame at having told him over the past six weeks so many things that were untrue. Then she confessed her real name, Lily Shiel. By 1937, just to say this name was almost physically unbearable, opening a door to a chaos of memories, old fears, stale smells of poverty, and the accumulated guilt of what she had done to escape. Once she had blurted it out—*Lily Shiel!*—the rest was easier. She had never dared to pause long enough in her forward flight to look back on these things before: the orphanage, stealing food, wetting her bed, how she had slapped her mother who was dying of cancer, or caused a man to commit suicide. She remembered every moment of every bad thing she had ever done. The unresolved past was with her still, the tension she felt every time she sat in Bob Benchley's bungalow while the fine people discussed intellectual things, leaving her on the outside—she with her paltry education that had ended when she was fourteen.

She told Scott everything. Or nearly everything. There were some secrets so terrible the true words simply refused to form on her lips. She admitted she was "part Jewish," rather than Jewish from head to toe. It made it easier somehow. Sheilah's shame of being Jewish was very great, and she carried an even greater shame of concealing it so many years, knowing what a weak person this made her out to be. She was certain the Hollywood

Jews would despise her if they ever found out. She also kept from Scott her true age and the full extent of her sexual experience. But except for these matters, she told him the lengthy saga of Lily Shiel who had been so bold as to reinvent herself.

She talked urgently for several hours, a flood of words. When at last she came to a stop, she felt wonderfully cleansed and free. For the first time in her life she had told the truth. When Scott continued to hold her and speak soothing words, it appeared that someone truly loved her at last. She did not have to pretend anymore.

Shortly after this drive to Malibu she wrote Lord Donegall in England to break off her engagement to be married. She would not be a marchioness after all, but Scott Fitzgerald's final love.

7

MOVING PICTURES

More than anything in the world he wanted to make pictures.
He knew exactly what it was like to carry a picture in his head as
a director did and it seemed to him infinitely romantic.

—F. Scott Fitzgerald, from an early draft of *Tender is the Night*

SCOTT WAS TORMENTED by the pictures he carried in his mind of
Sheilah with other men. He could imagine the settings themselves with gut-wrenching clarity, the darkened bedrooms, the
arms of other men around her, other lips kissing his girl—all the
damp secretive things lovers do. Fitzgerald's jealous imagination
transformed him into an unwitting voyeur.

Shortly after Sheilah confessed the secrets of her past, at the
end of summer 1937, Scott attempted to exorcise his demons by
putting his jealousy into verse. He meant to write a love poem,
but the final product was more concerned with the eight lovers
he believed had preceded him than with Sheilah. He spelled
Sheilah's name wrong, which was sad for a love poem, but this

in itself had no hidden meaning—throughout his life he spelled
nearly everyone else's name wrong as well

For Shielah: A Beloved Infidel

That sudden smile across a room,
    Was certainly not learned from me
That first faint quiver of a bloom
    The eyes initial extacy,
Whoever taught you how to page
    Your loves so sweetly—now as then
I thank him for my heritage
    The eyes made bright by other men.

No slumbrous pearl is valued less
    For years spent in a rajah's crown
And I should rather rise and bless
    Your earliest love than cry him down
Whoever wound your heart up knew
    His job. How can I hate him when
He did his share to fashion you?
    A heart made warm by other men.

Some kisses nature doesn't plan
    She works in such a sketchy way
The child, tho father to the man
    Must be instructed how to play
What traffic your lips had with mine
    Don't lie in any virgin's ken
I found the oldest, richest wine
    On lips made soft by other men.

The lies you tell are epic things
    No amateur would [ever] try,
Soft little parables with wings,
    I know not even God would cry.
Let every lover be the last
    And whisper, "This is now—not then"
The sweet denial of the past
    The tale you told to other men.

I'm even glad someone and you
    Found it was joyous to rehearse,
Made it an art to fade into
    The passion of the universe.
The world all crowded in an hour,
    Textbooks in minutes, that has been
Your fate, your wealth, your curious dower,
    The things you learned from other men.

The little time you opened up
    A window, let me look inside,
Gave me the plate, the spoon, the cup,
    The very coat of love that died
Or seemed to die—for as your hand
    Held mine it was alive again
And we were in a lovely land
    The world you had from other men.

But when I join the other ghosts
    Who lay beside your flashing fire
I must believe I'll drink their toasts
    To one who was a sweet desire.
And sweet fulfillment—all they found
    Was worth remembering. And then
He'll hear us as the wine goes around
    A greeting from us other men.

                              -S.

    No one had ever written Sheilah a love poem before and she was deeply touched—so flattered that it would be many years before she realized on closer inspection what a very ambiguous piece of writing it was. At the time it seemed Scott had given her more than a poem, but her own special word; she was an infidel. The word delighted her and somehow changed everything. It explained her pagan amorality and put her past history into a more glamorous light. Best of all, she was beloved. Forever hence she would think of herself in an altered way, as Scott's beloved infidel—a phrase which transformed her faults into virtues and gave a name to something that had existed before only in darkness.

Sheilah was blinded by love and her sudden conversion to a life of truth. She told herself she would never lie again. Even her letter to Donegall breaking their engagement had been written in an orgy of candor, like throwing open a window and letting sunlight and air into a fetid place. She told Donegall she was in love with another man; she admitted everything. Joyfully she burned her bridges to the dishonest past.

A few days after breaking with Donegall, she was soaking in the tub at Scott's bungalow when he walked into the bathroom and put a small pillow under her head so she might be more comfortable. He smiled at her with kindness and then left without once glancing at her submerged body. Sheilah was astonished at this simple act. It wasn't the pillow that impressed her so much, though that was very nice. It was the fact that his eyes had refused to take advantage of her nakedness, to scan her up and down in the hard appraising way that men had always done before. With her lifelong embarrassment about the size of her breasts, Scott's sensitivity won her heart forever.

It was a small incident, but in the future Sheilah always dated this episode in the bath as the moment she gave herself completely to Scott Fitzgerald. And it was at just this time when she had let down all her defenses, only days after she decreed herself totally his, that Scott left her with hardly a word of explanation to see his wife in North Carolina.

"I'll be out of town for a week or so—I'm going to visit Zelda," he told her quite casually one evening. It was all he would say about it.

"All right, Scott," she answered unhappily. "Let me know when you get back."

And so it seemed the pillow had been yanked from behind her head, and her bath flooded with an icy rush of unexpected cold. As Scott left for the East Coast, it had never even occurred to him that Sheilah might be shattered.

Scott had not come to Hollywood to fall in love but to work: to write, to save himself, and to reestablish his reputation. The trip east to see Zelda came at an awkward moment for him not because of his new love affair, but because he had begun a movie that promised to be very good. He hated to tear himself away at just this strategic moment. Unfortunately, Zelda could not be denied; he had responsibilities toward her and old ties. Though they had hardly been together during the past seven years, she was still his wife, bound to him always by a thousand memories. Scott and Zelda Fitzgerald. It was more than a family identity; it was a path backward to the good old days of fortune and fame and youth. Scott knew very well that he and Zelda would never be a couple again, but he was not prepared entirely to break with the past. As for Sheilah, he assumed a woman with her experience understood the rules governing an affair with a married man.

At the moment, Scott was inclined to put all the women in his life (Zelda, Scottie, and Sheilah) out of mind so that he could get on with his work. Looking back over the past two months, Scott had to acknowledge that writing for the movies was not as easy as he first thought. He had a great deal to learn about his new craft. Soon after starting at MGM in early July, he took advantage of the studio's library of films to screen dozens of movies for him every week, and he studied their form and content with the same fascination as he had once studied the construction of short stories in the *Saturday Evening Post*.

Scott's first project at MGM was polishing dialogue on *A Yank at Oxford*, a film which would inaugurate Metro's new studio in England and star Robert Taylor as an American Rhodes scholar and Maureen O'Sullivan as his British love. It was on this assignment that Scott encountered for the first time the assembly-line system for producing screenplays which had been dreamed up by Irving Thalberg, a man who had aspired to be the Henry Ford of the American cinema. In Thalberg's system, different groups of writers worked piggyback on a single movie, often at the same time and sometimes under the illusion that no one else was working on the script. For *A Yank at Oxford*, the original script had been started by John Monk Saunders and then turned over to Frank Wead, a veteran Metro screenwriter. When Frank Wead had finished 101 pages, Scott Fitzgerald was put on the script behind him; after Scott, the script was given to the screenwriting team of Malcolm Stewart Boyland and Walter Ferris, and then received a final revision by a respected script doctor, George Oppenheimer. Often it seemed as if the revisions might go on forever. As a novelist accustomed to working on his own, Scott found this all very strange. Producers loved your work one day, said you were better than Shakespeare—and the next day they fired you and gave your script to someone else. What counted in the end, as far as a writer's career was concerned, was getting credit—that fragile moment at the start of the first reel when your name flickered across the screen.

Scott did not last long on *A Yank at Oxford*. When the movie was released he wrote Zelda's mother in Alabama: "Very few lines of mine are left in 'A Yank at Oxford.' I only worked on it for eight days, but the sequence in which Taylor and Maureen O'Sullivan go out in the punt in the morning, while the choir boys are singing on Magdalene Tower, is mine, and one line very typically so—where Taylor says, 'Don't rub the sleep out of your eyes. It's beautiful sleep.' I thought that line had my trademark on it." Despite his one line, Scott did not receive that most important ticket to a Hollywood career: screen credit.

Then Scott's luck changed dramatically. In mid-July, a few days before he met Sheilah at the benefit for the Screen Writers Guild, he was assigned to write a movie adaptation of *Three Comrades*, Erich Maria Remarque's novel of post–World War I Germany. Quite miraculously he was given the script to do alone, without a collaborator; he would be under the supervision of one of Hollywood's most literate producers, Joseph Mankiewicz. Scott respected Remarque's novel, a story considered quite left-wing in Hollywood because of its anti-Nazi sentiment, and he had a sense of landing very much on his feet. On July 19, he was able to write to Max Perkins, his old editor at Scribner's, "Everyone is very nice to me, surprised and rather relieved that I don't drink. I am happier than I've been for several years."

"The work is hard as hell, at least for me, and I've lost ten pounds," he added to Anne Ober on July 26. But he liked the work and a few weeks later he wrote Margaret Turnbull, the mother of his future biographer Andrew: "After almost 3 years of intermittent illness it's nice to be on a steady job like this—a sort of tense crossword puzzle game . . . a surprisingly interesting intellectual exercise. You mustn't miss my first effort, *Three Comrades,* released next winter." And so Scott had set to work in good spirits—happy to be involved in a new love affair, and happy to find himself the sole screenwriter on a serious and important movie. The story concerned three friends, former members of the German Air Force, who start an auto repair shop together after the war and do their best to survive the deepening economic depression and the growing shadow of Nazism. Robert Taylor was again set to be the star of the movie, this time with Franchot Tone and Robert Young as his two comrades, and Margaret Sullavan as his love interest, portraying a girl slowly dying of tuberculosis.

Scott divided the story into three "acts": a structural device still practiced today by Hollywood screenwriters. *Three Comrades* offered a chance for Scott not only to tell a poignant love story— always his forte—but also make a political statement about the dire economic conditions in Germany that were giving rise to fascism. He would have an opportunity to shed his image as a writer of the rich and identify himself in the camp where he felt he belonged—the left-wing. Unfortunately, Scott had little experience expressing himself in moving pictures. Trying to add social commentary to the story, he came up with the heavy-handed idea of flashing onto the screen a graph depicting Germany's postwar inflation rate. He veered from style to style, passing quickly from documentarylike realism to sheer Hollywood fancy. In one wildly inappropriate love scene, Robert Taylor was to telephone Margaret Sullavan through a switchboard located in heaven, with angels and satyrs and Saint Peter himself connecting the call. Scott appeared uncertain if he was Serge Eisenstein, Walt Disney, or Jean Cocteau—and in his inexperience seemed determined to try every cinematic device he could think of, all at once.

Still, he was delighted to have a free hand with such an important project and he was learning fast from his mistakes. Joe Mankiewicz said he was thrilled so far with the script; he could hardly give Scott enough praise. But this was the movie Scott must leave to visit Zelda. On September 4, after finishing nearly two-thirds of the first draft of the screenplay, he was scheduled to take one week off to fly to North Carolina. He became anxious that matters might somehow change at MGM in his absence. So much in Hollywood depended on being there, constantly selling yourself. He was tormented by the fear that he might return to find Mankiewicz had hired another writer, a collaborator, to work with him on the script.

Scott got himself into a fine state of worry. On the day before he left for the East Coast, he thought it best to drop Mankiewicz a line to plead his case for continuing *Three Comrades* on his own:

> Dear Joe:
>
> This letter is only valid in case you like the script very much. In that case, I feel I can ask you to let me try to make what cuts and rearrangements you think necessary, by myself. You know how when a new writer comes on a repair job he begins by cutting out an early scene, not realizing that he is taking the heart out of six later scenes which turn upon it . . . .
>
> If a time comes when I'm no longer useful, I will understand, but I hope that this work will be good enough to earn me the right to do a first revise to correct such faults as you may find. Then perhaps I can make it so strong that you won't want any more cooks.
>
> Yours,
> Scott
>
> P.S. My address will be, Highlands Hospital, Asheville, N.C., where my wife is a patient. I will bring back most of the last act with me.

Scott had an uneventful visit with Zelda, taking her briefly from Highlands Hospital to a family reunion in Charleston. Zelda's obsessions had changed over time, from ballet to painting to writing, and now to religion—at the moment she claimed to be in direct communion with Christ. Scott was always depressed to see Zelda at such an end, her beauty gone and all the promises of youth unfulfilled. He was careful not to upset her by any mention of Sheilah Graham. Zelda's mental balance was precarious, her jealousy had always been profound, and he believed he could drive her over the edge into raving insanity within fifteen minutes of any conversation simply by saying he was interested in another woman. Scott wrote of this visit a few months later: "Zelda is not better . . . I've become hard there and don't feel the grief I did once—except sometimes at night or when I catch myself in some spiritual betrayal of the past."

None of this was pleasant; it was a difficult thing to visit your wife in a mental hospital. And so Scott was relieved and greatly heartened to receive on September 9 a telegram from Joe Mankiewicz answering his letter and putting his mind to rest about *Three Comrades*—to know at least that his new life in Hollywood was going well:

DEAR SCOTT YOU MUST STOP READING ALL THOSE NASTY STORIES ABOUT MOTION PICTURE PRODUCERS THEYRE NOT TRUE I KNOW THAT IMPOSSIBLE IS ONE WORD AND I WOULDN'T TRY TO HIRE SHAKESPEARE BECAUSE BRITISHGAUMOT HAS HIM TIED UP STOP I HAVE READ THE STUFF AND THINK IT IS SIMPLY SWELL WHERE DID YOU GET THAT BUSHWAH ABOUT ANOTHER WRITER BEST WISHES FOR A HAPPY THIRD ACT AND COME BACK AS SOON AS YOU CAN=

JOE

This was such good news that Scott felt silly for his suspicions. He had so much riding on *Three Comrades*. It was more than a movie for him, it was a new career, a fresh start. Scott returned to California on Saturday, September 11, in a cheerful mood but soon received a tremendous blow. The "bushwah," as Joe had put it, was all too true. It wasn't that Mankiewicz had lied in his telegram; most likely his words were passionately true for the few moments in which he wrote them. In Hollywood matters like this changed according to mood, box-office receipts, and a new opinion handed down from the front office.

Whatever Joe's reasons, Scott found himself with a cowriter to help revise and finish *Three Comrades*, a man even Mankiewicz conceded was a hack—Ted E. Paramore. As it happened, Scott had known Ted Paramore years ago in New York, and had mercilessly satirized him as a barely disguised character, "Fred E. Paramore," in his second novel, *The Beautiful and Damned*. As a result of this satire, Ted was a friend no longer. The writer with whom Scott was now expected to collaborate was in fact an enemy from the past.

*   *   *

In the first weeks of their love affair, Sheilah had dared to ask Scott about Zelda only once. He stiffened noticeably, put her off with a few evasive remarks, and was clearly so uncomfortable discussing his wife that Sheilah thought it best to leave the subject alone. "In everything I took my cue from Scott," she admitted later. "Whatever he wished was how it must be." Still, with no definite knowledge of Zelda, she could only imagine the worst. During the week of Scott's absence, she suffered continual onslaughts of insecurity.

She went to her old standby Eddie Mayer for stray bits of information about Zelda. Eddie told her some of the more fantastic stories: how Scott and Zelda had ridden on the tops of taxis and swum in fountains in their evening clothes, and driven their car onto a train track in France and fallen asleep. Sheilah did not find these pranks particularly amusing; they seemed silly and adolescent to her. All in all she was glad she knew the dignified, charming Scott Fitzgerald of 1937 rather than the outrageous brat of a decade earlier.

Zelda remained a shadowy and frightful figure in Sheilah's imagination. Zelda, she understood, was beautiful and talented and had set about to make all of Scott's friends fall in love with her. She was marvelously self-confident and came out constantly with witty and memorable remarks; she could dance, write, and paint . . . and yet she was mad. Sheilah had an old childhood horror of two things: insanity and drunkenness. There was something nightmarish about Zelda locked away in a mental institution. Did they have bars on the windows? Late at night, were there horrible cries and moans floating down darkened hallways? It gave Sheilah goose bumps just to imagine such a place and she told herself she shouldn't be jealous. Scott obviously had to care for this woman: He couldn't simply abandon her. Still, she did not like the situation, she *was* jealous, and when Scott returned to California she punished him sometimes with brooding long silences which he pretended not to notice. What she hated most of all was that he did not confide in her. He told her nothing about the visit, one way or the other, as if Zelda were a sacred subject he could not discuss with someone like her. And this after she had told him everything about herself.

But it was difficult to stay angry with Scott, particularly when she saw how unhappy he was to have *Three Comrades* taken from his creative grasp and turned into the usual studio hash. Scott did his best to keep his problems from Sheilah, but sometimes his frustration got the better of him. "Paramore's a hack," he complained bitterly about his most unwanted collaborator. "They've taken away his originality and talent." Scott was outraged when this studio hack dared to tinker with his dialogue. One evening he told Sheilah in disgust that Paramore had written a line for a German sergeant to say, "Consarn it!" Sheilah laughed, but Scott assured her it was not at all funny. It was an outrage that he, a serious writer, must endure such a collaborator. It would have been easier if Ted Paramore had been on the project from the start; as it was, Scott was heartbroken to be led on and then have his hopes so thoroughly dashed.

Sheilah worried about him, and her worry caused her jealousy to fade away. Each evening after work she would hear the raspy horn of his automobile as he came up the hill to her house, and he appeared as full of charm as before, entirely the enthusiastic, boyish man she had come to love. But underneath the facade she was aware that for Scott things were not going well.

She said to him one night, hoping to cheer him up: "I feel badly. Here you are, a famous writer, and I've not read a thing you've written. I want to read every one of your books."

"Do you really?" he replied. Scott regarded his work with great seriousness; she never once heard him make a joke about his writing. "All right, Sheilo. I'll get you my books. Let's get them tonight."

After dinner they strolled along Hollywood Boulevard to the Pickwick Bookstore where Scott and Sheilah had sometimes browsed before. Los Angeles was not a city with a high regard for the written word; movies were important, not books. "Out here," Scott observed, "though the bookstores were bulging, reading was becoming a mere skill in the middle income brackets—a sort of technological accomplishment."

"Have you books by F. Scott Fitzgerald?" Scott asked the clerk in the bookstore.

"Sorry—none in stock." The clerk was a young man and he turned brusquely to another customer. Scott interrupted, unwilling to let the matter die.

"Do you have any calls for them?" he persisted.

"Oh—once in a while, but not for some time now."

As they walked from the store, Sheilah did not dare look at Scott; she felt the darkness of his silence. "Let's try another place," she said hopefully.

But it was the same at the second bookstore. A clerk told them that they had no books of F. Scott Fitzgerald in stock, nor was there ever any demand for them. Sheilah was sorry she had set this hunt in motion, but now that they had begun, Scott was determined to continue. His face was grim and even more pale than usual; he said they would try a third store. Sheilah walked miserably by his side as they went in silence farther along Hollywood Boulevard; it was no longer a pleasant evening. The third store they found was a small one, chaotic, with stacks of books piled everywhere. An old gray-haired man stood perched on a ladder among his musty volumes. He moved slowly down the ladder when Scott asked his increasingly terse question: Did they carry the books of F. Scott Fitzgerald?

The proprietor shook his head, but said he might be able to get hold of one or two. "Which ones are you interested in?"

In a voice that was carefully neutral, Scott pronounced the titles of his most famous novels: *This Side of Paradise*, *The Great Gatsby*, and *Tender Is the Night*. The old man promised nothing but he said he would do his best.

"I'm Mr. Fitzgerald," Scott said defiantly when it came time to leave his name and address.

The old man's eyes opened very wide. After a stunned moment he reached with awkward enthusiasm to shake the author's hand. "I'm happy to meet you, Mr. Fitzgerald. I've enjoyed your books very much . . . I'll really get these for you," he promised. "And if there aren't any about, I'll order them from the publishers."

Scott thanked the man with grave courtesy and then he and

Sheilah walked from the small bookstore back out onto Hollywood Boulevard where the lights were bright and fame was the official religion of the land. Sheilah was afraid to speak and Scott's silence was not inviting. It was clear to them both why the old man had been so surprised when Scott had revealed his name; he had believed quite simply that F. Scott Fitzgerald must surely have died years ago along with his era.

Despite the pain of finding himself passed over as an author, and the various indignities and difficulties he encountered in Hollywood, Scott always found time to guide Sheilah with her career. In September 1937 Sheilah was glad to have Scott's advice, for her career was about to undergo an enormous change: She was poised to become a radio personality in a network coast-to-coast variety show in which she would have a five-minute spot to broadcast the latest gossip about Hollywood. It was the deal Sheilah had concluded earlier in the summer before meeting Scott; the show was to originate live from Chicago, with her five minutes cut in from a studio in Los Angeles. It was a great opportunity for her, a chance to become a household name—as famous perhaps as Walter Winchell. But she was terrified of the upcoming show. She had never done radio before and her nerves were at a fevered pitch. While Scott was in North Carolina, she wrote and rewrote her five-minute script, and when he returned, she anxiously showed it to him on the night before the first weekly broadcast. He read the script through carefully and then asked if she would mind if he changed a word here and there. Sheilah assured him he could change all the words he liked.

Scott sat down at a table with a pack of cigarettes and a stubby pencil, and set to work on her script with deepening concentration. He always wrote with his left hand, though he was right-handed in everything else. His pencil moved quickly, slashing at her prose and adding new sentences. "Cut out all these exclamation points," he lectured. "An exclamation point is like laughing at your own joke." A few moments later he added, "When you tell an anecdote, tell it so your listeners can actually *see* the people you are talking about." When Scott finished his rewrite, he went over the script a final time to underline the words she was to emphasize.

At last he handed her a script that was hardly recognizable from what she had given him. Sheilah saw that the language was beautiful and flowed like poetry, but after some hesitation she dared to voice a timid objection: "This won't be over the heads of my audience, will it? People who listen to movie gossip aren't usually intellectuals, Scott."

"It will be good for them," he told her with a grim smile. In prep school Scott had earned the nickname "Bossy" for telling people what to do, but Sheilah did not mind his tendency to take over. She had so little faith in herself, that it was easy to put her faith in him.

The radio broadcast was the next day and as the time for it approached, Sheilah became steadily more nervous. The show began in Chicago at seven in the evening their time, and at five o'clock in California. Scott was still at Metro at that hour, but he could not bear to miss his prize pupil. He left his office and crossed the street to a garage that was fixing his car to find a radio so that he could listen to Sheilah's voice. Sheilah knew he was across town listening and it did not make her less nervous. She sat waiting in a soundproof booth with a huge microphone in front of her and all sorts of intimidating electronic gadgets she had never seen before.

The waiting itself was unbearable. First she had to sit through the interminable progress of the variety show in Chicago before it came time for her segment. At last the Chicago announcer said, "And now we take you to the well-known columnist, Sheilah Graham in Hollywood." But even now she had to wait, a delay of forty seconds in which engineers across the country moved the dials and pulled the switches which would connect her with all of America; it seemed the longest forty seconds of her life. On her end, she watched through the soundproof glass as a director with headphones held up his arm; when he lowered his arm, this was her cue to start reading her script. But she could hardly breathe, and the sudden dryness of her throat was terrible. She began to swallow continuously, gulping air and clearing her throat.

At last the director brought down his hand with a flourish and she was on the air. She swallowed hard, began to speak in a high shrill voice, and then swallowed again. Her heart was pounding so violently she was certain it would be heard through her microphone coast to coast. "Hello, everyone, this is Sheilah Graham in Hollywood," she began. She struggled through the script, gulping and swallowing every few words. She knew she was a disaster. After four years in America, she had lost much of her British accent. But now in her nervousness her accent returned with a vengeance—an exaggeration of long vowels, more British than she had ever sounded in her life, as though she were a parody of some absurd colonel's daughter in an India regiment. There was nothing she could do but keep reading and somehow get to the end.

Scott was very kind. He telephoned immediately after the show to say she was "quite good."

"Oh, Scott, I was terrible and you know it," she told him miserably.

"No, no," he assured her. "You sounded a little breathless, but that was all."

Unfortunately, the sponsors in Chicago agreed with Sheilah's assessment rather than Scott's. They objected most of all to Sheilah's British accent which they believed would be impossible for an American audience to understand. "They didn't mind Cary GRA-ah-ant," Sheilah said afterward, "but George Ra-ah-ft was too much." Mr. Wharton, the producer, phoned the next day to say they would continue with her under one condition: She would write the script, but they would hire a professional actress to read it in her place, an actress who would be introduced as Sheilah Graham.

Scott was outraged by the suggestion. "Absolutely not," he declared hotly. "There's nothing wrong with your voice. You have a contract, they must use *you*. You'll get over your nervousness if they'll give you a chance."

Sheilah believed she could relax and do the show quite well if only there was not that dreadful forty seconds' wait while the Hollywood studio hooked up with the national broadcast—forty seconds in which she might clear her throat a hundred times and still be garbled and out of breath. Scott entered this discussion as passionately as if his own career were on the line. He had an idea: She must fly to Chicago to do battle for her cause. In Chicago she could do next week's show without the fatal forty seconds of delay and after a relaxed performance, the sponsors would forget about hiring a professional actress.

Sheilah did not need much convincing; faced with a problem she always preferred action to sitting in doubt. She telephoned Mr. Wharton who was skeptical about her plan to come east but would not stop her from giving it a try. Sheilah hung up the receiver to see Scott smiling triumphantly. This was his favorite role, to be quarterback barking out plays for his team to follow. Caught up in the moment, he said that he would go to Chicago with her. She needed him there to take care of all the details and see that she was relaxed. Sheilah was overwhelmed by his enthusiasm and show of support—really, it was so typical of Scott, why she loved him. But she worried about his work. It was an overnight flight to Chicago and he would miss a few days at the studio.

"Are you sure you can leave? . . . You know we can't get back before Tuesday."

"Don't worry about that," Scott assured her. "I'll arrange it."

It seemed there was no way she could stop him. Unfortunately, there were a few days remaining before the plane trip east, time for a single desperate complication to occur.

On October 6, Scott received a telegram from the legendary girlfriend of his youth, the beautiful Ginevra King; she had thrown him over many years before, but now she was in Santa Barbara and wished to invite him for lunch. Ginevra was more than an old love: She had become the heroine for much of his early fiction. He had used her to advantage, capturing the sort of wild and beautiful, free-spirited and flirtatious young woman who was to become a trademark of his writing. To hear from Ginevra again threw his life into turmoil. On October 8, Scott wrote to his daughter:

> [At Princeton] I used to write endless letters throughout sophomore and junior years to Ginevra King of Chicago and Westover,

who later figured in *This Side of Paradise*. Then I didn't see her for
twenty-one years. . . . Yesterday I got a wire that she is in Santa
Barbara and will I come down there immediately. She was the first
girl I ever loved and I have faithfully avoided seeing her up to this
moment to keep that illusion perfect, because she ended up by
throwing me over with the most supreme boredom and indifference. I don't know whether I should go or not. It would be very,
very strange. These great beauties are often something else at
thirty-eight, but Ginevra had a great deal besides beauty.

In the same letter, Scott mentioned in a very off-hand manner
that "Sheilah . . . by the way, has broken her engagement to the
Marquess Donnegal [*sic*]. (The poor man was about to get on a
boat, but it was a sort of foolish marriage in many ways.)" To
refer to Sheilah and Ginevra King in the same letter was to invite
a difficult comparison. Ginevra was the model for not only
Rosalind in *This Side of Paradise*, but Judy Jones in *Winter Dreams*,
Daisy Buchanan in *The Great Gatsby*, and Josephine in an entire
series of short stories. She was the golden girl, moving in a
graceful world of romance and wealth, a girl such men as Jay
Gatsby and Scott Fitzgerald might yearn for but never fully possess.

Sheilah could not compete with such a potent memory. For
Scott to meet Ginevra King after all these years created a difficult
confrontation between his youth and his exhausted middle age.
"Life hasn't much to offer except youth and I suppose for older
people the love of youth in others," he had written with great
arrogance in 1917. But now this misfortune, age, had happened
to him. He was forty-one years old, his life had not worked out
well, his books were not in the stores—it was unbearable for
Scott to acknowledge what he had become. The telegram from
the past threw him into a precarious emotional state. At some
point after receiving Ginevra's wire, he decided he would be
young again, if only for an afternoon.

Scott went to Santa Barbara to see Ginevra King on October 9.
He encountered an intelligent and still attractive thirty-eight-
year-old woman, the wife of the extremely rich William H.
Mitchell III. Ginevra had settled down from her wild youth to
follow the well-worn path of her class. She was now a proper

matron of society, an avid horsewoman, a supporter of many worthy charities; she spent her days between such leisurely places as Palm Beach and Santa Barbara. Mrs. Mitchell remembered her lunch with Scott in a 1946 letter: "[We] had a much better time than I had anticipated. Afterwards . . . he suggested we go to the bar—I settled for a lemonade but he insisted on a series of double Tom Collins. I was heartsick as he had been behaving himself for some months before that. For the next few days I was besieged with calls, but as he was in love with someone in Hollywood, I believe, he soon gave up the pursuit."

The gin in those double Tom Collinses meant a major sea change for Scott Fitzgerald. It is unclear at what exact moment Scott fell off the wagon. Perhaps he braced himself with a few cocktails before his lunch with Ginevra, or seeing her may have brought on the need for the pixie wings of inspiration. Certainly there were many pressures on him besides this confrontation with his youth, particularly the ongoing struggle at MGM with Joe Mankiewicz and Ted Paramore. Perhaps it had been simply too long since the last drink, and some inner clock now dictated a binge.

Whatever the reasons, Scott was drinking again, and he himself had a neat explanation for the fact: It was Sheilah's fault, there was no doubt in his mind. She made him do it.

While Scott visited the love of his youth in Santa Barbara, Sheilah accepted an invitation for dinner from Arthur Kober, the East Coast writer once married to Lillian Hellman who had made a name for himself with his "Bella" stories in *The New Yorker* and was in Hollywood writing screenplays for the Marx Brothers. Sheilah believed herself in love with Scott, but found nothing wrong with an occasional dinner with another man when Scott was busy, or out of town in Santa Barbara. Arthur Kober seemed particularly harmless: He lived at The Garden of Allah and was part of the amorphous Benchley crowd, a pleasant fellow who was somewhat long-winded and in no way a rival to Scott.

But Scott was alarmed. It was fine for him to spend a week in North Carolina with Zelda, and have an intimate luncheon with an old girlfriend at her hotel, but when Sheilah mentioned she planned to have dinner with Arthur Kober, he was overcome with mistrust. He knew what a great flirt she was; anything might happen. Scott made her promise that she would be home alone by eleven o'clock, and to make certain she met her curfew, he insisted he would telephone at exactly that hour. Scott was unrelenting.

Sheilah was accustomed to her independence and felt claustrophobic at being watched over so closely. She knew Scott really wanted her to cancel her date but she was defiant and went to dinner with Arthur Kober anyway. But as the dinner progressed, she began to feel guilty. She glanced at her watch from time to time to make certain she would meet her curfew. Arthur always seemed in the midst of some interminably long story and she had to hurry him along a bit. With urging, she managed to get him to the curb outside her house on Kings Road at a few minutes before eleven. Unfortunately, he was in the middle of one of his endless stories as he came around to open the car door for her. It was clear he wanted Sheilah to invite him in. She now felt doubly guilty: Scott would be phoning at any moment, and this man who had taken her for an expensive dinner must be abruptly dispatched. It seemed best to let him finish his story as he stood by the open car door. He was still talking when she heard her telephone ringing from inside the house. Sheilah felt awkward about the whole thing; it seemed impossible to run for the phone without inviting Arthur Kober inside, and she judged it best to let him finish and leave the telephone unanswered. She could always call Scott back.

It was half an hour before Sheilah managed to get rid of her date and phone Scott—a fatal half hour, time in which Scott was able to work himself into a frenzy of imagined cuckoldry. He was angry on the telephone, but also strangely loquacious; he told Sheilah that her tardiness had caused him to start drinking again. It was all her fault and now she must accept the consequences. Sheilah laughed, for she was used to his dramatic exaggerations and thought he must be joking. Scott's voice was hoarse as though he had a cold, but he'd been such a strict teetotaler on every occasion she had seen him that she simply couldn't imagine him with a drink. On the contrary, there had been moments at parties when she wished Scott *would* take a cocktail to relax. It seemed almost unnatural in Hollywood for a man to be so sober.

Sheilah and Scott were busy during the next few days getting ready for their trip east and they did not see each other. She spoke with Scott on the phone several times and his cold seemed to be getting steadily worse. He really sounded dreadful, hardly himself at all.

8

A BAD BROWNIE

> Often people display a curious respect for a man drunk, rather
> like the respect of simple races for the insane . . . There is
> something awe-inspiring in one who has lost all inhibitions.
>
> —F. Scott Fitzgerald, *Tender is the Night*

SCOTT AND SHEILAH AGREED to meet at the airport in Burbank for
the evening flight to Chicago. Scott made his way directly after
work from MGM in Culver City, and Sheilah came from her
house above Sunset Boulevard. They had not seen each other
since before the Santa Barbara luncheon with Ginevra King.

It was a crisp fall evening, the middle of October 1937, with a
gusty wind blowing across the open fields and orange groves of
Burbank. Sheilah was invigorated by the wind and the challenge
before her, and excited that she and Scott were taking a trip
together, flying to a strange city she hardly knew; she had gone
to Chicago once with John Wheeler, but with Scott it would seem
brand-new. Then she saw Scott at the airport and she barely recognized him. His face was flushed and he grinned at her in an

exaggerated way that was entirely too merry for the occasion. His Brooks Brothers suit, ordinarily so subdued, seemed somehow askew on his body. All this struck Sheilah as strange since Scott was normally fastidious—quite formal, really, in his suit and tie, refusing to give in to the casual styles of California. Now he did not seem entirely clean or even well-shaved.

A press agent, Mary Crowell, had brought Sheilah to the airport to help with her luggage and ticket—one of the perks of being a Hollywood columnist. After they located Scott inside the terminal, Mary asked Sheilah to come with her to meet a young actress who was leaving on another plane, promising Scott she would keep Sheilah only a few minutes. Perhaps it would be best if they met up with him shortly in the bar? Scott grinned and said that the bar would be a swell place to meet.

Sheilah went to meet the actress, but her mind was on Scott's puzzling appearance. The actress babbled briefly in a self-important way about her upcoming projects, then Sheilah followed the press agent back to the airport bar. Scott was sitting at a table with a glass of water in front of him. As Sheilah and Mary approached, he picked up the glass and drank it down in a single gulp. The women joined him and Mary signaled the waiter and asked if she could buy them all a drink. Sheilah ordered a brandy; it was rare for her to drink but flying frightened her and she hoped it would settle her nerves. She expected Scott to order his usual Coca-Cola, but instead he said cheerfully, "Bring me a double gin." Sheilah was dumbfounded. And then everything about his unfocused appearance made a horrible sense. The water he had just poured down his throat was not water at all but straight gin. When the waiter reappeared with their order, Scott took his drink, tossed it down in one quick motion, and ordered another double gin before Mary had finished paying for the first.

Sheilah was alarmed. She never seen anyone drink like this, one glass after another, poured down his throat without so much as a civilized pretense of taste. Scott ran his hand through his hair and turned to the women with a disheveled leer. He began talking all sorts of flirtatious nonsense. He told Mary she was adorable, utterly adorable. He told Sheilah she had "skin like peach note paper." *My God, he's tiddly,* Sheilah said to herself. *Tiddly* was a kinder word than *drunk.* Drunk was something terrifying that took her back to leering red-faced men who lurched in her direction outside the East End pubs of her childhood. She simply could not believe this was her Scott, the quiet, dignified man she thought she knew. The waiter reappeared at their table with a double gin. Scott took it from the tray and called out his happy refrain, "And when you come back, bring another one."

For Sheilah this was getting to be a problem. She had watched him drink three double gins in less than ten minutes and he had just ordered a fourth. It was a staggering amount. When the new drink came, she reached for it in what she hoped was a playful manner, trying to push it aside. Scott reacted with startling speed, slapping her hand away from his glass. He glared at her furiously with owlish red-rimmed eyes, as if daring her to try it again. Sheilah could hardly believe the change that had come over him. His eyes seemed to crowd together toward the center of his face and he was no longer handsome. Sheilah was angry herself now. Then unexpectedly, just as her anger was building, he winked at her—a slow, exaggerated wink. She had to laugh for it was really quite funny. Well, she said to herself, why shouldn't he drink if he wants to? All the men she knew drank— Benchley certainly did, Eddie Mayer, even boyishly pleasant Lord Donegall. Sheilah knew Scott was worried that his six-month contract at MGM was coming up soon for renewal; he had so many pressures on him that perhaps it was harmless to explode a little.

She watched Scott down two more double gins before their plane was announced; he drank each in the same urgent way, draining the glass in a single swallow. This made six now; she felt unpleasantly like a schoolmistress counting them, but she couldn't help herself. She would be tiddly on just one. Mary Crowell hardly looked her in eye when she said good-bye. Scott staggered as he rose from his chair and made a comical struggle with his raincoat. It was a challenge to fit his arms into the proper sleeves. The raincoat had become a difficult animate object with a drunken life all its own. Scott finally gave up on the buttons and the coat flapped wildly in the wind as they walked together out to the open tarmac and on toward the plane. Sheilah was afraid he might simply blow away.

Scott made his way unsteadily up the metal steps into the DC2, and then lurched along the aisle of the small plane until at last he collapsed safely into his seat. Sheilah hoped the worst was over. But then she noticed a bottle sticking out from one of the deep pockets of his raincoat. She had a foreboding this could be a difficult trip. Scott once had told her that when he was little his mother used to call him a good brownie when he behaved, and a bad brownie when he was naughty. What Sheilah had to deal with now, she thought, was a very bad brownie indeed.

The plane taxied and rose high into the twilight sky above the San Fernando Valley. Scott wrestled the bottle free of his difficult raincoat and took a deep swallow.

"Scott, please. . . ."

"Shh!" he whispered, putting his finger dramatically to his lips. "Do you know who I am? I'm F. Scott Fitzgerald, the writer." He slapped Sheilah's knee as if this were a great joke. Sheilah held onto his hand, nervously hoping he wasn't about to make a scene.

The stewardess came down the aisle. "Do *you* know who I am?" he demanded.

"No, sir. I don't have my passenger list with me."

"I'm F. Scott Fitzgerald, the very well-known writer," he assured her. Sheilah blushed with embarrassment. When the stewardess drifted past to the other passengers, Scott leaned toward a man across the aisle. "Do you know me?" he challenged.

"Nope. Who are you?" replied the man tolerantly.

"I'm F. Scott Fitzgerald. You've read my books. You've read *The Great Gatsby*, haven't you? Remember?"

"I've heard of you." The man seemed momentarily surprised that this was no ordinary drunk, but the literary variety. Scott was glad someone remembered him and he fastened onto the fellow as a great friend, embarking on a semicoherent conversation. Sheilah was mortified—not only for herself, but for Scott. She had always respected him so greatly. How could he disgrace himself like this? Then she heard Scott talking about her, bragging to the man that she was "a great lay." Sheilah could hardly believe her ears. Scott, the old-fashioned puritan, whom she had never even seen naked! She was furious and did her best to let him know this by ignoring him for nearly a thousand miles. When the plane came down in Albuquerque for its first stop, Sheilah told Scott coldly to get off the plane and find his own way back to California.

"It was a mistake for you to come," she told him. "I don't like you this way at all."

"Okay, baby, okay," he agreed. "You'll always be a lone wolf like me. I'll go. Goodbye."

When the plane came to a halt by the terminal, Scott stood up and tipped his hat to her with exaggerated courtliness. He said that two lone wolves could never be together, and that was just the way it was. Sheilah was afraid he was saying good-bye forever, and she hadn't meant it to go as far as that. As Scott walked off the plane she made a point of telling him that she would see him in a few days in Hollywood, but he only smiled sadly and walked away. The image of a lone wolf was too close to the mark. He was right, she thought: "He is a lone wolf because of his great talent, and I because I have so many secrets and am never satisfied . . . I'll never belong anywhere."

In Albuquerque the flight crew made up the sleeping berths for the overnight trip to Chicago. Sheilah climbed into her bed, hugged her knees, and cried softly as the plane floated through dark skies. She had liked him so much and now it was over. She was still crying when the curtains to her berth were pulled open and she saw Scott peering in at her, grinning mischievously. There was a new bottle of gin sticking out of his raincoat pocket, but Sheilah was so glad to see him she didn't care.

"Oh, Scott, I thought you'd gotten off!"

"Sure I got off . . . needed another bottle."

She pulled him into her berth and he fell asleep in her arms as the airplane made its long continental glide below the stars. In the morning, Scott looked wretchedly ill, pale and fragile in his wrinkled suit. He rode in silence with Sheilah in a taxi from the Chicago airport to the Ambassador East Hotel. They had reserved a suite of two bedrooms with a sitting room in between; the separate bedrooms were necessary not only for appearances but because of Scott's chronic insomnia. Scott wandered into her room while she was unpacking; his face was once again flushed full of color and there was a bottle in his hand that had only a few fingers left of gin. As she watched him, he raised the bottle to his lips and drank until it was empty. Then he used her bedside phone to call downstairs for another. Sheilah couldn't imagine what to do with him. It was as if he were showing off, determined to prove what a naughty brownie he could be.

Before long a very small bellboy appeared at the suite with a bottle in a paper bag. Sheilah was not certain if he was a midget or only a child; he wore a neat, small uniform and seemed very strange to her. When this tiny bellboy lingered for a tip, Scott let out a whooping cry and began to chase him merrily around the sitting room. They went round and round in circles, until the bellboy managed to flee out the door into the hallway. Sheilah felt as if she had fallen down some rabbit hole into a new world of nightmare possibilities. The drunk Scott Fitzgerald had no inhibitions, no limits to his behavior. At last, out of breath from his unaccustomed exercise, Scott took his new bottle of gin into his bedroom and closed the door.

Mr. Wharton, the producer of the radio show, arrived at the hotel suite in the late morning. He was a pleasant slender man in his early thirties who wore a conservative business suit and a polite smile. He had the look of a man on a delicate mission. Sheilah was nervous about Scott in the next room and hoped he would stay away, but moments after Mr. Wharton arrived, Scott ambled dangerously into the sitting room and peered at the producer with red unfriendly eyes. Mr. Wharton rose to his feet and said what an unexpected pleasure it was to meet the famous F. Scott Fitzgerald. Fortunately, he knew who Scott was, and for the moment this mollified Fitzgerald to inaction. He accepted the acknowledgment as his due and collapsed heavily into an armchair to oversee the proceedings.

Sheilah pitched her cause, doing her best not to look at Scott. "Now, I've brought my script with me, Mr. Wharton. I know I can do the show to your satisfaction if I don't have that appalling forty-second wait. That throws me off completely."

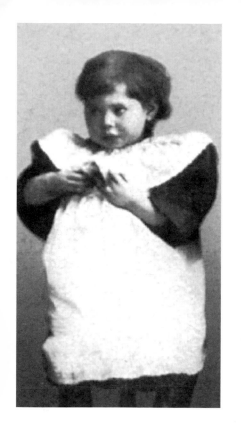

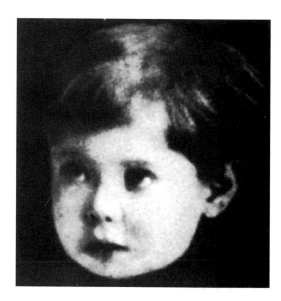

Lily, age two. Soon after she
married Major John Gillam,
Lily took the original of this
photograph to an artist who
skillfully added the dress and
the hairstyle, and transformed
a wooden spoon in her hand
into a flower. Sheilah used the
resulting portrait to fabricate an
upper-middle-class past.
*(Courtesy of the Sheilah Graham
Westbrook Estate)*

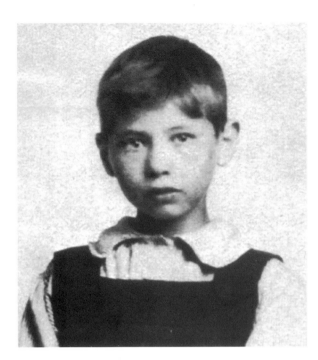

A subdued Lily at age nine, in the orphanage. *(Courtesy of the Sheilah Graham Westbrook Estate)*

Lily's mother and father. *(Courtesy of the Sheilah Graham Westbrook Estate)*

Lily at seventeen. *(Courtesy of the Sheilah Graham Westbrook Estate)*

Lily's first appearance—at nineteen—as "Sheilah Graham," ecstatic winner of a silver cup as London's most beautiful chorus girl, and soon to become the toast of London's musical-comedy stage. *(Courtesy of the Sheilah Graham Westbrook Estate)*

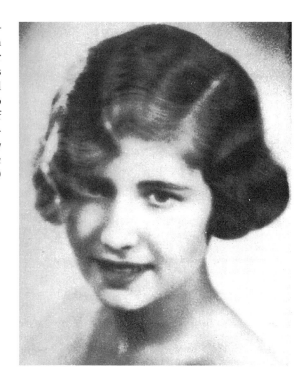

On June 9, 1931, Lily Shiel, orphan, achieved the summit of her social dreams: She was presented at Buckingham Palace to King George V and Queen Mary. *(Courtesy of the Sheilah Graham Westbrook Estate)*

Major John Gillam, winner of the DSO at Gallipoli, resplendent in the court costume he wore the day he escorted Sheilah to Buckingham Palace. *(Courtesy of the Sheilah Graham Westbrook Estate)*

Scott at fifteen. (*Courtesy of the F. Scott Fitzgerald Estate*)

Scott as a young army officer in 1918. He had his uniforms made at Brooks Brothers, but to his eternal regret he never actually saw battle. *(Courtesy of the F. Scott Fitzgerald Estate)*

Scott in 1920, shortly after the publication of his first novel, *This Side of Paradise*. He was nearly as famous for his good looks as for his prose. *(Courtesy of the F. Scott Fitzgerald Estate)*

Scott and Zelda soon after their marriage, probably 1920. *(Courtesy of the F. Scott Fitzgerald Estate)*

Scott, Zelda, and Scottie en route to France in April 1928. The bloom was off the marriage, and the bad years had begun. *(Courtesy of the F. Scott Fitzgerald Estate)*

Sheilah in 1936, shortly before meeting Scott. These three photographs taken on the same day were publicity stills to promote her syndicated column, "Hollywood Today—A Gadabout's Notebook." *(Courtesy of the Sheilah Graham Westbrook Estate)*

Scott in the early summer of 1937, several weeks before he met Sheilah. Life had dealt him some hard blows: He was nearly $40,000 in debt, out of fashion as a writer, and desperately hoping to do well in Hollywood. (*Courtesy of the F. Scott Fitzgerald Estate*)

Scott in 1936 in North Carolina during his "Crack-up," a year before he met Sheilah. *(Courtesy of the F. Scott Fitzgerald Estate)*

Scott and Sheilah in 1939 on the lawn of Edward Everett Horton's estate, Belly Acres, in Encino. This is one of only two photographs that exist of Scott and Sheilah together. *(Courtesy of the Sheilah Graham Westbrook Estate)*

In the early summer of 1940, Scott and Sheilah took a weekend trip to Tijuana and posed for a sidewalk photographer. *(Courtesy of the Sheilah Graham Westbrook Estate)*

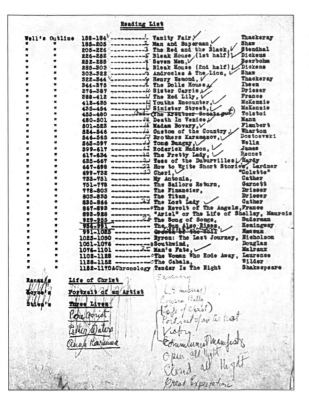

Reading List

Well's Outline				
188-184	Vanity Fair	Thackeray
185-205	Man and Superman	Shaw
205-226	The Red and the Black	Stendhal
226-252	Bleak House (1st half)	Dickens
252-285	Seven Men	Beerbohm
285-303	Bleak House (2nd half)	Dickens
302-322	Androcles & The Lion	Shaw
322-344	Henry Esmond	Thackeray
344-376	The Dolls House	Ibsen
376-387	Sister Carrie	Dreiser
388-412	The Red Lily	France
412-435	Youths Encounter	McKenzie
435-454	Sinister Street	McKenzie
455-480	The Kreutzer Sonata	Tolstoi
480-501	Death In Venice	Mann
501-523	Madam Bovary	Flaubert
524-546	Custom of the Country	Wharton
546-565	Brothers Karamazov	Dostoevski
565-597	Tono Bungay	Wells
599-617	Roderick Hudson	James
617-634	The Pretty Lady	Bennet
635-667	Tess of the Dabervilles	Hardy
667-698	How to Write Short Stories	Lardner
699-732	Cheri	"Colette"
732-751	My Antonia	Cather
751-778	The Sailors Return	Garnett
778-803	The Financier	Dreiser
803-835	The Titan	Dreiser
835-866	The Lost Lady	Cather
867-893	The Revolt of The Angels	France
893-928	"Ariel" or The Life of Shelley	Maurois
929-955	The Song of Songs	Suderman
956-991	The Sun Also Rises	Hemingway
991-1025	Growth of the Soil	Hamsun
1025-1050	Byron: The Last Journey	Nicholson
1051-1076	Southwind	Douglas
1076-1101	Man's Fate	Malraux
1102-1128	The Woman Who Rode Away	Laurence
1128-1152	The Cabala	Wilder
1152-1176 & Chronology	Tender Is The Night	Shakespeare

Ransom's	Life of Christ
Joyce's	Portrait of an Artist
Stolz's	Three Lives
	Don Quixote
	Esther Waters
	Queen Marouna

(handwritten, right)
Seminary
(4 novels)
Cousin Bette
Life of Christ
Portrait of an Artist
Victory
Communist Manifesto
Open all Night
Cloud all Night
Great Expectations

One of Sheilah's many reading lists for the Scott Fitzgerald College of One. *(Courtesy of the F. Scott Fitzgerald Estate)*

Scott set about giving Sheilah an education, assigning to her three hours of reading every day. This is a bookmark on which he wrote out a list of Byron's poems that he wanted her to study. *(Courtesy of the F. Scott Fitzgerald Estate)*

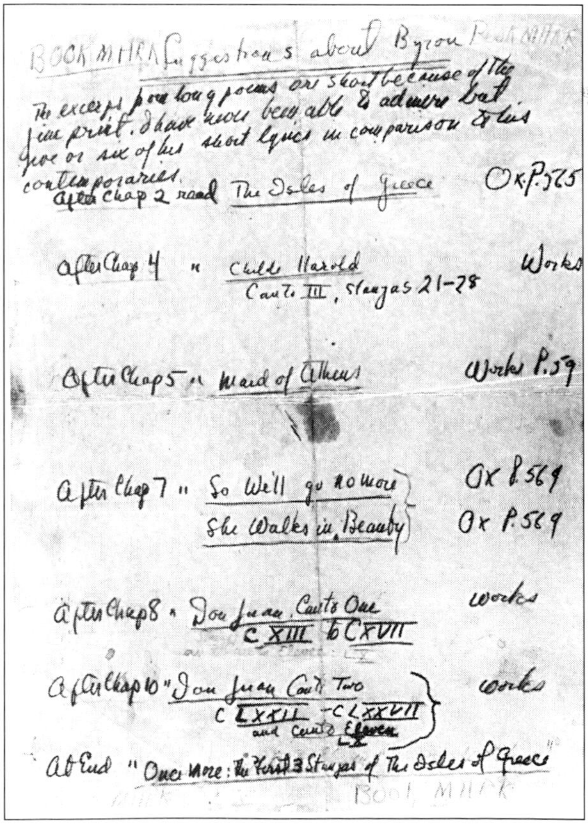

BOOK MARK Suggestions about Byron

The excerpts from long poems are short because of the fine print. I have never been able to admire but five or six of his short lyrics in comparison to his contemporaries.

After chap 2 read The Isles of Greece — Ox. P. 525

After Chap 4 " Childe Harold
Canto III, Stanzas 21-78 — Works

After Chap 5 " Maid of Athens — Works P. 59

After Chap 7 " So We'll go no more
She Walks in Beauty — Ox P. 569

After Chap 8 " Don Juan Canto One
C XIII to CXVII — Works

After Chap 10 " Don Juan Canto Two
C LXII - CLXXVII and Canto Eleven — Works

At End " Once more: The First 3 Stanzas of The Isles of Greece"

BOOK MARK

For Shielah, a Beloved Infidel

That sudden smile across a room
Was certainly not learned from me
That first faint quiver of a bloom
The eyes initial extacy
Whoever taught you how to page
Your lovers so sweetly—twas as then
I thank him for my heritage
The eyes made bright by other men.

No slumberous pearl is valued less
For years spent in a rajah's crown
And I should rather use and bless
Your earliest love than cry him down
Whoever wound your heart up knew
His job. How can I hate him when
He did his share to fashion you?
A heart made warm by other men.

Some kisses nature doesn't plan
She works in such a sketchy way
The child, the father to the man
Must be instructed how to play
What traffic your lips had with men
Don't lie in any virgin's ken
I found the oldest, richest wine
On lips made soft by other men.

The lies you tell are epic things
No amateur would ever try
Soft little parables with wings
I know not even god would cry

Let every lover be the last
And whisper "This is now—not then"
That sweet denial of the past
The tale you told to other men

I'm even glad someone and you
Found it was joyous to rehearse
Made it an art to fade into
The passion of the universe
The world all crowded in an hour
Textbooks in minutes—that has been
Your fate, your wealth, your curious dower,
The things you learned from other men

The little time you opened up
A window, let me look inside
Gave me the plate, the spoon, the cup
The very coat of love that died
Or seemed to die—for us your hand
Held mine & was alive again
And we were in a lovely land
The world you had from other men

But when I join the other ghosts
Who lay beside your flashing fire
I must believe I'd drink their toasts
To one who was a sweet desire
And sweet fulfilment—all they found
Was worth remembering. And then
He'll bless us as the wine goes round
—A greeting from us other men

S.

When I finally came to myself last Tuesday I found this, which seems to be yours.

It is very quiet out here now. I went in your room this afternoon and lay on your bed awhile, trying to see if you had left anything of yourself. There were some pencils and the electric pad that didn't work and the autumn out the window that wont ever be the same. Then I wrote down a lot of expressions of your face but one I can't bare to read, of the little girl who trusted me so and whom I loved more than anything in the world—and to whom I gave grief when I wanted to give joy. Some things should have told you I was extemporizing wildly— that anyone, including Scottie,

(over)

"For Shielah, a Beloved Infidel." In the fall of 1937, soon after Sheilah confessed the truth about her past, Scott wrote this poem to celebrate her lies and amorous history. As was often the case, he misspelled Sheilah's name, reversing the *i* and the *e*. (Courtesy of the F. Scott Fitzgerald Estate)

②

should ever dare criticize you to me. It was all fever and liquor and sedatives — what nurses hear in any bad drunk case

I'm glad you're rid of me. I hope you're happy and the last awful impression is fading a little till someday you'll say "he can't have been that black."

Goodbye, Shielo, I won't bother you any more.

Scott

Scott's note of apology to Sheilah after their last fight in November 1939.
(Courtesy of the F. Scott Fitzgerald Estate)

A glamorous Sheilah Graham in the mid-1950s. *(Courtesy of the Sheilah Graham Westbrook Estate)*

Mr. Wharton's smile turned so vague that Sheilah was suddenly nervous. "You are going to let me on tonight, aren't you? I've come all this way. . . ."

"Well, I can't promise anything, Miss Graham. I'll have to talk it over and I'll let you know this afternoon."

Sheilah tried to appeal to his chivalry. "I know you're going to let me on that program tonight. You simply must, Mr. Wharton."

Scott had been watching silently but now he leaped to his feet. "Well, does she or does she not go on the show tonight?" he demanded.

"Well, I don't know, Mr. Fitzgerald—I can't give you a decision. I have to check with. . . ."

Scott moved closer. "Take you hands out of your pockets," he said gravely. He put up his own fists in the melodramatic posture of a gentleman boxer, and he began to prance about the room. Mr. Wharton was astonished; he tried to back gracefully out the door but Scott leaped forward with a wild swing—so wild it connected only by an unfortunate miracle with the producer's mouth. When Sheilah saw that Mr. Wharton was bleeding, she began to scream. In the midst of this pandemonium, the producer hastily agreed that yes, of course Miss Graham could do the show tonight. Before any more damage could be done, Sheilah hurried him out of the room and closed the door.

Scott was pacing the floor, reliving the glory of his punch. "That s.o.b. . . . he'll see," Scott muttered ominously. "You're going on and he's not stopping you. Just let him try."

But Sheilah had reached her breaking point. She lay down on the carpet, screamed, and kicked her legs like a small child, and threw a tantrum. "You have ruined me! I hate you!" she cried. "I never want to see you again." She continued to holler, feeling outraged and sorry for herself, until at last she penetrated the haze of Scott's alcoholic stupor and he understood that she was angry at him. Now it was his turn to be dumbfounded. Everything he had done had been done for her. Eventually Sheilah realized she was alone in the sitting room, and her tears and hollering gradually subsided. Scott had silently left her, slipping away into the bright October Chicago morning to nurse the wounds of Sheilah's ingratitude.

*   *   *

The incident remained a series of gaudy impressions in Sheilah's mind that took some sorting out. Had Mr. Wharton really agreed to let her do the show tonight? Or had he said that only to escape safely from the room? Sheilah could not proceed in any clear direction until she found out what the producer meant to do. She telephoned Mr. Wharton later in the morning to apologize. She was prepared for a difficult conversation but in fact he was very gracious and assured her, sadly, that "these things happen." Then she pressed him delicately about the show. To her amazement he said yes, he would stand by what he had said—he would let her go on the air.

Sheilah was thrilled. The circumstances were bizarre but she had succeeded in getting what she wished. But this left her in a dilemma about Scott. She was furious at him, of course, but she had to acknowledge that his drunken antics had done the trick: Mr. Wharton had come to the Ambassador East prepared to tell her no, but he had left with a yes on his bloody lips, all due to Scott's sodden chivalry. So what was she to think? *And where was he?* Each hour he stayed away increased her worry. On one hand she felt she could easily kill the man; but on the other, she worried terribly that in his condition he might fall in the street or be hit by a car, or suffer a dozen other calamities she could only imagine.

She now suspected the truth, that Scott was AWOL from the studio, and had disappeared from work without a word to Joe Mankiewicz in order to be her knight errant and do battle for her cause. This also gave her pause; he had risked his career for her. It was wonderfully romantic. So how could she hate him? Surely this transformation into a raving maniac was a temporary aberration. The real Scott Fitzgerald was the sober, slightly old-fashioned gentleman with the poetic smile. The thing now was to get him back to Joe Mankiewicz in some sort of shape to resume work on *Three Comrades.* MGM must not put him down as a drunk or he would be finished in Hollywood forever.

And so Sheilah gradually came around, from throwing a temper tantrum on the floor to the romantic vision that Scott needed her in this moment of crisis. She must save him from himself.

Then in the afternoon, she received a puzzling and not altogether coherent phone call from the film editor of the *Chicago
Daily News,* a paper which ran her column. As the conversation
unraveled, Sheilah began to understand that somehow Scott had
hooked up with this man and they had gone on a spree together.
The newspaperman said they were in a bar not far from the
Ambassador East and Sheilah should join the party. Sheilah
imagined Scott standing with his ear close to the receiver, repentant, too ashamed to make the call himself. She said she would
be right there.

She left the hotel with grim determination, galloping down
the street to the rescue. But the bar she found was dingy and
smelly and her spirits sagged as she walked in from the glare of
the street, entering an indoor gloom, a room hazy with smoke
and vague menacing figures who slouched sullenly at the bar.
Scott and the newspaperman were at a small table, laughing and
carrying on, giving the only life to a place where everyone else
might just as well be sleepwalking. As Sheilah sat down she felt
waves of repulsion; she still carried from childhood a primal
horror of men in places like these. Scott was flushed and greasy
and his handkerchief was filthy. He looked like a traveling sales-
man down on his luck.

Scott was telling loud stories with a mouthful of four-letter
words, one after another, like some fourteen-year-old boy showing off to his friends. Sheilah was more amazed than angry, for
this was a man who when sober visibly winced at the word
damn. They ordered more drinks, then Scott started bragging
about her to his new friend. Chortling and grinning, he said
what a great cunt Sheilah was, a fabulous lay. Sheilah refused to
take him too seriously. He seemed to her almost a parody of adolescence. This was just Scott being a bad brownie again. But he
was getting awfully tiresome and she wished he would grow up.

She left the two men to their drunken pleasures and walked
out of the foul-smelling bar into the pure relief of sunshine. The
hell with Scott, she thought. She had a show to do.

At five o'clock, Sheilah made her way alone to the Chicago
CBS studio for a rehearsal of the radio show. She was nervous,

but not as nervous as she had been that first broadcast from Los Angeles. She knew now that Scott could not help her; she was on her own, as she had always been before, the lonest wolf there ever was.

Sheilah sat on stage waiting her turn, watching different acts rehearse, singers and comedians. The stage faced an empty auditorium where the live audience would be seated tonight; Sheilah prayed that this phantom audience would love her. She was pagan enough to believe that if you said the right words in your most secret mind, and willed something to happen with all your might, then it could not fail but come to pass. It was nearly time now and she took deep breaths trying to relax. But shortly before she was set to begin, an incredible thing happened: Scott Fitzgerald appeared.

Sheilah could hardly believe her eyes. She watched Scott make his way clumsily through the empty auditorium to sit by himself in the very center of the first row. His clothes were askew, he was filthy, and he grinned at her in his most flamboyantly pixie manner. Sheilah put her finger to her lips, warning him to stay quiet. Scott mimicked the gesture back at her, making an exaggerated show of how good he was going to be. She wondered how he had managed to talk his way in here. And why, dear God? Why?

When it came to her segment, she did her best to forget about him. Sheilah began to read her script, but she did not get far before Scott stood up unsteadily and interrupted the rehearsal:

"Now Sheilah, don't you be afraid of them. Nothing to be afraid of. Speak slowly and distinctly. . . ." Scott raised an imaginary baton and began to conduct her as if she were an orchestra.

"Scott, please sit down and be quiet," she whispered in an agony of embarrassment. But Scott refused to sit down; he continued beating time with his invisible baton, guiding Sheilah through the rhythms of her script until two stagehands appeared to escort him firmly from the theater. Sheilah was humiliated and distraught and furious, all at once, but somehow she managed to finish the rehearsal. Mostly it was her anger that carried her through; every time she found it in her heart to forgive him, Scott committed some new outrage. It was unbelievable, really: He wouldn't quit or simply pass out as drunks were supposed to do.

Sheilah remained in the safety of the CBS studio until seven o'clock came and it was time for the live broadcast. With the rest of her life in chaos, a mere radio show seemed suddenly nothing to worry about: She was relaxed on the air, and read her Hollywood gossip without a snag. She thought she did quite well.

Finally, exhausted by the ordeal of the day, she returned to the hotel. But when she opened the door to her suite she was greeted by a sight so improbable it took her brain a moment to take in the picture: Scott was there, alas, and still going strong. He was on a chair in the sitting room with a filthy bib tied around his neck and a tray of food alongside him. A younger man, a stranger Sheilah had never seen before, was on the floor kneeling in front of Scott trying to force a steak sandwich into his mouth with his fingers. Both Scott and the stranger were splattered with coffee and food. As Sheilah walked in the door, Scott bit down hard on the hand that was feeding him. The stranger let go an operatic howl of pain.

"*Yeeoooohh!* . . . The son of a bitch bit my finger!" the man cried to Sheilah.

"Hi, Sheilo," said Scott happily, with pieces of steak drooling from his mouth.

Sheilah gazed back and forth from one man to another, fearing she had entered some nightmare where she did not quite know the rules. The stranger rose to his feet, brushing bits of food from his clothing. "Sorry you had to walk in on this Mack Sennett comedy," he apologized. "You're Miss Graham, of course." He introduced himself as Arnold Gingrich, editor of *Esquire* magazine, whose offices were in Chicago close to the Ambassador East.

"Show her those articles, Arnold," Scott ordered. When Gingrich didn't jump to do as he said, Scott let loose a stream of obscenities, telling him to get the son-of-a-bitch "Crack-Up" articles that had nearly fucking destroyed him.

"Oh, this is awful, just awful!" Sheilah sighed. "Have you ever seen him like this before?"

Gingrich said yes, unfortunately he had seen Scott Fitzgerald almost exactly like this on a number of occasions. As far as the publishing world was concerned, Arnold Gingrich was Scott's last friend and admirer, a true fan. Gingrich personally liked Fitzgerald and since 1934 he had used *Esquire* to advance Scott money for unwritten articles whenever the author was in a particularly desperate situation—which was often. For his part, Scott had never treated the young editor very well, complaining endlessly about how little *Esquire* paid. Gingrich told Sheilah that Scott had telephoned his office and asked him—ordered, was more the word—to come over to the Ambassador East with a copy of the "Crack-Up" pieces to read to Sheilah when she returned. Unfortunately, Gingrich had been busy at the moment firing someone at the magazine and couldn't come right away. Scott in his drunken exaggeration took this as a betrayal of their friendship. When the editor was able to cross the street from his office he found Scott sitting before a long row of shot glasses that were set up on a table, each full of gin.

Arnold Gingrich recalled years later that Scott "could hardly talk, slurring all his words, trying to tell me about Sheilah, this great new English girl . . . he kept saying, 'I just got to have this cunt.'. . . I thought, My God! let's see if we can't get this son of a bitch sobered up a little. I ordered a steak sandwich and a big pot of coffee." But when the food arrived, Scott refused to eat unless Arnold fed him by hand. Gingrich was a good sport about it. He held Scott by the nose to pour coffee down his throat; this seemed to work until Scott gathered the coffee in his cheeks and spat it out into the editor's face. It was in the middle of these unlikely proceedings that Sheilah had arrived.

"I've got to get him back to Hollywood," Sheilah told Gingrich uneasily, gazing at Scott in an appraising manner; in his food-splattered bib, Fitzgerald looked like a very large and difficult baby. She explained that Scott's option was coming up for renewal at MGM and it was essential that he be in Hollywood tomorrow morning for a meeting with Joe Mankiewicz. They had a reservation for a midnight flight, though at this moment it seemed unlikely that Scott would be in any shape to travel.

Arnold managed to get more coffee into Scott. Then Scott remembered the "Crack-Up" articles for which he had called the editor in the first place, and he insisted noisily that Arnold read them aloud to Sheilah. "Sheilah was perfectly willing to read them herself, but no, *I* had to read them," Gingrich remembered. "He lay down on the couch and pretended to be napping, but he was listening to every word, watching Sheilah's reaction. She was watching him and I was doing a bad job reading because I had one eye on him, too. It was an odd way [for Sheilah] to meet *The Crack-Up*."

Eventually Scott did fall asleep fitfully on the couch for a short time. Gingrich took advantage of the quiet moment to tell Sheilah something of the background of the "Crack-Up" pieces: How Scott in 1934 had come up hard against a creative block, complaining that everyone wanted him to write about young love, but young love was the last thing on his mind. The confessional pieces Gingrich suggested in their place may have helped unravel the final threads of Scott Fitzgerald's reputation, but at least they got him writing again. Sheilah was struck at how little she knew about this man she loved; he had told her nothing about his desperate years, nor his alcoholism, and she had been too willing to take him at face value—the charming, sensitive man with the sad lines around his eyes that made him so interesting. Now she was learning fast, a crash course on F. Scott Fitzgerald.

Soon it was time to leave the hotel for their midnight flight to California, but Scott refused to wake up. Eventually Gingrich picked up Scott and simply hauled him out of the room, down the elevator, and through the lobby. But halfway across the lobby, Scott opened his eyes mischievously and said to Gingrich, "I'm all right now." He stood up easily on his own feet and made his way jauntily into the waiting airport limousine—making the young editor feel like a great fool. Arnold told Sheilah to give him a call if there were any more problems.

When the limousine pulled away from the hotel, Scott turned to Sheilah with a conspiratorial grin. "Did I do a good job?"

What job? she wanted to know.

"Pretending to be drunk," he told her cagily. "That little snot was putting me off all day long. He was too busy to see me and I wanted to make him sweat a little."

Scott was not quite finished with his games. The limousine

was empty except for himself and Sheilah, and a man and young woman in the seat behind them. Shortly before they reached the airport, Scott glanced at the young woman behind them, and then said to Sheilah in a loud whisper, "Doesn't she have lovely hair?"

The young woman heard the compliment and smiled. Scott waxed on about her to Sheilah: "Isn't she pretty? Such lovely hair, such poise—a very lovely young woman."

The girl in the backseat beamed with pleasure. Scott now turned to face her directly. "You silly bitch," he said.

Her mouth fell open in astonishment; the man beside her was so angry that Sheilah was afraid there would be a fistfight. Fortunately, the limousine arrived at the terminal and the driver moved around quickly to the passenger doors to let everyone out. Scott did not go far. He stepped out of the limousine, tripped on the curb, and fell down hard on the pavement. The driver offered a hand but Scott pushed him away angrily. Sheilah wisely stood to one side and waited for him to rise to his feet by himself. Then she guided him toward the ticket counter inside the terminal, urging him to be quiet, for if the airline saw he was drunk they wouldn't let him on the flight. But there was no disguising Scott's condition. The clerk at the counter took one look at Fitzgerald and said politely that he was sorry but he could not permit the gentleman on the plane.

Scott was outraged at this new assault upon his dignity. He stood unsteadily at the counter and loudly insisted that a private plane immediately fly him and Sheilah back to California; he said he would *buy* a plane if necessary. Sheilah was at her wit's end. She learned that the next flight to Los Angeles was at five in the morning—five hours from now. But what in the world was she going to do with a drunk and quarrelsome Scott Fitzgerald for five hours? Sheilah watched their plane take off without them and then she telephoned Arnold Gingrich for advice. He suggested she get Scott into a taxi and simply drive around until the five A.M. flight; perhaps Scott would be sober enough at that time to be allowed on the plane. Meanwhile Gingrich promised to telephone every bar in the vicinity of the airport and instruct them to give Fitzgerald only beer if he came in looking for something more to drink.

Sheilah got Scott into a taxi and told the driver to go any-where he pleased as long as he got them back to the airport to make the five o'clock flight. They had hardly left the curb when Scott put his head on Sheilah's shoulder and passed out. Sheilah was glad at first, but after a time the position became cramped and almost torturously uncomfortable. She was afraid to move lest Scott wake up and want to find a bar. Occasionally he shifted his weight and muttered, "Where are we?" "Going home," she assured him, and he fell asleep again. For Sheilah it was a long night in which to stare out her window into the dark sleeping city and wonder what in the world had possessed her to come so far in life only to fall in love with a man like this. They drove all night long, wide circles that went nowhere. When they returned to the airport in the early morning, Scott was noticeably drowsy and uncoordinated, but apparently this was not considered too unusual for the hour and he was allowed to board the plane. Sheilah was relieved when he slept most of the way to the West Coast.

In Los Angeles at last, she dropped Scott off at The Garden of Allah. He turned to her just before he stepped out of the taxi and he seemed suddenly sober; it was as if the old Scott, driven away by some naughty poltergeist, had now stepped back into his body, to look at her with eyes that were once again familiar.

"I'm going on the wagon," he told her quietly. "Don't worry. I can stop this whenever I want, but I must get out of it in my own way. I'll report sick to the studio and tell them I won't come in for several days. Then I will get a doctor and nurses. It will take at least three days." He told Sheilah that under no circumstances was she to telephone or try to see him during this difficult period of drying out; he promised to phone her when he was all right again.

"As you wish, Scott," she answered coldly. She was exhausted and disillusioned. It seemed a bitter irony that he had come to Chicago to look after her, but she had been the one to take care of him. It reminded her too much of Johnny; she was fed up with taking care of weak men. Wasn't there someone strong and won-derful to take care of her?

Scott phoned after four days. He told Sheilah about the horrors of the cure, days in which he could not keep down any solid food. He had told Joe Mankiewicz he was "ill"—the euphemism he always used to hide the shame of drinking. But Mankiewicz wasn't fooled; Scott was a man with a legend that traveled ahead of him.

Sheilah remained unforgiving and told Scott she would certainly go east alone for next week's show. In Chicago she was glad to be on her own, to feel again the old strength of her independence. She did her five-minute performance with less nervousness than before; she could write a script and deliver her lines without anyone's help. From the Ambassador East she telephoned John Wheeler in New York. She wasn't certain she liked Wheeler very much, but unlike Scott Fitzgerald, he was strong and independent and this suddenly seemed a very desirable trait in a man. Wheeler sensed opportunity and he invited Sheilah to come to New York from Chicago for a few days, to take in some theater and shopping and spend time with him. It sounded like a very good idea to her and she said yes; she told him she would be in New York the next day.

Sheilah was packing her bags when Scott telephoned from California. He wanted her to know that he had listened to the show and she had been very good. He offered to pick her up tomorrow morning at the airport in Burbank.

"I'm not returning to Hollywood until the end of the week," she said. "I'm going to New York."

Scott was quiet as he took this in. Then in a flat monotone, he said that John Wheeler must certainly be looking forward to her visit. She was startled by his intuition; he seemed to know everything about her, as if he could read her mind. "I suppose you will see him," he said.

"I suppose so," she answered cruelly.

She wanted to hurt him, and she had. He was dreadfully grave: "Sheilah, if you go to New York I will not be here when you come back. I'll give up my job and leave Hollywood and never return."

"You can't do a thing like that, Scott!"

"I will," he threatened.

She told him she would have to think about it and call him

back. But there was no question in deciding between John Wheeler and Scott Fitzgerald which man she preferred. The thought of losing Scott caused all her love for him to return in a sudden gush of feeling. It did not occur to her that his threat to quit his job and leave Hollywood forever was absurd and melo-dramatic. Sheilah had always been impressed by grand gestures, and she believed him because she was certain that, unlike her-self, Scott was a person who would not lie.

Sheilah left John Wheeler hanging in New York and took the midnight flight back to Hollywood and Scott.

9

EUPHORIA AND HANGOVER

When you once get to the point where you don't care whether you live or die—as I did—it's hard to come back to life . . . It's hard to believe in yourself again—you have slain part of yourself.

—F. Scott Fitzgerald, notes for *The Last Tycoon*

SCOTT WAS IN A BAD SHAPE after Chicago. He was a wraith, stretched thin, taut to the breaking point. He studied himself in his bathroom mirror and carefully recorded his findings: "Do I look like death (in mirror at 6 PM)." He hardly seemed real. He wrote and mailed to himself a postcard to make certain he did exist: "Dear Scott . . . How are you? Have been meaning to come in and see you. I have [been] living at The Garden of Allah. Yours Scott Fitzgerald." It was a relief when the card came back to him, delivered the next day. He was alive after all, a person with an address and a mailbox.

He suffered a succession of desperate days and nights, but it was an exquisite agony in its way. He knew he was very weak to break his vow not to drink; he might lie to others, but to himself he told the truth—he had always prided himself on this fact. Hangovers were an old friend; along with the physical misery, there came a grim and shadowless clarity in which inessentials were burned away. Drinking was for inspiration, and hangovers for contemplation of his sins. As a lapsed Catholic, he knew that pleasure was always followed by pain. This was the entire cycle of his addiction: euphoria and regret, heaven and hell. It was inconceivable to have one without the other, and it gave him the sense of dramatic motion that he required from life. Scott feared nothing except feeling nothing at all. When he had been young, he had sometimes written well on the bottle, tearing loose those old St. Paul inhibitions; but these days he often did his best work in the other state, the razor-sharp moments of wretched remorse when all the folly of the world was made clear.

In the "Crack-Up" articles that Gingrich read for Sheilah, Scott had written: "Through many an alcoholic mist, I felt each time a betrayal of a persistent idealism." The idealism remained, a heavenly city in his imagination, as bright and beyond his reach as it had ever been. He was a true believer in all that was wonderful in life—great art, noble men, beautiful women, inspiration always, the perfect football season played on eternal Saturday afternoons with the autumn weather always bright and sharp. Whenever he came up short against his ideal, he felt wretched. One evening Scott could no longer bear the deathlike image he saw reflected in his mirror. The failure was too much for him. He stood at the sink in the bathroom of his Garden of Allah bungalow and broke the porcelain tap until it made a sharp edge. He ran his wrists against the jagged break until he saw thin lines of blood appear. As he watched, the lines widened and the blood rushed free. It came like wine, a spilled glass running down the drain of his Hollywood bungalow. . . .

But the sight of his own blood brought him around. He became suddenly frightened, called a doctor, and saved himself just in time. It was just one more duality to add to all the others; teetering on the brink of self-annihilation, he discovered in himself the most startling urge to live.

*   *   *

He had never meant for there to be any real involvement with Sheilah. She was fun and vivacious and pretty, and he enjoyed her. Certainly he would do whatever was necessary to keep her—make dramatic telephone calls to Chicago should it appear she might be leaving him for another man. Nevertheless, Sheilah was a type of woman to whom he gave what he thought of consciously as his "second manner"; she represented to Scott the low state to which he had fallen, and the dreary decade in which he lived. By 1937 Scott believed the best years of his life were in the past. At times he could not help but admit to himself that Sheilah was something of a peasant.

She badgered him about his drinking, which struck Scott as very tawdry, as if they were low characters in the sort of shabby pseudoproletarian novels that were popular these days. She said she could not understand how an intelligent man could drink when it made him so ill. Scott hated to be on the wrong end of a lecture, and this seemed an intolerable assault upon his dignity. He told Sheilah stiffly that he preferred not to discuss the matter— his drinking was not her concern. Sheilah let the matter drop, but sometimes he caught her standing close and sniffing his breath for any telltale scent of liquor. It made him furious. Zelda had never badgered him about his drinking, and it would not have occurred to her to sniff his breath. Well-bred people might drop you if your behavior became offensive, but they did not try to reform you. Sheilah simply had no idea of how things were done.

For Scott, this was very maddening. There was, for example, the incident of her birthday present. On September 15 she turned twenty-eight (or this was what she told him; she was thirty-three). After careful thought, Scott decided he would give her a fur coat, a silver-fox jacket to mark the occasion. This was more than a gift, it was a subtle statement, a definition of their relationship. A fur coat had a certain meaning, after all. In society some things must never be spoken except in code, and here the code was very clear: When a young woman accepted an expensive fur coat from an older man, it marked her as his mistress and not as someone who might under any circumstances become his wife. It was a discreet monetary exchange, like slipping a girl a hundred-dollar bill for the powder room and then forgetting to ask for the change. The differences between a mistress and a wife, a good and bad girl, one's first and second manner, high and low, success and failure—these were the rankings that made life such a treacherous contest, and Scott always kept them in mind for it was a contest he wished to win. For a respectable woman, the gift of a silver-fox jacket would have been a tremendous insult. Anyone who understood the rules would know this.

But Sheilah did not know the rules, and that proved an unexpected problem. She was so innocent as to be delighted with the jacket and entirely failed to understand the symbolism underneath. Scott was strangely touched. She bubbled over about how no one had ever given her any sort of present on her birthday before, certainly not anything as fine as a fur coat. She had always been so alone in the world, without family or even real friends. Now she believed she had found someone who loved her.

Sheilah primped in front of the mirror in her new coat. She wore it proudly to restaurants and parties, as self-conscious as a young girl in high heels for the first time, certain that all eyes were upon her. She made Scott laugh because she wouldn't sit back in the car with the coat around her shoulders, afraid she might ruffle the fur. The silver-fox had a magic for her far beyond an expensive piece of clothing; she loved it, and when she wore it she glowed and looked more beautiful than she had ever seemed to him before. Indeed her love for the jacket completely transformed the meaning of the gift, from the badge of a fallen women to something wonderful that knew no sin.

Scott hardly knew what to do with her. Her innocence was magnificent and moved him greatly. With all his better instincts, and against his inclinations, he loved her very much.

It seemed to Scott that some strange turn of fate had placed Sheilah in his care. He liked being needed; it made him feel not such a forgotten man. At the end of October, not long after the Chicago debacle and during a time when Scott himself was in very bad shape, he found a chance for one of his odd moments of chivalry. Sheilah had just received an annoying letter from a fellow Englishman, Clayton Hutton, a producer with a high opinion of himself who wrote angrily to "Miss Mussolini Graham" after she refused to answer his phone calls. The letter arrived on Mr. Hutton's business stationery which listed at the top and in the left-hand margin a summary of his professional credits, such biographical tidbits as "Producer of FASCINATION with Madeleine Carrol and Freddie Bartholomew," "UPS AND DOWNS with Naughton and Gold," and "Forty-Six English, French and German Shorts."

Dear Miss Graham:

It would appear to me you are lacking both in sportsmanship and also good manners; in other words you are getting exactly like all the other British who reside here.

When I last saw you at Bodley's house, it was left you were to have dinner with me on the Friday evening. I waited specially for you, but you neither communicated with me or left any message, but went off to Chicago.

I have 'phoned you many times since and to say the least you must have had some of my messages.

It is a matter of complete indifference whether I meet you or not, but at any rate you might have had the courtesy to have communicated with me.

With kind regards,

Yours sincerely,
Clayton Hutton

Sheilah, in fact, had stood the man up, but for Scott this made no difference. He could hardly wait to annihilate such an unwanted suitor who dared to question Sheilah's good manners. He composed a reply, savagely mimicking Mr. Hutton's stationery with absurd biographical data of his own that he wrote up and down the margins—such capsules of information as "3rd Football Team, St. Paul Academy 1910," "Worked Unsuccessfully on REDHEADED WOMAN with JEAN HARLOW, 1927," "Won FIELDMEET (Junior) Newman School, 1912," "AFFAIR (Unconsummated) with ACTRESS, 1927," and "Wrote 22 Unsuccessful Stories 1920 Offered to SATURDAY EVENING POST ect." (*Ect.* was Scott's lifelong misspelling of *etc.*)

Scott threw himself into his reply with gusto:

Dear Mr. Hutton,

Unable to match the apt phraseology in your letter to Miss
Graham of recent date, I can only repeat it; "You show both poor
sportsmanship and manners"—the former because when a girl
neglects two dozen phone calls it is fair to suppose you didn't make
an impression—the latter because you wrote such a letter at all.

It is nice to know that it is all "a matter of complete indifference" to you, so there will be no hard feelings. But you worry us
about the state of the English colony in Hollywood. Can it be that
there are other telephones that—but no—and anyhow you can
always fake refuge behind that splendid, that truly magnificent
indifference.

> Very Truly Yours,
> F. Scott Fitzgerald

This was vintage Scott, and Sheilah laughed greatly when she
read his letter with the absurd biographical data in the margins.
As always she was grateful for his help and amazed at how
much trouble he was willing to take on her behalf. After
Chicago, the good brownie seemed to make a decided return
and the chaotic memory of their trip together receded into something improbable in her mind.

On December 7, MGM renewed Scott's six-month contract for
an additional year, giving him a raise in the process from $1,000
to $1,250 a week. This was a great relief, and a sign that he might
yet conquer Hollywood. Then a few days later Scott read in the
Los Angeles Times that the Pasadena Playhouse was about to present a dramatized version of his short story, "A Diamond as Big
as the Ritz."

Scott burst into Sheilah's house that evening full of the good
news; the Pasadena Playhouse was certainly not Broadway, but
for Los Angeles it passed as legitimate theater. Scott's spirits
soared; he was transformed with hope. A new generation might
discover his writing through this single play; perhaps he was not
forgotten as an author after all. This could be the start of something, a return to fashion, the pendulum of time swinging back
his way.

Scott decided to make a big event of the opening night. He rented a limousine and took Sheilah to the Trocadero, the most fashionable restaurant in town, where they had dined so unsuccessfully with Scottie and her two friends on their second date. Tonight Scott wore a tuxedo and his best dress shirt; Sheilah her finest evening gown of gray silk with the crimson velvet belt, the dress she had worn to the benefit dinner dance for the Screen Writers Guild. Scott gave her a lovely corsage to pin on the front of her gown, and her silver-fox jacket was wrapped proudly around her shoulders. After dinner, the limousine carried them in quiet luxury to Pasadena and Scott laughed as he always did to see how she refused to sit back in her coat in the car.

On an evening like this all things seemed possible. Scott spoke excitedly about a serious novel he planned to write about Hollywood. The main characters, he said, would be based on Irving Thalberg and Louis B. Mayer—the forces of art versus money, quality against commercialism. The novel had been simmering in his mind ever since he had met Thalberg in 1927 on his first trip to Hollywood and was struck by the grace with which this crown prince of Hollywood wielded his great power. Riding in the limousine, he told Sheilah about a conversation with Thalberg which had impressed him greatly.

"We sat in the old commissary at Metro and he said, 'Scottie, supposing there's got to be a road through a mountain—a railroad and two or three surveyors and people come to you and you believe some of them and some of them you don't believe; but all in all there seems to be half a dozen possible roads through those mountains each one of which, so far as you can determine, is as good as the other. Now suppose you happen to be the top man, there's a point where you don't exercise the faculty of judgement in the ordinary way, but simply the faculty of arbitrary decision. You say, "Well, I think we will put the road there," and you trace it with your finger and you know in your secret heart and no one else knows, that you have no reason for putting the road there rather in several other different courses, but you're the only person that knows that you don't know why you're doing it and you've got to stick to that and you've got to pretend that you know and that you did it for specific reasons, even though you're utterly assailed by doubts at times. . . .'"

Scott never forgot this conversation. Thalberg's words, he believed, embodied the very heart of leadership, what it took to be "the top man." It was astonishing that Thalberg was only twenty-six years old at the time. Ever afterward, Scott regarded this young man as the best of Hollywood, someone who had integrity, intelligence, and a huge dream. To contrast such a romantic figure with a sentimental money-grubber like Louis B. Mayer was to capture the two polarities of the movie industry: all that was magnificent about Hollywood, and all that was sordid. "No one's yet written *the* novel on Hollywood," Scott assured Sheilah excitedly. The books so far had taken only a shallow and predictable look at the movie industry, leaving the field wide open for a serious writer.

Sheilah was delighted to hear Scott talking so enthusiastically about a novel he wanted to write. She told him an anecdote she had heard about Irving Thalberg's funeral: how an invitation to be a pallbearer at this important event had been sent by mistake to Harry Carey, an out-of-work cowboy actor, instead of the well-known producer, Carey Wilson, for whom it had been intended. When the cowboy was seen carrying the casket of Irving Thalberg, everyone in town assumed his career had taken a major surge for the better, and from that day on, his phone never stopped ringing and he became a big star. Scott thought this was a perfect anecdote about Hollywood. He took out his notebook and wrote the story down, and assured Sheilah it would find a place in his book.

In this way—excited, discussing the future—Sheilah and Scott arrived at the Pasadena Playhouse. But they were greeted by a puzzling sight. The building was dark and there was no sign of the usual crowds and cars that were part of an opening night. The chauffeur came around to open the limousine door and Sheilah and Scott stepped out upon a silent sidewalk.

"Could I have gotten the date wrong?" Scott wondered. This did not seem likely as he had phoned the theater earlier in the day to say he was the author of the story and request that two seats be reserved for him "somewhere near the back." He left Sheilah in the darkened lobby and wandered into the theater to find out what was happening. When he returned his smile was strained. "It's the students," he said. "They're giving the play in the upstairs hall." He tried to make light of it and Sheilah did her best to be as nonchalant as Scott. Together they climbed the stairs to a small hall on the second floor where they found a tiny stage and a dozen or so rows of wooden benches. Scott and Sheilah were early and no other audience had yet arrived. They sat on the hard benches near the back and Sheilah spoke brightly of her day; when the conversation flagged she asked a barrage of questions about *Three Comrades* and how things were going at Metro. Eventually a dozen or so students drifted into the upstairs theater; they were dressed casually in slacks and skirts and glanced from time to time with curiosity at the couple in the rear in evening clothes.

At last the lights dimmed and the play began. It was an uneven amateur production but Scott laughed at every joke, more loudly than anyone else, and at the end he continued clapping long after the other applause had died away. "I'm going backstage," he told Sheilah. "It might encourage them to know the author came to see them."

He returned in a few moments. They walked down the stairs and into the waiting limousine. "They were all nice kids," Scott said. "They seemed a little awkward when I introduced myself. I told them they'd done a good job."

As they drove back into West Hollywood, Sheilah made a effort to keep up her bright line of chatter, but gradually her words faltered and died, swallowed by Scott's deepening silence. He sank back into the upholstery, staring out the limousine window at the passing sprawl of low houses, his face exhausted and proud in the flickering reflection of streetlights.

Sheilah was certain that if she betrayed even the slightest sign of pity, Scott would never forgive her.

Scott left her for Christmas and flew east once again to Asheville to visit Zelda. He told Sheilah he had no choice but to go: Zelda's doctor had recommended these visits as part of her therapy. He planned to take his wife out of the hospital on a small vacation and pretend they were a normal couple.

"You don't mind, do you?" he asked Sheilah.

She knew she had no right to mind, but she did—she minded terribly. She said only: "Scott, must you go?"

"I must take out my poor Zelda—I cannot abandon her there," he said. "I won't write you while I'm away."

And so Sheilah was left alone over Christmas to face the last days of 1937 by herself. It was a time of year when the legitimate people of the world fled back to their wives and families, leaving girls like her alone. She hated Christmas; it always made her feel such an outsider. A year earlier, over Christmas 1936, she had found herself unexpectedly abandoned when King Vidor, the movie director she thought she was going to marry, eloped with another woman. Now the holiday season found her miserable yet again. On Scott's first trip to Zelda in September, she had known him only two months, but by Christmas their love had deepened and his absence was more painful than before. Sometimes she forgot for weeks at a time that Scott Fitzgerald was a married man, but it always came back when she least expected, a slap in the face. At these times she understood she was in love with a man who offered her no status, no security— who at any moment might return to his wife, leaving Sheilah with nothing.

She had dinners out with whatever strays and lost spirits she could summon forth from The Garden of Allah. She flirted, hoping for some warmth in return, and all the time she felt a great ripping emptiness in her life waiting for Scott's return.

Scott did not tell Sheilah everything. He was careful to conceal from her that throughout the ongoing months of their love affair, he and Zelda had remained very much in touch, writing to each other long and often intimate letters at least once a week. Scott did not tell Sheilah about Zelda, and he likewise kept any knowledge of his new Hollywood love from his wife. He was leading a classic double life, anxious to keep his wife and mistress apart, though the circumstances were unusual and he did not believe he was doing anything wrong. It was a complicated matter.

The bottom line, as far as Scott was concerned, was that he

had not slept with his wife for a number of years, and had no desire to do so ever again. "I cannot live in the ghost town which Zelda has become," he confided a few months later to Dr. Robert S. Carroll, the director of Zelda's sanitarium in North Carolina. He told the doctor that clearly Zelda needed to find a life for herself that had some "provision for hope and for sex"—but it would not be with him. Perhaps eventually she might find someone new, "some man whose personality might be a rock on which she might steady herself more permanently." Meanwhile, he would not abandon her, or betray—as Scott put it—that "old bond of justice that existed between us." He added for the record: "Each time that I see her something happens to me that makes me the worst person for her rather than the best, but a part of me will always pity her with a sort of deep ache that is never absent from my mind for more than a few hours: an ache for the beautiful child that I loved and with whom I was happy as I shall never be again."

Zelda felt this ache as deeply as Scott. Week after week she sent to him in California contrite and wistful letters that were nostalgic of the past. "I wish we were astride the tops of New York taxis and a little hilarious in parcs [sic] and public places, and younger than young people," she had written recently. For Scott the memory of riding around drunk on the tops of taxis seemed very long ago, a subject best forgotten, but for Zelda in her asylum, time stood still. Scott was nostalgic in his own way for his lost youth and his "beautiful child," but along with his nostalgia there was a good deal of rancor. He nursed many old grievances. He never forgot that Zelda had turned him down the first time he asked for her hand; it was only after *This Side of Paradise* was accepted by Scribner's and it appeared that he might offer a glamorous ticket out of the provincial life of Montgomery, Alabama, that she changed her mind and agreed to be his wife. Initially Scott had excused this first refusal as a sensible decision: Clearly a clever woman did not marry a young man who had no money or prospects. But over the years the memory of Zelda's refusal grew in his mind and became part of a general resentment Scott had about money—how freely she had spent his earnings, forcing him to work for her luxuries rather than his art. Unfortunately, she was spending it still, for Highlands Hospital was not cheap, costing him approximately six thousand dollars a year plus a fifty-dollar-per-month allowance he sent to her separately. This complex issue, money, was connected in Scott's mind to a more general image of Zelda as the spoiled belle of the ball, decorative but useless, an eternal amateur whose flittering ways had caused him to misspend his talent and energy, health and time.

But there was another old grievance even more rancorous: In the mid-twenties, Zelda had accused Scott of having homosexual feelings toward Ernest Hemingway, a man she detested and whose pretense of robust manhood she often called "bogus." Scott violently denied Zelda's accusations and accused her in return of transferring to him her own inclinations. He thought it quite obvious that in Paris she had been in love with her ballet teacher, Madame Egorova, as well as Dolly Wilde, Oscar Wilde's niece, who was a well-known lesbian. Zelda certainly had been intensely attracted to Madame Egorova, sending her teacher a bouquet of flowers every day and sometimes falling at her feet in worship. Still it is doubtful that anything physical had occurred, just as it is also unlikely that anything had happened between Ernest and Scott. The Fitzgeralds were seeking hallucinatory reasons to explain their dwindling sex life and growing estrangement. Mutual accusations of homosexuality were easier to hurl than for either of them to accept the more mundane truth that far too much alcohol may have been the cause. The homosexual baiting of one another continued and a decade later in Hollywood Scott drafted an angry letter to Zelda about this issue at a time when she was hoping to be released from Highlands Hospital:

> When you come out you are of course free. Meanwhile if you should find it impossible to rid yourself of the idea that I am in *any* sense homosexual, I would find it impossible to live with you or even to see you again. I can't [believe] that this will be the case— first because the idea began in an attempt to implicate me in what you thought were your own tendencies (i.e. your accusation about Ernest occurred exactly one month after the Dolly Wilde matter) and secondly because the intensity of your conviction has always

been in exact ratio to the observed pathological condition of your nerves (so much so that putting the cart before the horse you have thought that your *suspicion* was the cause and your *neurosis* was the effect.)

Zelda infuriated him further in the mid-twenties by saying that his penis was too small to give her any satisfaction. Scott was so upset that he had Hemingway examine him in a Paris bathroom after lunch one day. Ernest had a good look and told Scott he was absolutely normal and that Zelda was merely trying to "put him out of business." Then Ernest took his friend to the Louvre where the two writers spent the rest of the afternoon looking at penises of every shape and size, from those on Greek statues to the appendages of little angels darting about the clouds. Scott and Ernest had consumed a bit of wine at lunch and had a raucous time in their search for a manly norm, only to have Zelda's suspicions rain down on him, Scott believed, most unfairly.

These and other unresolved issues from the past remained a tangible barrier between Scott and Zelda whenever he went east. He approached his wife with wary caution, never forgetting his wounds. They had begun with many gifts—youth, talent, fame, and good looks—and in a decade they had destroyed it all; now they took turns blaming each other for the debris. Scott believed the weak always destroy the strong. He wrote his daughter: "I think the pull of an afflicted person [i.e., Zelda] upon a normal one [Scott] is at all times downward, depressing and eventually somewhat paralyzing." It was no wonder that Scott's trips east were tense and difficult. The Christmas visit of 1937 was a depressing one for him, with the old accusations hovering near the surface. Their daughter remained north in order to save money, spending her vacation with the Obers and her friend Peaches Finney. Scott described the visit to her in a letter in February:

> Your mother was better than ever I expected and our trip
> would have been fun except that I was tired. We went to Miami and
> Palm Beach, flew to Montgomery, all of which sounds very gay and
> glamorous but wasn't particularly. I flew back to New York intend-

ing to take you out with your friends Saturday but I discovered
you were on bounds. My zero hour was Monday morning in
California so there was nothing to do except fly back on Sunday
afternoon.

Scottie was in her last year at the Ethel Walker School and
hoping to enter Vassar in the fall. Scott was outraged to find his
daughter "on bounds" at such a vital moment in her scholastic
career, astonished that she did not seem to understand the seriousness of her predicament. He concluded his letter with a
threat:

> It is either Vassar or else the University of California here
> under my eye and the choice is so plain that I have no sympathy
> for your loafing. We are not even out of debt yet, you are still [a]
> scholarship student and you might give them a break by making a
> graceful exit . . . You have got to make all the right changes at the
> main corners—the price for losing your way once is years of
> unhappiness.

As for Scott, he only lost his way briefly during his stopover
in New York before returning to California; the tension of seeing
Zelda exploded into a three-day drunk. He knew he shouldn't,
but away from watchful eyes it was a temptation too hard to
resist. Neither Sheilah, Scottie, nor Zelda was ever to learn of this
particular binge and so for Scott it was a free ride. He was able
for the moment to maintain the illusion that he was a man who
made all the right changes at the main corner, with only a small
detour every now and then into an undetected back alley all his
own.

10

THREE COMRADES

People don't seem to realize that for an intelligent man writing down is about the hardest thing in the world.

—F. Scott Fitzgerald to H. L. Mencken, May 4, 1925

SHEILAH SUFFERED DURING THE WEEK OVER CHRISTMAS when Scott went to Zelda, but soon he was back in California once again, coming up her hill each night and honking his wheezing horn. As the new year of 1938 got under way, she resolved to no longer accept dates with other men. This was more than a way to avoid Scott's jealousy; it was a gradual acquiescence to a change in her life. Somehow the drunken disaster of Chicago had led to a deeper commitment between them. It was as if the ice were now truly broken: She had confessed her past life of many lies, and he too had revealed his true hand, the good and the bad of him. Surviving this first icy shock of truth, their love affair now moved into a new realm.

Sheilah's five-minute radio spot had been canceled in November after her third show. The sponsors had decided to pay off her six-month contract rather than let her continue, more certain than ever that they hated her British accent. All in all, Sheilah was relieved it was over. Everything about the radio show had been difficult—the flying back and forth, her nervousness, and most of all, the problems it had created with Scott. Rarely in her life had Sheilah gotten anything for nothing, and now it seemed a great luxury to enjoy six months of an unearned salary of two hundred dollars a week.

With no radio show to distract her, and no further dinner dates with other men, Sheilah was glad for the snug winter evenings alone with Scott. The new year found them more reclusive than before. They had a secret world together with a language all its own. Scott often telephoned five or six times a day from work just to say hello. "What are you wearing?" he might ask. "What are you thinking of? . . . When will I see you? . . . How do you look?"

Boxes of flowers often arrived at her house on Kings Road accompanied by little notes: "For Sheilah—from her chattel, Scott." Or "Missing you is a luxury like everything about knowing you, lovely, lovely, Sheilah." And once after a small quarrel: "Darling, I am sorry I was difficult tonight. You are dear Sheilah and nothing can change that. Please feel better dear sweet Sheilah. Dear face, dear heart, dear, dear, dear Sheilah."

All this attention was hard to resist. In order to keep her evenings free, Sheilah began to pay Jonah Ruddy a weekly fee to cover the various industry events, premieres and parties, so that she could stay home with Scott. Often they turned on the phonograph and danced in her living room, doing elaborate pirouettes and bows. Scott might take off tap dancing across the floor in a wild parody of Fred Astaire. Sometimes he recited poetry as they danced; he made her helpless with laughter as he did the "Shuffle Off to Buffalo" to T. S. Eliot's "The Boston Evening Transcript" and invented a wooden-soldier dance to go with the chorus from Swinburne's *Atalanta in Calydon*, which he told Sheilah was "the dancingest poem." Sheilah followed him around the room, flapping her arms as stiffly as he did, dissolving into laughter, falling into his arms.

Boxing was another of his passions—a fact Sheilah had learned to her dismay in Chicago. But now it was a matter of fun. Scott would prance about her living room making all sorts of ferocious faces as he pretended to spar. "Sheilo, keep your chin in or I'll slug you!" he taunted. He was always entertaining her; he seemed to need the center stage of her attention, all her laughter, applause, and love. She had no idea that he had performed these same antics with other women; that he had recited poetry while dancing and had shadowboxed to delighted laughter in other rooms. It was not that Scott was insincere, it was simply that his charm for women was well rehearsed. As a writer he had often stripped good lines from his stories to put into his novels— "self-plagiarism," he called it—and it was even more natural to self-plagiarize for the purposes of romance, recycling lines that had worked in the past. In one early incident in 1917, he went so far as to court a young woman, Fluff Beckwith, by pretending to write her a poem, "When Vanity Kissed Vanity," which he had in fact written previously for someone else. Scott at the moment was hoping to restore his ego recently shattered by Ginevra King and he was willing to use any ammunition at hand. The girl was naturally flattered—and then greatly dismayed in 1945 to discover her poem in a book dedicated to Scott's cousin Cecelia.

But Sheilah suspected none of this. Scott was pleased to see her eyes light up with love and admiration. She thought him the most imaginative and spontaneous man she had ever known. And he was, of course. An artist simply had to work very hard to make his spontaneity seem easy.

They went to parties, though less often than when they first met. Sheilah felt inadequate to join in the intellectual chatter among the writers Scott knew, conversations which often involved intricate puns and literary and historical references to which she did not have a clue.

Sheilah felt she had made a fool of herself one evening when she overheard a young woman speaking of Willa Cather. "And who is Willa Cather?" she asked flippantly, trying to affect the casual and superior manner she had sometimes overheard Robert Benchley use so effectively. The young woman gave

Sheilah a withering look. "Doesn't Willa Cather's name mean anything to you?" she asked. "Oh, well, we have never heard of her in England," Sheilah managed, but she heard someone chuckle and knew she had made a stupid remark.

Word games were a part of nearly every gathering, and these also caused Sheilah a great deal of misery. Many of the games had evolved over the years from the famous lunches in New York at the Algonquin Round Table; it was said that the critic Alexander Woollcott thought up word games so elaborate, no one could understand them except Harpo Marx. Sheilah always felt left out and dreaded the moment these games would begin. In California, charades was the most popular game of all, generally called simply *The* Game at The Garden of Allah. It was taken so seriously that Marc Connelly often held rehearsals when his team was scheduled to take on Ira Gershwin's or Dorothy Parker's. Besides Sheilah, only Robert Benchley hated charades, but for a different reason—he found it trite and tiresome. One afternoon, Benchley was rehearsing *Of Mice and Men*, crawling about on the floor to indicate the word *mouse*, when he said abruptly, "The hell with you!" He crawled out the French door and couldn't be found until the next day. For revenge Benchley dreamed up an "anti-game" he called "Subway." No one could make heads or tails of it; it seemed to consist of Benchley pushing the actor Charlie Butterworth around The Garden of Allah swimming pool in a wheelbarrow.

Benchley was Sheilah's only ally when someone inevitably said, "Let's play The Game." Even Scott loved charades; it brought out his competitive spirit and he was always eager to win. Sheilah sat tensely while the others were having fun, certain she might be unmasked at any moment—afraid she would be put down as stupid if they discovered how little she knew. To compensate, she tried desperately to be vivacious and bright and tell everyone in a loud voice the latest studio gossip.

Scott watched her behavior with a critical eye. Finally he felt something must be done. "Sit back," he suggested to her one night. "Let them come to you. Don't be too eager—it makes you unattractive." Sheilah confessed how terribly inadequate she felt at these gatherings and Scott thought up a strategy for her. Any situation could be dealt with, he stressed, as long as you had a plan. On their way one night to Frances and Albert Hackett's house in Beverly Hills, Scott suggested that throughout the evening Sheilah pretend to herself that everyone at the party bored her. This would counterbalance her eagerness and give her the appearance of self-confidence and poise.

Sheilah dutifully followed Scott's suggestion. She spent the evening sitting quietly and saying to herself, "George S. Kaufman bores me. Oscar Levant bores me. Ogden Nash bores me." As long as she kept her mouth closed, the ploy was a great success. She repeated to herself what Scott told her, that she didn't have to prove anything; she was worthy in herself and did not have to perform as her price of admission. Eventually Scott and Sheilah became both so quiet in public that they were hardly noticed; Scott was content to circulate briefly, say hello to his friends, and then sit in a corner with Sheilah watching the passing parade. Alan Campbell once said to them enviously, "You two always look as though you had a secret you were going to talk about later."

One evening Alan Campbell gave a party for Somerset Maugham, who was visiting California. When the party was ending, Maugham said to Alan, "I'm told F. Scott Fitzgerald is in Hollywood. I should like to meet him." "You did, tonight—here," Alan assured him. Scott had simply been so quiet and self-effacing that he had made no impression. This was a far cry from the young Fitzgerald who when introduced to James Joyce in Paris in the twenties offered to jump from the fifth-floor window as a sign of eternal homage to the master. James Joyce assured the impressionable American that such homage was not necessary; later he remarked to Sylvia Beach, "That young man must be mad. I'm afraid he'll do himself some injury."

Life was calmer now, some days almost tranquil. There was not so much energy left to carelessly throw away. Eventually Scott convinced Sheilah that it was best to simply stay at home and live in a world of their own.

One evening they were sitting in cozy silence in Sheilah's living room. She was working on her column while Scott read a book of Tennyson. Without any preamble he began to read to her aloud in the melodramatic tenor voice he reserved for poetry:

> Now sleeps the crimson petal, now the
>   white,
> Nor waves the cypress in the palace walk;
> Nor winks the gold fin in the porphyry font.
> The firefly wakens: waken thou with me.

Scott stopped to make certain he had her complete attention. Then he continued his florid recital, as smooth as any matinee idol pulling forth emotion from a darkened theater:

> Now folds the lily all her sweetness up
> And slips into the bosom of the lake.
> So fold thyself, my dearest, thou, and slip
> Into my bosom and be lost in me.

"Oh, Scott," Sheilah murmured. She would slip into his bosom anytime. There were tears in her eyes and he took her in his arms. Sheilah was greatly moved. "If only I could walk into your eyes," she said, "and close the lids behind me, and leave all the world outside. . . ."

Scott recognized a literary moment. He held her tenderly, and when he could he slipped from her arms and found a pencil and a piece of paper to write down her last romantic utterance. It was a good line: *If only I could walk into your eyes. . . .* He might use this somewhere, in a novel or a story. Good dialogue was almost as hard to come by as true love, and perhaps more lasting.

Sheilah was bored. She hated to admit it, but it was true. By the middle of January nearly three weeks had passed since her desperately lonely Christmas, and three months since the Chicago debacle. For Sheilah, this was an awfully long time without a crisis. Sometimes it felt as if her life were slipping away in a regular succession of unmarked days.

Sheilah began to think a trip somewhere might be fun and one night she suggested to Scott that they spend a weekend in New York. Scott was amused by her youthful restlessness and he counseled her in the wise tones of a patient philosopher.

"Why do you want to go to New York, Sheilah?"

"I'm not really sure why. To go to the Stork Club and '21' and places like that."

"Why do you want to go to the Stork Club and '21' and places like that?"

"To see the people, I guess."

"But who are the people you see at such places?" Scott insisted gently. "They're not real. I have been there. I have given all that up. What can you get from such people? What can you get from New York?"

Being young—though not quite so young as Scott believed—Sheilah had trouble accepting such ageless wisdom. "Oh," she said, struggling to express herself, "New York excites me. It thrills me."

"Sheilah, what you are looking for, you have found. You are looking for love, for someone to understand you. You have me. I love you and understand you. There's no need for you to go to New York."

Scott convinced her with the quiet force of his mature personality that they need go nowhere at all. Then he picked up the telephone and reserved seats for the flight east. She had made New York sound awfully good—the Stork Club, "21," Broadway, a real city. He too was bored and ready for action.

They stayed at the Ambassador Hotel on Park Avenue. As usual they took a suite with two bedrooms in deference to Scott's insomnia. At night Sheilah heard him pacing restlessly in his room and she called to him to see if he was all right. He poked his head into her bedroom and said he would be fine: He had just taken five sleeping pills and soon would be fast asleep.

Five sleeping pills! Sheilah was alarmed. Had she heard him correctly? Now she was wide awake. Occasionally she split a Nembutal in half when she had trouble sleeping—five of these pills seemed positively suicidal. She became so worried that she decided to telephone Scott's doctor at his home in Los Angeles. She whispered into the receiver, knowing that Scott would be angry at her for going behind his back. The doctor told Sheilah not to worry. He had a Hollywood practice and much of his business was devoted to dispensing strong sedatives and stimulants to busy people. Fitzgerald was one of his best customers and normally took three teaspoons of chloral and two Nembutals every night to get to sleep, and in the morning Benzedrine to wake up and jump-start the day. "[Scott] has built up such immunity, he could take eight Nembutals and they wouldn't hurt him," the doctor assured her. But Sheilah was not assured and she spent an anxious night until she saw that Scott was all right in the morning.

Despite the worry of this one night, they had a good weekend. Scott did not tell his daughter that he and Sheilah were close by in New York; perhaps he believed it would rob him of moral authority were Scottie to think he was traveling with a woman. But Scott introduced Sheilah to two of his oldest friends, Gerald and Sara Murphy. This was not a casual introduction, for the Murphys comprised a special and very meaningful corner of his past. They were a rich and charismatic couple, wonderfully cultivated, who had lived in France in the twenties gathering around them a glittering crowd of artists and intellectuals—a crowd which included at different moments Stravinsky, Picasso, Braque, Jean Cocteau, and Americans such as the Fitzgeralds, Ernest Hemingway, and John Dos Passos. Gerald and Sara had discovered Cap d'Antibes in the south of France before it was fashionable: They made it fashionable by their presence. *Tender Is the Night* is dedicated to "Gerald and Sara, Many Fêtes," and it was widely known that they were Scott's models for Dick and Nicole Diver in the first half of novel, though the second half, the dissolution of this golden couple, was entirely Scott and Zelda.

Scott must have been apprehensive about introducing Sheilah to a couple whose opinion he so greatly valued, and who were linked in his mind to an artistic and personal past that was vastly more important to him than his current life in Hollywood. Sheilah passed the test; the Murphys were pleased to find Scott among the living and in the company of a pretty young woman who seemed to care about him in such a supportive way. As for Sheilah, Scott was able to write to Gerald a few months later: "Sheilah, of course, was fascinated by you both, and I looked up old pictures in old scrapbooks for her."

Sheilah was unaware that she had been tested and found

acceptable. She liked the Murphys; they were charming and easy people to know. But she had a small fight with Scott afterward when he mentioned that Gerald had at one time wanted to be a painter, but gave it up when he realized he did not have the talent to be first rate. Scott thought this very admirable. "But he enjoyed painting," Sheilah protested. "That was not the point," Scott insisted stubbornly. The point, for Scott, was that he hated amateurs, those dabblers who were not willing to devote their entire energy to art; for Scott either you aimed to be among the immortals, or you were some silly housewife taking a course in basket weaving for self-enrichment—there was no middle ground. Sheilah with her more practical nature could not understand why Gerald Murphy should sacrifice something he enjoyed to what seemed to her a very remote ideal. It was the first time Sheilah had ever dared to disagree with Scott about an intellectual matter. By 1938 she still was awed by his great learning and intelligence, but in secret she had begun to suspect that he was not a god.

Scott and Sheilah flew back to California through a winter storm which tossed and battered their small airplane—a storm he would use eventually in the opening chapter of his Hollywood novel, along with the brief appearance of a drunk who was not allowed on the airplane. A writer in need of reforestation could afford to waste nothing, not even memories of his own humiliation. Flying into Los Angeles, Scott "could see a line of lights for the Long Beach Naval Station ahead and to the left, and on the right a twinkling blur for Santa Monica. The California moon was out, huge and orange over the Pacific. However I happened to feel about these things . . . they were home, after all. . . ."

During all this time—throughout the autumn of 1937 and the first months of 1938—Scott had continued to work on the screenplay of *Three Comrades*, though not with the same enthusiasm with which he had begun. He had never recovered from the shock of being assigned a collaborator—Ted Paramore, the old friend from the past he had dismissed with sarcasm in *The Beautiful and Damned*, now come back to haunt him. Scott did not want any collaborator, brilliant or bad. It was an outrage, unthinkable. He spent hours trying to manipulate his unwanted partner, hoping that Ted Paramore would simply stand aside— take a very long nap on the couch, if he liked—and let Fitzgerald do the actual work. It was all very frustrating for Scott and he worked himself up into a fine frenzy. Hollywood unfortunately was a town full of other people who had wills as strong as his own.

Back at the end of October, not long after Paramore came on the picture, he wrote his collaborator a letter to lay down some ground rules:

> Dear Ted . . .
>
> We got off to a bad start and I think you are under certain mis-apprehensions founded more on my state of mind and body last Friday than upon the real situation. My script is in a general way approved of. There was not any question of taking it out of my hands. . . The question was who I wanted to work with me on it and for how long. *That was the entire question* and it is not materially changed because I was temporarily off my balance.
>
> At what point you decided you wanted to take the whole course of things in hand—whether because of that day or because when you read my script you liked it much less than did Joe or the people in the office—where that point was I don't know. But it was apparent Saturday that you had and it is with my faculties quite clear and alert that I tell you I *prefer to keep* the responsibility for the script as a whole.

The "state of mind and body" he referred to was the desperate hangover of his Chicago binge. This complicated Scott's attempt to convince Mankiewicz and Ted Paramore of his basic superiority as a writer who would create a movie masterpiece, if only they would let him. As a last round of ammunition, he could not fail to remind Paramore who he was, not just any Hollywood hack but F. Scott Fitzgerald.

> . . . Ted, when you blandly informed me yesterday that you were going to write the whole thing over yourself, kindly includ-ing my best scenes, I knew we'd have to have this out . . . I want your help but I am not going to spend hours of time and talent

arguing with you as to whether I've chosen the best or second best speech . . . while you dredge through the book again as if it were Shakespeare—well, I didn't write four out of four best sellers or a hundred and fifty top-price short stories out of the mind of a temperamental child without taste or judgment.

Scott always came back to the pride and glory of his literary past, unaware that in the movie business this did not count for much. Only box-office receipts mattered, and Scott had not pulled off a real hit since his first novel, *This Side of Paradise*, all the way back in 1920. In Hollywood people often summoned forth the ghost of William Shakespeare, perhaps the only author they might all agree was synonymous with genius. But not even the Bard would have survived in the movies had he the misfortune to go without a hit for anywhere near that long.

Scott continued to assault his collaborator with memos and letters, and when these appeared to have little effect he went to the absurd length of writing an instructive fairy tale which he titled, "A Fable for Ted Paramore by F. Scott Fitzgerald." In this heavy-handed allegory, a great architect of an ancient city was asked to design a cathedral. Unfortunately, there were ignorant critics in the city who objected to the design, complaining particularly about two towers which they said were useless. And so a terrible blunder was made: A second architect was called in to revise the design of the first architect and a cathedral was built from the new plans. Naturally it was a very ugly cathedral, and the citizens of the ancient city did not like it one bit. Thirty years passed and the unhappy citizens of Fitzgerald's imaginary town finally dug up the design of the first architect and built from it a new cathedral which "seized the imagination of the multitude." The people then located the first architect in order to question him as to why his design was so brilliant. He replied nonchalantly that he did not consciously know the reason. Perhaps it was "because I felt good that day . . . and if I feel good I have a reason for what I do even if I don't know the reason."

Scott concluded this preposterous fable:

On that same day a young boy going to Mass with his mother quickened his step as he crossed the cathedral square.

"Oh, I like our new cathedral so much better than the old," he said.

"But the academy thinks it's not nearly so beautiful."

"But it's because of the mountains," said the little boy. "Before we had the tower I could see the mountains and they made every-thing seem little when you went inside the Church. Now you can't see the mountains, so God inside is more important."

That was what the architect had envisioned without thinking when he accidentally raised his forefinger against the sky fifty years before.

Scott was telling Ted Paramore as clearly as possible, "Leave my cathedral alone." However, while a river of memos and tele-phone calls are quite the thing in Hollywood, fables and alle-gories are not. Ted Paramore must have believed Fitzgerald was a pretentious quack whose career at MGM would not be a long one. He was certainly as unhappy as Scott to be saddled with a collaborator he despised, and he fired off some angry letters and telegrams of his own. DISAGREE VIOLENTLY WITH CERTAIN SCENES FINAL VERSION SCRIPT WHICH HAVE FINGERS LIKE BRAISED CHICORY, he wired Scott on January 25. Despite the stormy nature of their col-laboration, Scott and Ted Paramore were somehow able to com-plete six different drafts of *Three Comrades*, submitting their final draft on February 1, 1938. Joe Mankiewicz declared it one of the best screenplays he had ever read—and then he promptly rewrote it himself so that it was barely recognizable to its origi-nal authors.

This was a new complication and it took Scott by surprise. He had believed Paramore to be the Great Enemy standing between himself and artistic fulfillment—now his producer dared to rewrite him as well. Other Hollywood writers were not sur-prised. "Joe thinks he's Shakespeare," observed George Oppenheimer. "It is both Joe's strength and his weakness that he thought that he could rewrite anyone," said Edwin Knopf, who had brought Scott to Hollywood in July. Most Hollywood writ-ers accepted such indignities as merely the way of the movies. But Scott did not; he would not accept it. An artist had to have some control of his vision or it would all turn into a terrible mess—didn't they know this? Scott soon redirected his anger from his collaborator to his producer.

In mid-January, after Mankiewicz first began to add his own revisions, Scott wrote the producer what he believed was a diplomatic letter:

Dear Joe:

I read the third batch [of revisions] . . . with mixed feelings. Competent it certainly is, and in many ways tighter-knit than before. But my own type of writing doesn't survive being written over so thoroughly and there are certain pages out of which the rhythm has vanished. I know you don't believe the Hollywood theory that the actors will somehow "play it into shape," but I think that sometimes you've changed without improving.

Scott continued in his letter to go through the script page by page in a patient attempt to show Mankiewicz where he had erred. As a rule, writers anxious to continue finding employment in Hollywood did not criticize their bosses, but Scott went further still—he lectured Joe Mankiewicz on some general guidelines of writing dialogue:

. . . Pat's speech beginning "—if all I had, etc.," isn't as good as the original. People don't begin all sentences with *and, but, for* and *if*, do they? They simply break a thought in mid-paragraph, and in both *Gatsby* and *Farewell to Arms* the dialogue tends that way. Sticking in conjunctions makes a *monotonous* smoothness.

Again the not-so-subtle reminder that he was the author of *The Great Gatsby* and not someone to mess with. But Mankiewicz was unimpressed and refused to heed the lectures and advice of his hired hand; he went on by himself to completely revise the final draft. Scott felt desperately betrayed. On the cover page of his copy of the eventual shooting script, Scott crossed out the words, "Script okayed by Joseph Mankiewicz," and wrote instead: "Script Scrawled Over by Joseph Mankiewicz." On the top of the next page, so that posterity should know of this outrage, Scott added: "37 pages mine about 1/3, but all shadows + rythm [*sic*] removed." Further along in the margin of this same script, Scott could not resist the remark: "This isn't writing. This is Joe Mankiewicz. So slick—so cheap."

Scott's anger against Joe Mankiewicz became intensely personal; he began privately to refer to the producer as "Monkeybitch," and he heaped upon this name a fury of insults. "Joe: As a writer you're an amateur," he wrote in a note he never sent. "You smooth everything. Any actor would rather have a cacophony and dissonance. That's why in Hollywood dialogue by several writers often plays better than dialogue by one. It takes an old hand to change keys." From "Monkeybitch" Mankiewicz, Scott was inclined to let his disillusionment spread until it embraced movie producers in general as a despised low class of life. In a self-indulgent note scrawled in pencil, Scott wallowed in his venom:

The Hollywood producers have not had the early advantages which are considered standard—and it is not very kindly nor Christian to mock at them . . . They are less than people & I have never heard a writer or playwrite [sic] or an actress or a novelist say a nice thing about a producer except possibly the one they are working for at the moment—from Dorothy Parker's exhibit who was "only a ponys bottom"—on up. [It] is too much to ask that they have pleasant natures for it is a filthy job to debauch a nation—even though the nation wallows in the spew.

On their side they have their money and their strident molls and they accept mockery and hatred as their share. They do not mind—they lick it up with the oppression visited upon their parents in Oddessa [sic] and Lotz [sic]—they are having their moment among the fleshpots before returning to the darker and bloodier ghettos that lie ahead.

This was strong stuff—and possibly Fitzgerald was drinking strong stuff to write these lines. Throughout the late thirties émigrés had been streaming into Hollywood from Europe with warnings of the approaching holocaust: Otto Preminger, Ernst Lubitsch, Billy Wilder, Fritz Lang, and Peter Lorre were just a few who arrived with tales of what was happening in Hitler's Germany, so Scott had some notion of "the darker and bloodier ghettos" that lay ahead for the Jews. At the moment, however, he was more concerned with producers who dared to rewrite him. Each evening he appeared at Sheilah's house full of barely suppressed fury. She saw how greatly he suffered over the script, but did not understand why he was so surprised. After all, what did he expect? Didn't Scott realize that this was just the way it was in Hollywood? All the other writers accepted the system—why couldn't Scott? You had to bend a little in this town, maybe bend a lot. Scott was simply bashing his head against a wall. One night Scott showed Sheilah a letter full of outrageous insults which he planned to send to Joe Mankiewicz. Sheilah persuaded him to tear it up, certain it would harm his career.

"You'll only antagonize him and he'll never restore your script," she argued diplomatically. At last she was able to convince him to send a much milder one in its place:

> Dear Joe:
>
> Well, I read the last part and I feel like a good many writers must have felt in the past. I gave you a drawing and you simply took a box of chalk and touched it up. . . . I guess all these years I've been kidding myself about being a good writer. . . .
>
> To say I'm disillusioned is putting it mildly. For nineteen years, with two years out for sickness, I've written best-selling entertainment, and my dialogue is supposedly right up at the top. But I learn from the script that you've suddenly decided that it isn't good dialogue and you can take a few hours off and do much better.
>
> I think you now have a flop on your hands . . . inexcusable because this time you *had* something and you have arbitrarily and carelessly torn it to pieces . . .

Scott continued for a number of pages in this manner and then concluded:

> My only hope is that you will *have a moment of clear thinking. That you'll ask some intelligent* and *disinterested* person to look at the two scripts . . . I am utterly miserable at seeing months of work and thought negated in one hasty week. I hope you're big enough to take this letter as it's meant—a desperate plea to restore the dialogue to its former quality . . . all those touches that were both natural and new. Oh, Joe, can't producers ever be wrong? I'm a good writer—honest. I thought you were going to play fair. Joan Crawford might as well play the part now, for the thing is as groggy with sentimentality as *The Bride Wore Red*, but the true emotion is gone.

Many years later, in 1969, Joe Mankiewicz had the opportunity in an interview to tell his side of the story, complaining bitterly how various biographers had dealt with him: "When I rewrote

Scott's dialogue, people thought I was spitting on the flag." He continued:

> I didn't count on Scott for dialogue. There could be no greater disservice done him than to have actors read his novels aloud as if they were plays. Mr. Hemingway, Mr. Steinbeck, Mr. Fitzgerald, Mr. Sinclair Lewis—all of them wanted to write plays and none of them could write one to save their soul. After all, there is a great difference between the dialogue in a novel and in a play. In a novel, the dialogue enters through the mind. The reader endows it with a certain quality. Dialogue spoken from the stage enters through the ear rather than the mind. It has an immediate emotional impact. Scott's dialogue lacked bite, color, rhythm.

Mankiewicz was even more stubborn than Scott Fitzgerald; he was a man who would have it his way, or no way at all. But Joe's stubbornness earned Scott's respect in one instance. When *Three Comrades* was finished, MGM became worried it might be perceived as too critical of Nazi Germany. In the winter of 1938, Louis B. Mayer invited a representative of the Nazi government as well as the official industry censor from the Hays Office, Joseph Breen, to join with him and Joe Mankiewicz for a screening of the movie. The Nazi was indeed upset at what he saw; he assured the Americans that it was the vilest Communist propaganda to paint his government as being in any way anti-Semitic. He was very sincere and Joseph Breen was inclined to believe him.

The Hays Office had recently been created by the movie industry itself to deal with accusations by certain Christian groups that movies flaunted immorality; the idea was that if the industry censored itself, the government would leave them alone. As the person appointed to this task, Joseph Breen was in many ways the most powerful man in Hollywood, the final arbitrator of what could and could not be shown. In an earlier battle, Breen had forced Walt Disney to remove an udder from an animated cow, afraid such a sight might prove too suggestive to Americans of all ages who enjoyed milk. Specific words were prohibited, such as *cripes, fanny, Gawd, goose, hell, madame, SOB, son of a,* and *whore,* as well as all traveling-salesmen and farmer's-daughter jokes, no matter how sanitized. Breen also dreamed up the iron-clad formula that in any love scene at least two feet out of four must be firmly on the floor—giving way among the writers to a standing joke, so to speak, of various sexual positions that would not violate the ban. After viewing *Three Comrades*, Joseph Breen suggested that several scenes might be refilmed so that it would appear that Germany's problems were due to the Communists rather than the Nazis. Louis B. Mayer was happy to agree.

But Joe Mankiewicz stubbornly refused. He said he would not make any cuts or changes, and that he would in fact resign loudly and publicly from the studio if any Nazi were allowed to tamper with his film. Louis B. Mayer hated to offend Germany, but he hated even more to lose one of his most prominent producers—and in this case he bucked both the Nazi and the American censor to side with Joe Mankiewicz. When Scott heard about this, he was so moved that for a moment he forgot his bitter feud. The following day, in a great splurge of enthusiasm, he threw his arms around Mankiewicz in the MGM commissary and kissed him. Unfortunately, the original anti-Nazi theme of the script had already been watered down, transforming it into a more conventional love story instead. Anti-Semitism was as much an accepted fact of life in the United States as it was in Germany, and Jews such as Joe Mankiewicz and Louis B. Mayer had to be careful not to rock the boat.

Scott and Sheilah went together to the premiere of *Three Comrades* in June 1938. They dressed in their best evening clothes and entered the theater by the front door this time rather than the side, drifting through an ocean of celebrities and screaming fans.

"At least they've kept my beginning," Scott whispered to Sheilah when the movie began. But as the reels played, Scott slumped deeper into his seat. As he watched the ending, she heard him murmur sadly, "They changed even that." He was inconsolable. Later that night at Sheilah's home, she was startled when he suddenly punched the wall hard with his fist. "That s.o.b.," he cried. "My God, doesn't he know what he's done?"

For Scott it seemed that all his hopes for Hollywood had come crashing down around him. He disappeared the next day on one of his three-day drunks, pouring gin down his throat until he made himself violently ill; Sheilah did not see him until after the round-the-clock nurses and the vomiting and the drying out. Already the cycle was familiar to her.

As it happened, *Three Comrades* was the closest thing to success Fitzgerald was ever to know as a Hollywood screenwriter. For the first and final time, Scott saw his name appear briefly on the magical surface of a movie screen, with credit for the script given equally to F. Scott Fitzgerald and E. E. Paramore.

11

INFIDELITY

... I'm through. From now on I go nowhere and see no one because the work is hard as hell, at least for me, and I've lost ten pounds. So farewell, Miriam Hopkins, who leans *so* close when she talks, so long, Claudette Colbert, as yet unencountered, mysterious Garbo, glamorous Dietrich, exotic Shirley Temple—you will never know me ... There is nothing left, girls, but to believe in reincarnation and carry on.

—F. Scott Fitzgerald, in a letter
soon after arriving in Hollywood

IN FEBRUARY 1938, the producer Hunt Stromberg called Scott into his office, paced the floor restlessly, sucked on his pipe, and then uttered a single tantalizing word: "infidelity!" It was a subject he wished Fitzgerald to consider. Then after a meaningful pause, he added a name: "Joan Crawford!"

Scott was being offered an assignment rather than an assignation. This was all Stromberg would tell him on their first meeting—infidelity and Joan Crawford, a concept and a star. His job was to connect these two intangibles and dream up a movie. It was a common Stromberg strategy to get a writer's attention with such a ploy, a few key words to start the creative juices flowing. Later he gave Scott a short story entitled *Infidelity* by Ursula Parrott, but he made it clear that Fitzgerald was free to let his imagination run wild.

Scott was intrigued. Hunt Stromberg was important at MGM, a producer who had more prestige than Joe Mankiewicz and for whom others in Scott's circle had worked in the past, including Dorothy Parker, Alan Campbell, and Frances and Albert Hackett. In appearance Stromberg was a tall and eccentric man whose upward extension ended in an untidy shock of hair. He walked about the studio with an abstracted air in three-piece suits and round-lens glasses, looking more like a professor from Heidelberg than a Hollywood producer. He was notoriously messy, holding script conferences in a heavy cloud of pipe smoke, pacing back and forth in his office with his shoe laces often dragging on the floor. He had a large collection of pipes, but he managed to keep none of them lit for long; and so he fussed and sucked and tamped and fiddled, and left a trail of wooden matches in his wake. Generally he tossed the matches toward the ashtray on his desk from wherever he happened to be standing in the room, but his aim was not good and the flaming missiles might end up anywhere. A month earlier, one of Stromberg's flying matches had set fire to a chair in which Dorothy Parker was sitting nearly comatose with boredom; she was nearly asleep and perhaps the fire under her chair was not entirely accidental.

For Scott, Hunt Stromberg represented a fresh start and his spirits soared. He easily forgot Monkeybitch and his bad experience with *Three Comrades*. Now he loved Hollywood once again and everything was going to be wonderful. "This time I have the best producer in Hollywood, a fine showman who keeps me from any amateur errors, and I hope to finish the picture alone," he wrote enthusiastically to the parents of his daughter's best friend, Peaches Finney. And in another letter to Max Perkins: "I am writing a new Crawford picture, called *Infidelity*. Though based on a magazine story, it is practically an original. I like the work and have a better producer than before—Hunt Stromberg—a sort of one-finger Thalberg, without Thalberg's scope, but with his intense power of work and his absorption in his job."

After Joe Mankiewicz, Stromberg seemed a producer sent from heaven; to compare his new boss to the romantic figure of Irving Thalberg, even missing nine fingers, was for Scott high praise. He set to work with enthusiasm and on February 22 completed a memo for Stromberg detailing his concept of the story and a precise schedule of how long it would take him to write the script. He concluded: "My plan is to work about half the time at the studio but the more tense and difficult stuff I do better at home away from interruptions. Naturally I'll always be within call and at your disposal." It was unusual in the thirties for a screenwriter to ask to work at home, almost brazen; nine out of ten producers would have said no. Jack Warner often said about writers that he liked "to see the bodies." It was a widespread sentiment among the studio bosses that writers were a lazy bunch who drank too much and needed to be kept at their desks under watchful supervision. Fitzgerald's happiness was complete when Stromberg agreed to let him work at home. It seemed to him a sign of respect for his stature as an artist. Scott much preferred pacing about his bungalow in an old dressing gown with a stubby pencil and pad of yellow paper to making a forced appearance at the writer's building at MGM, the dismal "Iron Lung." And if perchance he became "ill," no one would know.

Scott approached the new movie in an organized fashion, drawing up charts and lists of characters. Joan Crawford was to portray Althea Gilbert, a woman whose husband Nicholas, "a Cooper–Gable type," has an affair with an old girlfriend from his past, Iris Jones—"an attractive girl, not strikingly pretty, presentable, very sweet and serious." Scott wanted to present Iris Jones not as a siren seductress but as a girl Nicholas might have married except for an accident of fate; the movie would show there was a thin and often arbitrary line which drew people into marriage with one person rather than another. Under the right circumstances, he believed nearly anybody could stray. "In everyone's lives there are locked doors," he wrote in his notes.

"Even married couples are not so possessed that the chance opening of these doors may not lead to trouble."

Scott saw Joan Crawford on the MGM lot and he went over to say hello. "I'm going to write your next picture," he told her pleasantly.

The star smiled grandly at the news, then fixed the author with her most smoldering stare. "Good," she said, "Write hard, Mr. Fitzgerald. Write hard." That evening, Scott threw his head back to laugh as he repeated this incident to Sheilah—it was one of the few times she heard him actually laugh out loud. Joan Crawford had a huge ego and she was a terrible actress, but Scott refused to be discouraged. The success of his film depended on her and he was determined to find a way to accent her virtues and minimize her faults. With this in mind, he set about to study Joan Crawford in minute detail. He had three of her movies run off in a Metro screening room—*The Divorcée, Possessed,* and *Chained*—and he dissected each film carefully. He drew up charts of how the action progressed and how many pages of script it took to reach various cornerstones of the plot, but most of all he scrutinized the star.

"Don't like her smiling to herself—she will ham everything like that," Scott noted. "Why do her lips have to be glistening wet?" After viewing the three movies, he realized that writing for her would not be easy: "Giving Joan such stage direction as 'insecurely' or 'with private reservations' or 'Cynically' are like giving matches to a baby. With Joan it all comes out as a leer— she cannot fake or bluff or pretend to."

Possibly he studied Joan Crawford more thoroughly than anyone has ever done before or since. She would be his instrument, the violin to give voice to the music he wrote for her, though, unfortunately, she was not exactly a Stradivarius. "She gets too excited when she listens," he observed. On the other hand: "Very good when she is tired. When she is tired and bored her vitality shines through." He concluded: "Her best expression is sadness." But he must be careful not take this sadness too far because he hated the tremulous quality of her voice when she cried—fake Hollywood tears if he ever heard them. On March 11 he summed up his findings in a letter to Gerald Murphy:

I am writing a picture called *Infidelity* for Joan Crawford.
Writing for her is difficult. She can't change her emotions in the
middle of a scene without going through a sort of Jekyll and Hyde
contortion of the face, so that when one wants to indicate that she is
going from joy to sorrow, one must cut away and then cut back.
Also, you can never give her such a stage direction as "telling a lie,"
because if you did, she would practically give a representation of
Benedict Arnold selling West Point to the British.

Unfortunately Joan Crawford was only the beginning of
Scott's problems with *Infidelity*: He had a more serious battle
looming with Joseph Breen, the industry censor from the
dreaded Hays Office. Scott's friends knew very well the problems he would encounter trying to write a story that dealt honestly with adultery, but they were afraid to tell him. "We felt so
desperately for Scott," Frances and Albert Hackett later recalled,
"because we knew it couldn't be done. They wouldn't allow it
just because it was about infidelity. About the only infidelity you
could have in pictures in those days was a man taking another
man's wife to lunch. We didn't tell Scott that it was impossible
because we couldn't bear to break his heart. He was enthusiastic
about his script; he wanted very much to do it. It was the first
thing he really came to life on."

Scott continued to enjoy working on the screenplay and he
liked Hunt Stromberg, but he was finding the atmosphere of
Hollywood increasingly unpleasant. The movie industry seemed
to him "a jungle. . . full of prowling beasts of prey." This was a
town which placed "an emphasis as in a mining camp on the
lower virtues." Late in the winter, Sheilah took Scott to the
Academy Awards presentations of 1938, held at an elaborate dinner ceremony at the Coconut Grove. Scott came along out of
curiosity, and to keep Sheilah company, but he found the self-
puffery of the event absurd. The producers, directors, and actors
strutted about as if they had accomplished something meaningful (like *Gatsby*, perhaps, or *A Farewell to Arms*) instead of their
slick panderings to popular taste—children's tales, really, that
were dressed up for adults. As the speeches droned on, Scott
took out his notebook and jotted down an idle poem:

THE BIG ACADEMY DINNER

The men were wearier and wearier,
    The women were thinner and thinner,
The speeches drearier and drearier
    At the Big Academy Dinner.

Writers were more and more pensive
    Except for an occasional beginner,
Women were horribly expensive
    At the Big Academy Dinner.

At the Metro-Goldwyn table
    Winner sat next to winner
And cheered at much as they were able
    At the Big Academy Dinner.

Garbo, the lovely barber,
    Cooker, the tall mule skinner,
Had sailed into harbour
    At the Big Academy Dinner.

But also the pimp and crook,
    Also the pious sinner,
And none of them got the hook
    At the Big Academy Dinner.

May the peritone cause me pain,
    May ulcers puncture my inner
Tubes if I go again
    To the Big Academy Dinner.

Infidelity was a subject more tranquil to imagine in fiction than in fact. Scott always liked to appear in public with the top girl that all the other men wanted, but this had a dangerous side to it as well. "I was on fire for sex most of my waking hours," Sheilah recalled in later years, "and men knew it. I exuded an odor of sex more compelling than a mating call." It was a call Fitzgerald was determined would remain unanswered by anyone except himself. But this was not easy in a place like Hollywood, land of the lower virtues. He must be constantly vigilant.

The movie stars were the most worrisome of all. Scott had a particular hatred for Errol Flynn, who was always after Sheilah, calling her up, pestering her for dates. And also Randolph Scott, who had the nerve once to appear at Sheilah's door at four in the morning, ostensibly to return a bathing suit she had left at the beach house in Santa Monica he shared with Cary Grant. Fitzgerald worried what this bathing suit was doing left behind at such a beach house; he worried endlessly, not only about the present but the past, and he continued to pry from Sheilah any details he could learn of her disturbing early life.

Scott was fascinated, and very shocked, when she told him about a movie producer who had followed her about the *Aquitania* on her 1933 crossing from England to New York, and then one night burst into her cabin to beg for "quick relief." This was loathsome, and just the sort of thing you might expect from a movie producer, but it made such a good story that Scott wrote it down, thinking he might use it in a book one day. He continued to mine Sheilah's memories, sifting and sorting through her past; if something nasty had happened, he wanted every last detail.

Scott was jealous not only of men but of any person or thing in her life which threatened his dominance. "Life was something you dominated if you were any good," he wrote in "The Crack-Up." It was a philosophy which doomed him to constant anxiety and devious machinations. In March, Scott set about to guard Sheilah from the influence of the only woman friend she had made during her five years in America, Margaret Brainard, who lived in New York.

Sheilah's friendship with Margaret Brainard began in a Manhattan bar soon after she arrived from England in 1933. Sheilah was waiting for John Wheeler, and as she sat in the bar she ordered five drinks, whiskey sours, to be set up in a line on the counter in front of her. It was a serious spectacle, almost F. Scott Fitzgeraldian in nature. Margaret Brainard, sitting nearby, was surprised to observe a young woman who was clearly such a great drunk. But as she watched more closely it became apparent that Sheilah had ordered the drinks only for the bright red maraschino cherry in each glass; she was not touching the whiskey at all. Margaret laughed. It was absurd— very much Sheilah, of course, to take what she wanted, the bright red cherry, and throw away the rest—all with an appealing innocence of how things were generally done. The two women began to talk and discovered they had much in common. As usual, Sheilah was juggling several complicated love affairs at just that moment, and so apparently was Margaret. Sheilah had never confided to a woman before about such matters and it was very satisfying to find a kindred soul; by the time John Wheeler appeared the two young women had decided that they were great friends.

In the winter of 1938 Sheilah was delighted to receive a letter from Margaret saying she had just landed a job at the newly opened Saks Fifth Avenue in Beverly Hills and would arrive in California at the end of the week. That evening, Sheilah couldn't wait to tell Scott the news; she recounted the funny story of the five whiskey sours, and how Margaret had been so warm to her when she first came to America. Sheilah had already written back to invite her friend to stay with her during her first few weeks in Los Angeles, and she was looking forward to showing Margaret the sights of the city and introducing her to her friends. Sheilah was so bubbly with her news that she became aware only gradually that Scott was very thoughtful as he sat listening to her, and not his normally enthusiastic self at all.

"When will she be here?" he asked quietly.

"She arrives Saturday."

Scott delicately changed the subject. But a few days later, on Wednesday night, he unexpectedly returned to it again. "I've been thinking about Margaret staying with you, Sheilo. Are you sure that's a good idea?"

"Oh, of course," she said, surprised he could imagine otherwise. Again Scott dropped the subject but on Thursday night he said that he had decided to take Sheilah away to Santa Barbara for the weekend.

She blinked at him, not quite comprehending. "Scott, we can't.

You know Margaret is coming on Saturday. I'm going down to meet her and bring her here."

"But I would like to go away. I'm tired," he complained. "I must get away. I could use a weekend out of town—"

"But Margaret—"

"Well, you know, I think Margaret would be happier in her own apartment. These last few days I've been looking for one for her."

Sheilah could hardly believe what she was hearing. Scott explained that he had spent the past few days finding an apartment for Margaret near Saks Fifth Avenue; he had paid the deposit so there could be no further discussion of the matter. He even presented Sheilah with the key. She was flabbergasted; it was almost beyond her comprehension that Scott should take time off from his busy schedule to search for and rent an apartment for her friend. She tried to tell him that Margaret would be terribly hurt when Sheilah was not at the train station to meet her.

"No, I don't think so," Scott said firmly. "As a matter of fact, she can move in the moment she arrives. It's all set." Then his voice became persuasively gentle: "If she were with you all the time, Sheilah, perhaps I couldn't see you as much. And I do want to get away this weekend. Now that she has an apartment, we can go. You can leave this key for her with a note."

Scott had touched upon a delicate point and the question of being free to see one another gave Sheilah pause. Unfortunately, it was necessary to put up a facade of respectability. Once already a nosy neighbor, a woman, had been shocked to see Scott leave one morning from Sheilah's house after clearly having spent the night. The neighbor complained to Sheilah's maid, Christine, that she was on the verge of calling in "the chief of public morals." Scott and Sheilah had laughed about this at the time, and Scott had suggested that the answer to their problem was to get two houses side by side with a connecting tunnel underground. But though it was funny, the incident came as a reminder to both Scott and Sheilah that they must at least pretend to respect society's rules. And so the argument that Margaret Brainard might interfere with their nocturnal visits was at least partly convincing.

As usual, Sheilah gave in to what Scott wanted; she left a note
for her friend and went off with Scott for the weekend in Santa
Barbara. It was awkward and Sheilah had to do some patching
up with Margaret when she got back to town. It was only many
years later that Sheilah understood that Scott was afraid some
late-night woman-to-woman talk might have gone against
him—that Margaret would have seen too plainly the truth of the
situation: Scott was an alcoholic, he was married, he would
never divorce Zelda, and from a practical point of view Sheilah
was wasting her time on him.

Later that winter, Scott found an even more urgent cause for
jealousy: John Wheeler was coming to Los Angeles for two days
as part of a nationwide tour of newspapers that subscribed to the
NANA syndication.

"You're not going to see him are you?" Scott asked.

"Of course I am, Scott. I have to see him. He's my boss."

But John Wheeler had also been Sheilah's lover and as the
time approached for his visit, Scott grew visibly more gloomy
and apprehensive. Sheilah tried to reassure him that she no
longer had any romantic feelings for Wheeler, but Scott refused
to be assured. He became so impossible about the visit that she
could not imagine what she was going to do; she hated for Scott
to be jealous, but at the same time she could not afford to offend
her boss. Scott was bothered by this fact as well, that Wheeler
might have any kind of hold over her; he wished to be the only
one in that position in Sheilah's life.

Sheilah was in a bind. Then on the night before Wheeler
arrived, she came up with a solution: She would check into the
Good Samaritan Hospital and have a small operation for a
female problem that a doctor had been urging her to undergo at
her convenience for a number of months. It was a cunning
answer to the problem and Scott was touched. He drove Sheilah
to the hospital in a more loving mood than she had seen him in
since the specter of Wheeler's visit had arisen between them.
When she awoke from the ether she found a note in Scott's
handwriting on a memo pad by her bed: "So glad it went well,
my blessed. Will be back when you wake up in the late after-

noon." And below this: "Second note. I am here—it is 5:30—and you are getting rapidly out of the ether and very sick. You asked me several questions and said you couldn't believe they did it while you were asleep. I love you and I am coming back in the morning quite early and sit with you. It has been a day for all of us and I must go eat and get a bit of sleep. Thank God it is over and you're well again."

Scott came the next day to sit by Sheilah's bed and watch over her as she slept. Three days passed in this fashion and by the time she was allowed out of the hospital, John Wheeler had come and gone.

Shortly after the surgery at the Good Samaritan Hospital, Scott told Sheilah that Zelda wished to see him and he must go east. He did not say how long he would be gone, nor would he discuss Zelda or his feelings about the trip—only that as usual he would not write to Sheilah while he was away. As with the earlier visits, it did not occur to him that Sheilah might have any cause to be upset; after all, Zelda was his wife.

Despite Scott's pretense of spontaneity, the trip had been carefully planned, and it came about as a result of his idea rather than at Zelda's request. Sheilah might represent his new life in California, but the old life still had priority—Zelda and Scottie both, his legitimate family that required his support. If he were ever inclined to forget this fact, there were always Zelda's many letters to remind him, full of ornate and often maudlin memories that continued to arrive in his mailbox at least once a week. "I am yours forever—whether you still want me or not—and I love you," she had written recently. "I think of boat houses in Atlanta with scaffolding and big dead moons and a drink behind the boats. I thought I was happy, or, at least, there was some pleasurable sense of things being in the world to conquer. . . . You have been so good to me. My Do-Do. I wish I had not caused so much disaster. But I know you will be happy someday."

These letters filled Scott with alternating currents of guilt, claustrophobia, sadness, rage. In early March, he wrote Dr. Robert Carroll that he was planning to take Scottie to Virginia Beach over the Easter vacation and have Zelda meet them there, making something of a family reunion out of the occasion. In his letter to Dr. Carroll, Scott once again made it clear that as far as he was concerned, his marriage was over:

> I have, of course, my eternal hope that a miracle will happen to Zelda, that in this new incarnation events may tend to stabilize her even more than you hope. With my shadow removed, perhaps she will find something in life to care for. . . Certainly the outworn pretense that we can ever come together again is better for being shed. There is simply too much of the past between us. When that mist falls—at a dinner table, or between two pillows—no knight errant can traverse its immense distance. The mainsprings are gone.

Scott always took great pains in his letters to Dr. Carroll to dazzle the psychiatrist with his skill as a writer. The doctor, after all, knew every secret of his marriage and to some extent acted as a referee between himself and Zelda, and—more delicate still—between Scott and Zelda's family. Scott very much wanted the good doctor on his side. He ended by planting a broad hint that there *might* one day come into his life a woman other than Zelda:

> And if the aforesaid miracle should take place, I might again try to find a life of my own, as opposed to this casual existence of many rooms and many doors that are not mine. So long as she is helpless, I'd never leave her or ever let her have a sense that she was deserted. . . I know scarcely a beautiful woman of Zelda's generation who has come up to 1938 unscathed.
>
> For myself, I work hard and take care of myself. . . If it ever comes to a point when a divorce should be in the picture, I think I would rather have you [than Zelda's family] watch over Zelda's interests.

In late March, Scott flew to Baltimore, where he met Scottie, and then together the father and daughter made their way to Norfolk, Virginia, where a nurse from Highland Hospital would deliver Zelda. On the train south, Scott let his daughter read the first 104 pages of *Infidelity*; he had only twenty pages more to finish the screenplay and he was proud of his work. At Norfolk, they met up with Zelda and the reunited Fitzgerald family made their way together to the Cavalier Hotel in Virginia Beach. The languid resort hotel had a country club atmosphere and the Fitzgeralds set about with the other guests to enjoy the spring sunshine. But there was a crack running through their small family, a broken mainspring, and this was not destined to be a happy Easter. Zelda might take a nostalgic tone about family life in her letters, but to experience these domestic idylls in the flesh was another matter.

Zelda did not look good. In the twenties, Gerald Murphy had observed that her beauty was "not legitimate at all. It was in her eyes. . . if she looked like anything it was an American Indian." Her beauty came from grace and vitality, something intangible which lay beneath her features; when the intangibles changed, her physical appearance was transformed as well. Now her face was craggy and immobile, like a wooden Indian's, and her eyes had the sharp predatory look of a hawk. She was dangerously on edge. She became unreasonably irritated first with her golf and tennis pros at the hotel, and then later with Scottie, tensely correcting her daughter over every small matter, then attempting to hide her irritation beneath a saccharine tone of voice. Scottie wouldn't stand for it. The sixteen-year-old girl had enough trouble dealing with the obsessive demands of her father; to have her mother jump on her was just too much. Scottie spoke back to her mother sharply, and Zelda became livid with rage. Clearly this must be Scott's fault. *He* had taught the girl to hate her mother. She was certain they were both ganging up against her. Zelda stormed off to Scott to report accusingly how badly their daughter had behaved to her. But Scott was on edge himself and instead of pacifying her in a calm, reasonable voice, there was a scene.

For Scott this was unbearable; Zelda and Scottie and himself, the saddest family there could ever be. It was simply too much for a hard-working man who only wanted to be left in peace so he could write and earn the money that everyone wanted— money for Zelda's doctors, money for Scottie's school, all of it draining away his remaining energy and resources. Scott found a dozen excuses to call downstairs and ask for a bottle of gin, each one as good as the other. He told himself that any man would drink under the circumstances; you would almost have to be crazy not to. He had wisely avoided liquor during his earlier trips to see Zelda in September and over Christmas; now with gin in the picture, what might have been a small family squabble turned into a full-scale disaster.

Things went downhill fast. Zelda was furious to see her husband reeling with liquor. It seemed so unfair that for years the world had called her insane and put her into an asylum when Scott with only a few glasses of gin was clearly more a lunatic than she could ever be. *He* was the crazy one; people should see what he was like when he was drunk. All at once it seemed immensely important to Zelda that the world know the exact truth about who was insane and who was not. She ran up and down the corridors of the hotel and knocked urgently on every door to warn the startled guests that there was a dangerous madman on the loose—Scott Fitzgerald. Zelda sounded the alarm. She pleaded that someone please call a doctor quick to send her maniac husband back to the hospital where he belonged, and when the doctor arrived she nearly managed to convince him that Scott was insane. If there was any grim humor to the situation, Scott did not see it. He complained later to Dr. Carroll that for a few desperate moments at the Cavalier Hotel, only he and Scottie knew the truth—that Zelda was the mad one, not him—though of course what the teenage girl thought of both of her parents is open to conjecture.

Scott managed to straighten things out, but it was a sordid business, very undignified for an author of his stature. He was so furious at his wife's behavior that he continued drinking past what "would have amounted to a two day bat"—as he put it to Dr. Carroll. He went beyond even the classic three-day binge that he once mentioned to Max Perkins, all the way into one of his epic drunks where at last he could drink no more, and he would require intravenous feeding and the care of a doctor and nurses.

Meanwhile Sheilah waited in California, not knowing when Scott would return and imagining all sorts of things—though nothing as colorful as what in fact was occurring in Virginia Beach. She received a single telegram from Scott on March 25, the day he left, wired to her from the airport at Tucson, Arizona:

US STOP THE SORT OF THING YOU READ ABOUT = SCOTT

It was charming, typically Scott, but the silence and long days which followed were not reassuring. Sheilah was not certain whether Scott was sleeping with his wife; he was not, as it happened, but since he told her nothing about his marriage she had no way of knowing. Still, it was not the idea of sex that made Sheilah jealous, for in this single area she could not imagine that Scott should prefer another woman to herself. Sheilah suffered in a different way, from being left out of a past she never knew, and a general sense of inferiority that she was not as brilliant or witty as she imagined Zelda to be, and that Scott would never love her as much. Most of all, his continual desertions made her feel that she was only the "other woman," with no rights in his life.

Sheilah wanted more. She wanted a husband and children, a family of her own. Although Scott was not aware of her true age, she certainly was; she was thirty-three years old and believed that this miracle would never happen to her if she waited much longer. Over the past months, she had allowed herself to fantasize that she and Scott might one day marry and have children. And if marriage was truly impossible, she told him she was willing to throw convention to the winds and have his child out of wedlock. But Scott was plainly shocked, not only at the thought of flouting conventional mores, but that anyone should believe he possessed the time or energy for an additional child, legitimate or otherwise. It was tough enough for Scott to deal long distance with the family he already had. He was so touchy about the subject that Sheilah did not dare bring it up again.

She often dreamed of Zelda, her rival, though she never told Scott. In her dreams, Zelda appeared as a dark and solemn figure who stared at her with insane eyes and never said a word. Her stare was infinitely reproachful, filled with hatred and silent accusations. Sheilah endowed Zelda's nightmare image with all her own primal fear of madness, and she woke always full of dread. Now that Scott was away, Sheilah dreamed of Zelda even more often. She wondered when Scott would return and deliver her from this evil image.

Empty days passed in which she told herself again and again how foolish it was to be involved with a married man. Then on April 3 she received a telegram from Washington, D.C.:

ARRIVING MONDAY AT NOON AFTER A WRETCHED WEEK DON'T MEET ME
PLEASE I LOVE YOU SO MUCH = SCOTT

Sheilah's heart leapt at the news and her own wretched week was quickly forgotten. Scott was coming back, and he loved her—nothing else mattered. Then he telephoned from the airport and he did not sound wretched at all. "Sheilo!" he cried gaily, "We're going to be married!"

For a moment Sheilah hardly dared to speak. "We're going to be married?" she echoed.

"I'm getting a divorce," he told her excitedly. "I'll tell you all about it when I see you. Wait for me—I'll be right over."

Sheilah hung up the telephone in a happy daze. It seemed that all her wishes were about to come true. She sat down at her desk and wrote out her new name on a piece of paper to see how it would look: *Mrs. F. Scott Fitzgerald*. She had to write it several times just to believe it was real. But when Scott appeared at her house she saw the true situation at a glance: his face was flushed, his hair disheveled, and his clothes untidy.

"Baby!" he cried. He held her in a bear hug and she smelled the liquor on his breath.

"Are you getting a divorce?" she demanded angrily. "Have you told her?"

"Yes, I am, I am!" He was emphatic, though a moment later he admitted that no, he had not actually told Zelda yet—but he would. . . oh, would he ever! Sheilah wiggled free of Scott's drunken embrace and he began to pace the floor, back and forth, his hands in motion, telling her of his wretched week. He was through with Zelda, absolutely through. "Do you know what she did this time? Tried to get me committed. Called a doctor and said I was insane and should be put away."

Scott lit a cigarette with trembling fingers; he could barely keep the match in place long enough to inhale. "Back in a minute," he said slyly, and then dashed out to his car. When he returned he was more flushed and more emphatic than ever. He told her again all about the unbelievable insults he had endured in Virginia Beach, and how he was going to get even. He hardly even glanced at Sheilah to see the bleak disappointment in her face. She sank into a chair, more drained than angry. She knew that there was no marriage in her immediate future, and it was very painful that he should taunt her with what she wanted most.

"They'll find out at the studio you're drinking and you'll lose your job," she told him coldly.

Scott put his finger to his lips. "Don't tell anyone!" he said dramatically.

She got rid of him at last, saying he should go back to The Garden of Allah and sleep it off. Scott somehow managed to drive down Sheilah's steep hill and maneuver the short distance along Sunset Boulevard to his bungalow. Then someone at the hotel phoned to invite him to the hotel bar—a dark and depressing bar that the guests generally avoided. Scott did something to his shoulder in the parking lot that he could not quite remember. For a man in his condition, a parking lot contained as many perils as a highway. At two o'clock in the morning Sheilah was awakened by the sound of her doorbell ringing urgently. She hurried downstairs from her bed and found Scott on her doorstep leaning against the bell. He looked terrible. He was clutching his shoulder, and there was a taxi on the street behind him with its engine running.

"I think I've broken my shoulder," he said thickly.

Sheilah threw a coat over her nightgown and steered Scott back into the taxi, telling the driver to take them immediately to the Queen of Angels Hospital. Scott protested loudly that he wasn't about to go to any hospital. "Stop babying me!" he slurred. He assured her that in his time he had broken every bone in his body, and this small mishap, a lousy broken shoulder, was nothing for a guy like him. But Sheilah was in no mood for nonsense. She told him plainly that if he ever wanted to see her again, he would go to the hospital and get his shoulder set.

He was impossible. He whined and complained about doctors and hospitals and how he would not be babied, but she managed to get him inside the hospital at last. However, Scott took one look at the emergency room with all its cold apparatus of life and death, and with a sly look on his face he made a sudden dash for the exit. Sheilah ran after him and would not let him leave. "Scott," she cried, "You can't go, you've got to have this set. Stop behaving so stupidly!"

As they stood arguing, a tall nun, the superintendent of the emergency room, came over to see what was wrong. She was dressed in a white robe and conveyed a sense of higher authority. "Sister, he wants to go, he won't stay," Sheilah complained, close to tears. "He has to have his shoulder set."

The nun took a very good look at the untidy spectacle of Scott Fitzgerald and said simply, "Come." Scott obeyed meekly; the lingering ashes of an Irish Catholic childhood could not resist such a summons. Sheilah sat in the reception area wondering what was to be done with such a man. Could she leave him? She hated Scott when he was drunk like this. But what would he do without her? Despite every rational instinct, she cared what happened to him.

Scott had overdramatized his injury. He did not have a broken shoulder after all, only a minor sprain. He was unaccountably meek as she took him in a taxi back to The Garden of Allah; the regal and authoritative figure of the nun had apparently curbed any further rebellion. Riding in the cab, Sheilah pleaded with him to stop his drinking. It was horrible, she said, degrading for an intelligent man to treat himself this way. Scott listened contritely to her lecture. "All right. I'll get the doctor," he agreed. And then he added with an unconvincing echo of old pride: "I can quit whenever I want. You know that, don't you?"

"I know it, Scott," Sheilah lied.

As always, he warned her not to telephone or try to see him during the period of drying out. His sense of drama never abated for an instant; in hushed tones he painted his coming days of detoxification as torture straight from the Spanish Inquisition—but he would do it, because he was strong. Three days passed in which Sheilah heard nothing from him. She had trouble sleeping, thinking about Scott far into the early hours of the morning, tossing about the question of her difficult lover. There were clear choices to be made: She could leave him, or she could stay. Sheilah decided at last that she would run the course; as much as she detested the bad brownie, she loved the sober and gentle Fitzgerald even more.

On the afternoon of the fourth day he sent her a box of flowers, and that evening he telephoned. "Sheilo, when can I see you?" His voice was weak and plaintive. "Can you come and see me now? I want to see you now, Sheilo."

She was ready for him. At The Garden of Allah she found Scott almost deathly pale but dressed neatly in a pink shirt and jaunty polka-dot tie; by now she had learned to read his sobriety by how carefully or carelessly he was dressed. Tonight he was loving and wan and all soft edges. Sheilah said she didn't want him to drink again, not ever. It frightened her.

He replied ever so gently: Don't let us talk about it.

She was used to his evasions and let the matter drop for now. It did not matter because Sheilah had a plan. She had little education, she was not in his league at all. Perhaps she had been to bed with too many men; certainly she had told outrageous lies. Nevertheless, though she knew she was quite a terrible person, she had decided that she was going to save Scott Fitzgerald.

12

MALIBU

I will cure him. I will take him away from the Garden of Allah, away from his friends and the temptation of the bar; I will take him to the sea.

—Sheilah, writing in 1958

THREE DAYS AFTER SCOTT'S DRUNKEN return to California in April 1938, while he was still in the care of nurses, Sheilah pointed her blue Ford westward on Sunset Boulevard and drove by herself to where the long boulevard finally gave out and the ocean began. She made a right turn onto the Pacific Coast Highway and headed north along the edge of the coastline to Malibu. She planned to rent a house on the ocean. She had decided that Scott stood no chance against alcohol in the smoke-filled rooms of The Garden of Allah, surrounded by old friends and ironic conversation. She envisioned for Scott a cure of sunlight and sand, crisp ocean breezes, and the soothing sound of waves crashing against the shore.

Sheilah herself worshiped these elemental forces. She had

fallen in love with the ocean many years earlier while still in the orphanage; each summer the older children had been taken to the seashore to stay for a week at the elegant home of a trustee, to sleep on clean beds, eat good food—sweet buns spooned full of jam—and play by the edge of the surf with no bells or routine to disturb them. The ocean was forever bound in Lily's mind to food and sunlight and delicious things. Now in California, Sheilah loved nothing better than to swim in the surf and then lie afterward all shivery wet on her towel, offering herself completely to the warm rays of the sun. It was her pagan ritual. The beach had always been a source of renewal for Sheilah, and she hoped for Scott it would be the same.

She found a white clapboard cottage for rent among the sand dunes at 114 Malibu Beach. The house seemed transported from New England, as if some MGM cyclone had carried it from the dunes of Cape Cod to this Oz world of California. There were green shutters on the windows, a widow's walk on the second floor, and a small fragrant garden to one side that was entered through a white latticed archway. Colored lanterns were hanging in the garden from the latticed archway and it all seemed very romantic to her. Across the highway, the Malibu hills were emerald green, fields of long grass swaying in the wind, dotted everywhere with the yellow of wild mustard, rising upward sharply from the coast toward the high meadows above. There were two seasons in California, green and gold; a time would come in the midsummer when the Malibu hills would turn overnight wheat brown, dry as tinder. Sheilah loved all this; she wanted to inhale everything about the landscape, the ocean and hills, through her pores into her soul. She found the inside of the house charming as well. There were four bedrooms, a sunroom, a dining room, and many vases filled with flowers. In the bright and tidy kitchen, she discovered a black woman baking cookies, filling the house with a warm and nostalgic aroma.

Everything about the cottage suggested health and domestic order. Scott could even save money by living here. The rent was two hundred dollars a month with a six-month lease, and Flora, the housekeeper, agreed to stay on for an additional fifty dollars. Even with Flora's salary, it added up to a fifty-dollar-a-month

savings from the three hundred dollars Scott paid for his bungalow at The Garden of Allah, not to mention the economy of staying home for meals. MGM was forty-five minutes away in
Culver City—perhaps a bit longer the way Scott drove—but this
was only slightly longer than Scott's commute from The Garden
of Allah. With four bedrooms, Sheilah might keep an office here
and visit evenings and weekends. The owner of the house was
someone Scott knew: Frank Case, the manager of the Algonquin
Hotel in New York, where the Round Table crowd had once
gathered so gaily for lunch. This also seemed auspicious.

Sheilah was already in love with the house. She imagined
Scott swimming in the ocean and becoming tan and healthy. It
would be a cozy life for two far from traffic and crowds. In the
evenings Scott might read poetry to her or they could simply listen to the waves crashing rhythmically against the sand. What
could be more romantic? Most of all it would be a real home for
them both.

"If Mr. Fitzgerald takes this place will you promise to keep the
cookie jars filled?" Sheilah asked the maid.

"Oh, yes, ma'am!" Flora said with a smile.

For Sheilah, this was the clincher—an endless cookie jar,
something Lily might have dreamed about while sneaking into
the kitchen at the orphanage. She decided to put the matter to
Scott the following day, when he was still weak from his binge
and in a repentant mood. She described the house in glowing
detail: the cookies, the widow's walk, and each sunny room. She
told Scott he would be able to work there, he could save money,
it would be perfect—and if he needed to be in town for any reason, of course he could always stay at her house on Kings Road.

"If you think so, Sheilah," Scott said quietly. At the moment he
was dysfunctional with his hangover and content to leave all
practical matters to her.

And so on an afternoon toward the end of April, Sheilah
picked up Scott in her car and helped him move his few belongings, mostly books and papers, from The Garden of Allah to the
cottage in Malibu. Scott had spent his life in hotels and rented
places and had accumulated little. Driving up the Pacific Coast
Highway, Sheilah stopped at a florist to fill every remaining

nook and cranny at the rear of her car with flowers for the new house. She never stopped to consider that this was her fantasy and not Scott's, that Scott in fact detested cut flowers and disliked the sun; he had a phobia about taking off his socks under any circumstances, certainly not to walk in the sand, and as far as the cookie jar went, he had in mind an entirely different source of sugar to satisfy his persistent need.

Scott Fitzgerald was the most determinedly pale individual ever to be marooned on Malibu shores. He had no intention to swim, or sunbathe, or roam with Sheilah with his cuffs rolled up along the edge of the ocean. He would not even dress the role, refusing to transform himself into a beachcomber in sandals or gaudy shirts. On the warmest summer day, Scott remained heroically aloof from the lure of the ocean, often in his old raincoat and battered hat, a woolen scarf around his neck, city shoes, and sweater.

Sheilah was astonished at Scott's resistance to the beach. Each day she began a battle of wills trying to get him in the ocean for a swim, but he always answered, "I'm too busy—I have work to do." She failed even to get him out of his heavy shoes and socks—and certainly it was one of the great pleasures of life to walk barefoot in the sand, or squiggle your toes in the shallow tide pools. "As a child I had a mysterious shyness about showing my feet," he confessed. Scott described a trip he had taken with his parents to the beach at Atlantic City when he was very young; he let them believe he was afraid to swim in the water when he wouldn't take off his shoes, but it was simply the prospect of bare feet that bothered him. The phobia remained as an adult and Sheilah now understood why Scott always kept his socks on when they made love. Sheilah didn't mind his eccentricities as much as his refusal to live out the healthy scenario she had planned for him.

Soon after the move to Malibu, Scott bought a Ping-Pong table and this became almost his only form of exercise. Fortunately, Scott's idea of Ping-Pong included pirouettes and much crossing of his eyes, and this made the game at least slightly more physical. There was also shadowboxing when he was in the mood, and sometimes Sheilah cajoled him into walking with her to the Malibu Inn, where he liked to play the football slot machines. The walks were a success—and Sheilah appreciated each small victory—but she was frustrated when he insisted on keeping to the shady side of the road. This was a man who needed the sunshine on his moonlike face. Sheilah was so physical herself, blond and full of sunlight, that she could not understand how Scott could resist such simple pleasures.

The exercise program did not turn out as she hoped, but at least Malibu was the start of a new domestic life together. Sheilah kept her house on Kings Road, but for all practical purposes she and Scott now lived together. During the day, Scott worked at home dressed in an old gray flannel bathrobe which was torn at the elbow and showed patches of the gray pullover sweater he always wore underneath. Scott often wrote in bed, as if he were an invalid. He kept a stubby pencil lodged behind each ear, and a row of fresh pencils lined up and ready in the breast pocket of his dressing gown. At the start of the day, Scott sharpened all these pencils by hand with a pen knife; they had to be just right, not too sharp because he wrote furiously fast, pressing down hard on the pages of his yellow legal pads. When the pages were full, he tore them off to float carelessly down around him. Scott's room was on the second floor off the widow's walk, and Sheilah sometimes saw him pacing on this narrow balcony deep in thought, his hair in disarray, the pockets of his old dressing gown bulging with at least two spare packs of cigarettes. Scott paced whenever he could not find an elusive word or phrase. He refused to use a dictionary or thesaurus — the perfect word would come in its own time, he assured Sheilah. And besides, once he opened a dictionary, his working day was shot for he would not be able to close the book for hours.

He ate eccentrically and less than Sheilah liked. Lunch was often nothing more than a few pieces of fudge and highly sweetened black coffee. For dinner he might ask Flora to cook him up a chocolate soufflé and a bowl of turtle soup. Sugar was the mainstay of every meal. Scott and Sheilah's life settled down into a quiet pattern. Each day she drove into town to have lunch at one of the studios, and then returned to Malibu to write up her gossip into the latest edition of "Hollywood Today—A Gadabout's Notebook." She tried not to bother Scott as he roamed the top floor in his tattered dressing gown. On Sundays they often sat together in the living room listening to the world news on Frank Case's big console radio. Terrible things were happening in Europe. They heard radio broadcasts of Hitler's speeches, angry German words which filled the beach cottage, and then the thunderous reply of great crowds chanting, *"Sieg Heil! Sieg Heil! Sieg Heil!"*. . . the drone of these distant voices was like the surf breaking outside their window. It was hard for Sheilah to believe there was a world which existed outside the snug reality of their beach house. Scott hated Hitler and could barely sit still for the speeches. "They're going to do it again. They're going to have another war—and we'll be in it, too," he told Sheilah one afternoon. His green eyes were ablaze; he seemed strangely energized by the prospect ahead. He lit a cigarette and said, "I'd like to fly over there and assassinate Hitler before he starts another war. I'd do it, too, by God!"

As a literary animal, Scott was certainly remembering Pierre's plan to remain in Moscow to assassinate Napoleon in *War and Peace*—a favorite novel of Scott's which he often reread for inspiration before starting something serious of his own. One of Scott's personal disappointments was that he had missed the last war, and in 1936 he complained about the fact in an article for *Esquire* titled "I Didn't Get Over." It wasn't the blood that Scott was so sad not to experience, but rather the great war novel he would have written. He was eternally envious of Ernest Hemingway who *did* get over, believing Ernest owed much of his success to his wartime experience. Scott tried to make up for this lost experience by poring over historical accounts of various battles. He kept close at hand a book full of gory battlefield photographs in which he tried to imagine himself in trenches full of dead bodies—but to no avail. Scott was wise enough to write only about what he knew, and it remained a bitter disappointment that this source of literary material was out of reach.

So should there be another war, it would certainly be tragic, but Scott planned to get in on it, as a journalist if he could not contrive something more heroic. It was intolerable that Hemingway should have the field forever to himself.

After Scott endured several weeks without drinking, Sheilah said to him unwisely, "Now, don't you think it was silly to have gone through all that agony for the stuff in a bottle?"

He visibly stiffened. "It's none of your business. I don't care to discuss it," he answered sharply. His nostrils became thin with irritation; his anger was one of great reserve and dignity. Then majestically he changed the subject. "About dinner—will you ask Flora to make me a lettuce salad and oyster broth?"

It was what a later generation would call denial; but Scott did not intend to be denied. In Malibu he began to drink in a different way than Sheilah had seen before—not in the great dramatic binges, but rather in a slow cycle which built gradually over a number of weeks to arrive at a climax. It always began with beer, which Scott considered a harmless brew, hardly alcohol; he felt entirely justified in maintaining, with a great show of virtue, that he was still on the wagon. When medical people spoke about drinking, he was certain they did not mean beer—or wine either, for that matter, a beverage which was surely the right of any civilized man who had lived in France. And in fact at this stage of the cycle, Scott appeared entirely sober; Sheilah would never have guessed alcohol was passing his lips except for the occasional discovery of an empty bottle. But once the beer started, the number of bottles consumed increased gradually until he was drinking as many as thirty-five a day—nearly six six-packs in his thirsty quest to have the small percentage points of alcohol add up into something meaningful. Sheilah by now definitely *did* know what was going on; the stench if nothing else was ever present, a hated aroma which took her back in time to the pubs of Stepney Green and the brewery near her mother's flat. By the time Scott had reached thirty-five bottles a day, the physical transformation was well in progress: the sly leer, the unshaved face, filthy clothes, and occasional four-letter word which slipped from his mouth. And then he turned finally to gin—after thirty-five bottles of beer a day, gin seemed wonderfully light, a translucent elixir, almost healthy by comparison—

and the amount of this grew also from a few fingers to a crescendo of a quart a day, sometimes more. Once the gin began, Scott shunned any solid food and the cycle quickly arrived at its inevitable conclusion—Scott so ill that he must put himself in the care of nurses for the painful drying out. Then he would remain sober a week or two before starting with a single bottle of beer the entire cycle once again.

Sheilah watched all this with feelings of dread and helplessness. She hated Scott when he was drunk, and she was outraged at the lies he told attempting to conceal his condition. She often found bottles of gin hidden in strategic places throughout the beach cottage; Scott's favorite hiding place was inside the water cabinet behind the toilet. It was mortifying to flush the toilet and open up the back to discover a bottle of gin jamming the plunger. She found it nearly incomprehensible that a man with his old-fashioned sense of personal dignity would lower himself to such absurd subterfuge.

But sometimes at a certain point in the cycle—not too early, not too late—he came to her flushed with desire. Sheilah hated to admit it, but she found this very exciting, to be taken by him when he was drunk. All his inhibitions were gone. It was as if the old puritan censor had taken the train back to St. Paul and left them alone in a room together. Anything might happen at such a time, wild variations on a missionary theme, forbidden pleasures—sometimes it seemed as if he might even take off his socks. Sheilah was young and sexy; she was thrilled to feel Scott cutting loose. But of course after too much liquor, Scott fell into a stupor and could not make love at all, nor would he try. He passed beyond the physical realm into a land of pure befuddlement all his own, transformed into a grinning, slobbering, unshaved thing who could barely stand on his feet. Sheilah grew to hate it all, and her horror of drunkenness outweighed the brief pleasure of liberated sex.

He had a strange sense of humor—almost cruel, really. Sometimes he spoke in silly baby talk to her. One time he said, "Mama, I wanna walk on a floor covered with babies." Then he crossed his eyes and added, "I wanna hear them squish." Sheilah laughed—what else could she do but laugh?—but the remark left an odd impression. Often she was not certain when he was joking and when he was not.

There was a morning in Malibu when Sheilah by mistake lifted Scott's coffee cup to her lips and was about to take a sip—then to her astonishment, he slapped the cup violently from her hands, sending it skittering across the floor.

"Don't ever use my cups or spoons or towels or anything else of mine," he said dramatically. He paused for effect, and added, "I have tuberculosis."

Sheilah was thoroughly alarmed; she had been told her father had died of tuberculosis shortly before her birth and the disease held an old dread for her. "Scott, are you sure? How do you know?"

"I've had it on and off since college," he assured her. "It's not bad now but it flares up if I don't watch myself."

After her initial alarm, Sheilah was never certain if this was only one of Scott's strange pranks. Whatever the case, dashing the cup from her hand had certainly been a useless gesture for they shared far greater intimacies than coffee cups. He had strange fears and phobias; she began to suspect he was quite a hypochondriac. Once, when she was driving and had carelessly allowed her speed to drift above twenty miles per hour, he screamed at her: "My God, slow down, you're killing me!" When they went to the movies, Scott often insisted they change rows three or four times during the course of a single film, complaining that the person behind him was kicking the back of his seat, though these phantom feet never touched Sheilah's seat. She concluded that Scott's tuberculosis must be a similar phantom and she was not surprised when the disease seemed to vanish mysteriously during the longer stretches when he was sober.

It was in Malibu that Sheilah finally began to read the books that had once made Scott Fitzgerald famous. Six months had now passed since the awkward autumn evening in 1937 when she had walked with Scott along Hollywood Boulevard searching for his books in the stores. She had remained curious about his writing, but was nervous to bring up the subject after such a painful night. Probably Scott had managed to find copies of his novels at some point during the winter, but apparently he hesitated, waiting for the right moment to give them to Sheilah. He was sensitive about his work, very much aware that Sheilah had little education, and perhaps anxious that she might fail to appreciate his genius. But now in Malibu he began to feed her belatedly his books one by one. As Sheilah read, he tended to hover nearby, pretending not to watch her but in fact taking in each subtle change in her expression.

He started her off with his first novel, *This Side of Paradise.* But Sheilah was disappointed; she did not like the book and found the characters immature and callow. She hated the love scenes in particular because Amory Blaine was so boorishly insincere, plotting seductions as though they were military campaigns, then losing all interest once he had managed to get a kiss. She wished Amory were more like Scott somehow, a person who was truthful, warm, and romantic. There was a difficult moment when she finished the final page and Scott turned to her blandly expecting praise. "Well," she said carefully, "it's not as good as Dickens."

"Of course it's not as good as Dickens," he fumed. Fortunately for their continued relationship, Sheilah loved the next novel he gave her, *Tender is the Night.* At last she saw his literary genius, that he *was* a great writer as he had been telling her all along. The language and poetry of the novel swept her away; unlike *This Side of Paradise,* it was desperately romantic, and this enticed her most of all. In fact, the book was so overpowering, so... something she could not put into words, that she had to look at Scott in a different way than before. The man she loved was no ordinary person. He awed her with his knowledge and understanding, and his ability to put quite marvelous things into words. Her favorite part of the book was where Dick Diver inspects an old trench from the war, and says so sadly to Rosemary, "This land here cost twenty lives a foot that summer." And then a few sentences later: "See that little stream—we could walk to it in two minutes. It took the British a month to walk to it—a whole empire walking very slowly, dying in front and pushing forward behind. And another empire walked very slowly backward a few inches a day.... " All

of Sheilah's romantic inclinations for heroic poetry were rekin-
dled with lines such as these. The part about the two empires
positively gave her goose bumps. She had always respected Scott,
but after she read *Tender is the Night,* he became for her, not a god
exactly, because she saw how deeply he was flawed, but something extra. From that moment on, she never entirely forgot his
enormous talent, even during those implausible moments when
he was drunk and filthy and seemed the last person on earth to
be entrusted with such a gift for poetry.

Scott was happy she liked his novel. He told her that *Tender*
was his own favorite of all his books, even though it had serious
structural problems; he had never completely recovered from the
unkind reception the critics had given the book, nor its modest
sales. He wanted to rewrite it one day; he believed now it should
have been two books instead of one. Unfortunately, in the nine
years he spent writing the novel, he had experienced so many
changes in his life and marriage that the artistic unity of the
work had been lost. It was not easy to concentrate on a novel
when your wife was going insane.

Tender is the Night had so much to do with Zelda, her insanity,
even the mental institutions where she had stayed in Switzerland,
that it was a natural progression for Scott now to speak of his
wife, a subject which had once been off-limits between them. He
told Sheilah small pieces of the story at different times throughout
the spring and summer of 1938. The conversations often began
after he received a letter from Zelda—disturbing letters which he
read aloud to Sheilah so that she would know what he had to put
up with. Sheilah was struck by Zelda's ornate language. "This is
beautiful writing," she told him cautiously, stifling her jealousy,
hoping Scott would find her majestically fair. "Yes," he agreed,
"but it doesn't lead anywhere. It doesn't add up."

Scott gradually warmed to his narrative and told Sheilah the
unhappy story of his marriage, from the early years when he
first fell in love with Zelda Sayre at a country club dance and
thought her the most beautiful girl he had ever seen, through the
drinking, the fighting, and, finally, to the moment a French doctor came to him with the terrible words, *"Votre femme est folle."*

Sheilah was fascinated. She heard anecdotes that were incredible to her: how he had once run to stop Zelda at the last moment from throwing herself in front of a moving train, and the terrible time in 1929 when Scott was driving Zelda and Scottie back to Paris from the Riviera and Zelda suddenly grabbed the wheel and tried to steer them over a cliff.

There was one story about Zelda that Sheilah found particularly horrifying: a time in Baltimore when a young writer, Charles Warren, visited the Fitzgeralds' house. Zelda was jealous to be left out of the conversation, and while Scott and Charlie were standing together talking about writing, she came up stealthily from behind and without warning dug her fingernails deeply into the young man's face perilously close to his eyes, then ripped downward through the flesh, turning his face into a bloody pulp. Scott had to rush Charlie to the hospital. This anecdote reinforced all of Sheilah's primal fears of Zelda's madness. Now in her recurring dreams, Zelda was even more terrible than before, lurching forward from dark shadows to attack Sheilah as she had done to Charlie Warren, coming after her with dreadful long fingernails.

"She would never bend," Scott explained to Sheilah about his wife. "That is why she broke. You know how to bend."

Sheilah had an unexpected reaction to these stories. Earlier she was hurt when Scott kept silent about his marriage, but now she was even more upset to learn the details. It seemed so unfair that he would marry such a destructive person rather than herself. She punished him with brooding silences. Scott sometimes came downstairs from his bedroom to find Sheilah staring out the window, lost in thought, refusing to look at him.

"Dear, is there anything the matter?" he asked finally.

"No."

"There must be—you look so sad."

"No. There's nothing the matter," she sighed.

When she continued to stare out the window in a nearly catatonic stupor, Scott said gently, "Perhaps—perhaps if you took a walk along the beach you'd feel better."

"No," she said tragically, and still refused to meet his eyes. She hoped he got the point: Nothing would make her feel better except a quick divorce and even quicker marriage to her, but since that apparently was impossible she would stare out the window until she went as crazy as Zelda. It would serve Scott right.

"Well. . . I'll go up and finish some work," he said at last, apologetically, and then returned upstairs to his room. Of course he knew exactly what was going on, but he chose not to delve any further. Zelda's hold on him was greater than he was willing to admit to Sheilah, and despite endless complaints about her and hints of divorce in letters to Dr. Carroll he could not do without this old anchor to his past. Sheilah knew this instinctively and it made her miserable. She chided herself for being so stupid, for making the classic mistake of falling in love with a married man.

But the brooding was only a phase; she was a realist and at last she simply hardened herself to the situation. It wasn't Scott's fault, she told herself many times. He could not help it if his wife was in a mental institution; in all conscience, he could not abandon her there. But Sheilah was not in possession of all the facts. Though Scott willingly read to her Zelda's letters, this was only one half of the correspondence. He did not share his replies which were often full of love and tender phrases, and even occasionally—in Scott's own moments of nostalgia—a hint that one day Zelda might join him in California.

It was only many years later, after Scott's letters were published in 1963, that Sheilah learned the truth, how emotionally tied Scott was still to his wife. As with Fluff Beckwith who discovered her own special poem from Scott in a collection dedicated to someone else, time would reveal the duplicity of his romantic lies; Fitzgerald's eventual fame betrayed him.

Scott was discussing a scene from Shakespeare when he looked at Sheilah and noticed that her face was blank. In public she would have tried to muddle through, pretending she knew the scene in question, but alone with Scott she confessed the truth. She had no idea what he was talking about.

"But *everyone* knows that!" he said, astonished at her ignorance.

"You mustn't make fun of me. You see I'm so vulnerable," she told him, trying very hard not cry. She remained extremely sensitive about her lack of education, an issue that was connected in her mind to the orphanage, the East End of London, her onetime Cockney accent, and all those odious and coarse things she had endured while Scott was at Princeton learning how to be so superior.

Sheilah continued to dread social gatherings in which her ignorance might be exposed. One day in the late spring she confided to Eddie Mayer that she could not understand why Scott was in love with her. From what she understood of Scott's past, he had always fallen for rich, confident girls—she was simply not Fitzgerald's type.

Eddie replied with a maddening literary reference to Proust's *Remembrance of Things Past* that he assumed Sheilah would understand. He mentioned Swann and Odette, and how Swann was insanely in love and ruined himself for her, and when it was all over he said, "And she was not even my type." Sheilah was intrigued; she saw that literature could be useful and explain quite practical things—why, for instance, Scott Fitzgerald was in love with her—and she promptly made her way to Martindale's bookstore in Beverly Hills and purchased all seven volumes of *Remembrance of Things Past*. She took this heavy load back to Malibu, where Scott was amused to find her struggling through the dense and difficult prose. He immediately took charge of the situation, for Sheilah had strayed unwittingly into his favorite domain—Scott, the frustrated pedagogue. "You must not read more than ten pages of Proust a day," he ordered. "It is too difficult and you will find it hard to finish if you take on too much." He set up a schedule for her, a concrete plan. She was to read precisely ten pages a day until she had completed the first one-third of *Swann's Way*—then she could go to thirty pages a day for the second third, and forty pages for the last. Meanwhile, he would keep the other volumes carefully out of sight until she was ready for them so that she would not be daunted by the magnitude of her task.

Sheilah was the perfect pupil and did exactly as Scott told her. For Scott, this was something of a miracle; despite his bossy nature, no one had ever done what he had told them to do before. Certainly not Zelda or Scottie. Eventually Sheilah made her way through all the long volumes of *Remembrance of Things Past*. She came to like Proust, though it was awfully difficult going at first. Unfortunately, at the end of this gargantuan task, she still believed herself inadequate. Nor did she have any clearer idea than before why Scott Fitzgerald loved her.

In the spring of 1938, not long after Scott had moved to Malibu, his daughter arrived at one of life's major's corners: She was set to graduate from the Ethel Walker School in Connecticut and face the many hazards waiting ahead in college. Scott was terrified for her future and determined to guide her every step. To fuel his worry, Scottie was voted the most popular girl in her class. The father could only ponder what dangerous acts she had committed to win such a title. When he was young, he had done everything he could to be popular, but despite endless plans and poses it always eluded him. Now that his daughter had succeeded where he had failed, he was not happy. He could only believe that she was adrift in shallow things.

He worried also that Scottie would need an expensive graduation present to keep pace with the other girls. In March he wrote to Anne Ober, the wife of his agent:

> We will have to make a mass pilgrimage to her graduation this June. I am hoping her mother can come too, and we will watch all the other little girls get diamond bracelets and Cord roadsters. I am going to a costumer's in New York and buy Scotty some phony jewelry so she can pretend they are graduation presents.
> Otherwise, she will have to suffer the shame of being a poor girl in a rich girl's school. That was always my experience—a poor boy in a rich town; a poor boy in a rich boy's school; a poor boy in a rich man's club at Princeton. So I guess she can stand it. However, I have never been able to forgive the rich for being rich, and it has colored my entire life and works.

Scott seemed to lose sight of who was graduating, himself or his daughter. With his own adolescence still not entirely finished, he often appeared unwilling to step out of the way, join the foggy ghosts of the older generation, and allow Scottie the full possession of her own youth. In the end he did not go to his daughter's graduation, nor did he buy her any costume jewelry; he was only letting off steam about his own frustrations. But Dr. Carroll allowed Zelda to go north for the ceremony at the Ethel Walker School, and she reported proudly to Scott: "Scottie is the prettiest girl. . . She wore white gardenias and white flannel and white hopes and the freedom and grace of the best and we are very proud and devoted. . . Meanwhile—life is so nice, when one can have some. . . Scottie is a very good thing to have. I'm so glad we've got her."

But then with such great white hopes and everything looking good, Scottie risked her entire future. She had applied to Vassar for the fall term, but while remaining at school after graduation to study for her college entrance exams, Scottie and a classmate broke bounds and hitchhiked to Yale for a dinner party. The headmistress at the Ethel Walker School sent Scottie home in punishment—to the Harold Obers' home, that is, which served as her foster home during Scott's long absence. Scott was furious when he learned of this hitchhiking spree. He was certain his daughter had ruined her chances at Vassar and had thrown her life away with a single wild act. He wrote her a letter that was so abusive Sheilah made him tear it up, convincing him that it would alienate his daughter forever. Scott then sat down and wrote a second, much milder, letter:

Dearest Scottie:

I don't think I will be writing letters many more years and I wish you would read this letter twice—bitter as it may seem. . . .

When I was your age I lived with a great dream. The dream grew and I learned how to speak of it and make people listen. Then the dream divided one day when I decided to marry your mother after all, even though I knew she was spoiled and meant no good to me. I was sorry immediately I had married her but, being patient in those days, made the best of it and got to love her in another way. You came along and for a long time we made quite a lot of happiness out of our lives. But I was a man divided—she wanted me to work too much for *her* and not enough for my dream. She realized too late that work was dignity, and the only dignity, and tried to

atone for it by working herself, but it was too late and she broke
and is broken forever. . . She never knew how to use her energy—
she's passed that failing on to you.

Scott eventually passed from the failures of the mother to
those of the daughter:

> . . . When you began to show disturbing signs at about four-
> teen, I comforted myself with the idea that you were too precocious
> socially and a strict school would fix things. But sometimes I think
> that idlers seem to be a special class for whom nothing can be
> planned, plead as one will with them. . . .
>
> My reforming days are over, and if you are that way I don't
> want to change you. But I don't want to be upset by idlers inside
> my family or out. I want my energies and my earnings for people
> who talk my language.
>
> I have begun to fear that you don't. You don't realize that what
> I am doing here [in Hollywood] is the last tired effort of a man who
> once did something finer and better. There is not enough energy, or
> call it money, to carry anyone who is dead weight and I am angry
> and resentful in my soul when I feel that I am doing this.

Scott went on to complain that she had done nothing to make
him proud since she had learned to dive at summer camp. He
berated her for being "'a wild society girl,' vintage of 1925"—a
vintage he knew too well, since such girls had been the heroines
of nearly all his fiction. He ranted on, a flood of hyperbole and
self-indulgence, a confusion of identities in which he didn't seem
to know where he ended and where his daughter began. At last
he ended with two postscripts: One, that when she went to
Europe this summer, she must keep a diary to be written according to his specifications: "Please don't let it be the dry stuff I
could buy in a ten-franc guide book," he insisted. And as a final
P.P.S.: "Will you please read this letter a second time? I wrote it
over twice."

Scottie's reaction was normal for a sixteen-year-old girl: She
shook the letter to see if there was a check enclosed, and when
there was not, she stoically ignored the rest. The summer trip to
Europe had been arranged some months earlier as a graduation
present—"a tourist-class, station wagon tour of Europe," as Scott
described it to Dr. Carroll, hoping to keep news of the trip from

Zelda as long as possible for fear she would be jealous. By 1938 Scott believed there was going to be a war soon in Europe, and he wanted his daughter to see the Old World while it was still intact. While Scottie was abroad, Scott wrote a number of pleading letters to Vassar begging for her admission—and as with many a youthful folly, breaking bounds to hitchhike to Yale did not turn out to be quite the end of the world after all. Vassar agreed to admit Scottie Fitzgerald, and upon her return to the United States, she set out to California with her friend Peaches Finney for a quick Hollywood visit before starting college.

Scottie was well aware that Sheilah often took her side in the endless father-daughter feuds. Just before Scottie had set out for Europe, Sheilah sent her a present of a sweater, and Scottie wrote back:

> . . . waited until we were safely on the Atlantic to tell you how much I love the sweater. It's so marvelously soft and really I just adore it because I love nice sweaters more than anything in the world. . .
>
> . . . let me congratulate you on doing such a good job on Daddy—you are *definitely* a good influence. I hope he isn't going to get so upset every time I do anything wrong. . . Anyhow thank you so much for all your trouble.

Despite Scottie and Sheilah's growing friendship—or perhaps because of it—Scott worried about the moral impression Sheilah's presence in Malibu might have on young minds. Shortly before Scottie and Peaches arrived in California, he faced Sheilah with a painful decision. He asked her to move out of the beach house for his daughter's visit, to take away all her clothes and belongings, to cleanse the house of any hint that she and Scott were living in sin.

Sheilah was devastated. She had courted Scottie's affections with such small gifts as sweaters hoping she might be accepted as a sort of stepmother. She longed to be part of the family grouping. It came as a slap in her face to be treated as if she were something unclean, a mistress who must be hidden from view. Besides, she loved the beach house; Malibu had been her fantasy of a real home and it was a bitter disappointment to be sent away. Sheilah wept, she was very crushed, but she did what Scott asked of her—she took her things and left.

Scott was now free to set a high moral tone. When Scottie and Peaches arrived in Malibu, he did his best to maintain the fiction that Sheilah was simply a good friend who dropped in from time to time. Scottie, of course, knew very well what was going on, and Sheilah sometimes felt the girl's blue eyes upon her in a wondering way, at a loss to imagine how an attractive young woman could put up with an old ogre like her father. Scott continued to rail at Scottie about her hitchhiking to Yale; he referred to the incident again and again until finally Sheilah could not stand it anymore. "Now, Scott, you stop picking on her. What she did was perfectly harmless. Let her alone." Scott was grumpy about Sheilah's defection, but he finally let the Yale matter drop.

He was pleased whenever Scottie came to him for advice; if only she would *take* his advice—that was the problem! At one point during the vacation two young men from back east were coming over and Scottie had no idea how she and Peaches were to entertain them. This was right up Scott's alley. "Scottie," he said, "you must have a plan. I'll give you one. Go out and buy half a dozen of the latest dance records. When dancing wears off, remember—action creates conversation. Take them into the kitchen and make fudge. You'll be so busy mixing, buttering pans, talking about what you're doing, that no one will be bored. If you're still stuck after that, bring them to me. I'll show them my pictorial history of the war. It fascinates everyone."

Scott's pictorial history of the war was his extremely gory book of mangled soldiers which he had purchased in an attempt to invade Hemingway's literary turf; he often delighted in showing these pictures to shocked visitors. Scottie was understandably eager to escape her father whenever possible; she and Peaches often went off with Sheilah, who acted, if not like a stepmother, at least like the perfect older sister, arranging for the girls to visit the movie studios and go to Hollywood premieres.

One afternoon, Sheilah took Scottie and Peaches to a Warner Brothers set where she introduced the girls to Errol Flynn. After a photographer took their picture together, Scottie was so excited she found a pay phone to call her father. But Scott hated Errol Flynn; he told his daughter the actor was a facetious, swaggering idiot, and then he chided her for being so shallow as to be impressed by meeting such a man: A well-brought-up sixteen-year-old girl of sound moral character should not be influenced by Errol Flynn simply because he was fabulously handsome, rich, and one of the most famous movie stars on the planet. Scottie stormed out of the phone booth with angry tears in her eyes. "Daddy was making fun of Errol. He's always trying to ruin things," she told Peaches.

Sheilah, of course, knew entirely well why Daddy despised Errol: The star was easily aroused and accustomed to having his way with women. Later that afternoon, after work, Errol in fact showed up at Sheilah's house hoping to swagger his way into her bedroom. Sheilah was flattered but not interested. Fortunately, when she answered the bell she was dressed to go out and soon managed to get rid of him. Later she told Scott about this—she could not help but let it slip. It made Fitzgerald even more sarcastic on the subject of Errol Flynn, but Sheilah wanted him to know that some men appreciated her.

All in all, it was a difficult few weeks for Scott. No one quite appreciated how hard he must work to guide his daughter and meanwhile keep Sheilah on hold, absent from Malibu but safely out of the grasp of swashbuckling movie stars. Then he had to fight with Scottie about her upcoming freshman year at Vassar. He believed he must plan everything for her: her academic curriculum, her social life, even her political ideologies—he insisted she was under all circumstances to remain a liberal. They even clashed over her choice of roommates. Scottie wanted to share a room with Dorothy Burns, a beautiful girl from the Ethel Walker School—too beautiful, Scott believed, a fact which would cause the appearance of hordes of young men who would certainly lead Scottie astray. As the day came closer for Scottie's departure, Scott loaded her up with last-minute advice. After all his consuming worry, he was astonished when Peaches had the nerve to tell him off, saying that he should stop bullying everyone and leave his daughter alone.

*   *   *

Scott was in a state of nervous exhaustion by the time Scottie and Peaches finally left. Unfortunately, he had other pressures on him besides the nerve-racking juggling act he must constantly do to keep his wife, daughter, and mistress in line. *Infidelity*, which had begun so well, had turned sour for Scott soon after he moved to Malibu. This time it wasn't his screenwriting or producer which caused him misery, but rather the Hays Office with its moral guidelines for American films. Concerning infidelity, the edict was very clear: "Adultery, sometimes necessary plot material, must not be explicitly treated, or justified, or presented attractively." At MGM, Louis B. Mayer, "the pious sinner" of Scott's poem about the Academy Awards, was particularly anxious to make family pictures that portrayed a sentimentalized small-town Anglo-Saxon America full of smiling moms and apple pies. At the same time, every movie also required a sex goddess to go along with the apple pies, and this created problems for an ambitious screenwriter, who must navigate a dangerous minefield between hypocrisy and titillation.

When Scott realized he was going to have difficulties with Joseph Breen, the censor, he came up with a clever strategy: He changed the title of his movie from *Infidelity* to *Fidelity*. Unfortunately, Breen in a rare moment of insight saw through the ploy. He strongly objected that *Fidelity* even with its new name still had a happy ending; the unfaithful husband got his wife back and suffered neither hellfire nor eternal damnation for his adulterous act. In the following months, Scott and Hunt Stromberg did their best to rewrite the story so that Joseph Breen might finally approve. At the end of his wits, Scott came up with an elaborate argument that the movie wasn't really about adultery at all, but thievery—the theft, that is, of another person's spouse. In various memos to Hunt Stromberg, Scott went to torturous lengths to bend words and convince the producer that adultery was basically nothing more than a dishonest business transaction; therefore, since the Hays Office had issued no edicts on this subject, the movie could be made.

But Breen knew sin when he saw it; he refused to accept

Fitzgerald's convoluted reasoning, and Hunt Stromberg simply lost patience and canceled the picture.

Scott wrote his daughter:

> We have reached a censorship barrier in *Infidelity* to our infinite disappointment. It *won't* be Joan's next picture and we are setting it aside awhile till we think of a way of halfwitting halfwit Hayes and his Legion of Decency. Pictures needed cleaning up in 1932–33 (remember I didn't like you to see them?) but because they were suggestive and salacious. Of course the moralists now want to apply that to *all* strong themes—so the crop of the last two years is feeble and false, unless it deals with children.

So once again Scott had come to a disappointing end on a picture. Hollywood was a very hard nut to crack and after the strain of his daughter's visit Scott was in a dark mood. Hoping to cheer him up, Sheilah suggested they have a few friends over to the Malibu house. Scott lit up very brightly and agreed this was exactly what he needed—a party.

It would be no ordinary party. As always, Scott had a plan. He organized a Ping-Pong tournament, complete with handicaps for each guest, and a game to see who could get to the bar first—a game Scott easily won, though this afternoon he let everyone know that he himself was drinking only water. Eddie Mayer was the first to arrive, bringing his seven-year-old son, Paul. Scott took it upon himself to entertain the boy, playing a game of Ping-Pong in the same manner as he did with Sheilah, crossing his eyes and acting the clown. When the game was over, he took Paul into the garden for a mock boxing match, dancing about throwing jabs and absurd uppercuts until the seven-year-old was helpless with laughter. Scott was in rare form.

Other guests soon arrived: Dorothy Parker, Alan Campbell, Nathanael and Eileen West, Cameron Rogers and his wife Buff Cobb, John O'Hara, the screenwriter Nunnally Johnson with his wife Marion, and Charlie Warren—the young writer Scott considered his protégé whose face Zelda had once gouged with her fingernails. Charlie was only twenty-two and he annoyed Scott by calling him "sir"; he had come this afternoon wearing a back brace because he had strained a muscle, and he was accompanied by a lovely starlet, Alice Hyde. All told, it was a congenial crowd of people who knew one another well, and Scott was at his most charming. This was the Dick Diver side of his personality—Dick Diver at the start of *Tender is the Night* rather than at its sad conclusion—amusing, magnetic, listening and laughing, and making each person believe he found him or her the most wonderful guest at the party. It was a brilliantly sunny summer day and everyone was dressed casually in swim suits and shorts except Scott; he wore gray flannel slacks and a gray pullover sweater, guarding himself against any subtle change in the weather.

Sheilah had not seen Scott this happy for some time. When the party was in full swing, Scott noticed two curious children peeking through the white picket fence into the garden; they were the sons of Joe Swerling, a screenwriter who lived next door, and Scott invited them to join the fun. When they seemed bored with grown-up conversation, Scott set about to entertain them, bringing out a deck of cards from the house to perform magic tricks. He assured the two boys in a stage whisper that only one other person in the world could do the trick they were about to see, and he was in a jail cell in San Quentin for life. Then Scott rolled up his sleeves, said "Abracadabra," and twirled about three times with his eyes closed. After the fanfare, he produced four cards on demand—an ace, a king, a ten, and a four.

Sheilah was as delighted as the children to watch Scott's magic. It was a side of Scott she adored: his childlike imagination and the generous way he gave of his time.

"Aren't you kids thirsty? How about something to drink," he asked.

One of the boys answered politely, "I'd like a glass of champagne, thank you." The fun stopped abruptly; the child was eight years old and Scott was deeply shocked. He excused himself and telephoned Joe Swerling next door to demand if he was aware that his son drank champagne. The father laughed and said they sometimes gave the boy ginger ale, calling it champagne, and a crisis was avoided. Scott turned his attention now to his adult guests and showered them with the same determination to delight and entertain that he had given earlier to the children. He performed tricks, he told jokes, he was the life of the party. As the afternoon went on, Scott became funnier and funnier. Suddenly Sheilah had an inkling of suspicion. She thought to herself: *He's too gay.* She found an opportunity to stand next to him and sniff the sea air; sure enough, there was the subtle perfume of gin wafting on the breeze. She wondered how she could have been so stupid—the water he was drinking with such a show of virtue was of course straight gin.

For the time being, Scott remained the perfect host, apparently unaffected by the liquor except for his infectious joie de vivre. Then he played a puzzling joke on Charlie Warren. Scott approached Alice Hyde, the pretty starlet Charlie had brought as his date. He lowered his voice and said he must speak to her; he took her aside and swore her to secrecy about a difficult matter. Charlie was a fine young man, but unfortunately he suffered from an advanced case of syphilis. This was the real reason for Charlie's back brace—he was literally falling apart. Scott assured Alice that Charlie's fingers were about to fall off, and that if she danced with him she would be able to feel where the back brace held his crumbling body together. Scott felt he must tell her these things lest she wander blindly into a tragic romance.

As the afternoon deepened, Charlie Warren was surprised when his date appeared to avoid him. Eventually Alice told Sheilah that she had a headache and must leave the party at once. She barely said good-bye to Charlie as she made her escape. Scott watched his joke unfold with great pleasure, and when Alice was gone he wandered over to Charlie to commiserate.

"What's the matter, old man? Seems she can't stand you. You haven't said anything offensive to her, have you?"

"Oh, no, sir," Charlie said unhappily. "I can't understand it."

Scott pretended great concern. He mentioned that he often saw Alice Hyde at the studio and he offered to try to fix it up. But Charlie shook his head and said with a sigh that it probably wouldn't do any good. He was mystified as to the ways of women; she had been so friendly and he couldn't imagine why she had changed her mind about him. Scott enjoyed his prank so much that he did not enlighten his young friend as to the truth of the situation.

Eventually, inevitably, Scott's mood turned sour. Sheilah had seen this before—an early ebullience when all seemed right with the world, and then without apparent warning he became a raving, falling-down drunk. As the afternoon sun sank into the ocean, the guests gathered their belongings, located their husbands and wives, and began to take their leave. Nunnally Johnson and his wife Marion were on their way out of the house when Scott unexpectedly came up behind Nunnally and gave the screenwriter a violent shove into a bedroom. Scott slipped in after him and locked the door, dropping the key into his shirt pocket with a melodramatic flourish.

"Listen, Nunnally, get out of Hollywood," he said. "It will ruin you. You have a talent—you'll kill it here." Scott held up a hand and began to list on his fingers all the people he knew whose talent had been ruined writing for the movies—he did not mention himself.

Nunnally objected, "Look, I don't think I've been chosen by destiny to be a great writer, Scott. I haven't felt the call. I'm just a guy who makes his living writing and I make a better living writing in Hollywood than anywhere else. Why should I leave?"

"Why, you sonofabitch, you don't know what's good for you," Scott exploded. "I'm warning you—get out of here. This place isn't for you. Go back to New York."

Scott continued for more than twenty-five minutes to enumerate the many evils of the great whore, Hollywood. Nunnally soon realized that argument was useless and he pretended to agree. He promised Scott that yes, he would leave town immediately. But Scott was too clever. "Oh, no—now you're lying," he said, advancing forward in his boxer's stance, fists ready. "You tell me the truth."

The screenwriter backed away. "Have I got to fight to get out of this room?" he asked nervously.

Sheilah and Marion meanwhile were pounding on the locked door. Sheilah tried subterfuge: "Scott, everyone's leaving, they want to say goodbye to you." Finally Scott unlocked the door and Nunnally made his escape. But Scott had worked himself up into a rage. He went about the house ordering all the remaining guests to leave. He tried to get into a fight with Cameron Rogers, who was a large man. When Cameron refused to be goaded, Scott turned to his wife, Buff. "God damn that big Harvard lug—if he doesn't knock me out, I'll kill him. I got to be knocked out. . . Come on, Cameron, put up your fists like a man."

Scott began his famous shadowboxing while Sheilah fluttered nearby, not knowing what to do. Cameron finally gave Scott a light tap in the stomach and Scott collapsed on the floor with a great show of injury. As a small group carried him to a nearby sofa, he was heard to mutter: "That big, hulking brute. . . and me dying of tuberculosis."

"Oh, be quiet, Scott," Buff said. "If he hadn't done it, I would have."

They dumped Scott on the sofa but he was up in a moment. He ran into the driveway to scream insults at the departing guests. He found Nunnally and Marion Johnson about to drive off in their car.

"You'll never come back here. Never!" he cried at them.

"Of course I will, Scott," Nunnally replied patiently. "I want to see you and Sheilah again."

"Oh, no, you won't," Scott shouted. "Because I'm living with my paramour! That's why you won't."

Nunnally Johnson had seen the word *paramour* in print but never in his life had he heard it spoken in real conversation. "Good God," he said to Marion as they drove away, "I didn't know Scott was a Methodist."

By 1938 the word *paramour* was painfully old-fashioned, but Sheilah had a general sense of its meaning—he had called her a whore. That was how she took it: *whore, whore, whore*! She could hardly believe Scott would insult her like that in front of their friends. For a moment she wanted to slap him, slap him hard, the bastard. But she could not—instead she ran breathlessly onto the beach to cry.

Everyone had gone now. From where Sheilah stood on the dark sand she saw Scott inside the lighted house tearing through the rooms searching for his car keys. Earlier in the summer, in a calmer moment than this, they had agreed that Sheilah was to hide his car keys whenever he started to drink, and she had done this in the afternoon as soon as she understood that Scott's glass was not filled with water. But he was too sly for her and managed to find the keys in her top dresser drawer. Sheilah watched as he staggered from the house out into the driveway and drove off with a roar at a reckless speed far greater than his usual twenty miles per hour. She worried about his driving but felt helpless to stop him. At times like this, she always tried to remember what Robert Benchley had once told her: "God takes care of drunks and little children."

Though Scott could barely walk, he managed to drive to the liquor store in Malibu and return shortly with a new bottle of gin. He stepped out of the car with the bottle raised to his lips and began walking erratically toward Sheilah on the beach. She wasn't certain what he meant to do. Insult her? Apologize? But to her horror, Scott continued walking past her down the beach to the edge of the water. He kept going, still in his shoes and flannel pants and gray sweater, and stepped fully dressed into the ocean. She screamed after him but he would not stop. He fell into an oncoming wave and flailed his arms about drunkenly in the foam.

"Scott!" she shrieked. "You'll die of pneumonia! Scott—"

He swam a few strokes out to sea, and then turned back to shore. He stepped onto the beach with his clothes dripping wet and the hiss of the ocean swirling about his soggy city shoes, the bottle of gin still in his hand.

Sheilah could not help herself—she began to laugh. She found the sight of him hideously funny. It was, after all, absurd. She had brought Scott to Malibu to save him, hoping he would swim each day and become tan and healthy in the sun. But this nighttime dip was the only time she had ever managed to achieve her goal and see Scott Fitzgerald in the ocean.

13

BELLY ACRES

> Sometimes I wish I had gone along with that [Cole Porter,
> Rodgers and Hart] gang, but I guess I am too much a moralist
> at heart and really want to preach at people in some acceptable
> form rather than to entertain them.
>
> —F. Scott Fitzgerald to his daughter, November 4, 1939

SCOTT HAD NEVER LIKED MALIBU; it was cold and damp and the
ocean was not fun to fall into after you had too much to drink.
Shortly before the six-month lease on the beach house was due
to expire in October 1938, he told Sheilah he wanted to move.
Sheilah was disappointed. She imagined the ocean in winter as
very romantic: lonely sunsets, extreme tides, even an occasional
storm lashing against the windows of their cottage. But Scott
shivered at the very thought of such possibilities; a man with
nineteenth-century lungs had to be careful. So he sent her in
search of a new home, hopefully someplace where it was warm
and dry.

Sheilah had to acknowledge that the Malibu experiment was a

failure. Fortunately, she enjoyed house hunting as a kind of recreational sport. It was very pleasant for her to walk through strange living rooms and kitchens with a critical eye, trying to fantasize what life might be like in such a place. Would it feel like home? Could she end her restless travels and finally belong somewhere? She pictured tables and chairs in different positions, colors of paint, which bedroom would be for Scott, which would become her office. After several days of projecting herself and Scott into all sorts of imaginary domestic situations, she found at last a house she thought was perfect. It was a guest cottage on the estate of the actor Edward Everett Horton at 5521 Amestoy Avenue in Encino, a sleepy tree-lined country lane in the San Fernando Valley.

In 1938 Encino was mostly ranch land and citrus groves, one of the driest and warmest parts of Los Angeles County, ten to twenty degrees warmer than the coast. It was protected from the fog and vagaries of the Pacific Ocean by a line of squat hills known grandiosely as the Santa Monica Mountains. There was a lazy Southern California peace upon the land, a stillness quite opposite to the ceaseless motion of wind and water at Malibu. In Encino in the hot days of autumn, time seemed to come to a geriatric halt.

The house Sheilah rented for Scott was one of three white clapboard cottages on Horton's sprawling estate, set down among fir and beech trees, rolling lawns, and carefully tended gardens that were blooming with red and yellow roses. Edward Everett Horton, the landlord, was a comic actor with a trademark prissy voice, famous for his exaggerated double takes; sensing perhaps that his fame in the movies was not eternal, he had invested wisely in land. The "guest cottage," as Horton called it, was below the main house and despite its modest description it was larger than the house at Malibu. Downstairs there was a paneled living room, dining room, spare bedroom, and study, as well as a huge kitchen, pantry, maid's room, and bath. Upstairs was a spacious master bedroom, dressing room, bathroom, and outside balcony, where Scott might pace lost in thought as he had done so often on the widow's walk at Malibu. From the upstairs balcony a flight of outside wooden steps descended to the perfect lawns and gardens below; a short path led to the tennis court and to a pool that had no water. The rent for all this country luxury was two hundred fifty dollars a month.

Sheilah helped Scott move for the second time, chauffeuring his few clothes and many books and papers to Encino. But Scott was not at all certain he liked the new home Sheilah had found. There was something unpleasant about the too-perfect lawns and white picket fences; the grounds seemed overdone, as prissy as Edward Everett Horton himself. An estate like this, more weathered with time, might be believable if it existed in North Carolina or Virginia; in Southern California it seemed like an invention of the movies, a copy of a copy, a stage set of something that never was. Above all, Scott was embarrassed by the name of the place, "Belly Acres." Scott found the pun positively loathsome; it summoned up images of slapstick comedians (the landlord, alas) slipping on banana peels around the swimming pool. "How can I tell anyone I live in 'Belly Acres'?" he complained to Sheilah, not even slightly amused.

Scott remained grouchy about his new home until Buff Cobb dropped by one afternoon. He gave her a tour of the grounds, complaining with much sarcasm about everything in sight, and then was surprised when Buff insisted that to her the estate seemed charming. She pointed to the white picket fence that Scott detested. "And all those little pickets look like little gravestones in a Confederate graveyard," she told him. Scott was taken with the imagery and ran inside to find Sheilah. "Sheilah!" he cried, "She's made the place livable! We've got romance in the house." It was apparently all he needed, the right poetic metaphor, and from that moment he found Belly Acres bearable. He told Sheilah she might as well give up her large house on Kings Road and take a smaller apartment somewhere in town for the sake of appearances and an occasional overnight stay. He wanted to live in sin, for Sheilah to stay with him in Encino; if he were exiled to the San Fernando Valley, he might as well have company. To make the house more appealing to her, he paid to have the pool filled.

And so began a time of deceptive peace. The drowsy mood of

Encino was seductive. There was a smell of flowers in the air and freshly mown grass. Days passed in a delicious lull. Sometimes in the evening Scott and Sheilah sat outside on the upstairs balcony like an old married couple without the need to exchange a word. When it was very quiet in the early evening they could hear distant voices from the RKO Western lot next door that spread out for many acres beyond the trees. Someone would cry: "Everybody-quiet! Camera—shoot!" And there would come the pounding of hooves on the earth and the far-off crackling of guns.

At such times Scott and Sheilah would smile across the twilight and feel themselves under an enchanted spell. How strange to have ended up here, Scott on his long journey from St. Paul, and Sheilah from the wrong part of London—so much motion and flight to find each other at last in this land of papier-mâché and make-believe.

Sheilah loved to be outdoors. On the weekends, she often played tennis with the landlord's two brothers, playing with all her might, eager to smash the ball hard and win a point. After Scott had the pool filled, she swam everyday as well, long laps back and forth until she was exhausted. She never gave up trying to get Scott into the pool with her. Come on, she would say, it will feel good. You need the exercise. But Scott smiled wistfully and replied every time that he was too busy.

He did find time to stand by the side of the pool, dressed in wintry city clothes, and coach Sheilah on the finer aspects of swimming technique, how to breathe, how to move her arms— barking instructions at her as she went back and forth on her laps. This was more than simple bossiness; the artist in Scott liked to be in charge, to rearrange the universe to his liking. It was the same with football. On Saturday afternoons throughout the autumn, he took Sheilah to the Los Angeles Coliseum where they watched UCLA's legendary halfback, Kenny Washington, score fabulous touchdowns. Scott considered himself a master of strategy and he enthusiastically explained the rules of this most American sport to her and supplied a running commentary of what each team should have done in every situation. At prep school, he had once humiliated himself during a scrimmage by running with the ball in the wrong direction to escape being tackled; nevertheless, as an adult he believed he understood the game better than anyone else and he liked to oversee the action from the safety of his bleacher seat.

"I have two scoring plays that will make a coach's reputation in one season," Scott bragged once in a 1933 article for the *Saturday Evening Post*. Throughout the thirties he sometimes telephoned the Princeton football coach, Fritz Crisler, or Asa Bushnell, the graduate manager of athletics—often in the wee hours of the morning—to tell them of new plays he had dreamed up that would surely destroy the great archenemies, Harvard and Yale. Eventually Coach Crisler, after one of these late-night phone calls, said he would use the play under one condition— that Scott make himself publicly responsible for its success or failure. This gave Fitzgerald pause and he told the coach that maybe he should simply keep the play in reserve.

Scott and Sheilah often went to movies in town. One night they drove home from a preview of a new film singing loudly in the car as Scott guided them (slowly) up the twists and turns of Laurel Canyon Boulevard, over the summit and down into the San Fernando Valley on the other side. They sang an improvised duet of "Don't Bring Lulu" by Billy Rose which for some reason—or no reason at all—seemed excruciatingly funny. They sang and laughed and when at last it was quiet for a few moments in the darkened car, Scott was moved to recite a poem to her in his musical voice:

> Fair youth, beneath the trees, thou canst not leave
> Thy song, nor ever can those trees be bare:
> Bold Lover, never, never canst thou kiss,
> Though winning near the goal—yet, do not
> grieve:
> She cannot fade, though thou hast not thy bliss,
> For ever wilt thou love, and she be fair!

He glanced at Sheilah to make certain she was listening; he knew she often drifted away from him, thinking about her column or some problem she was having with a star. But Sheilah was listening intently, enthralled with the mystical rhythms of words, and the evening, and Scott's voice.

"Who wrote it?" she asked.

"Keats," he told her. He recited more stanzas of the "Ode on a Grecian Urn," and when he couldn't remember anymore, he did a few stanzas of "Ode to a Nightingale," from which he had taken the title for his fourth novel:

> . . . tender is the night,
> And haply the Queen-Moon is on her throne,
>   Clustered around by all her starry Fays;
>   But here there is no light,
> Save what from heaven is with the breezes blown
>   Through verdurous glooms and winding
> mossy ways.

Scott was well aware of the effect of Keats upon romantic women when recited in a certain voice in darkened automobiles; he had used poetry often enough in the past to woo and impress—once he had even recited the "Ode to a Nightingale" to a prostitute who was working the Grove Park Inn in Asheville, North Carolina, in the summer of 1935. But though there was an element of calculation in these recitals—and Sheilah was never to know how many times in the past these recitals had taken place—Scott was himself always freshly and sincerely moved by the eloquence of great language. He once told Sheilah that in another century he would have been a poet himself, but these days it just wouldn't pay the bills. Sheilah proved to be the most attentive listener he had ever found. She loved to hear him recite poetry and wanted more.

Scott hardly needed further encouragement. When they arrived home, he hurried to his bookcase and pulled out a handful of volumes. First she must hear the full version of "Ode to a Nightingale" and then "Ode on a Grecian Urn." Later he read Andrew Marvell's "To His Coy Mistress" and Shelley's "Ode to the West Wind." Sheilah adored the sheer opera of sound, even though she did not understand every word, and was happy to listen all night. When Scott came momentarily to a halt, she asked hesitantly, "Will you tell me what to read? Will you give me a course in poetry?"

Scott's smile took on an ecstatic quality. Would he give her a course in poetry? It was like asking the Big Bad Wolf if he would

care for a dinner date with Red Riding Hood. After years of seeing his pedantic efforts resisted by Scottie and Zelda, this was a
dream come true: The frustrated teacher had found at last his
perfect match, an unresisting young woman who saw education
as the cure to most things that ailed her. With Sheilah, Scott could
play Pygmalion to his heart's content; she actually *wanted* him to
make her over. It was incredible. Just as the Tin Man wished for a
heart, the Lion courage, and the Scarecrow a brain, Sheilah
hoped her personal Oz might give to her an education. She was
bright and curious about the world, but there was more to it than
that; she believed in almost a mystical way that an education
would make her a legitimate person at last.

Scott was certain Sheilah would never untangle the secrets of
poetry on her own. As he wrote later to his daughter:

> [Poetry] isn't something easy to get started on by yourself. You
> need, at the beginning, some enthusiast who also knows his way
> around—John Peale Bishop performed that office for me at
> Princeton.
> Poetry is either something that lives like fire inside you—like
> music to the musician or Marxism to the Communist—or else it is
> nothing, an empty, formalized bore around which pedants can
> endlessly drone their notes and explanations. "The Grecian Urn"
> is unbearably beautiful with every syllable as inevitable as the
> notes in Beethoven's Ninth Symphony or it's just something you
> don't understand. . . Likewise with "The Nightingale" which I can
> never read through without tears in my eyes. . . . For a while after
> you quit Keats all other poetry seems to be only whistling or hum-
> ming.

Despite his love of Keats, he began Sheilah with Shelley, giving her a book of poems as well as *Ariel*, André Maurois's biography of Shelley's life. Scott drew up a formal assignment sheet. At
the top he wrote, "How to learn from a Frenchman about an
exiled Englishman (by an American)." Then he specified the
poems she was to read each day, along with the designated chapters in the biography.

After Shelley came Byron, and then the entire *Oxford Book of
English Verse,* which Scott went through carefully to cross-reference

with various biographical and critical sources. Sheilah had always loved poetry as a child, and now she was astonished and grateful for this opportunity to learn more. "He dazzled me," she wrote many years later. "I was overwhelmed by the excitement he engendered in me, by his infectious enthusiasms, by the delight he took in opening new horizons for me, by the intense interest he concentrated upon me. I gave him every thought I had. I turned to him for every judgement."

In the orphanage Sheilah had memorized poems for a six-pence prize; now she memorized them to please Scott, reciting long verses to him proudly the moment he stepped from his car returning home in the evening from work. "I'm student one in your college," Sheilah said to him one day. "The F. Scott Fitzgerald College of One." Scott was very much taken with the fanciful name; it seemed to formalize their arrangement and from that day the F. Scott Fitzgerald College of One kicked into high gear. Poetry was only the beginning. Over the next weeks, Scott spent hours organizing a complex curriculum tailored to Sheilah's most immediate needs. There would be no math, science, Latin, or French—for this was an education for a woman in a hurry, and a professor who had more than a few gaps in his own schooling.

"We must first create a facade for you so that you can handle yourself in company—at least you'll know the general subject if it comes up. Then we will go into detail," he said. He promised that she would graduate in 1941 from the F. Scott Fitzgerald College of One, dressed in cap and gown and wearing blue stockings. There would be a special diploma presented from the founder himself, Prof. Fitzgerald—a founder, though Sheilah did not know it, who possessed no college diploma himself. For though Scott spoke of dear old Princeton proudly throughout his life, and let it be widely assumed that he had graduated from this fine institution, in fact he had not managed to pass the required courses.

Shortly before he met Sheilah, Scott analyzed the state of his own learning in one of his many lists:

How I Would Grade My Knowledge at 40

Literature and attendant arts	B+
History and Biography	B+
Philosophy	B-
Psychiatry	C
Military Tactics & Strategy	D+
Architecture	D
Art	D
Marxian Economics	D

Everything else way below educated average, including all science, natural history, music, politics, business, handicrafts, etc. save for some specialized sport knowledge—boxing, football, women, etc.

This was a modest assessment, for Scott was ruthlessly honest in his self-observations, and he measured himself against the very highest standards. Sheilah would have been surprised to note that he had put his knowledge of women in the category of sports, next to boxing and football, but for the time being he was able to keep this small slip of the pen to himself.

Like many young people of an original bent, Scott had done poorly in school. He liked the football and dances, the clothes and pranks and late-night conversations with his friends—the atmosphere of school, but not the substance. His grades were so bad in prep school that he was required to take a special exam to be admitted to Princeton. Once at college, he continued to ignore his studies with such a sublime and superior attitude that one of his English teachers, Gerald Gerould, later refused to believe that the arrogant, lazy boy in his class had gone on to write *The Great Gatsby*. Scott was on academic probation almost from the start and only managed to avoid expulsion by a strategic attack of tuberculosis in his junior year, which allowed him to go home ill rather than in disgrace. When he returned, he was put back a year, which he hated since this was a kind of social suicide, but he did no better with his classes. Finally, the World War provided an excuse to leave Princeton forever for officers' training school in the South, and his three-and-a-half-year college career dribbled to an inconclusive end. As with the attack of tuberculosis, the war came at a very convenient moment for Scott Fitzgerald.

Scott remained extremely touchy and secretive about his academic failure in later life. He complained to his daughter that his English professors at Princeton really hated poetry and had no idea what it was about. The English department had "an uncanny knack of making literature distasteful to young men," he wrote in another instance. Almost without exception, he had found his teachers dull and unimaginative, and he was determined with Sheilah to give her what he had missed. The F. Scott Fitzgerald College of One would put some spark back into learning. "The schools are neglecting their most important responsibility," he told her, "to make education interesting, to make you love and enjoy it, to apply it to your own life after you leave school."

With Sheilah's education, Scott was able to redress an old wound. He took his College of One very seriously and for the next two years often spent hours every day, time he could not really afford, working out his curriculum and teaching his prize student. Classes convened whenever possible—riding in a car, or at breakfast, or across from each other at the dinner table. Sheilah also took these classes seriously and she worked hard. Though she was as busy as Scott with her own career, gathering gossip and writing seven newspaper columns a week, she generally managed to put in three hours of work a day on her new education.

For Scott, one of the joys of his College of One was that it allowed him to surrender to his lifelong mania for making lists. From his earliest years, though his life might be in chaos—ruined love affairs, liquor, wild parties, insanity, and disorder of every kind—these lists were something he could cling to. Scott now drew up long outlines and schedules: the books Sheilah was to read and detailed projections of how she was to spend her time. She would study Greek and Roman History, "Literature Through the Ages," Philosophy, Art, Music, Decorative Arts and Furniture, and more—all of it culminating with Oswald Spengler's *Decline of the West*, which Fitzgerald believed to be the ultimate description of the modern era.

Scott tried to make all this fun. He used thick pieces of red or gold paper to make covers for the many books he gave Sheilah, marking them as "Special Encino Edition." Often he wrote humorous comments on the covers or in the margins of the books themselves. On the inside back cover of Palgrave's *Golden Treasury* of poetry, he wrote a tough-guy spoof of "Ode on a Grecian Urn":

A Greek Cup They Dug Up. S'as good as new! And think how long it was buried. We could learn a lot of history from it—about the rubes in ancient history, more than from any poetry about them. Those pictures on it must tell a story about their Gods, maybe, or just ordinary people—something about life in the sticks at a place called Tempe. Or maybe it was in the Arcady Valley. These guys chasing the dames are either Gods or just ordinary people—it doesn't give the names on the cup. They sure are tearing after them and the dames are trying to get away. Look—this guy's got a flute, or maybe it's an oboe and they're going to town, ect., ect.

He gave everything his special imaginative touch. Inside *Greek History* by C. B. Newton and E. B. Treat he wrote:

For S.G. For her proficiency in pre-Socratic Philosophy, Hellenistic Anthropology and Trojan Archaeology,
                              from her loving
                              Prof. T. Thermistocles Smith
                              Olympic Games, 1910.

To bring literature to life, Scott and Sheilah acted out scenes together from books. When she read *War and Peace,* Scott became Pierre and Sheilah alternated between Natasha and Helene; they spoke to each other for hours at a time in these personas without a shred of self-consciousness, making up new adventures as they went along. It was a world of make-believe they entered eagerly, happy to forget MGM and Hunt Stromberg and the many movie stars Sheilah continued to offend. One afternoon Scott sent her flowers from the studio with a note that read, *"Helene, je t'aime. Pierre."* When Sheilah read *The Brothers Karamazov*, he became Alyosha—or "Yosh," as he called him—and Sheilah was "Grue"—

Grushenka. These games, like the playacting of children, might go on for many weeks at time; sitting in a car or at dinner, they could instantly step into their make-believe characters. Eventually they branched out from Russian novels and became characters from such classics as *Bleak House* and *Vanity Fair*, though with the British novels Scott sometimes tried a Cockney accent that was so bad it made Sheilah wince, since she knew Cockney all too well.

Scott often had to keep Sheilah from stealing a peek at the last page of a novel before she had arrived there legitimately. He scolded her and said that if the author wanted the last page read first, he would have written it that way. He also had to keep supplying her with fresh bookmarks so she wouldn't bend pages; she simply had no inborn respect for things. But despite an occasional reprimand, Scott did his progressive best to make every subject amusing and relevant. In the margin of *Das Kapital*, at a place where Marx wrote of the "small thefts of the capitalists from the laborer's meals and recreation time. . . the petty pilfering of minutes," Scott added: "They do this at M.G.M. in a big way; so the secretaries say." When it came to getting straight the names and dates of French history, Scott wrote a poem to aid Sheilah's memory. Among its verses:

Lest We Forget
(France by Big Shots)

Frankish Period 500–1000

Clovis—baptized "en regnant"—
Was ancestor to "rois faineantes"

Hammer! Hammer! Charles Martel!
At Tours he sent the Moors to Hell
Mayor-of-the-Palace, Boss of the Gang
He cleared the way for Charlemagne

Charlemagne stands all alone
One pine in a burned-over zone.
He passed—and Europe should cry
    "Merde!" on
the fatal treaty signed at Verdun. . . .

The House of Valois 1350–1600

For Charles the Wise and Charles the Mad
And Jehan's Charles the times were bad;
But Jehan and the Bastard met
And glued that dome on Charles-le-sept.

Life was no heaven seventh
For foes of Louis Eleventh
With marriage, guile and hate
Created he The State

The Renaissance—France sings and dances
Fights and fails with handsome Francis

Catherine de Medici
In fifteen hundred seventy-three
With her sons (two lousy snots)
Massacred the Hugenots. . . .

The Revolution

Mirabeau the swell began it
Then Citoyan Marat ran it
    Hey! Hey!
    Charlotte Corday. . . .

Robespierre was a sea-green incorruptible
They broke his jaw to prove he was
    interruptible. . . .

The Nineteenth Century

The Consulate and Empire blaze:
    And freeze at last at Borodino
Then Elba and The Hundred Days
    And Waterloo—and St. Helena

The Monarchs of The Restoration
Were not favorites of the nation
But even more did Fat Cats hate
The Barricades of Forty-eight

Republic Two was soon to falter. . .
The Décor, now by Winterhalter,
Starred Napoleon the Little
Bluff—a bushel, brains—a tittle

The Prussians take Sedan and Metz
The commune dies on bayonets
The Third Republic comes to stay
—or rather ended yesterday.
VIVE LA FRANCE!

As a poem it wasn't great; it owed more to Ogden Nash than John Keats. But Sheilah loved it because it was written for her, a gift of Scott's seemingly endless talent and generosity of time and energy. It even helped her keep French history straight—or at least French history à la Fitzgerald, which was not always the same as the history of books and universities. Along with her studies, Scott also encouraged Sheilah to try more serious writing than her daily column. They began a play together called *Dame Rumour* about a Hollywood gossip columnist who got into trouble through knowing too much about the stars. Always stick to what you know, he told her. After a few dozen pages and several completed scenes, Scott became too busy with his own work and *Dame Rumour* was never finished.

Then Scott began to encourage her to write her autobiography. He assured her that nobody had a story like she did; she must write it down. One day he presented her with a large black leather-bound ledger with red corners in which she was to confess everything, all the infidel secrets of her past. Scott organized her story into seven different parts, and made headings in the ledger for each section. He then wrote, "Each of the seven parts to have *theme* and dramatic idea, *plot, cast of characters, occupational*. Put it all down." Finally, on the front page of her unwritten life story, he wrote, "The Book of Lillith." Sheilah assumed this was simply a play on her real name without quite understanding who Lilith was. It was only many years later that she glanced through a dictionary and was dismayed to learn that in the Bible Lilith was the first wife of Adam who flew away to become a demon. Once again, even as he educated her, Scott managed to express his eternal ambivalence about the girl from the East End of London who had become Sheilah Graham.

Sheilah continued to study. She was so eager for all of his teaching, from Greek history to decorative arts. Then one night during a game of charades at Bob Benchley's bungalow, she took a bold step and joined Dorothy Parker's team. It was a premeditated act, carefully rehearsed, the summation of months of work. Scott had done his Svengali magic, transforming her almost into a cultured young woman. This was the test. She was nervous but he assured her that charades was nothing; her life had been a charade beyond other people's imagination. At the last moment, he spent several hours briefing her on the definition of the pronoun, because, as he told Sheilah, "at charades, they always ask, 'Is it a pronoun?'"

Ogden Nash guessed almost immediately that Sheilah was acting out a period of art history, Picasso's Blue Period, and Sheilah had rarely felt so happy to be found out in her life.

For Scott it was wonderful to dazzle Sheilah and the hours he put into her education were some of his happiest times; unfortunately, the rest of his life was not going so well. Throughout the passing months, the summer and fall of 1938, his work at MGM had run into one problem after another. After Scott failed to transform *Infidelity* into a moral tale to please the censor, he began a new picture for Hunt Stromberg, *Marie Antoinette*, that would star Irving Thalberg's widow, Norma Shearer. Scott saw the assignment as a chance to pay indirect homage to Thalberg, but Stromberg was becoming increasingly difficult—eccentric even for a producer, and Scott thought he had seen it all with Monkeybitch. There were the endless script conferences that he hated, an ocean of talk that left him feeling empty. Stromberg paced the floor at these meetings, sucking on his foul pipe and throwing wooden matches everywhere. Then without warning he would become distracted and send everyone angrily from the room. Scott didn't have a clue as to what was going on.

To make matters worse, Stromberg had a habit of reconvening these interrupted meetings hours later, telephoning Scott to return to his office or home sometimes late at night. Scott never knew when an evening with Sheilah or friends might end abruptly with such a royal summons. One night Stromberg managed to find Scott at a dinner party at Frances and Albert Hackett's home in Beverly Hills, and he had to hurry off and leave Sheilah stranded for hours. The next day, he sent a short poem to the Hacketts to apologize for his sudden departure:

> Sing a song for Sheilah's supper, belly void
>   of rye;
> Gone before the cocktail, back for the pie.
> Stromberg sent for Poppa, though Papa
>   hadn't et,
> To do what Jesus couldn't—
> Save Marie Antoinette. . . .

It was a clever little rhyme but Scott couldn't save Marie Antoinette any more than Jesus could, and he was taken off the picture after only a few days. His next assignment for Hunt Stromberg was to adapt for the screen a smash Broadway play, *The Women* by Clare Boothe Luce, which would have an entirely female cast. It was while working on this picture that Scott at last discovered Stromberg's secret, which many in Hollywood already knew: The producer was a morphine addict. Now Scott understood the reason for the interrupted story conferences; the producer needed to clear the room so he could phone his obliging studio doctor to hurry over with an injection. Scott was appalled; this was a new low, a hellish opium den in which he found himself. Stromberg had begun taking morphine to ease the pain of a slipped disc, but it had now become a necessity. In the 1930s it was not entirely uncommon for quite ordinary people to become addicted to morphine after a legitimate medical procedure, but Scott was not sympathetic. As a persistent idealist he found it hateful that a person might have such a secret crutch. A drug addict was particularly shoddy and depressing, a creature who lived in a moral shadow.

"Hunt's—run the gamut," he concluded in his notes. Later, his last hero, Monroe Stahr, would become "tired of his own rhythm and the rhythm of the people of Hollywood. He wanted to see people with more secrets than the necessity of concealing a proclivity for morphine." Certainly the lax offscreen ethical climate of Hollywood was disturbing, and Scott the moralist used the screenplay of *The Women* to express his outrage at tarnished things. The story concerned a wife who discovers one day at the beauty parlor that her wealthy husband has taken a paramour: He is having an affair with an ambitious but vulgar shop girl, Crystal Allen, who would be played by Joan Crawford, an actress Fitzgerald could not easily escape. Scott needed a quick way to indicate to the audience exactly what kind of creature this shop girl was. He came up with the idea of having the husband give the shop girl an expensive fur coat to cement their illicit affair—a silver-fox jacket, Scott specified, just like Sheilah's beloved birthday present. When Joan Crawford accepted this jacket without a moral qualm, he was certain everyone in the audience would instantly know she was little more than a prostitute.

It was a low blow to write Sheilah's jacket into the screenplay, but Scott found a chance to take a few shots at his wife and daughter as well. At least prostitutes, shop girls, and gossip columnists worked for a living, and Fitzgerald believed this was very fine. Work was ennobling; work was salvation. But there was another class of women who were idlers, who had never done a day of real work in their lives. Zelda was a prime example of this sort, and it looked to him like Scottie was too. Fitzgerald used the opportunity of a memo to Stromberg to deliver a brief lecture on this sort of lazy creature:

> She is a member of a group, a clan who are brought up with a curious dualism. They are given the best education, tutoring, instruction and chaperonage, but at the same time they are told in a subtle way that they have no special obligations to fulfill, no price to pay for these advantages. Their brothers are at least expected to attain the minimum requirements at Yale, Harvard, Princeton, to fit them to become part of New York's ruling caste—but not the women. Merely satisfying high school requirements is enough to saturate them with expensive cars, mink coats, fabulous jewelry, so at the age of eighteen they have anything they want, no sense of reward or punishment. They own the earth.

A memo like this would be hard to film, but Scott wrote it anyway, to let off steam. He worked on *The Women* throughout the summer of 1938, managing to put a curious transference of his own feelings about women into the script. But despite the silver-fox jacket and various moral lessons intended for his family, MGM did not consider his script bitchy enough and he was taken off the picture. The movie was released in September 1939 and it was a hit, but without Scott's name in the credits; once again he had failed to advance his Hollywood career. Then about the time he and Sheilah moved to Belly Acres, Scott was given a promising new assignment, *Madame Curie*, the story of the humble woman scientist who discovered radium and won the Nobel Prize. Scott had a new producer, Sydney Franklin, and as had happened so often in the past, he forgot his previous disappointments—his spirits soared. This time he believed he was really onto something. *This* would be the great motion picture to establish his reputation as a film dramatist. Sheilah was happy to see Scott more enthusiastic about a script than she had ever seen him before. And as it happened, this plum assignment arrived just in time because his contract at MGM was coming up once again for renewal, and he knew it was important for his future that he deliver something good.

"I am intensely busy," he wrote his daughter. "On the next two weeks, during which I finish the first part of *Madame Curie*, depends whether or not my contract will be renewed. So naturally I am working like hell—though I wouldn't expect you to understand that. . . ." He was convinced Scottie was slouching her way through her first term at Vassar, falling in love, as Scott put it, with "cro-Magnons, natural-born stevedores, future members of the Shriners and plain bums," taking all the easy courses, and tragically ignorant of the saving grace of work. He hoped *Madame Curie* would set her right, and all the spoiled women in America like her. He wanted to hold the French scientist up as a fine example, a new sort of heroine, a symbol of what women could be if only they avoided debutante balls. There was a moral here, and Scott was prepared to hit his audience over the head with it until it penetrated their skulls. "I approach [*Madame*

Curie] with honest reverence," he wrote in a memo to his bosses at MGM. "The picture will be doing a great wrong if [we] do not present Madame Curie as an image of everything woman of the future should aspire to."

Unfortunately, while Scott's new producer, Sydney Franklin, was in agreement with his conception of the script, the executive producer, Bernie Hyman, was not; he was less interested in a moral treatise than a common love story. To Scott's dismay and utter astonishment, Hyman simply took him off the picture before he finished a completed draft. "Bernie Hyman like Zero," he wrote bitterly in his notes. "Looks like nothing, acts like nothing—add him to anything and he decreased it."

It was a terrible disappointment to be taken off *Madame Curie*, a film which would eventually become a hit like so many of the projects on which Scott worked, but once again without his name on it. "I disagreed with everybody about how to do *Madame Curie* and they're trying it another way," he wrote to his daughter with a stubborn pride. "I'm convinced they're not going to make me Czar of the Industry right away, as I thought 10 months ago. It's all right, baby—life has humbled me. I am even willing to compromise for Assistant Czar!"

But Assistant Czar was optimistic; in late December Scott received a termination notice from the MGM accounting department, an impersonal note placed in his paycheck envelope informing him that his one-year contract, due to expire on January 27, 1939, would not be renewed. There was no further explanation. Scott tried to put a good face on it but he was anxious about his future. "Baby am I glad to get out!" he told Max Perkins in a letter in late December. "I've hated the place ever since Monkeybitch rewrote 3 Comrades!" But now he had to consider matters of basic survival. As much as he despised Hollywood, he had been making steady money there for the first time in his life—$1,000 a week for the first six months, and $1,250 for the past year—a fortune by the standards of the thirties. With Sheilah's help he had managed to be frugal and by December 1938 he had paid off most of the $40,000 debt with which he had arrived in California: He was entirely free of his debts to Max Perkins and Harold Ober and owed money still only to his publisher, Charles Scribner. He had managed to transfer to his own name the life insurance policy Scribner had been holding as security, keep Zelda in her expensive sanitarium, and pay Scottie's tuition at school—all this was quite a juggling act, and it left Scott without a cent of savings to show for his eighteen months under salary at MGM. Without a steady job, he had no idea how he would manage and he "began to have that harassed and aghast feeling of those who always live on the edge of solvency."

Then three weeks before he was to leave MGM for good, there seemed to be a last-minute reprieve: He was loaned to David O. Selznick to doctor the dialogue of several scenes of the great epic *Gone With the Wind*. Scott knew that Selznick had gone through nearly every screenwriter in Hollywood endlessly fussing over the script, and that few writers had lasted for long. Still he hoped he might stretch a few weeks into a few months. Scott began with Selznick on January 6, 1939, after first reading the novel. He wrote Scottie about the book:

> I read it—I mean really read it—it is a good novel—not very original, in fact leaning heavily on *The Old Wives' Tale, Vanity Fair*, and all that has been written on the Civil War. There are no new characters, new technique, new observations—none of the elements that make literature—especially no new examination into human emotions. But on the other hand it is interesting, surprisingly honest, consistent and workmanlike throughout, and I felt no contempt for it but only a certain pity for those who considered it the supreme achievement of the human mind.

Scott's new boss, David O. Selznick, was one of those who considered *Gone With the Wind* the supreme achievement of the human mind; he insisted that Scott underline and justify even the slightest change he made in Margaret Mitchell's story. A month later, Scott complained in a letter to Max Perkins: ". . . do you know in that *Gone With the Wind* job I was absolutely forbidden to use any words except those of Margaret Mitchell; that is, when new phrases had to be invented one had to thumb through as if it were Scripture and check out phrases of hers which would cover the situation!"

Despite his scorn—and possible envy of Margaret Mitchell's

phenomenal success—Scott did his best to make Selznick happy. At the moment George Cukor was the director, though the directors would change on this epic nearly as fast as the writers. George Cukor was considered a woman's director, since he had helped make great stars of such actresses as Greta Garbo and Katharine Hepburn, and this made Selznick somewhat nervous. He took Scott aside and explained that between the two of them they would have to protect Clark Gable from George Cukor's giving Scarlett O'Hara too much of the movie. It was a heavy responsibility. Scott also was entrusted to transcribe Miss Mitchell's various descriptions as accurately as possible to the screen. During one script conference, he was asked to figure out a way to make visual a phrase concerning Aunt Pitty, that she "bustle quaintly across the room." Scott returned to Sheilah that night in a foul mood. "How," he asked sarcastically, "do you bustle quaintly across the floor?" Sheilah did her best to give an impromptu demonstration, swinging her rear end from side to side as she made her way quaintly across the living room at Belly Acres. It was ridiculous and they laughed, or at least Scott smiled so deeply he appeared to be laughing. But it was a serious matter if he was to keep his job. "They won't change a word of the book," he complained wearily to Sheilah. "They think Margaret Mitchell is Shakespeare."

For a week, Scott wrote and rewrote the famous staircase scene, constantly asking himself, "What would she say to him? What would he say to her?" Hoping for inspiration, he had Sheilah act out the scene with him from the novel, as they had acted out scenes from so many novels before. Sheilah became Scarlett O'Hara, Scott was Rhett Butler, and they used the winding staircase at Belly Acres for their set. While Scott stood at the bottom, Sheilah descended the stairs grandly, holding the hem of an invisible evening gown with one hand.

"Miss O'Hara," Scott drawled with Southern chivalry.

"Captain Butler, I believe—" She waved an imaginary fan, but it was all too silly and they began to laugh. Sheilah dropped her grand manner and ran giggling into his arms.

"Am I really such an awful actress? I tried to help—"

"Sheilah, it might be better if I work it out on paper," he admitted.

But it was all useless anyway; Selznick had only been window-shopping in hiring Scott Fitzgerald for the job. After two weeks, Selznick fired George Cukor and Scott in tandem, and went on to hire a new director and yet another screenwriter to see what they might do. By the end of January 1939, Scott found himself unemployed and without a steady paycheck for the first time in a year and a half. It was a frightening situation but he was determined to get back to some serious writing of his own. There was a novel left in him yet; he was sure of it. In all, he was more relieved than disappointed to give up the strange craft of screenwriting.

He confessed his Hollywood failure to Max Perkins: "I just couldn't make the grade as a hack—that, like everything else requires a certain practiced excellence."

14

THE PROFESSOR
GOES TO COLLEGE

My whole theory of writing I can sum up in one sentence. An author ought to write for the youth of his own generation, the critics of the next, and the schoolmasters of ever afterward.

—F. Scott Fitzgerald, in a letter to the Booksellers' Convention, 1920

IN FEBRUARY 1939 a young writer named Budd Schulberg was about to serve a literary apprenticeship that he would remember for the rest of his life.

Budd Schulberg was a child of Hollywood, a charter member of the first homegrown generation spawned by the movie industry, the son of B. P. Schulberg, the production head of Paramount Pictures. Budd grew up in Beverly Hills surrounded by wealth and power, a shy and sensitive young man who spoke with a painful stutter. Eventually a family friend, the producer Walter

Wanger, steered him eastward to college—to Dartmouth, which happened to be Wanger's own alma mater. Hollywood was still a rude new empire; those who ruled this industry loved what they had built, but meanwhile they tended to send their children far away to school, to the legitimacy of New England.

Budd did well at Dartmouth; he was bright and he graduated with honors, Phi Beta Kappa. After college, as a thoughtful member of his Depression generation, he joined the Communist Party. Nevertheless, this was a young Communist who loved the movies and he returned to Hollywood determined to support himself as a screenwriter. His father helped him a little, but not too much. By 1939 Budd Schulberg had been out of Dartmouth for three years. He was twenty-five years old, recently married, tall and gangling and very earnest; his stutter remained a difficult speech impediment and he had a tendency to knock things over, and then apologize in a mumble of broken words. Trying to make a living, he came up with an idea for a movie set at Dartmouth during the annual Winter Carnival. It seemed a good premise, at least—the Dartmouth carnival with all the photogenic snow and young people. College pictures had done well in the past. The only thing Budd didn't have was much of a story. Still, he patched together a treatment of sorts and sent it off to his old family friend, Walter Wanger, hoping the producer might feel sufficient nostalgia for his own years at Dartmouth to take the bait.

Budd guessed right. Walter Wanger was known in Hollywood as an "intellectual producer." Few people remained long in his presence before they learned he was "a Dartmouth man," an Ivy League distinction that he wore in California like a badge. He dressed in sports jackets tailored with East Coast caution, and he smoked a pipe—not a messy, gurgling pipe like Hunt Stromberg, but one that managed to stay lit and imply a kind of intellectual superiority to mere cigarettes. Wanger was often seen at the studio with a briefcase bulging with books that local cynics suspected he never actually read.

In early February this well-cut figure of a producer summoned Schulberg into his huge office at the Samuel Goldwyn Studio to discuss the treatment of *Winter Carnival*. His verdict was not encouraging.

"It's lousy. Terrible," Wanger began. Budd expected this to be the end of the matter. But the producer went on to say that *Winter Carnival* might have unplumbed possibilities; all it really needed was a plot and halfway believable characters. "What I think I'll do," Wanger said thoughtfully, "I'll put another writer on it with you."

Budd didn't mind this a bit, as long as he had a job. "Well, okay, who?"

"Scott Fitzgerald."

The shy young writer felt as if he had been struck by a bolt of lightning. As it happened, he had reread *The Great Gatsby* only a few days earlier and Fitzgerald was one of his biggest literary heroes. "My God, isn't Scott Fitzgerald dead?" he asked in awe.

"On the contrary," Wanger replied with a superior smile, "He's in the next office reading your script."

Wanger led the astonished Budd Schulberg into the next room to meet Scott Fitzgerald, who was sitting at a table reading the treatment of *Winter Carnival*. The two writers shook hands, and then with a paternal smile Wanger left them to become acquainted; he was certain that two old Ivy League men would have a lot to say to each other. Scott finished reading the treatment while Budd respectfully waited, casting an occasional curious glance at the older author. Fitzgerald still looked like his photograph from the dust jackets of books Budd had seen; he had the straight nose and fine features of a matinee idol, but it was as if all the living color had been drained from his face to give a spectral impression of death. Scott's mouth was gentle and quick to smile, but his eyes seemed inexpressibly sad.

"Well, it's not very good," Fitzgerald said judiciously, looking up when he was done.

"I know, Mr. Fitzgerald," the young writer agreed quickly. "I don't think it's very good either."

Scott had never been in quite this position before; for the past year and a half, each movie he began was something he thought might become a good film: In every case he was quickly disillusioned, but *Winter Carnival* was obvious trash from the start. The story, such as it was, concerned a glamour girl named Jill who is on her way to Canada when she gets stranded at Dartmouth and after a few misadventures is elected Queen of the Carnival. It was unbelievable from start to finish, lightweight fluff without a moral or new type of heroine anywhere in sight. However, Walter Wanger was offering very good money, fifteen hundred dollars a week, for Scott to guide the young Budd Schulberg (at two hundred dollars a week) through the process of writing a story. Scott was depressed that he must accept such an assignment, but he needed the money too badly to turn down the job. It seemed ironic to him that he could never escape his first novel, *This Side of Paradise.* As a supposed expert on collegiate youth, he was now required to dredge forth some of the old youthful magic one more time.

Fortunately, Scott and Budd Schulberg hit it off from the start. The two writers met the next day for a script conference, but instead of discussing the movie, they found a more interesting topic—*The Great Gatsby.* During Schulberg's last year at Dartmouth, he had taken an honors course called "The Sociology of the American Novel," and the college senior had focused on the writings of F. Scott Fitzgerald. As a result, Budd knew the novels, the short stories, the essays, and nearly all of Scott's work. For Fitzgerald it seemed miraculous that a young man should know his work so well. "Scott was flattered and stimulated and it seemed to me, pathetically pleased to find any product of the Depression Thirties who knew, admired and could talk his books," Schulberg later recalled.

"I didn't think anyone your age read [my] books—they're practically out of print," Scott confessed. He told Budd that between his two best novels, *The Great Gatsby* and *Tender is the Night,* he had in the past year sold five of one and three of the other, earning a grand total of thirteen dollars in royalties; the short-story market had dried up for him as well, and he had not been able to earn a living as a serious writer for years, which was why he had been forced to take "this stinking job," as he put it, in Hollywood. For Scott, Budd Schulberg was more than a nice young man; it was a reprieve from a literary grave to find one youth, at least, who still admired him.

All this made for much more interesting conversation than

Winter Carnival. A week went by too fast. Each day one of them would say, "Today we *have* to work on the story," but then something would take them off in a more lively direction: art, politics, literature, and the fascinating difference between Budd's generation (dour, practical, old before their years) and Scott's "Lost Generation" of the twenties—any subject at all but the movie for which they were being paid. Budd was amazed by Scott's enthusiasm for talk: He might seem prematurely old in appearance, but the moment he warmed to a topic, he was youth itself, on fire with words and ideas; Budd hadn't gone on like this since those late-night discussions at Dartmouth when all of life seemed up for grabs.

Budd was not a bit worried about the neglected screenplay. He considered Scott Fitzgerald "one of the Immortals," and had complete faith that when it came time to face Walter Wanger, a genius like Scott would easily come up with a plot, interesting characters, and profound dialogue. However, by the end of the first week, Scott had done little more than dream up a single new character for the story, a girl he named Florine, who was modeled on his daughter: "She is a freshman at Vassar and completely dazzled by New York—so much so that she has neglected her work and is on probation in college, a probation which she has broken to come to Dartmouth Winter Carnival, pretending she has been summoned home by the illness of her father. She is wild and feverish—in 1920, she would have been a flapper. At present she thinks she is ahead of the times, but she is really behind them."

Scott couldn't resist this little dig at Scottie. As for "the illness of her father," Scott was in fact not feeling well. At Belly Acres, Sheilah slept in the guest bedroom on the ground floor and often heard Scott pacing above her head far into the night, unable to sleep. "My T.B.'s flared up," he complained to her one morning. He monitored his temperature throughout the following days with absorbing interest, fascinated by the slightest variation of the red vein of mercury as it rose and fell. He was alarmed when his temperature soared occasionally to 99.3. But the insomnia was worst of all. At night he lay in pools of sweat; sometimes he changed his sheets two or three times before the dawn finally broke. In the morning he rose exhausted, lit a cigarette, drank his sugared coffee, and began another enervating day in which he never felt entirely physically well.

At the end of a week, Walter Wanger called the two writers together into his office to ask how the screenplay was going. "Great," they lied; they said they were making fabulous progress. No screenwriter in the history of movies has ever told his producer anything less, but Wanger must have felt a chill of suspicion. He warned they had better come up with a story line fast because he was going to send them east the following weekend to New Hampshire for the actual Dartmouth Winter Carnival. A second unit would come along to film background shots that would be spliced into the movie. Of course the second unit had to know the story so that it would know where to film.

This was the first news Scott had that he was expected to travel to New Hampshire. "Walter, I really don't think that's necessary," he said. "Budd is out of there only two or three years and he certainly knows what a Winter Carnival looks like. I remember college parties pretty well from my Princeton days — and I doubt that they've changed that much."

Scott did not feel well; the last thing he wanted was to go to New Hampshire in the snow on a movie he wished he never had to write in the first place. But Wanger had made up his mind. "Scott, I insist on it," the producer said in his most autocratic manner. Wanger in fact was looking forward to a triumphant return to Dartmouth to show off F. Scott Fitzgerald as a literary prize, a symbol of his own progress in the world as a successful Hollywood producer. Even Budd felt a little of this thrill; it would be fun to parade Scott about the campus in front of his old professors. The object of this attention, the prize himself, might be damaged goods on today's market, but academia generally lagged a decade or two behind the times and would hardly know. Scott was not happy to go, but he could not afford to lose the job.

And so with a slight fever and not much sleep, Scott boarded an airplane for the long flight east to film background shots for a movie for which there was still no story. There was an element of absurdity from the start, and to add to the gathering shreds of

comedy Sheilah, who was worried about Scott's health, decided
to come along secretly on the same plane as far as New York. The
secrecy was necessary because Walter Wanger was a possessive
man when people were on his time; he wanted his writers to
think of nothing but the movie at hand and he made it very clear
that wives and girlfriends were not invited.

Sheilah kept to herself at the airport in Los Angeles. She maintained a casual distance in the waiting room and tried not to look
at Scott. After Scott and Budd had boarded the plane, she
stepped on herself at the last moment and took a discreet seat far
in the rear. The cloak-and-dagger routine was Scott's idea and it
appealed to his obscure sense of humor, particularly since Budd
had never met Sheilah and had no idea of what was going on.
Then just before take-off, Budd's father, the head of Paramount,
showed up with a bon voyage present—two vintage bottles of
Mumm's champagne. All the ingredients for the coming farce
were now in place.

Budd opened the first bottle of champagne soon after the
plane was in the air and proposed a toast. Scott tried to beg off.
He said he wasn't feeling well and that he was on the wagon; he
was almost convincing. But Budd was excited at the adventure
that lay ahead—his first real screenwriting job, returning to
Dartmouth, flying east with an author he greatly admired—and
he convinced Scott that just a little one wouldn't hurt. Put like
this, Scott felt it would be almost churlish to refuse. It was very
good champagne and when the first glass was finished, Budd
pressed Scott to have another. Scott was feeling better than he
had for several days and had a third glass.

The two writers had planned to kick the story line of *Winter
Carnival* into shape during the long flight east; they had to dream
up some sort of coherent plot so the second unit would have
something to film. But the champagne was so festive it seemed a
pity to discuss anything so dreary. The bubbles stirred Scott's
enthusiasm and he soon launched forth with a flood of stories
about H. L. Mencken, Ernest Hemingway, Edmund Wilson, e. e.
cummings, and other famous people he had known. Budd was
dazzled at how incredibly smart Fitzgerald was; he seemed to

have read everything, to have known everybody, and with some
champagne to fuel his exuberance he spoke marvelously well.

They were an odd couple: Fitzgerald with his eloquence, and
Schulberg, whose every phrase came out elongated in a torturous stutter. Budd was totally under the older man's spell. The
conversation drifted to politics and Schulberg was surprised to
discover that Scott was a Marxist, entirely left-leaning in his outlook, though he did not like Stalin very much. Budd had been
chafing under Party discipline for some time and he found
Scott's views refreshing. It was difficult for him to think of
Fitzgerald as "a decadent writer" simply because his themes did
not advance the cause of the proletarian revolution. All this
made for great conversation and the second bottle of champagne
was soon opened. Scott listened as skillfully as he spoke, drawing the young man out. He was particularly interested in Budd's
stories of his childhood, what it was like to grow up in a place as
strange as Hollywood. Budd assured Scott that when you grew
up in the film industry, Hollywood had little glamour—it was
just a company town like any other. A year and a half later,
Schulberg would be astonished to read many of his exact state-
ments about a Hollywood childhood coming from Cecelia, the
narrator of *The Last Tycoon*.

In the midst of all this bubbly conversation, Sheilah strolled
occasionally up the aisle from the rear of the plane. Scott and
Sheilah had played make-believe so often in the past that it was
nothing for them to pretend polite surprise at seeing one another
on the same plane east, and to act as if they were only casually
acquainted. "So nice to see you," Scott said courteously, and
turned to introduce her to Budd—"Do you know Sheilah
Graham?" Occasionally as the night flight continued, he said in
an offhand way to Budd, "I think I'll go back and sit with
Sheilah." It was the sort of subtle practical joke that Scott loved.

Sheilah, from her position in the rear of the plane, was suspicious that Scott had become entirely too merry, sliding in next to
her from time to time, his eyes full of mischievous glee. Was this
a good brownie or a bad brownie? she wondered. He chuckled
about Budd, the poor idiot, so completely in the dark. Sheilah
was glad to see Scott in such fine spirits, but she remained decid-

edly uneasy. When she leaned too close to sniff his breath, and asked pointed questions about how he was feeling, Scott simply returned to the front of the plane. He spent the night in this manner going back and forth, with a wonderful sense that he was putting it over on everybody—first Budd, then Sheilah.

The next day in New York, Scott and Budd checked into a suite on the tenth floor of the Warwick Hotel on West 53rd Street, while Sheilah went discreetly to the Weylin Hotel a few blocks away. She set about to wait for Scott with a vague but insistent foreboding of disaster.

For Scott the party was just getting under way. As soon as he and Budd arrived in their suite at the Warwick, he picked up the phone and ordered a bottle of gin. Budd assumed this was how the Immortals did their stuff. With a belly full of liquid inspiration the two writers finally sat down to thrash out the details of *Winter Carnival*. But each idea seemed more absurd than the last—stale clichés, mechanical story plots that were particularly laughable after a bottle of gin. Sometime in the afternoon, Budd got a call from a group of old Dartmouth friends who wanted to see him; it seemed a good chance to clear his head. But when he returned to the Warwick an hour later the suite was empty and there was a note on his bed, the strangest note he had ever seen, entirely devoid of punctuation. It read: "Pal you shouldn't have left me pal because I went down in the bar pal and then I came and looked for you pal and then I went down in the bar again pal and I'll be waiting for you pal when you get back pal."

Budd sensed his screenwriting partnership was in big trouble. He rushed down to the King Cole Bar on the ground floor of the Warwick, but Scott was nowhere to be seen. He described Fitzgerald to the bartender who nodded wisely—yes, such a man had been there earlier but had wandered off down the street. Budd hurried along Sixth Avenue searching in every bar he passed until at last he found Scott Fitzgerald. Scott was in terrible shape—smashed, staggering drunk, there was hardly an adjective to describe it. Budd had never before seen anyone in quite this condition and he felt the first faint stirrings of panic. They had a nine o'clock meeting with Walter Wanger the next morning at the Waldorf Towers and by then they had to have *something*—a plot for the damn movie. He tried to impress upon his grinning partner that now was the time for cold showers and cups of black coffee. Scott assured him this presented no problem whatsoever. They would kick the thing into shape, pal. Why, he had written hundreds of the best short stories ever and some novels, too, so the kid should just relax and watch how the old pros did their stuff.

Budd guided Scott back to their hotel suite and ordered a pot of coffee. They got out their notebooks and pencils and Budd was desperately ready to watch the old pro come to life with brilliant ideas. But there was something about *Winter Carnival* that was as slippery as trying to climb up a mountain of ice; it seemed physically impossible to even concentrate on it for more than five minutes at a time. Distractions were everywhere. A waiter with a German accent appeared with their coffee and Scott became convinced the man was a Nazi spy. *"Sieg Heil!"* Scott said cunningly, hoping the waiter would give himself away by replying in kind. Scott then tried a Nazi salute, but the waiter only looked increasingly mournful and anxious to leave the room. As soon as he was gone, Budd objected, "Scott, that really wasn't fair—he might be a refugee from Hitler, he might be as much anti-Hitler as we are." Scott saw the point right away and he felt terrible. "I should go and apologize," he insisted, and darted down the hall after the German waiter to express his effusive and lengthy regrets. All these things took time away from artistic endeavor.

By nine the following morning, the two screenwriters had consumed quite a bit more booze but they still did not have a movie. They showed up at the Waldorf Towers bedraggled and exhausted to face an impossibly crisp and perfectly shaved Walter Wanger.

"How was the trip?" the producer asked pleasantly—not yet apprehending that there was a basic flaw in his plan to shoot a lighthearted comedy in the snow. "Did you see anyone you knew on the plane?"

Having no idea of the need to keep Sheilah's presence secret, Budd replied innocently, "Oh, yes, Sheilah Graham was on the plane." Wanger did a double take and turned angrily to

Fitzgerald, "Scott, you son of a bitch." Wanger was always unpleasant when his will was thwarted. "She's a bitch," he snorted.

"I wouldn't say that if I were you," Scott objected, moving closer.

"Sheilah Graham is a bitch," Wanger repeated.

Scott put his nose inches from Walter Wanger's face and said once again, quietly but full of threat, "I wouldn't say that if I were you." Only the lingering memory of fifteen hundred dollars per week kept Scott from taking a slug at the man, as he had done more freely with Sheilah's producer in Chicago.

Wanger backed down. "I was joking," he said with a thin smile. But bad feelings lingered. At least the showdown over Sheilah forestalled a serious script conference. Budd and Scott managed to mumble a few wild generalities about the story line and make their escape, promising to meet Wanger later that evening at Grand Central Station for the journey to New Hampshire.

In 1939 there was a special Winter Carnival train that once a year wound through New England from Manhattan to Hanover, picking up its cargo of eager young faces from all of the collegiate spots along the way. Scott and Budd, worse for wear than in the morning, met Wanger at the train and everything began to unravel at an alarming speed. The producer was in high spirits at the prospect of returning to his old college and he suggested that Budd and Scott walk the length of the train with him to ogle the pretty college girls. Scott demurred, but Wanger was feeling entirely too pleased with himself to take no for an answer and he insisted the two writers accompany him. Scott could hardly stand to look at all the eager faces, seventeen and eighteen years old; they seemed so unbearably young, children with their illusions intact.

Wanger grandly led the procession up and back the length of the train, smiling here and there at a pretty girl, suggesting to one that she might be right for a part in his movie. Scott found it all positively loathsome and perhaps it was from an unconcealed sarcastic glint in his eye that Wanger seemed to realize for the first time that matters were not as they should be. He took

Schulberg aside and asked, "Budd, tell me the truth—has Scott been drinking?"

Budd hesitated. "Well, a *little* bit," he admitted.

Wanger was furious. "God damn it, his agent gave me his word of honor—his word of *honor* that if I hired Scott on this assignment that he would not touch a drop. You know, Scott is an alcoholic and if he takes one drop there'll be no end to it."

Budd was at a loss. He had no idea Scott was an alcoholic and as with the matter of Sheilah's presence on the plane, he felt someone should have clued him in. He was getting a little angry himself now. He returned to Scott determined to get the author in some sort of shape to get down to work. But this was not easy. Scott produced a new pint bottle of gin from his pocket, like a magician pulling a rabbit out of a hat. Budd had no idea where he got the bottle since it seemed they had been together constantly since leaving the hotel. This was all getting crazy—and the bottom line was that Budd needed the job too. He was feeling more and more desperate.

In the middle of the night they arrived in Springfield, Massachusetts, and Budd urged Scott off the train for a quick cup of coffee—anything to sober him up and get his mind working on the plot. It was bitterly cold outside and Budd wished he had thought to bring their overcoats along. They hurried into a small brightly lit station coffee shop and Budd ordered the strongest, hottest coffee they had. While getting up to leave, Scott staggered and an envelope fell from his pocket onto the floor beneath a railing; it contained his fifteen-hundred-dollar paycheck, so desperately important, which he had not found time to mail to his bank in Los Angeles. Scott knelt on the floor but in his condition picking up anything as slippery as an envelope was a challenge. Scott was still on his knees when they heard the train whistle blow. Budd managed to haul Scott to his feet and they hurried back to the platform—but the train was already pulling away. The two writers stood on the platform and shouted as loud as they could for the train to stop, then watched helplessly as the red taillights disappeared into the snow-covered landscape.

Scott was philosophical. He was in a state where it was easy to accept all of life's misfortunes with an owlish smile. But Budd felt like pulling his hair. He could hardly believe this new disaster, to be abandoned on a bitterly cold February night in the deep snow without their luggage, without even their overcoats to keep them warm. Budd led Scott back to the coffee shop where he made a fuss and managed to find an ancient taxi, a Model A Ford, and a languid driver who scratched his head at the thought of two Hollywood fellas in such a fix, but said he was willing to try to catch the train.

The Model A had no heater and there did not appear to be any shock absorbers as they bounced over the frozen road. The driver handed his passengers a jug of applejack to keep warm and also a thin blanket which they put over their heads like a tent. After an hour's drive they overtook the train and raced it to the next station. Scott and Budd were not certain this was a scheduled stop so they took no chances; they stood defiantly on the tracks and flagged the iron monster down. With a grinding of wheels and groan of steam, the Hanover Special came to a halt and let the writers back on board. Walter Wanger never even knew they were gone.

The Hanover Special reached its wintry destination later that morning. Among the festive crowd meeting the train was a Hollywood technician, a second-unit director who had arrived with his equipment a few days earlier. He was a man who did not yet suspect he would be immortalized in two separate novels: as Robinson, the technical whiz who could fix just about anything at Monroe Stahr's studio in *The Last Tycoon*, and as Hutchinson —"Hutch"—the overeager second-unit director in Budd Schulberg's 1950 novel *The Disenchanted*, which would fictionalize the events of this Dartmouth weekend. The second-unit man was a wonder of energy, eager to get his cameras rolling. He approached the bedraggled writers as they stepped from the train. "Where's the first set-up?" he asked brightly. "I'm all set to go—just tell me where the first set up is!"

His health and enthusiasm came as a slap in the face to the two writers, who had hardly slept for two nights and had been drinking heavily since Los Angeles. "Now there's a man—that

Robinson. He was a trouble-shooter—fixed the telephone wires in Minnesota blizzards—nothing stumps him," Scott wrote sarcastically in the second chapter of *The Last Tycoon*, after an earthquake has tossed the movie studio to and fro. At present, however, this apparition of energy was not yet a figure of fun; he represented the moment of reckoning for Scott and Budd. The cameras were set to roll on the various background shots which later would be projected upon huge screens at the Goldwyn Studio in Los Angeles; the actors would stand before these screens and say their lines, well-protected from the bitter New Hampshire cold. All that was missing was the script. Scott extemporized wildly; he sent the second unit off to film in front of the skating club, hoping this would give them some time.

From the station, the writers made their way to the Hanover Inn where Walter Wanger and the crew from Hollywood had their accommodations. But here they encountered a new problem: No one had thought to make reservations for Scott and Budd. After some confusion, they were put in a bare attic which contained a metal double-decker bed and a table, but no chairs. Scott found this howlingly funny, and symbolic of how Hollywood treated writers. Later in the afternoon, one of Budd's old professors dropped by, Red Merril, who had taught the course in which Budd had first encountered the writings of Scott Fitzgerald. Red Merril was a great fan of Fitzgerald and brought along a bottle of whiskey as a small token of his esteem; here was one professor, at least, who knew the way to a writer's heart. Scott, Budd, and Red sat on the bunk beds, polished off the bottle, and talked happily from one subject to another. The visit was certainly the high point of the Dartmouth weekend, and Red Merril the only representative of the English department to show Fitzgerald any honor. But the whiskey added to a deteriorating situation.

From this point on, the memories became confused. Budd remembered later that they trudged through the deep snow to the ski jump for some reason or another. But they were dressed all wrong for such a trek in city clothes. Scott's disheveled suit, his battered hat, and old overcoat were laughable to the young college kids who were so fresh and sure of themselves in their brightly colored ski clothes. It was different when a young person was drunk; to watch a middle-aged man slip and fall about in the snow was a terrible spectacle and brought forth malicious laughs and sneers from the passing crowd. Budd was nearly as drunk as Scott, but he was younger and more resilient; he managed to point Scott back to their attic room, which seemed the best place to hide.

Scott passed out for a while on the bunk bed, and Budd thought this was the very best place for him. But then Scott suddenly got up and wobbled toward the door. "I'm going to Zelda, she needs me," he said thickly. In his drunkenness, he did not call out for Sheilah, but for his lost wife. "I'm going to Zelda. . . ."

Budd knew this was a crazy idea so he headed Scott off at the door and dragged him back to the bed. Then Scott seemed to pass out again and Budd started taking off his shoes. But Scott was only pretending to be asleep. He opened his eyes and said bitterly, "Oh, you must be enjoying yourself, feeling so strong, so young, so damn sure of yourself. . . . " This was when Budd finally lost his patience; he had put up with a lot since leaving Los Angeles and now he stormed off by himself to a fraternity bar he knew from his undergraduate days to drown his frustrations and maybe find some people his own age. But Scott showed up like a recurring hallucination. It was incredible—the man wouldn't quit. They both ordered a few rounds and soon they were the greatest of buddies all over again, carousing "out into the Carnival night laughing and improvising scandalous songs like any other two Carnival celebrants."

Scott was feverish, he was drunk, his feet were nearly frozen in the snow. But Budd was continually astonished at the things he said. He appeared hardly capable of standing on his feet, but ideas poured forth from him as though his mind were an endless fountain. "You know I used to have a beautiful talent, baby," he confided to Budd. "It used to be a wonderful feeling to know it was there, and it hasn't all gone yet. I think I have enough left to stretch out over two more novels. . . ."

In the midst of this flow of whiskey and wild talk, the second-unit director returned as a sort of unavoidable leitmotiv wanting to know what to film next. "Okay, we're ready, goddammit, just

tell us where the next set-up is and we'll get it for you!" he cried.
The man seemed positively deranged; with increasing hilarity,
Budd and Scott sent him off in different directions on his fool's
errand around the Dartmouth campus. In the evening, Wanger
had arranged a small reception to show off F. Scott Fitzgerald to
the Dartmouth English department and give the two writers an
opportunity to explain the story of *Winter Carnival* to the curious
academics. Scott and Budd appeared at this command performance with their clothes askew and eyes bloodshot, slurring
their words. It was no longer possible to obscure the facts of the
situation—not only were the screenwriters shamelessly drunk,
but it was obvious they had no story. Wanger was gravely
embarrassed.

The faculty room at Dartmouth was oak-paneled, heavy with
Ivy League respectability and muted Anglophilia. Scott and
Budd's disheveled presence came as an insult to the gathered
English teachers, gentlemen who seemed to prefer their authors
safely dead, arranged neatly on library shelves, rather than alive
in their midst in the somewhat rude and messy throes of creation. One professor, Alan McDonald, an old Princetonian,
regarded Scott with a particularly nasty expression. He said in a
loud aside, "He's really a wreck, isn't he?" Then the other faculty
members joined in the baiting of the drunk author. There was
something about the sight of Fitzgerald that made them want to
celebrate his ruin with all the petty jealousy to which cloistered
academics in small communities are often prone. Scott managed
some barbed comments of his own, including a savage assessment of Professor McDonald's old-school necktie—a school,
Scott was certain, that existed only in some haberdasher's fantasy. "Lotta nonsense," he said at last and managed to rise from
his chair. Then he gathered the remaining shreds of his dignity
and addressed the room in a loud voice: "You know, I'd love to
be a professor in a university like this with all the security and
the smug niceties, instead of having to put up with the things we
have to put up with out there in the world. I bid you good night,
gentlemen."

Scott walked from the room with Budd Schulberg in tow, leaving the professors to finish him off in his absence in a feeding

frenzy of scorn. They chortled over what a stumbling drunk the famous author had become; they said it was too bad that after such a brilliant start he should end up writing trash.

Only one person came to Scott Fitzgerald's defense, but it was not a professor from the English department: It was one of the Hollywood technicians, a camera operator from the hard-working second unit. "He walked out of here on his own feet, didn't he?" the cameraman said angrily to the room of gathered academics. And then he added with scorn, "He knows more than any of you will ever know."

Later that evening, dejected and miserable, Scott and Budd were staggering about in the snow outside the Hanover Inn when they encountered the apparition of Walter Wanger in full evening dress, white tie, tails, and top hat. At the sight of his writers, Wanger turned a number of colors including (as Budd later remembered), "Dartmouth green." The producer was nearly apoplectic that Scott and Budd had dared to destroy his Walter Mitty fantasy of a glorious college return and he fired them on the spot.

"I don't know what the next train is out of here, but you two are going to be on it!" he roared. Wanger would not even let them return to their room to fetch their baggage, but found someone to drive the two writers immediately to the train station. Budd and Scott were piled onto The Montrealer which passed through Hanover in the middle of the night and carried them southbound to New York. Scott finally fell asleep now that he could do no more damage. When the train arrived in Grand Central Station around eight the following morning, he was still out cold and Budd could not wake him. This presented a problem when the conductor came through and told them they had to get off. At last, with the help of a porter, Budd managed to get Scott off the train and into a taxi headed for the Warwick Hotel.

But the nightmare weekend had not yet come to an end. At the Warwick the desk clerk glanced briefly at the two disreputable figures without baggage, and then cast his experienced eye into his reservation book to say, alas, there were no vacancies. Budd declared hotly that they had just left the Warwick hardly twenty-four hours earlier—they *had* to have a room. But the clerk shrugged his shoulders with the ruthlessly polite manner of his profession and would not budge. Budd had no choice but to steer Scott back into a taxi and drive to another hotel. But it was the same story at every hotel they tried. No one would take in the two drunk screenwriters returned from their Arctic hell.

Scott was feeling deathly ill; all the drink and traipsing about in the snow had caught up with him. After six or seven hotels refused to give them a room, he said gently, "Well, Budd, I know where I can get in—at the Doctor's Hospital." The hospital had dealt with Fitzgerald before, though never in quite so bedraggled a condition. Scott was admitted, according to the hospital records, with a fever of 103.8 and "a mild to moderate upper respiratory infection." He was described as "confused, excitable and restless, with difficulty in coordinating his speech."

As soon as Budd had checked Scott into the hospital, he phoned Sheilah at the Weylin Hotel, where she was still anxiously waiting.

"I've got bad news, Sheilah—"

"Scott's dead!" she cried.

"No, no, no. But he's sick. I've been taking care of him. He went on a terrible bender—I should never have given him that champagne. . . . "

Budd related the whole saga of the Dartmouth weekend and was relieved to let Sheilah take over. He was only a young man, after all, and he had wandered into something over his head. Schulberg returned to Hollywood where Walter Wanger rehired him alone to work on *Winter Carnival*; he believed the young man deserved a second chance since he was a family friend and it was clear he had been led astray by the alcoholic insanity of Scott Fitzgerald.

As for Scott, this was a bender which would take some time to repair. Scott remained for three days in the Doctor's Hospital, and then another week with Sheilah recovering at the Weylin before they were able to return together to California. In New York, Sheilah found a psychiatrist, Dr. Richard H. Hoffmann, to visit with Scott for an hour every day. Dr. Hoffmann had met Scott and Zelda in Paris in 1925; he admired Scott's writing, knew about his drinking, and said he would do what he could. But Scott was not an easy patient. One afternoon Sheilah came into the room after a session and was dismayed to see that Scott had managed to reverse roles: He was listening to Dr. Hoffmann's problems and happily psychoanalyzing his psychiatrist. It was a typical Fitzgerald maneuver.

As far as Scott was concerned, New York psychiatrists "all seem a little bit overnervous themselves, to me." In fact, Scott was not about to entrust his psyche to a medical man—to a poet, perhaps, but none was available. He went along just to make Sheilah happy and on the strict condition that she never discuss him behind his back. "Anything Dr. Hoffmann has to say about me, I want to know—there'll be no whispering in corners," he insisted. It was only many years later, at Sheilah's request, that Dr. Hoffmann agreed to talk about the sessions. He told her that Scott suffered from hyperinsulinism, a disease which is the reverse of diabetes and results in a craving for sugar. The disease, he said, may well have been caused by Scott's drinking but now it had a life of its own. Scott's body craved sugar, and alcohol was the quickest fix at hand.

Beyond the physical problem, Dr. Hoffmann said Scott believed himself finished as a writer. "I don't have it any more. It's gone, vanished," he told the psychiatrist. The doctor did his best to convince Scott that what was gone was not his talent, but rather his adolescent illusions about life. He quoted Emerson: "On the debris of your despair, you build your character." He said, "This is not your death, it is the death of your youth. This is a transitional period, not an end. You will lie fallow for a while, then you will go on." Later, when Scott wrote asking for his bill, Dr. Hoffmann waived his usual fee. He replied in his letter, "Let's buy a wreath for the grave of your adolescence, and then go on from there."

Back home in California, Scott continued to telephone and send notes to Budd Schulberg whenever he had an inspiration for *Winter Carnival*. It didn't matter that he was no longer on the payroll; Scott believed his young friend could not manage without him. But he needn't have worried about Budd; the shy young

man with the stutter went on quite without Fitzgerald's help to
write such critically acclaimed movies as *On the Waterfront* and
Faces in the Crowd, both of which were based on best-selling novels Schulberg had also authored. Budd Schulberg would garner
the Hollywood laurels Scott himself longed for but would never
have.

As for *Winter Carnival*, a story was finally written and a movie
made. It enjoyed a vogue for a time on the Dartmouth campus
with midnight showings on Saturday nights. The students loved
to hoot and holler at the camp misrepresentation of their Winter
Carnival—laughter too young to understand that even a second-
rate comedy has its cost.

15

BLUE GIN

When drunk I make them all pay and pay and pay.
—F. Scott Fitzgerald to Ernest Hemingway, September 9,
1929

IN THE COLD EARLY MONTHS OF 1939, with no movie work in sight, Scott tried to convince Scribner's to republish his early writings. The money would be a godsend, and he could certainly use the lift to his morale.

"I have come to feel somewhat neglected," Scott wrote Max Perkins soon after MGM let him go. "Isn't my reputation being allowed to let slip away? I mean what's left of it. . . the recession is over for awhile and I have the most natural ambition to see my stuff accessible to another generation. . . A whole generation now has never read *This Side of Paradise*. . . You can imagine how distasteful it is to blow my own horn like this but it comes from a deep feeling that something could be done, if it is done at once, about my literary standing—always admitting that I have any at all."

Max Perkins wrote back tactfully to say that at present it was not feasible to reprint his old work. For Scott it seemed the world just didn't want him. Even Max had turned him down, his old mentor of long ago—Max, who had once threatened to resign his job if Scribner's did not accept *This Side of Paradise*. Scott wondered what in the world he was to do now. After the icy disaster of Dartmouth, the future was a cause for anxiety.

A new novel might change everything, if only he could summon forth the old magic. Scott spent some days tossing book ideas about in his head but he could not decide whether to tackle the Hollywood story which he had been mulling over for some time, or get back to an even older idea for an historical novel, tentatively called *Phillippe, Count of Darkness*, that would be set in medieval France. Scott's idea was to base the hero of this book, Phillippe de Villefranche, on Ernest Hemingway—a charismatic artist/man-of-action as he might have been in the tenth century. Unfortunately, either novel, France or Hollywood, would take time, and time was money, and he had neither—not with Zelda's hospital and Scottie's tuition and a dozen other expenses that were like the meter of a taxi constantly running. Scott never considered the expense of his own doctors' bills after going on a binge, but they were not so cheap either.

Along with the money, there was another reason that made Scott hesitate to throw himself into a long new work: He was no longer certain he had the knack, as he told Dr. Hoffmann. He felt used up. "I have asked a lot of my emotions—one hundred and twenty stories," he lamented in his notebook. "The price was high, right up with Kipling, because there was one little drop of something not blood, not a tear, not my seed, but me more intimately than these, in every story, it was the extra I had. Now it has gone. . . ."

Uncertain about his talent, badly in need of money, Scott believed he had but one option left: trash, as he succinctly called writing that was done not out of blazing passion, but cold need. On March 1 he made up a list of each studio and what kind of pictures they might want:

Columbia:	Story for Edward G. Robinson
Paramount:	Story for Lamour-Harlow type
Metro:	Story for Heddy LaMarr [*sic*]
20th-Fox:	Stories for Temple

And so on until he covered every studio in town. Scott hoped in this manner to organize his prospects and dream up an original story, a potboiler someone might buy. But then out of the blue, a job was dropped in his lap: H. N. Swanson, his West Coast agent, managed to come up with a freelance assignment on a picture called *Air Raid* for Madeleine Carroll at Paramount. Scott had no illusions about the movie; this was about as trashy as it got, but it would be nearly a month of work.

The money was fine, but Fitzgerald the artist found it depressing to lower his standards in such a way. "I expect to dip in and out of the pictures for the rest of my natural life," he complained to Scottie, "but it is not very soul-satisfying because it is a business of telling stories fit for children and this is only interesting up to a point. It is the greatest of all human mediums of communication and it is a pity that the censorship had to come along and do this, but there we are." A year later he said: "There's always some lousy condition [in making movies]. Our condition is that we have to take people's own favorite folklore and dress it up and give it back to them." Maybe Ted Paramore could do this happily, but not Scott Fitzgerald. He felt dirty, like a spoiled priest. At Belly Acres the worst months had begun.

It was a miracle that throughout the binges, melodramas, and occasional movie work, the F. Scott Fitzgerald College of One rarely closed its doors. The prize student continued to read and study her lessons at least three hours a day, and the professor used every possible moment to cross-examine and discuss what she had learned. Sheilah's new education occasionally emboldened her to make a literate comment about one thing or another. One evening as she stood with Scott on the lawn watching a California sunset, she tried to describe the sky in poetic language, but he stopped her before she could finish. "Don't ever tell me what the sky is like," he said irritably. Sheilah was crushed. She had to suppose that her observation had been trite, and that even with a bit of Proust and Keats under her belt, she was still far from being the sort of person—like Zelda—who could say interesting things.

Her quasi-education left her in a difficult limbo, neither in one world nor the other. She knew at last the difference between the Hundred Years War and the Thirty Years War, but she still did not feel entirely legitimate. Before Scott she had simply taken whatever she wanted without moral qualms; now she understood that this was wrong and she came to despise herself for all her trickery, past and present. And yet, how do you get integrity at the (secret) age of thirty-four when all your life you've been an absolute infidel stealing meat pies and any other goodies as long as no one was around to find you out? As far as Sheilah was concerned, Scott was the embodiment of a mysterious world of "values" that you probably had to go to Princeton to ever entirely understand. She made herself unhappy trying to emulate him, and she was ashamed often to find herself thinking of commonplace things—food and sex, and scooping Louella Parsons with some juicy bit of gossip. She was certain that Scott contemplated much loftier matters, entire empires that inched forward and backward at a foot a day in his splendidly poetic mind.

How strange then that he was a drunkard, this man who was so much better than herself—a fault she found absurd and elementary. In her black leather-bound ledger, "The Book of Lillith," she began a page about him, writing at the top, "The Story of an Inebriated Gentleman." Underneath, after a great deal of thought, she managed to follow this with only a single line: "Living with him was like sitting on top of a volcano—picturesque but uncomfortable." In fact, she never knew what to expect from Scott; on any particular day she might encounter a Scott Fitzgerald of consummate charm delicately reciting "Ode to a Nightingale," or a maniac with a sly smile and filthy shirt calling her a cunt and a paramour. It kept her on her toes.

She was not even entirely certain when Scott was drinking for he could be quite the pixie, bubbly as champagne, sober as well as drunk. Sometimes she kissed him for no other reason than to taste his mouth for gin—and then she felt guilty afterward for being so tricky. He saw very well what she was up to and some-

times teased her with wild stories of old debauches. He told her
that one time in 1935 he had the D.T.'s so bad he saw beetles and
pink mice running over his body and elephants dancing on the
ceiling. She was awfully gullible, ready to believe every shocking
word, but there was something about the image of elephants
actually *dancing* on the ceiling, and the glint in Scott's eye, that
made her suspect this was only his cruel sense of humor. It was
very maddening.

"Which is the real you?" she demanded finally. "The Dr. Jekyll
or the Mr. Hyde?"

"The sober man," he answered quickly, but of course Scott
might say anything. In fact—and this came as a shock to her—he
sometimes lied.

Sheilah did not give up. After Dartmouth, she urged Scott to
join Alcoholics Anonymous, but Scott received the suggestion
with the greatest disdain. He refused to admit he was an alcoholic and he certainly had no wish to be anonymous. "I was
never a joiner," he told her distastefully. "AA can only help weak
people because their ego is strengthened by the group. The
group offers them the strength they lack on their own." Exactly,
Sheilah thought. But Scott refused to regard himself as such a
weakling. *He* was a man of character who chose to drink, one
might say, in the heroic mode. It was a poet's prerogative to
destroy himself however he may choose—with a surfeit of
euphoria if it might be found. Some years earlier while in a similar debate with petty minds—one of Zelda's doctors—Scott justified his refusal to give up liquor by recalling Ulysses S. Grant: "I
can only think of Lincoln's remark about a greater man and
heavier drinker than I have ever been—that he wished he knew
what sort of liquor Grant drank so he could send a barrel to all
his other generals."

So send a barrel of gin to General Fitzgerald; he would continue to guard his flank against any attack. But Sheilah knew
how to wage a campaign herself, and she didn't always play by
the rules. One afternoon Scott went to his barber, leaving Sheilah
alone in the house with a difficult moral decision. Scott had
taught her that decent well-educated people, Anglo-Saxon peo-

ple, lived by a personal code that was more important to them than money, pleasure, or death; America had been built by such people—or at least some sections of New England and the Midwest. To get your way by stealth was not only dishonorable but, by implication, somehow Jewish. Alone in the house, Sheilah agonized as to whether or not she should commit a terrible act: search through Scott's drawers and private belongings for hidden bottles of gin. He would be furious, of course, and see it as a great breach of his privacy. After a brief struggle with her conscience—very brief—she gave in to the impulse to ransack Scott's bedroom. Her only hesitation was that he would come back too soon and catch her in the act.

She found what she was looking for almost immediately— eleven empty gin bottles among his socks and underwear. It was the confirmation of her worst fears. *Eleven bottles!* But what was Sheilah to do now? She understood that Scott must not discover she had been through his things. He would never forgive her. She considered various subtle ways to confront him, but she had no self-control. The moment he walked in the door she blurted out her discovery, her voice shaking as she held before him the evidence of his deceit, the eleven empty bottles he had tried to hide.

"What's that to you?" he answered sharply. He frowned so hard his features crowded all together into the center of his face. With a great show of insolence, Scott walked into the kitchen and pulled out a secret bottle from the back of a cupboard; he unscrewed the top and raised it to his lips and drank heavily.

Sheilah shouted at him. "Why don't you stop it? Any idiot can laugh at you! Why are you doing this? You don't know how silly you are! You're a good writer, why are you wasting your talent? You'll die. You'll drop dead. You'll have a stroke. You'll be through in Hollywood, through for good—then what will you do?" She had never shouted at him before and they were both surprised. He gave her a look of infinite scorn, and then retreated from the kitchen with his bottle of gin for the seclusion of his upstairs bedroom.

Sheilah hated fighting with Scott and yet the incident left her even more determined to do something—anything—about his drinking. She remembered now that in Chicago Arnold Gingrich had told her about a pill he had tried once on another *Esquire* writer, an alcoholic, with remarkable results; all Sheilah must do was drop one of these pills secretly into Scott's gin and he would become so violently ill that in the future even the thought of liquor would nauseate him. At the time Sheilah believed Scott would come to his senses and stop drinking on his own; she could not quite imagine playing Mata Hari, slipping a drug into Scott's drink when he wasn't looking. But a year had passed since Gingrich had made the suggestion and Scott was drinking more than ever; Sheilah was desperate enough to give it a try.

Unfortunately, the pill had a strange side effect: Only minutes after it dissolved in alcohol, it would turn Scott's gin a bright iridescent blue. A color, Sheilah shuddered to think, that was almost the same as that of her Ford. This meant she would have to work fast and find some way to doctor Scott's drink almost immediately before he had it. It made the whole operation more difficult. To pull it off, she would need all her trickery—this time applied to a selfless cause.

Scott had a regular nightly routine. Every evening at eleven o'clock he sat in the living room and listened to the late news on the radio, following the progress of the Spanish Civil War with intense interest. When the news was finished, he made his way into the kitchen to a secret bottle of gin he had stashed on a high kitchen shelf. Scott thought he was tricky, but he was no match for Sheilah. She spent a number of days developing a plan of battle that depended upon Scott's evening nightcap.

Sheilah waited until the weekend to make her move, for she did not want Scott to be sick and miss a day at the studio. She found a doctor to give her a prescription for the drug and then bought six bottles of Gordon's gin, Scott's brand, at a liquor store, receiving a frankly appraising glance from the clerk. Back at Belly Acres, she hid the six bottles in the kitchen. By the time evening arrived, she had lost and regained her nerve a dozen times. It worried her that the pill would make Scott ill—she hoped not too ill. While the eleven o'clock news was still in progress, she said good night to Scott with a deceptively sweet smile and made her way stealthily into the darkened kitchen.

She found one of her hidden bottles, poured enough of it down the sink so that it would be the same level as Scott's bottle on the shelf, then dropped a pill down its neck. She shook vigorously and substituted the doctored gin for Scott's in the cupboard. At last, with great misgivings, she escaped to the dining room to sit and wait for Scott to go to the kitchen for his nightcap. But tonight he did not come. He lingered for a maddening time in the living room. She couldn't imagine what he was doing with himself. After a few minutes, she knew she must return to the kitchen to do the entire operation again. Just as predicted, the gin in the cupboard had turned a vivid blue. She poured it quickly down the sink and then prepared a second bottle—this was why she had bought six. Finally she went back to the dining room to wait, but Scott still did not come for his nightcap.

Sheilah was frantic. She returned to the kitchen to doctor the third bottle, then the fourth, the fifth, and finally the sixth, pouring a small river of blue gin down the drain. Every moment she lingered in the kitchen she was afraid Scott would appear and catch her at this absurd task; it was funny, but she knew Scott would not laugh. He was a hypochondriac under the best of circumstances and would be appalled to discover her in the act of poisoning his drink. But Scott remained in the living room and refused the bait. Finally, in desperation, Sheilah put one of her pills into Scott's original bottle, hoping that if he did not come right away he might have his nightcap in the dark and not notice the unusual color. There was nothing she could do but leave the bottle on the shelf and go to bed.

Later that night Scott wandered into her bedroom with a glass in hand. "Funny, this gin is blue," he said, only moderately puzzled.

As soon as she saw the blue gin in his hand, she repented what she had done. "Don't drink it, Scott! Maybe it's poisoned!"

He glanced at her curiously and then swallowed his drink in a single gulp. For Scott gin was gin no matter what its color. Then he staggered off to bed. Sheilah was worried that he had consumed a good deal too much of the drugged bottle, perhaps even an overdose. Arnold Gingrich had used the expression "violently ill." But how ill, she wondered, was violently ill?

Eventually Sheilah tiptoed into Scott's room to make certain he was still breathing, ready to call an ambulance if necessary—but he was snoring loudly in a drunken stupor. She returned to his room at regular intervals throughout the night to check on him. In the morning he appeared fine, the same as always.

As far as she could tell, Scott was stronger than the miracle cure, the most stubborn man alive. The pill appeared to have no effect on him whatsoever—not then, nor later when Sheilah screwed up her courage and tried the treatment a second time. She alternately wept and raged, she pleaded and reasoned; sometimes she refused to see him for days at a time. But he would not stop drinking. Scott's resistance was of mammoth proportions. He was determined to drink, and it seemed beyond the power of modern medicine, beyond even Sheilah's considerable witchcraft, to stop.

Scott's TB flared up again, along with a steady fever, night sweats, and a racking cough which seemed to tear him apart. When it got bad enough, he called in his doctor, Lawrence Wilson, who continued to write him prescriptions for Seconal, Nembutal, and amphetamines. This was the Hollywood cure, the way to keep working no matter what.

Sheilah did not trust Dr. Wilson, and feared he was giving Scott too many drugs. Dr. Wilson in turn did not appreciate Sheilah's meddling in his domain. He believed she must surely be responsible for Scott's drinking and he ridiculed her naive fear of modern science; he urged her to leave these matters in the hands of experts. By early spring Dr. Wilson had put Scott in the care of a nurse who came to Belly Acres to look after him, but Scott had always found nurses easy to charm and manipulate and he continued to drink at least a pint of gin a day. One morning after a feverish night of gin and sleeping pills Scott woke to find himself tangled in his pajamas, too befuddled to understand why he couldn't move. "I can't move my arms!" he called in alarm to the nurse.

"Oh, Mr. Fitzgerald!" she said tragically. "Has it come to this?"

Scott was now thoroughly frightened. "What do you mean?"

"Has all that alcohol caught up with you? It's paralyzed you!"

He insisted she call Dr. Wilson at once. The nurse managed to untangle Scott from his pajamas as though it were an esoteric medical procedure and he was enormously relieved to find he could use his arms again. When Dr. Wilson arrived he continued the pretense that Fitzgerald had suffered a stroke.

"Scott, there is no doubt this was due to alcohol," Dr. Wilson said ominously. "You're lucky you got out of it so easily this time. You can continue drinking and it may never happen again. But, then again—it can. One drink might do it. And this time it could paralyze you for life."

"I'd just blow my brains out then," Scott assured him dramatically.

The doctor smiled coldly and suggested this might not be so easy to arrange. "Who's going to hold the gun? The Good Lord tapped you on the shoulder, Scott. Let it be a warning to you."

Dr. Wilson was of the school of medicine that believed a patient was the last person who should ever know the truth of a situation. Scott for his part was entirely willing to accept the fantasy that he had suffered a stroke. Such a dramatic event, in fact, was greatly preferable to him than the more comic truth of being so sodden and silly as to become entangled in his pajamas. Scott had a precious sense of his own dignity and the truth might have been a far more effective cure. As it was, he cut back his drinking for few days but soon returned to his daily gin.

Meanwhile, the supposed stroke provided ammunition for Scott against those who believed he was a mere hypochondriac. He wrote Scottie solemnly: "Since I stopped picture work three months ago, I have been through not only a T.B. flare-up but also a nervous breakdown of such severity that for a time it threatened to paralyze both arms—or to quote the doctor: 'The good Lord tapped you on the shoulder.' While I am running no fever above 99, I don't know what [a] return to picture work is going to do and when and if my health blows up you know what a poor family man I am."

Despite real and imaginary health problems, Scott could not entirely ignore family matters. Throughout the winter, he had a growing drama on his hands with the Sayre clan in Alabama. He had always disliked Zelda's mother and Zelda's sister Rosalind, whom he referred to once as "a smooth-faced bitch person." The Sayres in return never approved of Scott and blamed him bitterly for all of Zelda's misfortunes.

The Sayres were certain that Baby—as they still called Zelda—was as normal as any girl could be with such an awful husband. As an old and respectable Southern family, they knew something of mental illness and believed stoutly that any hint of such a thing must be denied and suppressed. The fact that the Sayre family was prone to what they delicately termed "nervous exhaustion" made the need for this concealment all that much greater. In 1933 Zelda's brother Anthony had committed suicide after experiencing a series of nightmares in which he murdered his mother; to conceal this unpleasant fact, the family bravely maintained to the world that Anthony had died of a mysterious "liver ailment"—even Scott would never know the full truth of this matter. It was therefore a grave embarrassment to the family when Zelda was placed in the care of psychiatrists. If Baby had done a few wild things—suicide attempts, arson, even try to steer her husband and daughter off a cliff—it was no wonder, really, when you considered the irregular life Scott Fitzgerald had forced her to live.

Mrs. Sayre began a campaign to get Zelda released from Highlands Hospital. She wrote her daughter directly, urging her to leave the sanitarium at once and come live with her in Montgomery where she belonged. Zelda needed little encouragement. As someone who was in direct communication with Christ and all his angels, she was ready to believe the world was mad rather than herself. The discipline of Highlands Hospital had been chafing her for some time. Dr. Robert Carroll, the head of the hospital, was the son of a minister and he had unusually puritanical ideas of how to treat mental disorders through a combination of rigorous physical exercise and an organic diet containing no starch, sweets, or red meat. Mirrors were forbidden to the female patients, along with rouge and lipstick. There was no tobacco or alcohol allowed and the days were filled with healthful calisthenics, five-mile hikes, volleyball, and gardening. Highlands Hospital might look like a luxury resort hotel from the outside, but Zelda was not fooled. She wanted out and her mother's letters fanned the revolt.

A complicated and angry correspondence began among Mrs. Sayre, Zelda, Scott, and Dr. Carroll over Zelda's release. Scott would have been pleased to save the money of Zelda's internment, but he was certain his wife could not survive in the outside world. Mrs. Sayre insisted her daughter was cured and that Scott was keeping her in the sanitarium for dark reasons of his own; Scott was outraged at the insinuation.

He wrote angrily (and ungrammatically) in his notes:

> Well, I don't know that Zelda is "cured" and needs only to "live quietly" is an *utterly false premise.* She has come up from depression & degrading insanity of two years ago by a *vigorous.* . . . discipline. All medical opinion is that Zelda's capacity to meet life is of about three weeks, that three consecutive months in the world will reduce her to a state of utter insanity. Against all this I'm asked to release her to a tired old woman [Mrs. Sayre] with a nurse who detached from the hospital will be without final authority.

Scott pointed the finger of blame back toward Mrs. Sayre. Zelda's insanity, he insisted, was due not to him, but to the spoiling mother who first encouraged "the mental laziness of the calculating girl, whose innocent-eyed 'what then mother?' conceded her utter indifference to the fate of any other creature in the world. . . ." He complained that Mrs. Sayre had nursed her daughter until she was old enough that "she could probably have chewed sticks."

Scott did his best to isolate Scottie from what he called "the Montgomery point of view" and he actively lobbied his daughter to side with him. Dr. Carroll stepped into this dispute cautiously on Scott's side—at least regarding the critical issue of Zelda's continued hospitalization. Dr. Carroll wrote Mrs. Sayre that although Zelda appeared quite normal at times, her mental state was precarious and it was probable that she would never be entirely cured. The doctor then urged Mrs. Sayre to please stop writing her daughter that she was well enough to leave the hospital; the effect of these letters was to confuse a schizophrenic patient who was not in any position to judge her own progress.

Scott felt vindicated to have Dr. Carroll's support against the hated Montgomery point of view, and for the time being Zelda remained at Highlands Hospital.

Now he only had to find a way to pay for it. New expenses for Zelda's treatment came up unexpectedly from time to time. Early in 1939, Dr. Carroll proposed to take a group of patients on a short vacation to Cuba, but by the time Scott could find the money it was too late and Zelda had to stay behind. Zelda was very understanding about her missed trip and wrote him a particularly loving letter, one of many which Scott did not show to Sheilah: "Havannah is probably a substantial sort of place and may be will stay there till next time. Anyway, its all very expensive, and we are so well adapted to spending money to-gether. When you come East there will be that much more justification for buying things. I am as grateful to you as if I were on board."

Zelda ended with an invitation which would have some consequence: "Come on! Let me see you fly East! We can go to Cuba ourselves, as far as that goes."

By April Sheilah decided she could no longer cope with the volcano that was Scott Fitzgerald. It was a periodic feeling of frustration. She couldn't stand his drinking, or her unaccustomed sense of helplessness that nothing she could do, no amount of reason or guile, would make him stop. It seemed the only power left to her was to stay away. Fortunately, she had her ground-floor apartment at 1443 North Hayworth Avenue, just south of Sunset Boulevard near Schwab's, the small place she had rented when Scott asked her to give up the large house on Kings Road to spend more time with him. Sheilah went into hiding on Hayworth Avenue whenever life at Belly Acres was too much to bear.

Early one morning before dawn, Sheilah was startled out of sleep by her ringing telephone. She turned on her bedside light and looked blearily at her clock to see that it was not quite five. She knew who was calling; there was only one person she knew who would not think twice about waking her at this hour. She had not seen Scott for several days and she picked up the receiver ready for anything. To her surprise, Scott sounded coherent and very sweet. He admitted frankly that he had been drinking around the clock, but now at last he was determined to quit. "I'm really going to sober up, Sheilo. I mean it," he said. "I called the doctor. He's getting me the nurse. He gave me a shot and I'm sleepy. Will you come over and wait for her?"

Scott said he was afraid he would be asleep when the nurse came and she wouldn't be able to get in. For Sheilah this was an irresistible summons: Scott was going to stop drinking and he needed her. She told him she would be there as fast as she could. She dressed in the predawn darkness and got into her Ford for the drive to Encino. The sun rose just as she crested the top of Laurel Canyon at Mulholland Drive and began the descent eastward into the wide plain of the San Fernando Valley below. It was going to be a beautiful April day; even at this hour there were sweet smells of spring in the air. Sheilah's mood was always affected by fine weather and this all added to her mood of optimism. She parked in the courtyard before the main house and walked along the path to Scott's guest cottage. The door was open and she went upstairs to find Scott in bed writing. He had a pencil in one hand, another tucked above his ear, and there was a yellow legal pad on his lap. The room smelled of gin but Scott smiled at her in a very nice way. He looked almost boyish—a sick little boy in bed.

He apologized for waking her but Sheilah told him she didn't mind. She was glad he was going to stop drinking, and that was all that mattered. He was exhausted, he had not slept all night, but he didn't want to be alone. She sat with him for a time silently holding his hand. Then he yawned and she said, "Why don't you go to sleep? I'll wait downstairs for the nurse."

"Okay, baby." She took his papers from the bed, and straightened his pillow and blanket and sheet. He snuggled down into the bed with a sigh. "You won't leave?" he asked sleepily.

"I'll be downstairs," she promised.

Sheilah was almost out of Scott's bedroom when she glanced at a photograph of herself in a frame on his mahogany dresser. It made her happy that Scott kept her picture to look at when she was gone. Then her eye traveled downward to a half-open drawer and what she saw made her feet stop moving: There was a gun in the drawer, bright and hard, partially hidden by a filthy handkerchief. Sheilah reacted instinctively. She kept her back to Scott so he wouldn't see what she was doing, and then reached into the drawer and slipped the pistol beneath her coat. She didn't mean to be sneaky exactly; she just didn't like the idea of Scott having a gun when he was drinking so heavily and often in despair.

"Give me that gun!" Scott said behind her. He wasn't asleep at all; he had been watching her. Before Sheilah could turn to face him, he flung himself on her and they fell together onto the floor.

"Give me that gun!" he cried again.

"No, no you can't have it. You might—"

Scott was all over her, fighting like a wild man. She had no idea how strong he was. They wrestled on the floor and he clawed at her, trying to pry her fingers loose from the gun. But she was determined that he not get it. One of Sheilah's fingers was caught in the trigger guard and Scott pulled so violently that he cut her flesh. Her hand was slippery now with blood and going numb—she knew she could not hold on much longer. But suddenly she was furious. He had hurt her! She was actually bleeding! The thought of this filled her with such a rage that she found the strength to yank the gun free of Scott's hand and throw it furiously against the far wall. Let the bastard kill himself, she thought. While Scott gazed stupidly at the weapon on the floor, Sheilah slapped him as hard as she could with her right hand across his face. Then she started screaming. "Take it! Shoot yourself, you son of a bitch! See if I care!"

Scott was speechless, stunned by the blow and Sheilah's animal fury. They were kneeling on the floor and she got to her feet and hovered above him. She was hysterical and kept screaming whatever came into her head. "I don't care what happens to you! You're not worth saving, you're not worth anything! . . . I didn't pull myself out of the gutter to waste my life on a drunk like you!" Then she turned and ran from him down the stairs and out into the placid California morning to the courtyard where she had left her car. Her hand was trembling and bloody and she could barely stop shaking to fit the key into the ignition. When she managed, she fired up the Ford and lurched out of the yard, spinning her wheels to make the loudest exit possible.

Scott watched her go in silence. She had outdone him, and he really hated that. Fortunately, he had a idea how he might upstage her.

The full impact of the incident only hit Sheilah afterward when she was driving home. They had wrestled over a gun. Was it loaded? What if it had gone off accidentally and she had killed him? What if he had killed her? All these things came to her in a blur of adrenaline and anger as she drove recklessly over Laurel Canyon, speeding along the curves, not caring, sobbing so hard she could barely see the road. She kept saying to herself she would never see him again. Never, oh never, again! This time the son of a bitch had gone too far. . . it was over for good. . . . God, how she hated him!

Yes, she truly hated him. She could think of nothing else. She relived over and over again the stark images of rolling about Scott's bedroom floor wrestling over a gun. Her hand still ached from slapping him. She wished she had hit him harder still. It was beyond imagination what she had put up with from this man. She thought of new insults, every mean, terrible thing in the world, and she said them all now belatedly as she drove home to Hayworth Avenue.

She was in a rage all day but by late afternoon her anger had ebbed away, collapsing in the weight of its own heavy inertia. She began to look at the incident from a different point of view: He was drunk, it wasn't the *real* Scott who had jumped on her but an evil twin. In a sense he wasn't responsible. She would miss him terribly, and she worried about the gun that was still in his possession. Most of all, he must be feeling awfully depressed right now, horrified at what he had done, desperate at the thought of living without her. In this manner, Sheilah came to doubt and revise herself until she began to imagine that perhaps the whole incident had been her fault rather than his. After all, he had telephoned her for help—and what had she done? She had resorted to her old trickery, trying to take his gun on the sly. Probably this wasn't right. And then she slapped him and said terrible things. Poor Scott, she thought. Poor Sheilah.

By six o'clock in the evening, Sheilah was ready to admit herself in the wrong and apologize. She telephoned Scott's number, but the housekeeper, Erleen Smith, answered and said that Mr. Fitzgerald was not there. "He left for the East this morning." Erleen seemed surprised that Sheilah didn't know. "Didn't he tell you? He said he's never coming back. I'm to stay on the job until I hear from him."

Sheilah let the phone fall slowly back onto the receiver. Her anger returned with a rush of bitterness. Oh, she knew where he was. *He had gone back to Zelda!* She could hardly bear it, her jealousy, her sense of abandonment. And worst of all, there was nothing she could do—no one even to scream at. It was like being halfway through a set of tennis and having your opponent walk off the court. Then within a few days she suffered a new indignity: Sheilah received in the mail a check from Scott for two thousand dollars. He said he wished to pay her off for her time so that there would be no further obligation between them. There was an unpleasant implication that she was the sort of girl who could be dismissed with money; it was the final closing of accounts between them, an ultimate rejection.

And yet she was certain it was all a game. Probably Scott expected her to tear the check in half, and be too ladylike to accept such a payoff. Well, wouldn't he be surprised! Feeling very gleeful—almost happy for the first time in days—she deposited the two thousand dollars into her account, knowing very well that Scott could not afford it. She was maliciously glad that he would be so seriously out of pocket. Let the bastard suffer. And as to his leaving Hollywood forever, this was nonsense too. Of course he would come back; he would have fired his maid if he had no intention of returning. But Sheilah did not plan to wait for him.

She threw herself into a whirl of activity, refusing to sit about and be depressed. Cecil B. DeMille had invited her to Omaha to attend the premiere of his new film, *Union Pacific* starring Barbara Stanwyck. Sheilah had originally said no, she could not come; she knew Scott would be jealous if she went out of town on her own. Now she called Mr. DeMille personally to say she had changed her mind. Of course she would go. She rode to

Omaha and back in a private train car with the cast; men flirted with her, and she flirted back—wealthy, successful Hollywood men who were vastly more influential than Scott Fitzgerald. She was wined and dined and treated like a celebrity. And she *was* a celebrity of sorts; she had almost forgotten this fact. The trip acted as a balm to her self-esteem. She had neglected her career for Scott, but she vowed this would never happen again. She was strong; she had an important job and a life of her own.

Two weeks passed and it was good to be on her own again, independent, answering to no one but herself. And yet when she returned from Omaha time passed more slowly than she thought possible; the Hayworth Avenue apartment seemed unaccountably empty, and there was a hollow ache that caught up with her at odd moments of the day, as though something very bright were missing from her life.

Scott careened out of California straight to North Carolina—to Zelda and the illusive pull of the past. Zelda needed him. She understood and accepted him. She was as ruined as he was; she did not try to make him over. He forgot everything bad he had ever said about her. Zelda was his kind of person. They were two wounded birds together.

Fired up with gin and soggy sentiment, Scott appeared at Highlands Hospital loudly demanding his wife, ordering her to pack. Zelda had missed out on Dr. Carroll's trip to Cuba; well, he would take her to Havana himself and they would have a wonderful time. He was determined to show her how much she still meant to him—that he had never wandered, no, not for a second, in the fleshpots of California. They would bring back the good old times when they believed in the philosophies of popular songs. Zelda seemed almost to be expecting him, waiting so patiently for him day after day in her asylum. She packed her Bible and an assortment of old-fashioned clothes, the short long-waisted dresses of the twenties, as though time had never passed and they were still the trendsetting couple of their youth.

They traveled together to Havana, a town Ernest had described to him in the past but which Scott had never seen. The heat and light were blinding. But nothing seemed completely clean and the people had dark complexions and body odors and they weren't very tall. This was not a good place for a wounded Yankee puritan who longed for a bright cleanliness of thought. There was an old vein in Scott which disliked foreign people. "I hated Italians once. Jews too," he confided to a friend in 1935. "Most foreigners. Mostly my fault like everything else. Now I only hate myself." But with a few glasses of gin, this self-hatred could easily turn outward. On the streets of Havana, Scott glared with disapproval at the sweaty crowds while Zelda prayed continuously, moving her lips silently as she read her Bible. When people stared at her old-fashioned clothing, she took refuge in their hotel room and refused to go out. She prayed for Scott and the world and many secret things she alone understood. There was an unearthly calm to her, a craggy certainty in her crooked smile.

In the afternoon, Scott left Zelda praying in their room to wander off by himself into the city. The streets were twisty and strange and they made him feel argumentative. When night came he found himself unaccountably in a courtyard full of dark men who were betting on a cock fight. Scott watched in horror as the two roosters slashed at each other with beating wings and a spray of blood. As far as he was concerned, this was a vision of hell. The men were even more vicious than the roosters, hollering in their strange language, urging their roosters on to the kill. Scott found it unbearable. Havana was worse than Hollywood, maybe the most terrible place he had ever seen.

Scott knew he had to do something about this. He had been dying for a fight all afternoon. He vaulted over the guardrail into the pit and tried to separate the two fighting birds. The dark men yelled at him, outraged at the interruption of their sport. Scott picked up a rooster and cradled it tenderly in his arms; it was broken and bleeding and he knew just how it felt. The thought of this broken bird made him so angry that he screamed over and over again at the incredulous crowd: "You sons of bitches!. . . You sons of bitches!"

The crowd surged forward and Scott felt himself lifted up and carried out of the pit. The men beat and kicked at him. They didn't fight like gentlemen, one at a time. For Scott the storm he had unleashed was a confusion of motion and pain. He wasn't entirely certain how it happened but somehow he escaped, or they let him go, seeing he was only a Yanqui drunk. He made his way back to the hotel, bloody and torn. In the hotel room he found Zelda where he had left her, sitting on the bed with the lights off, praying in the darkness.

It did not seem that Cuba was going to be the vacation of their dreams and Scott could hardly wait to get off the accursed island. He flew with Zelda to New York, where they had lived in the early years of their marriage. Perhaps they could bring back the magic here. They checked into the Algonquin, managed by Frank Case, Scott's Malibu landlord, and the Fitzgeralds tried to stir up the memories of carefree old times with gin and wild nonsense. He and Zelda made such a racket that the other guests complained; back in 1920 no one had ever complained about too much noise, but it seemed people didn't know how to have fun anymore. Later Scott got into a fight with a waiter; he couldn't remember what it was about exactly, though he recalled trying to throw the waiter down a flight of stairs.

Frank Case was a tolerant man; he had always encouraged a zany gathering of artists and writers at the Gonk, but this was going too far. Finally the manager could think of nothing else to do but put Fitzgerald in the alcoholic ward at Bellevue. Scott woke in the bedlam of this ward not knowing how he got there, but certain he had sunk below his usual class of drunks. He managed to find his clothes and sneak out of Bellevue, but he was worn down and sick and knew where he must go next: He checked into the Doctor's Hospital where he had arrived before in similar shape.

Alone at the Algonquin, Zelda telephoned her sister Rosalind and brother-in-law who lived in Larchmont to ask if they would help her get back to her hospital. Rosalind and her husband rushed into town to rescue her from this latest example of Scott's shocking behavior. Before Zelda left the hotel, she wrote Scott a note:

It seems useless to wait any more: I know that you are better: and being taken care of: and I am of no assistance; so I'll go back to the hospital on the 2:30 train. . . Why don't you come to Tryon? . . . we could keep a little house on the lake and let you get better. We might have a very happy summer in such circumstance—You like it there, and I am very clever at serving bird-song and summer clouds for breakfast. . . .

Please believe that I stayed over solely to the purpose of helping you if I could. I know from experience what a difference it makes in life where somebody cares about your troubles. . . .

To the Hospital, this version: We had a most enviable trip. And everything was according to the rules. This last refers to cigarettes and wine concerning which I will follow our agreement as to any irregularity of arrival. Your lungs are bad, and required attention, and I am capable of traveling alone so there wasnt any use in your adding another tiring journey to what you had before you.

D.O. please take care of yourself. So you will be well again and happier than these last times. There are so few people of our era who have made original contributions to the life about us, and not many who can be so charming, and almost not any with a greater capacity for enjoyment.

There are still a great many things which could give us pleasure. . . .

Rosalind put Zelda on the train south, where she made her lonely way back to Highland Hospital and the protection it offered from the world of sanity. At Highland, she lied admirably about their trip so that Scott might be allowed to take her out again—she even camouflaged Scott's alcoholic binge with his favorite fiction that he had suffered a relapse of tuberculosis. Scott remained at Doctor's Hospital for nearly two weeks before he was strong enough to face a return to California.

He was very touched by Zelda's letter and began to think of her as a sweet and wonderful person who always did her best to be supportive. Only the two of them really understood what tragedy was. But the trip to Cuba and New York was their last adventure. Scott and Zelda would never meet again.

Sheilah received her first report of Scott's movements from Mrs. Frank Case, who telephoned from New York to say she believed Scott was in trouble and perhaps Sheilah should come and help him. Sheilah listened quietly to the news and then put down the receiver. Scott could go to hell for all she cared. He was with Zelda—let his wife take care of him!

But she couldn't stop thinking about him. Mrs. Case said he was in the hospital at the tail end of a cycle she knew too well; he would be miserable now and repentant, unable to keep down solid food. She hated to think of Scott suffering. A number of weeks passed and when she knew he must be back in California, she expected her telephone would ring any day and Scott would be on the line asking to see her. Probably she would tell him no—she hadn't quite decided—but it was disturbing when he did not in fact telephone. Finally she decided it would be the decent thing to call him. With all his other worries, she wanted him to know she wasn't carrying a grudge. But when she dialed Scott's number, the housekeeper was strangely evasive; Mr. Fitzgerald was busy, she said. He was writing; he could not come to the phone.

"You mean he doesn't want to talk to me?"

Erleen was embarrassed but she said, yes, this was the case.

Sheilah was stunned. Suddenly it seemed urgent that he see her. She pursued him for two days, leaving messages with the housekeeper, but it was not until the end of the second day that Scott returned her call. His voice was cold and impersonal. "I'm returning your call," he said, "because I remembered how miserable you are when people don't call you back. I didn't want to put you through that."

Sheilah said she wanted to see him. Could she come over right away? Scott hesitated, but then he agreed. The terrible distance in his voice made Sheilah feel as if the ground had opened beneath her feet; at the back of her mind she had always believed there was time to repair the damage—time to luxuriate in her anger, and then try again. She believed in happy endings. She drove to Belly Acres and they sat on the balcony outside his bedroom overlooking the rose garden. Sheilah apologized for slapping him and for all of the horrible things she had said. She was glad to take the blame for everything. "I didn't mean it. I didn't mean all those awful things I said. You know that, don't you, Scott?"

"We won't talk about it anymore," he agreed magnanimously. Then he added with a small but devilish grin, "That gun was loaded."

The look of shock on Sheilah's face was so comical that Scott had to laugh. The ice was broken now and he went on with boyish enthusiasm to tell Sheilah about his bizarre trip with Zelda to Cuba and New York, telling her all the details of the cock fight and how he had tried to throw a waiter down a flight of stairs. Sheilah's head was spinning with his incredible stories; before meeting Scott she wouldn't have believed such antics were possible, but she had lived through too many of these adventures herself now to doubt his word.

It was so good to hear him laugh that she refused to consider its implications—that far from digging a grave for his adolescence, the oldest sophomore in the world was making his last great stand. But Sheilah didn't care. All that mattered was that she loved him, he had forgiven her, he was momentarily sober, and they were together again.

16

HEMORRHAGES AND HOPES

I only ask this of you—leave me in peace with my hemorrhages
and my hopes. . . .

—F. Scott Fitzgerald to Zelda, October 6, 1939

BY THE SPRING OF 1939, EXACTLY FIVE YEARS HAD PASSED SINCE SCOTT'S
last novel, *Tender is the Night,* was published in April 1934. This
was a long drought between books but Scott was ready to try
again. He was certain a novel was the one thing that could save
him.

His hope was a fragile one. He was terrified someone might
steal his idea; so many things could go wrong. He assured
Sheilah that all authors were great thieves, from Shakespeare on
down; it was a desperate profession, after all, and the person
who came up with the best idea first walked away with the
prize. Scott became so fearful of theft that toward the end of May

he deliberately misled Charles Scribner and Max Perkins, his publisher and editor, as to the theme of the new book:

Dear Max:

Just had a letter from Charlie Scribner. . . . He seemed under the full conviction that the novel was about Hollywood and I am in terror that this misinformation may have been disseminated to the literary columns. If I ever gave any such impression it is entirely false: I said that the novel was about some things that had happened to me in the last two years. It is distinctly *not* about Hollywood (and if it were it is the last impression that I would want to get about.)

In fact, the new novel *was* about Hollywood; Scott had at last rejected medieval France (along with Ernest in shining armor) as a possible subject. He now hoped to write the first true and serious book about the movie industry. The theme was a natural progression for him; he had always written about the American Dream. To have it all—grace, money, charm, a beautiful home, youth, a gorgeous automobile, endless inspiration, *and* the golden girl—this was the illusive quest that had led Jay Gatsby and Dick Diver to their separate ruins. Nowhere was this mirage of an American paradise more manifest than in California among the people who made the movies. There was romance here and tragedy to spare. The more he thought about it, he saw that Hollywood was the ultimate F. Scott Fitzgerald theme.

He needed a secretary to get under way, someone who was discreet, loyal, hardworking, inexpensive, unobtrusive, intelligent—pretty if possible, but not disturbingly so—and above all would not blab about his book to all the other writers in town. To be safe, he thought it best to hire someone who had no previous connection with the film industry. Scott contacted Rusty's Employment Agency on Hollywood Boulevard with a specific request for a secretary who had never worked for a movie studio. Before long, Rusty sent over a young woman, Frances Kroll, to interview for the job.

Frances came to the Edward Everett Horton estate for the first time on an April day in 1939 when all the fields and hillsides were green with California spring. She was a shy, dark-haired nineteen-year-old girl from a comfortable Jewish family that had recently moved to Los Angeles from New York. Her father was a furrier with a new shop on Wilshire Boulevard that he had rented in the mistaken belief that this was the Fifth Avenue of Los Angeles, teaming with wealthy pedestrians who would stroll past his display window. As a new arrival, Frances was lonely in California and hoped a job would give her a measure of independence from her overprotective family. Despite her unworldly air, she was a young woman who knew her own mind and she was ready to have some adventures. In this last area, Frances Kroll was about to get her wish.

The housekeeper, Erleen, met Frances at the front door and led the way upstairs to Scott's bedroom, where she found the author—quite to her astonishment—lying in bed in his slate blue bathrobe, a pencil above one ear. Frances had never been interviewed before by a man in bed and she found the situation uncomfortable. Scott regarded her with a penetrating expression and asked her to forgive him for not getting out of bed. He said he was ill with a fever. She thought he looked very poetic and handsome, ravaged by illness perhaps, but like a figure from a book. There was a Leslie Howard delicacy to him that she liked. She knew who he was, of course—the name F. Scott Fitzgerald had an old-fashioned ring of the past—though she had not actually read anything he had written. Like most of her generation, Frances was more familiar with up-to-date authors such as John Steinbeck and Ernest Hemingway.

Scott was pleased that she was shy and new to Los Angeles, since this would mean less opportunity for her to discuss his work with friends. He was very courtly with her. He asked her qualifications and seemed satisfied with what he heard. Then he lowered his voice and confided that he was looking for someone who was absolutely trustworthy. He was starting a new novel about the movie industry, he explained, and it was essential his secretary keep his work secret and never gossip about him to anyone, particularly movie people. He couldn't stress the importance of this enough; everything she saw and did at Belly Acres would be almost like a secret of state, guarded strictly between themselves. "I want to put your name down, Miss Kroll," he told her finally. "Would you get me my notebook in that top bureau drawer?"

Frances opened the bureau drawer and saw what was to be her first state secret: a dozen empty gin bottles in plain view lying next to the notebook. From the bed, Scott watched sharply for her reaction. But Frances did not betray a flicker of surprise; she picked up the notebook from the cache of empty bottles and gave it to him without comment. She had just passed Fitzgerald's test, though a basic error of communication had been made. What Scott took for tolerance was in fact merely innocence. The sheltered young woman had simply failed to make any connection between the empty bottles and the bed-ridden author. Certainly it never occurred to her that anyone might actually consume so much liquor. When the interview was over, Scott gave her thirty-five dollars in cash and asked that she stop at a Western Union office on her return to town and wire the money to his daughter at Vassar. Frances telephoned the following morning to say the money had been sent and Scott immediately hired her at thirty-five dollars a week to be his secretary. She understood later that the stop at Western Union had been her second test. She had passed with flying colors.

Scott was now ready to work. He began with hundreds of pages of general notes, then character sketches, an outline, and finally Chapter One. He preferred to write descriptive passages in bed propped up with pillows, working in longhand on his yellow pad, quickly filling up pages that Frances would later type. When it came to dialogue, Scott liked to pace the floor back and forth in his room, gesticulating and acting out the conversations of his characters, while Frances sat in a chair and worked as fast as she could to put it all down in shorthand. The next step for Frances was to type up a draft in triple space, leaving Scott plenty of room for corrections—and the corrections, she discovered, were never ending. She was amazed at how Fitzgerald continually revised and reworked his material, laboring over single words, phrases, and the overall construction—putting all the bits and pieces in different places like a jigsaw puzzle, and then changing it once again. In his youth, a critic once called Scott's writing "facile," a charge he never forgot and was determined to remedy with obsessively hard work.

At the beginning, Scott attacked the new novel in quick spurts

and stops. He was easily tired and often distracted. Frances seldom arrived at work knowing what to expect. "He was totally
lacking in energy and spent the better part of each day in bed,"
she said later. "There was no routine, no regularity. Each day
was different depending on how Scott felt, on his mood, on
whether he had been able to sleep the night before or sleep it
off." The novel was often neglected for other matters. Frances
was amazed by how much of his time and energy he gave to
writing letters—to Zelda, Scottie, friends, sometimes total
strangers. One of her first jobs was to type a letter from Scott to
Zelda which he dictated to her as he lay in bed:

> Dearest Zelda:
>
> Excuse this being typewritten, but I am supposed to lie in bed
> for a week or so and look at the ceiling. I objected somewhat to that
> regime as being drastic, so I am allowed two hours of work every
> day.
> You were a peach throughout the whole trip and there isn't a
> minute of it when I don't think of you with all the old tenderness
> and with a consideration that I never understood that you had
> before. . . .
> You are the finest, loveliest, tenderest, most beautiful person I
> have ever known, but even that is an understatement because the
> length that you went to there at the end would have tried anybody
> beyond endurance. Everything that I said and that we talked about
> during that time stands. . . .
>
> > With dearest love,
> > Scott

Frances knew nothing of the recent trip to Cuba and New
York, but she was deeply moved by the tone of Fitzgerald's letter
to his wife. As a romantic young woman, there was something
thrilling about her fragile employer lying in bed looking like
some pale prince from a story book, dictating such lines aloud in
his soft tenor voice; she could only imagine what he hinted at,
those things they talked about during "that time." Shortly after
typing this letter to Zelda, Frances took dictation for another letter, this time to Scottie, in which he said he was considering
bringing Zelda to California for a month's visit. The Fitzgeralds
were obviously very much in love. It was therefore confusing

when Sheilah appeared at Belly Acres about a week after Frances began her new job. Frances thought she had the most marvelous British accent. "She arrived late one afternoon," Frances recalled, "breathless, blond and smiling brightly as she stood in the doorway of Scott's room. . . . The change that came over Scott when Sheilah walked into the room held me spellbound. He could be several men—a romantic, tubercular poet as he lay back wan and wasted and softly said, 'Hello, Sheilo,' or the instantly nervous, responsive lover unable to wait another minute. . . ."

But if Zelda was "the finest, loveliest, tenderest, most beautiful person" Scott had ever known, Frances wondered who Sheilah was, and what she was doing in Scott's bedroom looking so blond and breathless? Scott and Sheilah did their best to conceal their relationship, but Frances soon understood what was going on—that Sheilah generally arrived toward the end of her work day to spend the night and often the weekends. Because of her sheltered life, Frances felt awkward at being a witness to what she regarded as a "clandestine affair." She had read about such things—she was no prude—but she didn't quite know how to act or even where to look without embarrassment when Sheilah was around. It seemed particularly odd how her employer meanwhile kept writing such loving letters to his wife. She was certain that Sheilah had no idea of these letters' existence.

There were in fact a number of odd things about Frances Kroll's new job, starting with the daily task each morning of sharpening Scott's pencils to just the right point where they wouldn't break when he pressed down hard. Then instead of working on the book, he might ask her to type up a long reading list for Sheilah's education, or send her to the used bookstores on Sixth Street in downtown Los Angeles in search of the various texts Sheilah was required to study. Scott seemed obsessively interested in everything, strangely unable to set the usual priorities between career and personal matters: He might put as much fervor into a list for Sheilah, or a letter bawling out Scottie, as the latest revision for Chapter One. There was no big or small— everything was important.

One day Scott had an idea for a desk like a breakfast tray on which he could work while he lay in bed; Frances had to take measurements and rush off to a fix-it shop on Cahuenga Boulevard to have the thing constructed; this was the project of the day and Scott was delighted with his new toy. Other times, when Scott was stuck for inspiration, he might have Frances read aloud to him from the King James Bible as he lay dreamily in bed listening to her. Scott was not after religious inspiration but rather a bath of beautiful language, hoping the poetry might jump-start his creative day.

Frances bought his groceries, she balanced his checkbook, and over the next twenty months she took her thirty-five-dollars-a-week salary irregularly, only when she knew Scott could afford it. He came to rely on her. He called her by a variety of nicknames, usually Françoise or Franny. Sometimes he telephoned her at home regarding small matters in the middle of the night when he couldn't sleep. He was oblivious to time. Once she received a telegram in the early morning: TRY TO MAKE DENTIST APPOINTMENT BETWEEN ONE AND FIVE FOR FULL HOUR. TELL HIM IT IS AN EMERGENCY. CALL ME AT NOON. REGARDS SCOTT. The telegram, she saw, had been sent at 2:30 A.M. Then a second telegram arrived which had been sent at 4 A.M.: FOLLOWING OTHER TELEGRAM TRY TO MAKE APPOINTMENT AS NEAR 2:30 P.M. AS POSSIBLE STOP DON'T WANT ANYTHING AS LATE AS 5 TO 6 SCOTT.

Frances bought his cigarettes—Raleigh Filters, three packs a day—but Scott took care of his own secretive liquor requirements, ordering his beer and Gordon's gin delivered from a small convenience store on Amestoy Avenue when no one was around. Despite this secrecy it was not long before the new secretary learned what the dozen empty bottles in Fitzgerald's bureau drawer were all about.

Edward Everett Horton was proud of having a once-famous author as his tenant; it made a pleasant addition to his rose gardens and neat lines of white picket fences. But he began to suspect Scott Fitzgerald was not entirely a sober individual. One afternoon Horton appeared with several guests who wished to meet the author. They were greeted by an improbable sight: Fitzgerald was sitting on the stairs outside his second-story bedroom tearing up planks of wood and throwing them angrily at the ground below. Horton and his friends beat a hasty retreat.

From that moment on the landlord kept his eyes open, as land-lords will, worried for his property. One morning Frances arrived at work to discover a man searching through Fitzgerald's trash barrel, shaking his head at the collection of empty bottles. Frances approached warily and asked, "May I help you?" When the man looked up, she saw it was Horton. "Looks like a case of the d.t.'s," he said.

Frances smiled vaguely but made no comment. Then she went inside the house to report the incident to her boss. Scott was glad she had; he did not at all like the idea of his landlord going through his garbage and knowing the extent of his drinking. He soon came up with a plan to foil Horton's curiosity. He had Frances buy a supply of burlap bags and from that time on she was given a new task to go with her many others: When the bags were full, she was to dispose of the bottles in the woods as she drove back to town at night. It was a case of flagrant littering, not an easy crime for a sensitive city girl. Frances found a quiet spot to do her dirty work in the bushy terrain of Sepulveda Canyon, where there is a busy freeway today; she felt a surge of appre-hension each time she pulled to the side of the two-lane road, looked around nervously to make certain there were no other cars in sight, and then dumped the empty gin bottles with a clat-ter into the brush. She was always glad to get away undetected.

Scott accepted her loyalty without comment; if he was aware of putting Frances in an awkward position, he did not give any sign of it. But as a writer Scott was never one to waste material and he would acknowledge the humiliating nature of Frances's garbage runs in his short story "Pat Hobby's College Days." In the story, an alcoholic screenwriter pressed his reluctant secretary into simi-lar service to dispose of his dead soldiers—his empty pints, half-pints, and quarts—asking her to dump them off in Topanga rather than Sepulveda Canyon (for one must disguise events slightly, particularly when a crime is involved). Unfortunately, Pat Hobby's secretary didn't have Frances's nerve; she couldn't go through with it and she returned the bottles to his studio office at the worst possible moment, embarrassing the bedraggled screen-writer before people he had been trying to impress. Now they all knew that Pat was a drunk. For Scott, as for Pat Hobby, the shame of these empty bottles was enormous. And so it was ironic. In life he might lie and pretend his drinking was of no importance, but in fiction he told the truth. It was devastating to his image of himself that he must succumb to such a low and sordid flaw.

By the summer money had become for Scott an increasingly desperate matter. "Sickness and no money are a wretched combination," he complained wearily to Zelda. However, it never occurred to him to cut down on his smoking or move into a house without a swimming pool and tennis court. He certainly was not willing to put Zelda in a state institution, or Scottie in a less Ivy League college than Vassar. He insisted on the grand life, or no life at all.

"Stray ideas as sending my daughter to a public school, putting my wife in a public insane asylum have been proposed to me by intimate friends," Scott wrote a few years earlier. "But it would break something in me that would shatter the very delicate pencil-end of a point of view." To maintain this delicacy, Scott put off paying his income tax and insurance premiums and he tried to sell a few short stories. *Esquire* was always good for a stray story here and there, but Gingrich paid at most $250, a drop in the bucket. Meanwhile the bills came flooding in. "Have paid Peck & Peck & Peck & Peck & Peck," Scott whined eloquently to his daughter about her clothes expenses, but he would not think of having her go to a less prestigious store.

At last Scott was reduced to his old habit of borrowing money from friends. Over the years he had developed a short list of supporters who might always be counted upon to come through in a pinch; at the top of the list was his agent, Harold Ober, a conservative New Englander, a graduate of Harvard who had supported Scott in not only the bad times, but the good times as well. Unfortunately, the Fitzgeralds had a way of living beyond their income no matter what it might be. High or low—it was never enough. And Ober had always come through; he had even provided a foster home for Scottie in the East—far beyond the normal duties of a literary agent. In June Scott sent an urgent cable to Ober asking for a five-hundred-dollar advance on two short stories he had mailed previously but which the agent had not yet been able to sell. Ober wired Scott the five hundred dollars, but he drafted a letter to indicate that his nearly twenty years of generosity had finally reached its limit:

> I was short of money when your telegram came because I had just paid up all my taxes and paid some money on a mortgage and some money that I owed on my insurance. I am still short, but I managed to wire the Culver City Bank the Five Hundred Dollars you needed. I think, however, it would be a great mistake for us to get back into the position we were in. I think it bad for you and difficult for me. . . I hope, therefore, we can keep things on a "Pay as we go" basis.
>
> I think you can do that if you will follow the old adage about "Watching the pennies and letting the dollars take care of themselves." I notice that both Scottie and you would always rather send a telegram or make an expensive telephone call than send a letter for three cents. You give tips four and five times as large as you need to. . . . I am sure that if you could look back over the years with some kind of celestial bookkeeper to note down your expenses, you would find that a large part of the money you have earned has gone for things that brought you no return.

Ober decided not to mail this letter. Perhaps he wanted to spare Fitzgerald a lecture along with his other woes. But he was fed up and two weeks later when Scott asked for another loan, he at last refused. Scott was dumbfounded and furious. He had accepted his agent's backing as a matter of course for so long that the refusal seemed like the betrayal of a natural right. He was so angry that he fired Ober in a fit of passion, determined to act as his own agent in the future, certain he could do a better job of it anyway. Still it was an emotional break, the end of a long association. Later in the summer, after some reflection, he wrote Ober mournfully:

> I have been and still am somewhat shocked by your sudden and most determined reversal of form. Only six months ago you were telling me "not to be in too much of a hurry to pay you back.". . .
>
> Your advice that I should have "taken on some movie work" with a lung cavity and a temperature of 102 was a new slant. The cavity evidently began to form about the time I started on *Air Raid*, and your implication that I had been loafing must have been based

on those two-day binges in New York, several months apart.
Anyhow, when the temperature was still a hundred and the cavity
still crackling I was asking Swanie to get me work and meanwhile
putting in five hours a day on a bed-desk.

... I don't have to explain that even though a man has once
saved another from drowning, when he refuses to stretch out his
arm a second time the victim has to act quickly and desperately to
save himself. For a change you did, Harold, and without warning—the custom of lending up to the probable yield of a next short
story obtained between us for a dozen years. Certainly you haven't
just discovered that I'm not any of the things a proper business
man should be?...

Whatever I am supposed to guess, your way of doing it, and
the time you chose, was as dispiriting as could be... Neither
Swanson nor Sheilah nor Eddie Knopf have any idea but that I
have labored conscientiously out here for twenty months and
every studio (except Wanger, but including Metro!) asked for,
according to Swanson, me at some time during April and May.

Scott closed with his oldest and saddest lie:

If it is of any interest to you I haven't had a drink in two
months but if I was full of champagne I couldn't be more confused
about you than I am now.

> Ever yours,
> Scott

After Harold Ober refused to help, Scott turned to his second
most reliable source of loans over the years—Max Perkins. In
early July he wired Max:

HAVE BEEN WRITING IN BED WITH TUBERCULOSIS UNDER DOCTORS NURSES
CARE. . . OBER HAS DECIDED NOT TO BACK ME THOUGH I PAID BACK EVERY
PENNY AND EIGHT THOUSAND COMMISSION. AM GOING TO WORK THURS-
DAY IN STUDIO AT FIFTEEN HUNDRED CAN YOU LEND ME SIX HUNDRED FOR
ONE WEEK BY WIRE TO BANK AMERICA CULVER CITY. SCOTTIE HOSPITAL
WITH APPENDIX AND AM ABSOLUTELY WITHOUT FUNDS. PLEASE DO NOT
ASK OBERS COOPERATION.

Perkins sent Scott the six hundred dollars, but this did not last
Scott for long. When the money was gone, he once again wired
Harold Ober asking for a loan:

STILL FLABBERGASTED AT YOUR ABRUPT CHANGE IN POLICY AFTER TWENTY
YEARS ESPECIALLY WITH STORY IN YOUR HANDS STOP MY COMMERCIAL
VALUE CANT HAVE SUNK FROM 60 THOUSAND TO NOTHING BECAUSE OF A
SLOW HEALING LUNG CAVITY STOP AFTER 30 PICTURE OFFERS DURING THE
MONTHS I WAS IN BED SWANSON NOW PROMISES NOTHING FOR ANOTHER
WEEK STOP CANT YOU ARRANGE A FEW HUNDRED ADVANCE FROM A MAGA-
ZINE SO I CAN EAT TODAY AND TOMORROW STOP WONT YOU WIRE SCOTT.

But Ober still refused, and though he and his wife continued
to offer Scottie a home on the East Coast, Scott was seething mad.
He could not fire his agent a second time, but he stormed
through the house and found his last will and testament and
angrily crossed out the name of Harold Ober as the executor of
his estate. Probably it had been a mistake to ever trust a Harvard
man; Scott rectified this situation by writing in by hand the name
of John Biggs, his old friend from Princeton who was now a
judge.

Money wasn't the only crisis: Scottie wanted to come to
California for the summer. Fitzgerald panicked at the very
thought of such a visit. He had just begun writing seriously
again and the last thing he wanted was a teenage interruption.
How would he entertain her? What would she do with her time?

"But Hollywood—why?" he had written Scottie in May:

> What do you want to do out here? I can no more see you as a
> reader in a studio wading through bad novels and worse magazine
> stories all summer and being so dog-tired at the end of the day that
> you would probably be ready for anything, even these empty-
> headed California boys. . . And what else can you do out here? Do
> you want to come out and be my secretary? *Let us laugh quietly and
> mirthlessly with a Boris Karloff ring.* As for some of the ideas you had
> before. . . I remember one of them was whether you should go to
> summer stock in one of those New England towns. Honey, I may as
> well hand you over to the white slavers and make a thorough job of
> it. For girls like you, it is nothing but a complete playtime job and
> strong competition between the girls to see who gets the honor of
> being seduced by the leading man.

Two months later, in early July, Scott was still doing his best to
discourage Scottie from coming to California, but now in a more
calm and tactful manner, without a single mention of white slav-

ery. First he assured her that "I am of course not drinking and
haven't been for a long time," but unfortunately "any illness is
liable to have a certain toxic effect on the system and you may
find me depressing, over-nervous about small things, and dog-
matic." All these traits he knew would come as a surprise to his
daughter. He warned her that he would be working hard and
the last thing he wanted at the end of a day was any kind of
problem. He ended:

> . . . you left a most unpleasant impression behind last autumn
> with many people, and I would rather not see you at all than see
> you without loving you. Your home is Vassar. Anything else to be
> supplied at present is a mockery of a home. . . .

Scottie showed this letter to her mother, who was angry at the
remark orphaning their daughter to a dorm at Vassar. The
Hollywood novel was put on hold through all this correspondence as Frances was kept busy at her typewriter. To Zelda he
wrote:

> Perhaps I was unwise in telling [Scottie] so succinctly that she
> had no home except Vassar. On the other hand, she doesn't see the
> matter in relation to the past. When I tried to make a home for her
> she didn't want it, and I have a sick-man's feeling that she will
> arrive in a manner to break up such tranquillity as I have managed
> to establish after this illness. Perhaps she has changed—but this is
> the first time in many years that you yourself have expressed plea-
> sure in her filial behavior.

For Scott, "all the old tenderness" for Zelda he had felt two
months earlier after their jaunt to Cuba, now evaporated quickly
as he and he wife wrestled over thorny family matters. Then
came a new domestic anguish; Scottie decided she wanted to follow in her father's footsteps and become a writer. This was all
very well in the abstract; in fact, nothing would make Scott happier, and he wrote to her some of his finest letters offering reams
of advice about how to transform burning emotions into English
prose. But unfortunately, Scottie actually sold a piece to
Mademoiselle which was published in their July 1939 issue. Scott
was angry on two counts: First, his daughter had used her real
name, Frances Scott Fitzgerald, which anyone could see sounded
too much like his own. And second, the *Mademoiselle* article—"A

Short Retort"—dared to criticize his own generation of the twenties, and implied that he and Zelda had not always behaved in a responsible manner as parents: ". . . in the speakeasy era that followed," she wrote about her childhood, "we were left pretty much to ourselves and allowed to do as we pleased. And so, we 'know the score.'"

Scott was furious. *Know the score, indeed!* He wrote his daughter a cutting letter, arriving at his main argument after first delivering a short digression on "post-Flaubertan realism." He told Scottie she must read *Roderick Hudson* and *Daisy Miller* before attempting *The Portrait of a Lady*, which he declared was in James's "'late second manner' and full of mannerism." Then he insisted she tackle *Lord Jim* and *Sister Carrie*—"almost the first piece of American realism. . . damn good and is as easy reading as a *True Confessions*." But finally he got to the angry point:

> I wish I could say the same about a recent article in *Mademoiselle*. I grant you the grace of having been merely a dupe as I warned you would be—for I cannot believe that you would announce that you pursued your education yourself while I went around to the speakeasies. There's nothing to do about it now, but in future please call yourself by any name that doesn't sound like mine in your writings. You must have wanted fifty dollars awfully bad to let them print such a trite and perverted version of your youth. . . .

After an extended and rancorous three-way correspondence—for nothing was easy anymore for the Fitzgeralds, not even a summer vacation—Scott at last agreed that his daughter could come to California in early August. He decided, however, that she must have a project to keep her busy: She would learn how to drive. This was necessary, Scott was convinced, because there were drunks on the highways. His daughter must know how to take over the wheel of a car if she were ever with a boy who had had a few too many—and with the sort of empty-headed stevedores she was inclined to date, this was entirely possible.

Sheilah meanwhile had begun to dread the visit even more than Scott. Over the past month she had followed the acrimonious exchange of letters, cautiously standing up for Scottie whenever she could. She thought Scott was being extremely unfair about his daughter's writing career. For Sheilah this was an emotional issue; as someone who had worked all her life, she believed a woman's right to a career was sacred. All the petty bickerings back and forth left an accumulation of bad feelings, and Sheilah became steadily more worried that Scottie's visit would trigger a binge.

Frances was sent to meet Scottie at the train station in downtown Los Angeles. After the many disapproving letters Frances had typed, she expected "some sort of Hollywood starlet." She was startled to find instead a soft-spoken teenage girl, not a great beauty but pleasant and pretty with natural blond hair. There was no flask of gin in her pocket, no cabal of leering boys in hot pursuit ready to abduct her into white slavery. Scottie in fact was a surprisingly normal seventeen-year-old girl— she would be eighteen in October—quiet but very much self-possessed. She moved into a spare bed in Sheilah's bedroom downstairs at Encino, and despite the constant father-daughter tension, Sheilah enjoyed sharing her room; it made her feel she was part of this family at last rather than some embarrassment who must be hidden from view. A few days into the visit, a boy Scottie knew in Pasadena showed up with a large happy group of young people who ended up staying the night. The boys slept on the living room floor, and the girls on the floor in Sheilah's bedroom. "I liked that," Sheilah remembered later. "I felt like everyone's mother."

But Scott did not enjoy the visit quite so well. He managed to control his drinking, though the tension this sacrifice caused him was palpable. Often he corrected his daughter in a fierce undertone when others were nearby, telling her how to behave with boys, or what she should have done in one situation or another. Scott was ready to explode over the smallest matter. At lunch one afternoon at the Hollywood Brown Derby, Scott and Scottie refought the battle of her article for *Mademoiselle*; he accused her of trading on his name, whereas Scottie shot back that he should not have named her Frances Scott Fitzgerald if she was not allowed to use it. Sheilah ate her lunch and wished she were someplace else.

"It's because I want you to be different from your mother," he told her finally, hoping to explain why he was so strict.

"Well, why doesn't *she* change?" Scottie snapped back with teenage frustration.

By August the weather was unbearably hot in the valley. Frances sometimes worked in a bathing suit and even Scott shed his gray sweater. Somehow Scottie got her driver's license, suffering a barrage of her father's obsessive advice. Frances was assigned to drive with Scottie on practice runs around the quiet roads of Encino; Scott didn't believe he had the nerves for it. Nearly a year later, he was still sending his daughter urgent last-minute thoughts on automobiles, adding in a P.S.: "I forgot to tell you that in the rain *don't depress the clutch*—use the brake only. And on the hills—go down in the gear in which you'd have come up."

In mid-August, Scott wrote a progress report of the visit to Zelda:

> Scottie is very pleasant and, within the limits of her age, very
> co-operative to date—on the other hand, she's one more responsi-
> bility, as she learns to drive and brings me her work and this sum-
> mer there is no Helen Hayes to take her on a glamor tour of
> Hollywood. All of which boils down to the fact that my physical
> energy is at an absolute minimum without being definitely sick and
> I've got to conserve this for my work.

Scott was relieved when she returned to college. He loved his daughter but he was besieged with worries. He could not come up with the $615 tuition for Scottie's fall term at Vassar and had to borrow $360 from Gerald Murphy and finagle an advance for the rest from *Esquire*. All of this took time away from his novel. But there was nothing he would not have done to keep Scottie in college; in his own harassed way, feeling the press of troubles all around him, this most anxious of all fathers did his best to catapult his daughter to safety.

In late August Scott landed a one-week job for Samuel Goldwyn rewriting dialogue on a romantic adventure story, *Raffles*, a film about a gentleman burglar starring David Niven and Olivia de Havilland. It was a rush job due to the fact that

David Niven, a British citizen, had just been called up for active duty in the army and needed to return home because England was mobilizing for war.

Scott noted to himself that he "liked Sam Goldwyn—you always knew where you stood with Goldwyn—nowhere." This was refreshing after producers like Joe Mankiewicz and Hunt Stromberg who had fooled him into expecting something more. Scott received twelve hundred dollars for the one-week assignment and he did his best to be businesslike about the job. He arrived each day at the Samuel Goldwyn Studio with Frances at his side and a briefcase full of Coca-Cola, working at a desk which was set up for him on the sound stage, off to one side among the lights and cables. David Niven was an elegant and intelligent man who enjoyed Fitzgerald's presence on the set and often walked over to the small desk to chat between takes. Niven confided that he could hardly wait to get into uniform to fight the Nazis; he would be in England already, but Goldwyn wouldn't let him out of his contract. Scott listened enviously and wished he too could do something heroic like go to war. There were times when being a writer seemed a very thin substitute for a real life.

Raffles once again ran afoul of Scott's old nemesis, the censor Joseph Breen. On September 6, Breen wrote to Samuel Goldwyn that the movie in its present form was unacceptable and could not be approved: "The general unacceptability of the material is suggested by the fact that you have here a criminal, who is permitted to outsmart the police, and to go off 'scot free.' Such a characterization, of course, is in violation of the Production Code." The censor went on to suggest that the movie might be saved with a few changes: an additional line or two to indicate to the audience that Raffles knew he could not escape justice. Breen asked also that a scene showing "ladies of the street" be omitted, as well as the words of one character who uttered, "Good Lord," and another who ventured unwisely, "Well, I'm a man of the world"— "this, for obvious reasons," Breen explained in an aside.

For Scott this was a depressing refrain of what he had suffered with *Infidelity*. Hollywood was beginning to appear to him a very dark comedy. In September, when money worries once again caused him to put aside his novel, Scott dreamed up a satirical character, the bedraggled hack screenwriter, Pat Hobby, whose misadventures in the movie industry would span seventeen short stories. The Pat Hobby series came into being through the pressures of the ever-patient Arnold Gingrich, who had been agitating for a number of months as politely as possible for some literary return for advance monies paid. Gingrich wrote:

> Dear Scott,
>
> They keep nagging me downstairs about the open items I continue to carry on the *Esquire* inventory. Whenever you can let go of a short script or piece of some kind, it will be a real act of appeasement against the pushing I keep getting for "an item of $200.00, against the next piece to be received, that has been on the books since February, 1937. . . . "

Scott was not thrilled with the scant money *Esquire* paid for his pieces, but over the past six months he had mailed Gingrich several stories. "Design in Plaster" was about a broken man in a cast (Scott Fitzgerald) whose obsessive jealousy drives an independent woman (Sheilah Graham) into the arms of a French lover—Edouard Jozan, with whom Zelda had an affair in the early twenties. Scott could always remix his autobiography to come up with a new work of fiction. In another story for Gingrich, "The Lost Decade," a man reappeared like Rip Van Winkle after losing ten years of his life to liquor. Pat Hobby was funnier than these other characters and not so much an autobiographical figure as an exaggeration of Scott and his own tribulations in Hollywood—a kind of nightmare image of what he might become if he stayed there too long. Poor Pat had neither dignity nor talent and he was always down on his luck. The first Pat Hobby story arrived at *Esquire* on September 16, 1939, and a second came in the mail a week later. All seventeen stories of the series were written quickly, often during a single day on the weekend, and Scott seemed nearly frantic to receive his money just as fast. With the second story, which arrived on September 21, Gingrich received a short note:

> Here's another story about Pat Hobby, the scenario hack, to whom I am getting rather attached. Also some enclosed pages with corrections for the first story about him ("Man in the Way").

Once again can I get a Western Union acceptance—that is if
you like it wire me and wire the money to the Bank of America,
Culver City.

I think I'll do one more story about this character Saturday or
Sunday. . . . I wish to God you could pay more money. These have
all been stories, not sketches or articles and only unfit for the big
time because of their length.

This letter set a pattern which Scott was to repeat throughout
his correspondence with *Esquire* about the Pat Hobby series.
Above all, there was the urgent question of money, the "Western
Union acceptance"—money which must be wired immediately
to Bank of America, Culver City. Then there were the barely
veiled insults that *Esquire* was not "the big time" and that
Gingrich was getting his stories at a steal. Acting as his own
agent, Scott pushed and whined for a raise in such a thoroughly
unpleasant manner that it must have left Gingrich nostalgic for
Harold Ober. But beyond the nagging question of money, each
letter contained revisions for a Pat Hobby story Gingrich had
already received. Scott was endlessly fussy about his work and
he had come to care greatly about his luckless screenwriter. He
wrote asking to change words, paragraphs, even the order in
which the stories would be published; many of the Pat Hobby
stories were revised as often as four times, generally long distance and through frantic last-minute telegrams. The stories
were written for quick money, but Scott as always was obsessed
with the quality of his work. He only wished he had the time to
make them perfect.

Still, the main project for Scott remained his serious novel
about Hollywood, which at the moment was called *Stahr*. All
other work, including the satirical stories for *Esquire,* was only a
means to making this book possible. Scott now began to read to
Sheilah at night what he had written each day. Sheilah was
pleased to discover that she was a central character in the novel.
In fact, she was the heroine—the English girl Scott called first
Thalia and later Kathleen. He used many of Sheilah's words and
phrases, the clothes she wore, actual incidents from their relationship, everything about her. For Sheilah this was miraculous;
it was flattering in the extreme. There could be no greater com-

pliment, she believed, than to be cast as the heroine of his new book.

"That's terribly exciting," she said after each installment. "What happens next?"

But Scott smiled mysteriously and refused to discuss scenes he had not yet written. "You lose the freshness," he explained. Sheilah could hardly wait for the next installment of the story, and Scott seemed on fire to oblige her. "Look! I have begun to write something that is maybe great," he wrote in an exultant mood to Scottie. "It may not *make* us a cent but it will pay expenses and it is the first labor of love I've undertaken since the first part of *Infidelity*... Anyhow, I am alive again."

On September 29, Scott sent a synopsis of the novel to Max Perkins at Scribner's and Kenneth Littauer at *Collier's* magazine, hoping for an advance from one of them or both. In the synopsis, Scott explained that the novel would focus "upon two principal characters—Milton Stahr and Thalia, the girl he loves." Stahr is the head of a movie studio, a romantic, doomed, and idealistic figure willing to battle a Louis B. Mayer–like opponent in order to make high-quality movies and fulfill his great dreams. Scott deliberately made his hero Jewish, sensitive to what was happening in Germany and aware that in the past he had been accused of being anti-Semitic, mostly through his unflattering portrait of a Jewish gangster in *The Great Gatsby*. The villain of the piece, Bradogue (later changed to Brady), would be Irish, Scott's own ancestry; he hoped in this way to take care of any charges, real or imaginary, that he was in any way racist.

He wrote in his summary:

Stahr is overworked and deathly tired, ruling with a radiance that is almost moribund in its phosphorescence. He has been warned that his health is undermined, but, being afraid of nothing, the warning is unheeded. He has had everything in life except the privilege of giving himself unselfishly to another human being. This he finds on the night of a semi-serious earthquake (like in 1935) a few days after the opening of the story.

Milton Stahr was soon renamed Monroe Stahr, because (as Scott explained to Frances) Jews often named their sons after

American presidents. Although Stahr was modeled upon Irving Thalberg, the character quickly evolved to become himself, as most Fitzgerald heroes had a way of doing. It was very pleasant to project himself as the head of a great movie studio. Thalia/Kathleen, however, was always Sheilah, from beginning to end, complete with all of Scott's ambivalence about her.

Thalia Taylor is a twenty-six-year-old widow, and my present conception of her should make her the most glamorous and sympathetic of my heroines. Glamorous in a new way... People simply do not sympathize deeply with those who have had *all* the breaks, and I am going to dower this girl, like Rosalba in Thackeray's *Rose and the Ring,* with "a little misfortune."

Sheilah was so happy about her new literary incarnation that she was able to gloss over a paragraph which came later in the synopsis:

Back to the main theme: Stahr cannot bring himself to marry Thalia. It simply doesn't seem part of his life. He doesn't realize that she has become necessary to him. Previously his name has been associated with this or that well-known actress or society personality and Thalia is poor, unfortunate, and tagged with a middle-class exterior which doesn't fit in with the grandeur Stahr demands of life.

But there was to be more to this novel than a simple love story. For the first time in Fitzgerald's fiction he planned to write about work, describing the inner life of an industry—the movie industry, a romantic business, perhaps, but a workplace with union problems just like everywhere else. He was hopeful this would make the book acceptable to the thirties. Art versus money, labor against management, communism and the American Dream—all this was to be included and analyzed in his novel—a social novel, in fact, which Scott believed would show the world that it had misunderstood him; he was not a man concerned only with the rich.

All he needed was money to fund his creative work; if Kenneth Littauer at *Collier's* bought the serialization rights he would be in business. Unfortunately, the editor expressed inter-

est in the synopsis but refused to give Scott an advance without
seeing at least fifteen thousand words of the manuscript itself.
Scribner's likewise would not commit itself. The time was long
past when an editor would advance money on Fitzgerald's reputation alone. Scott was disappointed—he needed the money
sooner rather than later. But he believed he was onto a good
thing and meanwhile it was fine to be sending out manuscripts
and proposals again, like a real writer rather than a Hollywood
hack. He had only to keep the faith a while longer, work hard,
and come up with fifteen thousand very persuasive words.

In October, John Wheeler surprised Sheilah by arranging a lecture tour for her to speak about Hollywood across America on
behalf of NANA. She was aware that this was a good chance to
boost her career; her main competitor, Louella Parsons, had just
gone on a similar tour and now Sheilah would have the same
opportunity to increase her standing. She would meet her readers around the country as well as the local newspaper editors
whose goodwill was so important—and to top it off, she would
be paid two hundred dollars a lecture. The only drawback was
that she had never done anything like this in her life and she was
terrified.

Mere terror had never stopped Sheilah from doing anything
before and it wasn't about to now. She sat down and over several
days wrote up a lecture with the irresistible title, "Now It Can Be
Told." It was full of froth and gossip of the Hollywood stars.
There were a few scandalous anecdotes and Cinderella sagas of
how various movie stars had reached the top, to live happily
ever after with their enviable mansions, servants, and cars. She
showed the finished draft to Scott who read it through with a
deepening frown.

"You don't believe this, do you?" he asked.

"No I don't, Scott—but it's what they expect to hear."

"If you don't believe it, don't say it," he told her. Then he read
through the speech a second time and finally shook his head
sadly. "This really isn't very good. I can't let you do a lecture like
this."

Obviously he would have to write the speech himself. And so

with his own career hanging in a precarious limbo—with everything depending on the progress of his new book—Scott put it
all aside for several days to work on Sheilah's lecture about
Hollywood. When he was done he had Frances type up the new
speech and he gave it to Sheilah to study.

"You can give them the gossip when you answer questions
after the lecture. But you are an important person," he stressed.
"You are coming to them as an authority on Hollywood. You
must explain the part films play in their lives in all areas. They
have a kitchen the way it is because that is how they saw it in a
Norma Shearer movie; they make up and dress the way they do
because this is how they see Joan Crawford on the screen. I have
kept some of your ideas, such as the difficulty of finding a husband in Hollywood, but that is far less important than explaining the enormous value of the director. The stars are merely pup-
pets who dance to his tune. Without the director, there would be
neither stars nor films. Now, let's rehearse the lecture. I have
written it carefully, and I want you to read it carefully. If you follow what I have written, you will have a success."

Scott got together a few props. The one time he had tried public speaking himself—at Princeton's Cottage Club—he had been
so drunk and shy that he made a complete fool of himself. But
this did not keep him from instructing Sheilah on how it should
be done. He built a raised platform in the living room out of
packing cases he found in the basement, then he put Sheilah on
the platform with her speech on a music stand in front of her—a
stand Scott managed to borrow from Frances's brother Herman,
who was a classical musician. The living room at Belly Acres
opened up upon a dining room, which led in a straight line to
the kitchen and a back porch, a distance of some sixty feet. Scott,
Frances, and Erleen sat on three chairs on the back porch while
Sheilah, at the far end of the house, attempted to project her
words at them. After a few moments, Sheilah giggled nervously.

"Stop that!" Scott commanded from the porch, outraged. "You
are an authority on Hollywood. You have something to say and
your audience has come to hear it. Don't be apologetic. You're
Sheilah Graham. Now, begin again."

Sheilah began again, but when she kept her eyes glued to the page, Scott once again interrupted. "Look up, Sheilo," he called to her. "There are people seated in front of you. You're a pretty girl, and they want to see your face: look up now and then."

The lecture itself—which Sheilah eventually got through—was a much more serious attempt to describe Hollywood than anything she might have written herself. Scott's main emphasis was that the director was the most important person in moviemaking, more important than the glamorous stars, certainly more important than the producer. Scott worked his own experience into the text:

> *Gone with the Wind* had three directors in as many months. First there was George Cukor. He had directed *David Copperfield* and *Little Women* for Selznick, so he seemed a natural choice for *Gone with the Wind*, which was another attempt to put a long novel on the screen.
>
> Now Cukor likes to direct women. In fact, he likes to direct women so much that he's liable to slight the male star—in this case Clark Gable. It was rather funny to hear Selznick telling one of the seventeen writers who worked on the script [i.e., Scott], "Look, don't let Scarlett romp all over Rhett Butler. George will try and throw everything to her. You and I have got to watch out for Clark."

Scott turned Sheilah into his puppet, giving her not only his own experiences to read, but also his point of view. He provided a sling of anecdotes to show how serious artists in Hollywood (particularly writers) suffered at the hands of producers:

> Ernest Hemingway visited Hollywood a few years ago. He and two producers were walking across the lot of a certain studio. Both producers were praising his works. Hemingway was naturally pleased and asked one of them which of his books he admired most. The producer looked a little blank, so Hemingway tried to help him out.
>
> "*A Farewell to Arms?*" "Yes," said the producer so eagerly that Ernest grew a little suspicious and asked (*Pause*): "Do you mean the play or the book?" (*Pause*.)
>
> "I mean the movie," the producer said. (*Pause*.)
>
> Hemingway was somewhat disappointed and turning to the producer on his left he asked, "Is that what you admire—the movie?"

"No," said the producer. "I never got around to seeing the movie—but I heard the song." (*Pause.*)

Scott was having fun, and getting a little revenge as well. Complete with stage directions for the proper delivery of his script, he let Sheilah take a swipe at his least favorite of all Hollywood producers, Joe Mankiewicz:

One of the producers at a big studio wanted to change the tragic ending of *Three Comrades*—he wanted Margaret Sullavan to live. He said the picture would make more money if Margaret Sullavan lived. (*Pause.*) He was reminded [by Scott] that *Camille* had also coughed her life away and had made many fortunes doing it. He pondered this for a minute; then he said, "*Camille* would have made *twice* as much if Garbo had lived." (*Pause.*) "What about the greatest love story of all?" he was asked. "How about *Romeo and Juliet*—you wouldn't have wanted Juliet to live, would you?" "That's just it," said the producer. "*Romeo and Juliet* didn't make a cent." (*Pause.*)

But despite this slapstick view of producers as barely literate chimpanzees, Scott concluded with a thought that was the central theme of his own novel in progress:

Once in a while a great figure has appeared on the horizon and led it through a mighty exodus. Griffith was one, Thalberg was another. There is no such person now in Hollywood—no single person whom we, of the movie industry, believe capable of controlling this vast art in all its many manifestations. But there's some boy growing up in America now who by some combination of genius and luck will answer Hollywood's great problem.

The lecture Scott wrote in Sheilah's name was an hour long, nearly ten thousand words—almost as long as the fifteen thousand words he needed to write for *Collier's* to get his own career back on track. Sheilah spoke his words, projected his opinions from the make-shift stage of packing boxes to the small audience on the porch. When she was finished, Scott, Frances, and Erleen applauded loudly. Then Scott put up his hand to ask a question.

Sheilah nodded to him. "Yes?"

Scott stood up. "Miss, I'd like to know—is it true that Shirley Temple is really a midget?"

"I have heard those rumors, sir," she replied. "But they are not true. I can assure you from personal knowledge that Shirley is a bright, normal little girl who happens to be extremely intelligent for her age."

"Thank you, Miss Graham," Scott said. And with a satisfied smile at his favorite student, he then sat down.

Despite Scott's help, Sheilah remained nervous about her lecture tour. Not only was she frightened of the live audiences she must face, but of the travel itself, flying in small planes from city to city. On October 27, before leaving Los Angeles, she had a lawyer write up a will in which, in the event of her death, she left all her worldly belongings to Scott. He was as much family as she had ever had. She signed the will, "Lily Gillam, also known as Sheilah Graham"— a confusion of identities, two beings who would barely recognize one another.

Scott was sorry to see her go. He "interviewed several kittens" hoping to find suitable company, but he decided instead that he would have lunch whenever he was lonely with John O'Hara—a good person with whom to share some gloom. At last, prepared for death in the air or at the podium, Sheilah flew to New York where she delivered her first lecture in a tense monotone without once looking up from her script. When she was finished, the audience was too dazed with boredom to ask a single question. Cleveland was slightly better; she glanced up from her script to manage an occasional tortured smile toward the back of the room. But by Kansas City she had reached her stride. At the end there was a good deal of applause and people in the audience were eager to ask questions.

"What is Loretta Young like?" one person asked.

Sheilah followed Scott's advice to be serious, never flippant in her replies. "Loretta is the most charming person. She always presents a happy appearance to the world. I have never known her to lose her temper," Sheilah said. And then, after a moment's thought, she added, "But, of course, it's always hard for one woman to know another woman. If you really want to know what she's like underneath, you must ask a man."

There was a roar of laughter, and when Sheilah realized her mistake, she gasped, "Oh, my God!" which caused more laughter still. Sheilah knew she was a terrible public speaker and the trip was a great strain on her. Knowing how hard it would be, Scott had given her his briefcase to take along, a tangible reminder of him, and for two weeks as she traveled the country there was a telegram waiting for her at each hotel.

KENNY WASHINGTON RUNNING WELL TODAY I THINK OF YOU
      SCOTT

In Boston, a telegram to SHILA GRAHAM AT THE COPLY PLAZA contained Scott's usual bad spelling:

THE POINT OF THE WHOLE THING SEEMS TO ME THAT YOU ARE GIVING THEM, AS A TYPICAL GROUP OF AMERICANS, A CHANCE TO KNOW THE DIFFICULTY THAT THE SAID PICTURE PEOPLE AND IN THE SAME HOUR TELLING THAT IF THEY WANT PICTURES TO BE HARDER HITTING IT MIGHT BE ARRANGED DO THEY WANT TO BE INTERTAINED [sic] OR INSTRUCTED. THE TWO THINGS ARE POSSIBLY COMPATIBLE BUT EXTREMELY DIFFICULT. CAN THEY HELP = YOUR HOLLYWOOD ADMIRER SCOTT.

To the Brown Hotel, Louisville:

THE COUNTRY IS BEHIND YOU NOW STOP JUST RELAX AND DO YOUR HOUR STOP NEWS JUST REACHED HERE ENGLAND IS AT WAR STOP IS DENIED AND AFFIRMED BY LOCAL PRESS SEEMS INCREDIBLE SIGNED CONSTANCE CAROL HEDDA STOP I STILL MISS YOU TERRIBLY = SCOTT.

And Scott's final message to St. Louis:

AM SO VERY VERY ANXIOUS FOR YOUR RETURN LOVE
      SCOTT

The telegrams were a great support to Sheilah as she struggled through the victories and failures of her nerve-racking tour. Meanwhile Scott managed to keep from her the truth of his own situation—that in her absence, all his own hopes had fallen apart.

Scott had sent off the first chapter of his new novel to Kenneth Littauer at *Collier's* just before Sheilah's trip east. Worried as always about the competence of the post office, he had Frances drive the manuscript directly to the plane in Los Angeles. Then he settled back to worry about its reception in New York, waiting for the reply which would determine his future. Everything now depended on Littauer's verdict. If *Collier's* bought the serialization rights, Scott would receive twenty-five hundred dollars per issue, perhaps as much as thirty thousand dollars in total (he fantasized) for eight, ten, perhaps even twelve installments. A yes from Littauer would put him in business again as a serious writer; no, and all his hopes for a second chance would be dashed and he must return to hack screenwriting—if anyone would still hire him.

Scott got his answer by wire while Sheilah was away. The telegram from Kenneth Littauer read:

FIRST SIX THOUSAND [WORDS] PRETTY CRYPTIC THEREFORE DISAPPOINT-ING. BUT YOU WARNED US THIS MIGHT BE SO. CAN WE DEFER VERDICT UNTIL FURTHER DEVELOPMENT OF STORY? IF IT HAS TO BE NOW IT HAS TO BE NO.

Scott was furious. Littauer must be an idiot not to understand the overall design of the book, the beautiful plan of it that was so tight and perfect in his mind. The son of a bitch actually implied he didn't know where he was going with the story—but he knew *exactly*. That was what was so frustrating. Frances watched anxiously as Scott paced up and down his room shouting expletives and insults. Finally, he called Littauer in New York to let loose his fury over the telephone. Frances had never seen Fitzgerald so angry and she was afraid he might have a stroke. He slammed down the receiver, drained of emotion. Scott then calmed down and tried to remind himself that Littauer had only deferred judgment while awaiting more pages, and that his six-thousand-word submission was in fact less than half of the fifteen thousand the editor had requested. Scott wired Littauer to say there were no hard feelings—it was important not to alienate *Collier's* completely—though in fact there were hard feelings and Scott would never forget this bitter refusal.

Meanwhile there were other magazines in New York. Scott wired Max Perkins to ask him to submit the manuscript to the

Saturday Evening Post. Max replied shortly that the *Post* was not interested, finding the material too strong for its readership, and that Scribner's also could not give an advance without seeing more of the manuscript. Perkins knew this would be a blow and he sent a wire to Scott full of encouragement as well as an offer of a personal loan: A BEAUTIFUL START. STIRRING AND NEW. CAN WIRE YOU TWO HUNDRED FIFTY AND A THOUSAND BY JANUARY. Scott was grateful but he recognized the gesture as more an act of friendship than faith in his ability as a writer. His feeling of rejection was overwhelming.

It was at this moment that Sheilah returned to Los Angeles from her lecture tour. Scott met her at the airport to welcome her home. He was determinedly jovial and she was too full of her own adventures to notice how tense he was. As they drove to Belly Acres, she rehashed her moments of success and failure and how the lecture had been received in different cities. Scott listened with a stubborn show of interest and said nothing about himself.

Then a few mornings after her return, Sheilah was astonished to read a front-page editorial in *The Hollywood Reporter* which savaged her lecture tour. The editorial was signed by the publisher, W. R. Wilkerson, who also owned the Trocadero restaurant; Wilkerson had never forgiven Sheilah for writing that his food was inferior and overpriced and this was his moment of revenge. He began by quoting from a report written by Jack Moffit, *The Hollywood Reporter*'s Kansas City correspondent:

> Sheilah Graham got $200 for a one-night stand at the Kansas City Woman's Club. The studios could have paid her two thousand to stay in Hollywood, and made money. The lecture was a dirt-dishing session that left none of the movie mighty unsmeared. Even Shirley Temple and her mother were exposed as having their hair dyed in Sheilah's shellacking. The nocturnal pastimes of an adult star were hinted at with Groucho eyebrows and streamlined innuendo. . . .

This apparently was a reference to Sheilah's innocent gaffe about Loretta Young. After quoting his correspondent, W. R. Wilkerson himself took over the slaughter:

Miss Graham's speaking tour was arranged by her newspaper syndicate, the North American Newspaper Alliance, which serves a
very important group of newspapers through the U.S., each of
which gets quite a bit of motion picture advertising. . . Hollywood,
its players, producers, writers and directors should tell Miss
Graham they won't countenance her further "dishing" to the ticket
buyers on this "lecture tour" and the industry should remind her
papers such "dishing" is NOT CRICKET.

Sheilah was devastated. She was sensitive to criticism at the
best of times and to find herself crucified so unfairly on the front
page of Hollywood's most important trade paper was a nightmare; everyone in town would read of her disgrace. She phoned
Scott in tears, barely able to read him the editorial.

Scott was immediately up in arms. "That's the most shocking
thing," he said when she had finished. "Sheilah, don't do anything. I'm getting a copy. They are going to give you an apology
and a retraction."

"Oh, those awful people!" she cried.

"Wait," Scott said dangerously. "Wait."

Scott had braved his own recent defeat in silence but this
was the last straw, one humiliation too many—the thumbs-down
of the crowd toward himself and Sheilah. And, of course, he was
the true author of the lecture that *The Hollywood Reporter* had
found so shocking. He drove furiously into Hollywood and
bought a copy of the *Reporter* from the stand outside Schwab's
drugstore. The columnist, Sidney Skolsky, walked by to find
Scott on the sidewalk, white with fury, holding a copy of the
rolled-up newspaper in his fist. "Did you see this?" he
demanded in a trembling voice. "Have you read this?" Then
Scott turned on his heels and walked off down the sidewalk with
murder on his mind. In fact, he had decided to kill W. R.
Wilkerson.

Scott telephoned John O'Hara to ask if he had read the attack
on Sheilah. "It's so damn unfair!" Scott said bitterly. "Sheilah did
a beautiful job and this man Wilkerson—John, I'm challenging
him to a duel. I want you to be my second."

John O'Hara believed he had seen pretty much all there was to
see in Hollywood, but this was something new. He tried to calm

Scott down; he explained patiently that people didn't challenge other people to duels anymore—it had gone out of style a few years back. "If you insist on going, I'll go with you," he said, "but I don't want you to go and I don't want to go with you."

"That's all I wanted to know," Scott replied curtly. "I thought you were my one real friend in this town. I'll get Eddie [Mayer]. He's diabetic and doesn't get into fights, but he's a gentleman."

O'Hara phoned Eddie Mayer to warn him what was up, but Scott apparently had decided that he needed no one's help. He drove directly to *The Hollywood Reporter*, where he stormed into Wilkerson's outer office and demanded of a frightened secretary that he be allowed to see the publisher at once. W. R. Wilkerson luckily was not in his office. Scott paced angrily back and forth outside the publisher's door for more than an hour before he gave up and left. Eddie Mayer meanwhile telephoned Sheilah to tell her about the duel; Sheilah hurried to Belly Acres and when Scott returned she managed at last to calm him down.

It was only now that he told her of the double rejection from *Collier's* and the *Saturday Evening Post*, two magazines which in the past had vied with one another to print almost anything Scott wrote. And Scribner's too—everyone had turned him down. Sheilah had never seen Scott so desperate. She had been too preoccupied with her lecture to suspect what Scott was going through.

"They don't want anything by F. Scott Fitzgerald," he told her miserably. "I'm not in fashion any more. No matter what I write, they don't want it."

It seemed his hopes for a fresh start had hemorrhaged to a premature end. What was he to do with himself now? he wondered. Scott Fitzgerald was ready for his last binge.

17

THE SILVER-FOX

[He] despised his own personality—he loathed knowing that
tomorrow and the thousand days after he would swell pompously
at a compliment and sulk at an ill word like a third-rate musician or a first-class actor. He was ashamed of the fact that very
simple and honest people usually distrusted him; that he had
been cruel, often, to those who had sunk their personalities in
him. . .

—F. Scott Fitzgerald, *This Side of Paradise*

DURING THE FINAL MONTHS OF 1939 SCOTT WAS IN A MOOD TO
BREAK things. In November he broke with his Hollywood agent,
H. N. Swanson—Harold Ober's West Coast representative. He
had never liked Swanie anyway. Years ago back east, in another
incarnation, Swanie had been a literary man of sorts, the editor
of a magazine called *College Humor* which had published some
of Scott's short pieces. Now Fitzgerald cut the tie with an
exhausted letter and a forlorn look at the past:

My destiny is probably not worth watching over. . . such as it is. I don't feel that you're sufficiently interested to continue as the watch-dog in the case. . . I thank you for the small favors in the past. Once you reviewed a book of mine in "College Humor." You said, "What would I give to write like that!" It was probably rather a thin dime, but you got what you wanted. And that's certainly your business. But so is my own, and I feel that I cannot do it with you any longer.

Scott found a new West Coast agent, Leland Hayward, with the hopes that a few morsels of movie work might be thrown his way. Even a week or two of salary would make a big difference now. Leland Hayward was a bright and charming man, but he could find nothing for Fitzgerald. It was a small town and Scott's reputation went before him, spread by the producers he had alienated in past.

There was nothing now to stop Scott from drinking as much as he pleased; his daughter was gone, he was out of work, and there was no need to keep up appearances. Sheilah still hounded him to stop drinking, but this only made him rebellious. He confided to Frances that Sheilah was "part Jewish," which he hinted explained a lot about her; without a thought, he betrayed one of the great secrets she had told him two years earlier sobbing in his car. Scott seemed to expect Frances to be shocked, but of course Frances was Jewish too. That was the problem in Hollywood, everyone was Jewish—Sheilah, Frances, Irving Thalberg, Monroe Stahr, everyone he cared about. It was enough to make a man cry. "Hollywood," he lamented, is "a Jewish holiday, a gentiles tragedy." And the tragedy was his; as an Irish Catholic at Princeton he knew exactly what it was like to be a despised minority and he hated the whole business. Like Sheilah he had done his best to pass. With a wardrobe full of Brooks Brothers suits and enough fame as the top American novelist, he had hoped to slip in among the beautiful people—Ginevra King's world of country club dances. He longed for an Episcopalian heaven where there were no strange words or smells or foreign rituals that set a person apart.

And so it was ironic for Scott to find himself now exiled to a

Jewish ghetto. It wasn't so much that he was a racist as a failed snob; an arriviste who had never quite arrived. Sometimes he asked Frances what it was like to be Jewish, as though fascinated to understand what it truly meant to be different. He wanted to know about Passover and Yom Kippur. Frances told him how once her father had bought a live carp to make gefilte fish, keeping it alive in a bathtub filled with fresh water until the holidays—then he banged the fish over the head and sent it into the kitchen. Scott found the story a little gruesome. He pondered the carp's fate in silence; then he brightened and with his best mischievous smile said that her father should have filled the bathtub with gin and "let the fish drink itself into oblivion." This at least was the Fitzgerald solution, and in Hollywood he, too, sometimes felt like a carp in a bathtub, waiting to be knocked senseless in celebration of some Jewish rite.

Scott complained to Frances about the two thousand dollars he had given Sheilah at the end of his last great binge—in a boasting way he exaggerated the figure to five thousand dollars. He gave the check, he said, "out of generosity" and now that he was broke he expected Sheilah to give it back—but she did not. Scott was resentful about the money, though he was too proud to actually ask for it back. He was nursing a slow grudge against Sheilah. Once when she was out of town on a film assignment, Scott made a tipsy pass at Frances, grabbing at her when they were working late. Frances pulled away quickly. Though she saw Scott as a romantic figure, "like an exiled prince in a period novel," he was not, as she said later, "her prince." Scott was ashamed of himself. "I won't do that again," he promised. "I wouldn't want to think of Scottie in such a situation."

Scott kept his word to Frances but he was ready for a romantic conquest. It wasn't lust, exactly—Scott was drinking much too hard for simple desire. But he wanted someone to look in his eyes adoringly and say yes to him. He was fed up with a world that kept telling him no.

Scott classified two groups of women who were most gullible to his charms: actresses and nurses. These days he saw a great deal more of the latter than the former, and he had perfected his sickroom manner to an art form few nurses could resist: a courtly, pale, tubercular poet lying among his pillows with a sad smile and the softest words. His skill was fatal. Ernest Hemingway might brag of killing lions on safari in Africa, but this was Fitzgerald's field of expertise. "Trained nurses on duty," he said cunningly, "should not be allowed to talk in their sleep."

In November, after a particularly drunken weekend, Dr. Wilson assigned an attractive young nurse, Jean Steffen, to come and live at Belly Acres. With a second nurse who alternated to give Jean an occasional day off, Scott now had round-the-clock care. Jean Steffen was slim and exotic with dark hair and dark eyes that were very appealing, though Scott confided to Frances that she was "part Indian," which for someone from the Midwest was almost worse than being "part Jewish." Jean was divorced with a young daughter and this gave her and Scott something in common, an opening to conversation of a personal kind. Scott put on all his sickroom charm and before long Jean appeared to believe her job at Belly Acres might last forever.

Sheilah and Jean Steffen hated each other on sight. Jean sometimes took Frances aside to complain that "Scott was fine until Sheilah came to visit." Dr. Wilson was also of the opinion that Sheilah was responsible for Scott's drinking, and he set up strict visiting hours to guard his patient from her harmful influence. To her surprise, Sheilah found that she was suddenly an unwelcome guest at Belly Acres, allowed only brief visits, kept from Scott by a glowering nurse who had an obvious agenda of her own.

Sheilah suspected that Scott was sleeping with Jean, but she did not know for certain and did not ask. She had always had a vastly practical attitude toward sex and now she wasn't so much jealous as disgusted by a situation which seemed to her seedy and predictable—and expensive as well, money which Scott could not afford and might save if only he stopped drinking. Sheilah knew instinctively that Jean Steffen was not a real threat. If nothing else, a nurse was no one's idea of "top girl" and Scott was too much of a snob to connect himself with such a person for long. It was pathetic how he kept trying to impress her. One day Scott asked Sheilah to take Jean's daughter onto a movie set, and Sheilah exacted a subtle revenge: She took the little girl to meet Scott's least favorite movie star, the flirtatious Errol Flynn, at the Warner Brothers set of *The Private Lives of Elizabeth and Essex.* Unlike Sheilah, Scott, of course, was extremely jealous; he had never forgotten how Errol had showed up at Sheilah's house in the summer of 1938 when Scottie and Peaches Finney were in town. It was just a gentle reminder that when it came to hurtful sexual games, Scott held the losing hand.

Sheilah continued to brood about Scott's gun, which seemed to her a very dangerous toy in the hands of someone who was drinking heavily and prone to fits of hysterical melodrama. One day toward the end of November when Scott was out, she and Frances took the pistol from its place in the kitchen drawer, wrapped it in newspaper, and hid it in the pantry on a high shelf where he could not find it.

A few nights later Sheilah drove to Encino and walked in on an improbable scene. Scott was in the living room dressed in his bathrobe giving away all his clothes to two tramps he had picked up on Ventura Boulevard. The men were filthy and unshaved and nearly as drunk as Fitzgerald—to Sheilah they looked like hobos straight out of central casting. One of the tramps had two of Scott's Brooks Brothers suits draped over one arm and Scott was filling the other's arms with shirts, neckties, and handkerchiefs. What was his was theirs, he assured them. Scott seemed to believe he was redressing social wrongs and establishing a state of instant Marxism.

"Meet my friends," he said grandly to Sheilah.

She tried to remain calm. "Don't you boys think you ought to go? And leave Mr. Fitzgerald's clothes here, please."

Scott frowned. "Why should they go, Sheilo? I told you they're my friends."

Sheilah ignored him. "Will you please put down those clothes and go?" she told the hobos. "Immediately? Get out of here!"

"Don't talk like that to my friends," Scott objected. "*You* go. These are my friends. Old friends."

The hobos smirked and blinked, not entirely comfortable as the focus of controversy. "I warn you," Sheilah told them, "if you don't leave at once I will call the police."

At the mention of police, the men made an elaborate show of placing the suits, shirts, and ties on a chair. "The lady says go, I guess we better go," one of them agreed. He waved at Scott. "So long, old fellow. Be seeing you."

The tramps shuffled out of the house and Scott stared after them dumbly as though he could not quite comprehend what had happened to his party. Upstairs Jean Steffen was straightening his bedroom, repairing the mess he had made while tearing through his drawers and closet to liberate his wardrobe for more equitable distribution. When Scott continued to stare sullenly at the front door, Sheilah took control of the situation with a bright, unnatural voice. "Scott, I'm getting you some food." She went into the kitchen to heat up a can of tomato soup and while it was heating she set the dining table for two. When the soup was ready, she poured it into two bowls and called Scott to the table. "Come on, Scott—hot soup will do you good." But Scott would not come. His mind was working with a slow, sodden logic, mulling over the insult he had endured. "Being rude to my friends," he muttered, "never so insulted in my life—"

Sheilah thought it best to ignore him. She sat at the table eating her own soup, trying to show by exaggerated example that it was very good and healthy. Scott seemed in such a stupor that Sheilah was not prepared for the explosion when it came. Without warning he sprang from his chair to the table with amazing agility, picked up his bowl of soup, and threw it as hard as he could against the far wall. The bowl shattered, leaving a sickly ooze of tomato soup dripping down the wall.

"Oh, Scott," Sheilah sighed. This sort of scene no longer shocked her, but she found it very wearisome. She went into the kitchen for a dishrag and returned to the dining room to mop up the mess. She picked up the shards of the bowl and was on her way back to the kitchen when Scott appeared in front of her, blocking her progress. "Scott, stop being silly," she told him wearily.

Scott slapped Sheilah hard, bringing his open palm against her face, sending her staggering backward. Sheilah had not expected the blow; her ears rang and tears came to her eyes. She felt disoriented, but when she saw Scott raise his hand a second time she knew enough to step out of the way. Jean Steffen mean-while had heard the commotion from upstairs and had come down to the dining room to see what was wrong. She was not entirely surprised to find that Sheilah's visit had upset Scott. "Mr. Fitzgerald, please," she said.

"Oh, you think she needs protecting, eh?" Scott cried. "You think she's somebody worth protecting? If you knew what she really is! She's a fake! She's out of the slums of London, she was raised in an orphanage, her name's not Sheilah Graham, it's Lily Shiel. Lily Shiel!"

Scott saw by the expression of horror on Sheilah's face that he had hit pay dirt—her weak spot, the way he could hurt her best. He began dancing about the room like a madman, chanting the name which he knew she hated: "*Lily Shiel, Lily Shiel, Lily Shiel, Lily Shiel. . .*" Then he taunted, *She's a Jew, She's a Jew*—he threw back everything at her, all the dirt, all the great secrets she had ever told him. Sheilah was still stunned from being hit, but this was worse. Scott was breaking their love apart as surely as he had shattered the bowl of tomato soup against the wall. There could be no greater betrayal than this, to shout out the secrets of her past before a stranger—a rival. An enemy.

Jean must have felt a brief moment of triumph, but it was her nursely duty to take charge of the situation. "Mr. Fitzgerald, please be calm," she said, and advanced upon him to take his arm. But Scott decided he was not going to be calm and he didn't like her patronizing manner. As the nurse stepped forward, Scott lashed out with his foot and kicked her hard on the shinbone. It was more the blow of an irate child than a gentleman boxer, but it was effective just the same. Jean cried out with surprise and pain and fled the room in a blur of tears; she did not return, not even later when she had every reason to believe Sheilah was in danger. Scott was just warming up.

He returned his full attention to Sheilah, leering at her with a very mischievous bad brownie gleam in his eye. With a show of deliberate calm, Sheilah turned and walked into the kitchen hop-ing to reach the back door. But Scott jumped in front of her and blocked her way. "Oh, no you don't. You're not leaving this house," he said.

"Why not?" she asked coolly. "I want to go."

"You're staying right here—Lily Shiel. You'll go when I say you can go."

"I hate you!" she burst out. "I don't love you any more! I don't respect you."

Scott lit a cigarette with trembling fingers. "I'm going to kill you," he said in a matter-of-fact tone.

Sheilah told herself she must not panic. Scott did not mean it; he was always so melodramatic. If she was very calm and deliberate she believed she could keep this nightmare from spinning out of control. She forced herself to sit quietly on a low kitchen cupboard. "All right, Scott, if you don't want me to go, let's talk," she said. "What would you like to talk about?"

"I'm going to kill you," he repeated stubbornly. He opened the kitchen drawer where he kept his gun, but the gun was not there and he turned to Sheilah angrily. "Where's my gun?" he demanded. She pretended innocence—how should she know where his gun was? Scott pulled at different drawers and began ransacking the cupboards trying to find it. Then he had a bright idea: Frances his loyal secretary would know where his gun was. He used a phone in the kitchen to call her. The phone was only inches from where Sheilah sat, so he could keep an eye on her and make certain she did not make a dash for the back door. He was very cagey. When Frances answered, Scott put on his most reasonable voice. "Frances," he said, "I've been hearing suspicious noises around here. Have you any idea where my gun is?"

Frances was not fooled. Sheilah was relieved when she heard the thin sound of the secretary's reply coming over the receiver: "No, I haven't, Mr. Fitzgerald."

"Did you see me put it anywhere? Maybe I hid it."

"No, Mr. Fitzgerald. I'm sorry, but I didn't."

Scott hung up the telephone and began to rampage more destructively through the shelves and drawers, pulling out pots and pans. "Scott, are you going to let me go?" Sheilah asked. "I want to go, Scott."

"No, you're not going," he said. "You're not getting out of here alive."

"If you don't let me go, Scott, I will call the police and there will be a frightful scandal. You wouldn't like that for Scottie, would you? You wouldn't like that at all."

Scott was searching the pantry at the far end of the kitchen, and Sheilah worried he was getting too close to his hidden pistol. She decided she must take a chance; she picked up the phone and dialed the operator. "Get me the police," she said. "If I am cut off, this is my number. . . ."

Scott staggered out of the pantry to face her, but he appeared confused at her tone of self-assurance and did not try to take the telephone from her. The police came on the line and Sheilah gave them the address on Amestoy Avenue and said she was being held against her will. The sergeant said a patrol car would be there immediately. She put down the receiver. "Now, Scott, you heard me call the police. I think you heard what they said. It will be very bad if they find me here. I think you'd better let me go now."

Sheilah stepped down from where she was sitting on the low cupboard. With a last pretense of calm, she walked to the kitchen door and out to her car in the yard. Scott did nothing to stop her. She almost felt sorry for him; when she called his bluff, he turned out to be nothing but a helpless child. The moment she was safely in her car, she broke down into sobs of rage and tears.

The phone was ringing as she stepped into her apartment. It was Scott.

"What do *you* want?" she shouted.

"I just wanted to be sure you got home safely," he said.

This seemed such a wild absurdity after everything she had endured that Sheilah could hardly find a fitting answer. "That's a joke!" she sputtered and slammed down the receiver. She was determined never to see him again. This time he had finally gone too far; this time it was really over.

She cried herself to sleep but in the middle of the night she was awoken by her ringing telephone. It was Scott and she hung up on him immediately. For the rest of the night, the phone rang every few minutes but she did not answer. At seven in the morning, Sheilah had finally managed to fall asleep when her doorbell rang. There was a special-delivery letter addressed to "Lily Shiel

Graham." Inside she found Scott's handwriting, large and uneven: "Get out of town, Lily Shiel, or you will be dead in 24 hours."

Scott was like a madman. Every few hours for the rest of the day, a new special-delivery letter arrived for Sheilah at her Hayworth Avenue apartment. "Leave town or your body will be found in Coldwater Canyon," said one. "Get out of Hollywood or you know what to expect," said another. Pat Hobby could not have written more lurid threats for a third-rate melodrama. Sheilah let her secretary, Pat Duff, answer the phone, and it rang continuously. "Is Lily there?" Scott asked. The secretary had instructions to hang up on him, but later in the afternoon Sheilah picked up the phone by mistake. "You haven't left town yet?" he cried in astonishment. "You'll be dead in twenty-four hours!" And this time it was Scott's turn to slam down the receiver.

Scott wanted the whole world to know her shameful past. Later in the day, John Wheeler called from New York wanting to know what sort of trouble she was in. He had just received a telegram from Fitzgerald which read: SHEILAH GRAHAM TODAY BANNED BY EVERY STUDIO STOP SHE IS RUINING NANA IN HOLLYWOOD STOP SUGGEST YOU SEND HER BACK TO ENGLAND WHERE SHE BELONGS STOP DO YOU KNOW HER REAL NAME IS LILY SHEIL? [sic] Sheilah explained as well as she could that this was Scott's idea of a practical joke. Wheeler was a brusque man; he was grouchy to find himself involved in a domestic quarrel, but he accepted the explanation—the telegram, after all, was ludicrous. Nevertheless, Sheilah was furious that Scott had tried to damage her career; it made her even more angry than when he had threatened to kill her, for this was overstepping a personal boundary where he had no right to go. One's career was sacred somehow, off-limits. Scott was fighting dirty—like kicking a woman in the shin. Now she had to worry what further harm he might do, who he might call, and what he might say. Hollywood was a town, after all, in which you could be ruined by rumor as easily as fact.

The harassment continued nonstop for days: phone calls, letters, telegrams, and threats. Sheilah was desperate. When she couldn't stand it anymore she went to a lawyer hoping to find some legal means to get Scott to stop. The lawyer listened gravely to her emotional outburst. She told him she could not sleep, she could not work—this maniac was driving her mad. Wasn't there anything she could do to make him stop?

The Hollywood lawyer was a man of the world. Sheilah had two options, he said. She could go to court, but this would take time and money and might result in unwanted publicity. Frankly he counseled a more informal solution. For five hundred dollars he would hire two policemen to show up at the Encino house at five in the morning and pound loudly on the door. They would make threats of an unpleasant nature, what they would do if Mr. Fitzgerald did not leave the nice lady alone. The lawyer had arranged such matters before. "We've found that a police visit just before dawn is pretty effective," he confided.

"Oh, no, you can't do that," Sheilah objected.

Why not? he wanted to know.

"He sleeps so badly," she explained. She added weakly, "He'd just be falling asleep about that time."

As it happened, Scott was enjoying his first good sleep in years. When he ran out of insults and threats, temporarily out of steam—when he had done all the damage his creative mind could conceive—he turned his anger at last against himself. He tried to commit suicide with an overdose of sleeping pills. But Scott was so accustomed to sleeping pills that they merely put him out for a single blessed night of rest. In the morning he was refreshed and ready for more.

Sheilah received a letter from Scott that was different from the others. This one was apparently written when he was sober:

Dear Sheilah:

I went berserk in your presence and hurt you and Jean Steffan [sic]. That's done.

But I said things too—awful things and they can to some extent be unsaid. They come from the merest fraction of my mind, as you must know—they represent nothing in my consciousness and very little in my subconscious. About as important and significant as the quarrels we used to have about England and America.

I don't think we're getting anywhere. I'm glad you no longer can think of me with either respect or affection. People are either good for each other or not, and obviously I am *horrible* for you. I loved you with everything I had, but something was terribly wrong. You don't have to look far for the reason—I was it. Not fit for any human relation. I just *loved* you—you brought me everything. And it was very fine and chivalrous—and you.

I want to die, Sheilah, and in my own way. I used to have my daughter and my poor lost Zelda. Now for over two years your image is everywhere. Let me remember you up to the end which is very close. You are the finest. You are something all by yourself. You are too much something for a tubercular neurotic who can only be jealous and mean and perverse. I will have my last time with you, though you won't be here. It's not long now. I wish I could have left you more of myself. You can have the first chapter of the novel and the plan. I have no money but it might be worth something. Ask [Leland] Hayward. I loved you utterly and completely. I meant to send this longhand but I don't think it would be intelligible.

Scott

Sheilah was not moved. Scott was not going to die; the end was not close. This was all melodramatic nonsense. He was simply doing his best to manipulate her emotions and bring her running back to him; it would have worked in the past, but Sheilah had learned her lesson. There would be no more wrestling over loaded pistols and getting slapped in the face. She had traveled too long a journey from the Jews Hospital and Orphan Asylum in Norwood to waste her life with a drunk. In order to forget Scott, she threw herself into a flurry of work and activity.

There were a good number of men about town happy to discover that Sheilah was single again. She went to the theater with Garson Kanin, the director, and to dinner with Louis Meltzer, a screenwriter she had known before Scott. Hollywood was a whirl of parties for a girl if that was what she wanted—and she wanted it now. She accepted dates with Irwin Shaw, Robert Benchley, Eddie Mayer, and John O'Hara. Even more intriguing, she dated the handsome young actor Victor Mature, who had wavy black hair and romantic brown eyes and a wonderful laugh. Victor Mature was one of those actors who enjoyed being a movie star without taking it too seriously; he was easy and fun and successful, all the things that F. Scott Fitzgerald was not.

Sheilah let everyone know that she had returned to circulation. When someone pressed her and asked what had happened with Scott, she replied with a thin smile that Mr. Fitzgerald was a closed chapter in her life.

Scott was surprised when his contrite letter to Sheilah did not bring her back; he had used, after all, his best tragic pose—the wounded literary genius—that was guaranteed to reduce any girl to jelly. Zelda once observed that "he liked women" and they in return "usually lionized him, unless he was intolerably scandalous: which was rare; then they usually forgave him because he kept all the rites and sent flowers and wrote notes world without end and was most ingratiating when contrite." With Sheilah, he had been both scandalous and contrite, but she did not keep her part of the formula and forgive him. It was surprising because he was accustomed to getting his way with her rather easily.

Then of course Hollywood was a small and gossipy town. Scott was aware that Sheilah was dating other men—writers he knew all too well, like John O'Hara, who was supposed to be his friend. For Scott, jealousy had always made women more interesting to him. Alone at Belly Acres he sometimes drifted aimlessly into the guest room where Sheilah used to sleep; he sat on her bed with such a sharp sense of regret and loss that it was unbearable.

Scott was wounded by this new turn of events. How could she forget him so quickly? It seemed awfully sad, and he was indeed very sorry for himself. If he was momentarily sober, he began drinking again heavily when she did not call or even write to answer what he was certain was a very moving letter. Soon he was angry all over again. If she did not come to him, he would have to go to her. One afternoon Scott got in his car and drove from the valley to Sheilah's apartment in Hollywood determined to do some new mischief—he did not know what exactly, but something really nasty.

Sheilah's secretary answered the door and told Scott that Miss Graham was not at home. Scott gave her a scathing look to indicate he had not been born yesterday. Then he pushed past her through the front door to search the apartment and find where Sheilah was hiding; she would not escape him so easily. But Sheilah in fact was not there. Pat Duff thought it best to return to her typing and let Scott roam where he wanted; she had a sense of how dangerous he could be when provoked.

Scott wandered into Sheilah's bedroom, probably not yet certain what he was going to do. Then his novelist's intuition took him to the heart of the matter, what he might do to cause Sheilah the maximum amount of pain. It was subtle and came from his deep knowledge of her. Just as he had known the name Lily Shiel was splendid ammunition, now he considered something new and deliciously cruel: He decided to steal the silver-fox jacket he had given to her on her birthday. It was the first birthday present she had ever had. Even now, more than two years later, Sheilah hardly dared lean back in the jacket lest she ruffle the fur the wrong way. Scott took the jacket from her closet and made off triumphantly with his stolen prize.

He was very pleased with himself as he drove back to Belly Acres. It was like sleeping with a prostitute and then taking back your money on the way out the door. He had to chortle just thinking how angry she would be. And then he did a very strange thing: He took Sheilah's jacket—this acknowledged badge of a fallen woman—and mailed it to his daughter as a Christmas present.

Sheilah did not discover the theft of her silver-fox jacket for several days. One evening Marc Connelly invited her to dinner—the bald little leprechaun playwright, author of *The Green Pastures*, whom she had hardly seen since sitting at his table at the benefit dance for the Screen Writers Guild more than two years earlier. Sheilah decided the occasion called for her best coat and when Marc appeared at her door she had him wait in the living room while she went to her closet.

At first she thought she must not be looking in the right place. Then she looked and looked and it was really not there. She went through her clothes again with a growing sense of panic, pulling at dresses and blouses. And then it hit her—Scott! Pat had told her about Fitzgerald's puzzling visit a few days earlier;

now its meaning was very clear. Sheilah rushed out to where Marc Connelly was waiting in the living room. "That man!" she cried. "That man stole my fur jacket!"

Scott's dirty work could not have been more successful. For Sheilah this seemed the ultimate betrayal and this time she did not hesitate to go to the authorities. She called the police and her insurance agent; they could wake Scott up at five o'clock in the morning and throw him in jail for all she cared. The next day Sheilah's insurance agent drove to Belly Acres to confront Fitzgerald about the theft. Scott admitted he had taken the coat, but pretended he had only lent it to Sheilah. The agent knew this was a lie because the jacket was insured in Sheilah's name. He gave Fitzgerald five days to return the coat; after that time, he said that he, not Miss Graham, would begin criminal proceedings. Scott had never expected Sheilah to act in such a decisive way and he agreed unhappily to return the coat. He asked only for more than five days; he had just mailed it to his daughter at Vassar and now he would have to write her and say a mistake had been made and wait for her to return it to California.

Sheilah was very glad to cause Scott some trouble. She wished him to suffer every torment in hell. Over the next few days her anger grew rather than diminished. Finally, it reached a climax one evening as she rampaged through her apartment and tore from cover to cover all the books he had given her, taking a terrible delight in ripping apart these books she had loved, along with their handwritten dedications and funny notes in the margins.

Nearly a week later she received a letter which was supposedly from Frances Kroll, but Sheilah knew very well that it had been dictated by Scott:

Dear Miss Graham:

Mr. Fitzgerald is himself again after six days in bed and everything he did seems perfectly abominable to him. He wants to know if there is any material way in which he can partially atone for the damage. He will, of course, replace anything, and more particularly he wants to know if it would be any help if he leaves Hollywood for good. He has no idea where you are nor has he any intention of trying to see you. He merely wants to remove as much of the unhappiness as is possible from what he did to you.

> Sincerely,
> Frances Kroll

Sheilah replied to Frances that she wanted nothing whatsoever from Mr. Fitzgerald except to be left in peace. Then a few days later a new letter arrived from Belly Acres: This time it was from Scott, a handwritten note on yellow paper that was wrapped around a small address book:

> When I came to myself last Tuesday I found this, which seems to be yours. It is very quiet out here now. I went to your room this afternoon and lay on your bed awhile to see if you had left anything of yourself. There were some pencils and the electric pad that didn't work and the autumn out the window that won't ever be the same. Then I wrote down a lot of expressions of your face, but one I can't bear to read, of the little girl who trusted me so and whom I loved more than anything in the world—and to whom I gave grief when I wanted to give joy. Something should have told you I was extemporizing wildly. . . It was all fever and liquor and sedatives— what nurses hear in any bad drunk case. I'm glad you're rid of me. I hope you're happy and the last awful impression is fading a little till someday you'll say, "he can't have been that black." Goodbye, Sheilo, I won't bother you any more.

> Scott

It seemed to Sheilah that Scott had said his eloquent good-bye a few times too often. Now she only wished he would truly leave her alone. In the past, she had forgiven Scott everything; he could seduce his nurse, threaten to kill her, and she would still not turn her back on him. But now a line had been crossed. There were three things in particular she could not forget or forgive: how he had betrayed her great secret, shouting out her name and her past; the theft of her beloved birthday present; and, finally, his attempt to get her fired from her job. These things, as far as Sheilah was concerned, had broken something that could not be repaired.

Five weeks passed in which there were no further communications from Scott. Sheilah did her best to put the love affair

behind her and take up again her old life as a single woman.
John Wheeler forwarded to her a telegram of apology he had
received from Fitzgerald, but it did not interest her:

I SENT YOU THAT WIRE WITH A TEMPERATURE OF 102 DEGREES AND A GOOD
DEAL OF LIQUOR ON BOARD. THERE IS NO REASON TO WORRY ABOUT
SHEILAH IN CONNECTION WITH THE STUDIOS. WE HAD SOME PERSONAL
TROUBLE IN WHICH I BEHAVED VERY VERY BADLY. PLEASE CONSIDER THE
TELEGRAM AS THE MUMBLINGS OF A MAN WHO WAS FAR FROM BEING HIM-
SELF.

                                        SCOTT FITZGERALD

Sheilah put the telegram aside with a curious feeling that none
of it concerned her anymore—not the liquor, or the temperatures,
or Scott's cycle of sin and repentance which she had seen too
often. She was free of all of this, and by the new year of 1940 she
told herself that she was enjoying her independence. Her column, "Hollywood Today," was a great success, appearing each
day in sixty-five different newspapers across the United States
and Canada. In January *Look* magazine asked if they might do a
picture layout of her as "the prettiest columnist in Hollywood."
Sheilah demurred when she learned she was expected to pose in
a bathing suit, but it was a flattering offer all the same. To be
pretty and successful and single in Hollywood was a winning
combination. The men she dated were impressed that she was
not only pretty but could quote poetry as well; she might now
add a line of Andrew Marvell or Keats to the dinner conversation. Sheilah was pleased one night when Irwin Shaw said to her,
"It's amazing how well read you are." She no longer had to
cringe when a serious subject came up. Scott Fitzgerald had
given her this self-confidence. There was always a faint echo of
him, a memory, a sense that something had happened—but what
a relief it was to be free of all his madness and moods!

Scott's doctor eventually got in touch with her to express his
concern about Fitzgerald's drinking. She told him that this was no
longer her problem. Sheilah had disliked Dr. Wilson from the start
and it seemed to her a bitter irony that this man who had blamed
her for Scott's drinking now was coming to her for help. She
drafted a reply to distance herself from both doctor and patient:

The only way to save Scott is to get him to a hospital where he can't get liquor otherwise you know better than I do what will happen to this very fine person. Everything else is utterly futile & you know it. At the present the situation is ridiculous. He has two nurses & one doctor & he is drinking at least a pint of gin a day if not more. . . you know Scott will not even hear from me. It is also stupid for you to regard me as the villain of the piece because I can't bear to see him drunk. I shall definitely not see him again for that reason. My absolutely last word on the entire unhappy matter is that if you [can't deal with Scott find someone who can]. . . . Please don't communicate with me in any way.

S.

When Scott came to himself, one of the first things he did was to discharge Jean Steffen. He could not afford her, and she was a constant reminder to him of how he had betrayed Sheilah. Scott was genuinely repentant for what he had done. Late as it was, he had decided that it was time to grow up; he was ready to celebrate the long-awaited funeral of his adolescence that the psychiatrist in New York, Dr. Hoffmann, had hoped to see. Though Sheilah did not know it, Scott Fitzgerald was in fact on the wagon and he would never again abuse alcohol.

A small miracle had happened, one that was more profound because it was so quiet. Scott had no one left to impress or to brag to, no one to even particularly believe he was finally sincere. He had turned forty-three years old on September 24; he was no longer a young man, but why he should change his ways at just this moment remains a mystery. Perhaps it was one binge too many. Or maybe it was that Sheilah had finally called his bluff. Few people had done this before, and never a woman.

Once in the south of France, Gerald Murphy had reached a similar point of exasperation with Scott after witnessing one too many pranks. Scott had just stretched out on the floor of a crowded restaurant to go to sleep, believing his behavior was very amusing. But Gerald had decided enough was enough. "Scott," he said, "this is *not* Princeton and I am *not* your roommate. Get up!" And Scott immediately rose to his feet. It was as simple as that. Like most children of twelve or forty-three, Fitzgerald had been waiting only for the irresistible voice of authority. Zelda, for all her originality, had always allowed Scott to do whatever he pleased. She was dependent upon him both emotionally and financially; she had complained about his drinking, but she had never threatened to leave him if he didn't stop.

But Sheilah was different; she earned her own money, she was accustomed to an independent life, and like Gerald Murphy she refused to tolerate his behavior any longer. When Scott understood that Sheilah meant business, that this time he really had gone too far, he was forced to examine himself as he had seldom done before. For one, he missed Sheilah. The house in Encino resounded with the silence of her five-week absence. He also had to admit himself morally in the wrong; he could not even pretend a sort of aesthetic superiority because in fact what he had done to her struck him as abominable. He may even have realized that he was not such a prize himself anymore—a sick, difficult, middle-aged man who was out of work. The chances were slim that he would ever again find a pretty and romantic young woman like Sheilah to put up with him. If she was "soiled goods," as he sometimes suspected, then so was he. Neither of them was so very perfect, and when Scott realized this, it was the beginning of wisdom and of real love. Chasing after a dream girl was something for teenagers.

Scott was tired. He was exhausted with making the same mistakes over and over again. He had worn himself out with drinking and suffering and foolish self-destruction. Without Sheilah he could envision only a life of loneliness and more failure, and then death. It seemed sordid somehow to come to such an end. Whatever the reasons, Scott did not write about them; he endured his transformation in private, but at the end of five weeks he emerged subtly different than before. The irony now was that Sheilah would never believe he had changed. How could he ever get her back? Despite his transformation, he was, of course, still Scott Fitzgerald. And so he sat down with himself and he came up with a plan.

One day in January 1940, Sheilah received a dozen red roses, delivered to her apartment with a note which read simply, "Scott." She debated throwing the roses into the garbage, but hesitated for a fatal second. The roses, after all, had no memory of what had happened. Why shouldn't she enjoy them? Sheilah put the flowers in a vase unaware of the cunning intelligence behind the gift—a man who was carefully playing his chances.

The next day Frances Kroll appeared at her apartment to deliver a final suitcase of her clothes and belongings that she had left behind at Encino. Frances sat down and gave Sheilah a carefully coached report on what was happening at Belly Acres. She said that Scott was working hard on his novel, nearly finished with the second chapter, and that he had stopped drinking. Sheilah smiled in a skeptical way, but Frances assured her it was true. Scott had learned his lesson at last; he had given up alcohol forever. Sheilah was not greatly interested. She had heard it all before.

Frances returned to Encino where Scott was waiting impatiently for her report. He had sent his all-purpose secretary as a spy into enemy territory to discover Sheilah's mood; Frances had agreed to act this part of go-between only because she believed that Fitzgerald was genuinely repentant. But her report was not encouraging. Scott wanted to know every detail, each word of the conversation, but he had to agree that it did not look good. Then he asked about the bouquet of roses he had sent.

"They're there, Mr. Fitzgerald," she said. "I saw them in a lovely vase on her desk."

All the worry lifted from Scott's face. He smiled with confidence, an expert in love, a man who knew all the angles as surely as a chess player might see ahead three, four, or even five moves to the inevitable end of the game.

"I've got her!" he said.

18

THE LAST NOVELIST

Like all those who habitually and instinctively lie, he had an
enormous respect and awe for the truth.

—F. Scott Fitzgerald, "Absolution"

SHEILAH WAS OUT ON THE TOWN, enjoying herself as a single
woman. On a Saturday night in mid-January 1940, she began her
evening with dinner at the Coconut Grove and then made her
way to Ciro's and the Mocambo on Sunset Boulevard, the two
most elegant night spots in Hollywood. There were stars and
writers and the top producers scattered among the tables; everyone was dressed in their best, the men in dinner jackets, the
women in gowns, determined to have a good time. The bands
played mambos and rumbas, the slinky Latin dance tunes that
were a craze. The war in Europe had made Hollywood suddenly
very gay; there was adventure ahead, romantic partings, and
heroic deeds—the very stuff of cinema, with the grit and blood
still far enough away to be glamorous. Sheilah dined and danced

and laughed and flirted; she was in a whirl of motion and it all
seemed a great deal of fun.

Her telephone was ringing when she arrived home breathless
late at night to her Hayworth Avenue apartment. She had to
fumble with her key and make a dash through the door to pick it
up in time. It was Scott. Strangely she was not at all surprised.
She had not been thinking about him—he was the furthest thing
from her mind—but the moment she heard his voice it seemed
inevitable that he should call.

"I'd very much like to see you, Sheilo." His voice was quiet,
certain of itself, and sober. "May I see you tomorrow?"

At first she could not physically answer. The sound of his
voice was more than familiar; it was like turning a corner and
finding unexpectedly that she was home. The glamour of her
single life which until just that moment had seemed so
immensely fun, appeared suddenly shrill and empty, a bubble
which a single telephone call might burst. Sheilah did not want
to appear too easy. She waited for what seemed a very long time
and then at last she answered gravely, yes, he could come to her
tomorrow.

Scott drove by early the next morning to pick her up in his
new car. His first California car had died recently and he was
now driving a 1937 Ford convertible, black with a beige top, that
he had bought secondhand from S. J. Perelman, paying it off at
twenty dollars a month. It was a quiet Sunday morning, sunny
but cold with patches of low mist hovering around the lawns
and trees. Sheilah sat without speaking by his side as Scott drove
the narrow country road that twisted through Laurel Canyon
and climbed into the Hollywood Hills. He parked at the summit
on Mulholland Drive and led the way on foot along a path
through the manzanita and scrub oak out to a small grassy knoll,
a viewpoint from which they could sit and gaze out across the
misty hills. Sheilah found it easier to look at the view than Scott.
Far across the hills she could see a hint of blue, the Pacific Ocean.
They were subdued and awkward with one another. It seemed
strange to her that they were vastly more formal now than at
their incautious beginning, that evening of casual words tossed
across the chasm of separate tables at the Screen Writers Guild

ball: *I like you*, he said. . . *I like* you, she answered. Now in 1940 the Screen Writers Guild was no longer a dream but a fact; the union train had come chugging into Hollywood to change the movie industry forever. The world was no longer what it had been that innocent summer of 1937 when Scott believed he was about to become the czar of the movie industry, and Sheilah was preparing to become the Marchioness of Donegall. It was a new decade—"the fearful forties," Scott called it, always willing to hazard a generalization even though this decade was only a few weeks old.

Sitting together in the grassy clearing, Scott began to speak slowly about his drinking. His voice was soothing, quiet. He wanted Sheilah to understand that as a young man he had learned to drink because everyone around him was drinking—it was the rebellious mark of his generation. "Zelda and I drank with them. I was able to drink and enjoy it," he said. "I thought all I needed anywhere in the world to make a living was pencil and paper. Then I found I needed liquor too. I needed it to write."

Scott confessed once in his fiction: "I found that with a few drinks I got expansive and somehow had the ability to please people, and the idea turned my head. Then I began to take a whole lot of drinks to keep going and have everybody think I was wonderful." Scott told Sheilah this in similar words as they sat together on the knoll. He told her that when Zelda broke down and his writing went out of style, he began to drink in a new way, in order to forget the pain of their wasted lives and his failed career. "I feel that I am responsible for what happened to her," he told Sheilah. "I could no longer bear what became of her. I could not bear what had become of me. But liquor did not help me forget. In these past years the escape has been more awful than the reality."

Sheilah had never heard Scott speak about his drinking like this, without boasting or putting on his usual show of wounded dignity. He said he was finally ready to stop. He knew it would not be easy. He was not a well man—he had his TB and his insomnia and God only knew what his exact temperature was at the moment—but he was determined to make a fresh start. He had found a new Hollywood agent, Phil Berg of the Berg Allenberg Agency, and he was feeling confident about his new novel.

"I am going to stop drinking, Sheilah," he vowed. "I have made a promise to myself. Whether you come back to me or not, I will stop drinking. But I want you back—very much."

Sheilah listened in silence. She felt there was a difference in him; he had never opened himself to her in quite this way. He was convincing, the very image of sober resolve, but Sheilah was still wary. She loved Scott, but she knew he was an awfully good actor—it was part of his terrible charm.

She turned to him finally. "Scott, how do I know I can believe you? *Can* you stop drinking, Scott? Do you really mean it?"

"I mean it," he promised. "Don't just take my words, Sheilah. Test me."

Scott jotted down a note for his new novel, little suspecting that it would become his most famous and often-quoted line: "There are no second acts in American lives." It was a sentiment born of the youth culture of the twenties, a sense that life contained one big bang—youth—an opening gambit and no further development of the plot until the disappointments of old age. Thinking of life as a three-act play, the missing act two was everything that should have connected youth and old age—middle age, a deepening of character, the slow glide to maturity. For a time it appeared that Fitzgerald himself was destined to be only a two-act man, but January 1940 saw the curtain rise on a belated middle age. Life on this new stage was different than before. There were to be no more wild scenes in airports or fights over a loaded gun; Scott would never again chase a frightened bellboy around a hotel room or challenge anyone to a duel. He kept his promise to Sheilah. . . or very close.

For Sheilah the trial period lengthened one sober day at a time until she fully accepted that Scott was truly changed. It seemed to her that they had both come of age. They settled down to a quiet domestic life together. The F. Scott Fitzgerald College of One resumed where it had left off in November. Scott ruefully replaced the books Sheilah had torn up in her rage at him, and gave them each new covers cut from wrapping paper, marking them as official "Encino Editions." He decided she was ready to tackle Christianity and he assigned her the Gospels of St. Mark and St. Luke and Joseph-Ernest Renan's *The Life of Jesus*. Occasionally Sheilah complained that her reading was too difficult. She was often discouraged and afraid she would never become truly educated. "Never mind," Scott assured her, "most college graduates are just as ignorant."

After dinner they took long walks in which Scott would question her in detail about what she had read. Or they might simply sit on the porch outside his second-floor bedroom and listen to the mesmerizing sounds of galloping hooves and pistol shots coming from the RKO Western lot next door. They rarely went out now except to the movies, the previews and premieres to which Sheilah received invitations because of her job. Scott and Sheilah both loved going to movies—the physical act itself of sitting in the dark, slinking down into one's seat, looking up at the big screen, and dreaming for an hour or two. Like most workers in the film industry, they retained the ability to be simultaneously cynical about the business and ardent believers in its celluloid dreams.

Sheilah no longer stood close to sniff Scott's breath, and she did not punish him anymore with brooding silences over the fact that they could not marry. Sometimes she found herself just a little bored, though she was careful to hide this from Scott. She was determined to be a more serious and decent person, for Scott's sake if not always her own. She tried her best to study hard and ignore the occasional faint call of the gaudy world: dancing and flirting and telling lies—all those things of her youth that were hard to give up.

As for Scott, he now began in earnest to write his novel about Hollywood. The reconciliation with Sheilah provided a calm harbor in which the succession of regular work days was possible. This was something new for Fitzgerald; he had produced all his previous writing in the midst of domestic chaos and drink, crises and disorder. In his youth, Scott seemed to need such turmoil to be creative; he had done his best writing in dramatic bursts, in all-night sessions full of stimulants and wild thoughts. But by

1940 he had worn himself out; it was only through a quiet daily routine that he was able to marshal his forces and get on with his book.

The new novel was ambitious:

> I want to give an all-fireworks illumination of the intense passion in Stahr's soul, his love of life, his love for the great thing that he's built out here, his, perhaps not exactly, satisfaction, but his feeling certainly of coming home to an empire of his own—an empire he has made.
>
> I want to contrast this sharply with the feeling of those who have merely gypped another person's empire away from them like the four great railroad kings of the coast—Crocker, Huntington and company or the feeling that L.B. [Mayer] would have.

Scott's novel would be a tragedy. It was his steadfast belief that the Louis B. Mayers of the world would always win the game, not the Monroe Stahrs; survival belonged to the faceless men who managed to finagle their small sinecure. Heroes were grand, but they were doomed to fail—though the fight was worth it, the only fight there was. He told Sheilah—gently as he was able—that life was a cheat and happiness was not possible. He and Sheilah argued about this often. She had a more senti-mental view, a belief in children and Christmas and logs blazing in the hearth. Though she had never known these things herself, she clung to the abstract idea of them as the carrot at the end of the stick, the reason one worked so bloody hard. And so she was aghast at Scott's conviction that nothing would last, and that defeat was the prize for anyone who aimed high. Sheilah assured him that *they* would last, *they* would be happy. Love would triumph and together they would beat the odds against them. But Scott only smiled at her innocence. As far back as 1920, in his first novel, he had written, "The sentimental person thinks things will last—the romantic person has a desperate con-fidence that they won't."

Meanwhile one carried on. Work was what a tragic hero did while waiting for the gods to do their mischief. Scott kept Frances busy typing and retyping the endless changes for his book. Each chapter went through four, sometimes five versions though he had not yet managed a "first draft" of the complete book. Scott wrote in the middle of the night when his insomnia woke him; he worked in the day whenever he was able, filling up the long pages of yellow legal pads in his large uneven hand. He was never satisfied. He was afraid he had too many characters; he searched constantly for ways to combine and reduce and tighten. His goal was to have a "constructed novel" like *Gatsby*, rather than one with a lot of side shows like *Tender Is the Night*—a book (he assured Sheilah) he would one day rewrite.

Writing was manic, wonderful, draining, euphoric, and enough to make any sane person pull out his hair. There was nothing objective to hang onto. After too many revisions Scott scrawled an angry note to himself on the first manuscript page of Chapter One: "Rewrite from mood. Has become stilted with rewriting. Don't look rewrite from mood." Nor was he altogether happy with Kathleen, his portrait of Sheilah. He set down in his notes: "Where will the warmth come from in this? Why does he think she's warm? Warmer than the voice in *Farewell to Arms*. My girls were all so warm and full of promise. What can I do to make it honest and different?"

He started once again his custom to read aloud to Sheilah each evening what he had written during the day. Before their fight at the end of November, Sheilah had heard Chapter One and the general plan. She knew she was the heroine, Kathleen, but now as Scott read each evening she heard a new array of intimate details taken from her life. It was unsettling: Scott had used everything, even their first meeting at Robert Benchley's bungalow and the mix-up of identities, how Scott had believed she was the girl with the belt of cut-out stars and had returned to the party to discover his mistake. Sheilah learned for the first time that she had reminded Scott of Zelda, Stahr's "dead wife." Some incidents were slightly disguised, others not at all. In the book, Stahr saw Kathleen for the first time on the back lot of his movie studio after an earthquake, a more dramatic setting than Benchley's bungalow at The Garden of Allah. Stahr and Kathleen met a second time at a dinner dance that was very much like the benefit for the Screen Writers Guild, though he combined this in a clever way with their Saturday-night date with Jonah Ruddy

and Eddie Mayer at the Clover Club. As Kathleen and Stahr
dance together, Kathleen says the same flirtatious words that
Sheilah had said to Scott: "When I'm with you, I don't breathe
quite right." Eventually they would make love for the first time
at a half-finished beach house in Malibu rather than Sheilah's
rented home on Kings Road, but this half-finished house was
suggested by the anecdotes Sheilah told him of her engagement
to the movie director, King Vidor, and the plans he had shown
her for a house he promised to build when they were married.

There were so many details large and small taken from their
own romance that Sheilah was overwhelmed. In the book,
Kathleen told Stahr about her mysterious past while sitting in
his limousine, just as Sheilah had confessed her secrets in Scott's
car—an old Ford rather than a limousine, but this was only window dressing. Scott used many of her phrases and observations.
He wrote that the Ping-Pong balls lying in the grass at night
were like stars in the sky, something she had said to him once in
the backyard at Belly Acres, and in another place that the
California rain came down so loudly it was like horses weeing.
She had said these things, uneducated Lily Shiel, and it was
nothing short of miraculous to find herself in Scott's novel. In
the second paragraph of Chapter One, he even managed to take
a swipe at her chief rival, Louella Parsons, in the voice of the
narrator Cecelia: "I was going to write my memoirs once, *The
Producer's Daughter*, but at eighteen you never quite get around
to anything like that. It's just as well—it would have been as flat
as an old column of Lolly Parsons'." Cecelia, for her part, was a
combination of Scottie at eighteen and Budd Schulberg with his
Hollywood background—and Budd would eventually be as startled as Sheilah to find so many of his casual remarks accurately
quoted.

Sheilah felt vulnerable, as though Scott had painted a portrait
of her naked for all to see. She was both flattered and uncomfortable. Kathleen, like Sheilah, was a quintessential outsider, a person who was part of nothing and who belonged nowhere, not
even in Hollywood, which was an industry of misfits. It was
eerie to be re-created so accurately on the page, a black magic of
sorts that caused a shiver to go up her spine. But despite her awe

of Scott's skill, Sheilah dared to make a suggestion or two. In the seduction scene at Malibu, Stahr in the original draft began to tremble and the lovemaking came to a premature halt. Sheilah had a practical answer for this problem. She suggested that Kathleen say something coarse and sexual, "making herself inferior" so that Stahr could relax and get on with it. The idea appealed to Scott and he wrote a revised scene in which Kathleen aroused Stahr so thoroughly that they made love a second time— in the light, no less, so he might see her. This second round of lovemaking began when Kathleen told Stahr that he should rest and take better care of himself. But this was not what Stahr was seeking:

> "Don't be a mother," he said.
>   "All right. What shall I be?"
>   Be a trollop, he thought. He wanted the pattern of his life broken. If he was going to die soon, like the two doctors said, he wanted to stop being Stahr for a while and hunt for love like men who had no gifts to give, like young nameless men who looked along the streets in the dark.
>   "You've taken off my apron," she said gently.
>   "Yes."
>   "Would anyone be passing along the beach? Shall we put out the candles?"
>   "No, don't put out the candles."

What nameless men—and trembling puritans—seek along darkened streets, of course, are prostitutes. For Sheilah this was not a flattering image but she recognized this particular scene as wild fantasy, since in life Scott would certainly have blown out the candle. Sheilah was often struck as forcibly by what Scott changed in the book as what he retained.

But some things escaped her attention entirely, such as the fact that throughout the novel Stahr had a fatalistic sense that he was going to die soon. Of course, Irving Thalberg died young and the character was modeled after him—but there was more to it than that, a premonition, a tone that would only strike Sheilah afterward. In Chapter Five a doctor examined Stahr, and the situation was so clear to him that he could only observe to himself:

Stahr... was due to die very soon now. Within six months one
could say definitely. What was the use of developing the cardio-
grams?... what it added up to was the definite urge toward total
exhaustion....

In the end, writing was more than hard work; there was magic
involved, a witch's brew of luck and intuition. "All good writing
is swimming under water and holding your breath," Scott said
in a letter to his daughter, after a lifetime of careful thought on
the subject. And indeed Fitzgerald was holding his breath and
swimming very hard, fighting off the exhaustion, hoping to cross
the water and come up on the other side. He had won a great
victory with himself; his only battle now was his race against
time.

Scott worried about his lungs. "My cough has become a public
nuisance," he complained to Scottie. He hinted darkly to Sheilah
and Frances that his TB had taken a turn for the worse, and he
monitored his temperature many times a day. But Scott was such
a hypochondriac that neither Sheilah nor Frances nor Scottie
took him very seriously.

On February 7, Scott wrote a letter to his new doctor, Clarence
Nelson, complaining about odd little "aches around the elbow
and shoulder... whenever I have had a great orgy of cokes or
coffee." Not long afterward, Scott reported to Frances that he
had suffered a mild heart seizure while trying to open a window.
When he raised his arms he felt a stab of pain that was so sharp
it took his breath away; later there remained an unusual stiffness
in his arms. Dr. Nelson decided this was not a heart attack but it
was a warning to take better care of himself. Scott related the
episode to Sheilah and Frances in such an understated manner
that they did not take it very seriously, particularly since he was
apt to complain more loudly if his temperature climbed above
ninety-nine.

At the moment, Scott was more worried about money than his
health. He complained to Zelda that it was hell trying to live
with only a hundred dollars in the bank. In every letter he urged
her to be more frugal. In February he wrote: "At the moment I
am hoping for a job at Republic Studios, the lowest of the low,

which would among other things help pay your hospital bill." In March: "Nothing has developed here. I write these 'Pat Hobby' stories—and wait. I have a new idea now—a comedy series which will get me back into the big magazines—but my God I am a forgotten man. *Gatsby* had to be taken out of the Modern Library because it didn't sell, which was a blow." Scott was forced to write Dr. Carroll asking him to wait temporarily on Zelda's bill; at the moment he simply could not come up with the money.

For a man prone to grand gestures, who had once hoped to impress and win the world, it was not much fun to be broke and in bad health. He made the best of it, though, squeezing out from each decimal point of fever the maximum amount of possible drama. In May he wrote to Zelda:

> I go according to the fever—if it stays around 99 I feel rash, if it runs up over a degree at a daily average I get alarmed and think we mustn't get stony broke like last fall. My ambition is to pay the government who've laid off me so far. I don't know what they'd annex except my scrapbook. . . .

> Yours at about 99.7,
> Scott

*   *   *

Lester Cowan was a producer, a short, dark-haired, dark-complexioned man, wiry and energetic, who usually had a cigar sticking out of one side of his mouth. He was not Ivy League like Walter Wanger, nor remotely "intellectual" like Joe Mankiewicz. His clothes generally appeared too large and did not in anyway hang in an elegant manner. He might have been a bookie or a New York cab driver. In his youth he had been an professional bantam-weight boxer and his nose still bore the reminder of being smashed several times.

As a Hollywood producer, Lester Cowan did not cut a very impressive figure; he had only one quasi-hit to his name, *My Little Chickadee* starring Mae West. Nevertheless, he loved Scott Fitzgerald's 1931 short story, "Babylon Revisited," and in the spring of 1940 he got in touch with Scott about turning it into a movie. Though he was no intellectual, the producer thought "Babylon Revisited" was the saddest story he had ever read, and every time he read it he cried and cried and cried.

It really *was* very sad, and possibly the best story Scott ever wrote. "Babylon Revisited" was about saying good-bye to ill-spent youth. In this autobiographical tale, a man by the name of Charlie Wales returned to Paris after the crash of the stock market to survey the damage of the twenties. The Ritz Bar, where he had once spent many fond and reckless hours, was now like a graveyard, emptied of Americans. Charlie was on the wagon, his wife was dead, and he was a recovering alcoholic. The thirties had not been kind years to him so far. He was in Paris doing his best to appear respectable and repentant in order to win back the custody of his daughter from his dead wife's sister.

Whenever Scott wanted a truly horrible woman to put into a story, he summoned up the image of Zelda's sister, Rosalind; he had used her as "Baby" Warren, Nicole's sister in *Tender Is the Night*, and in "Babylon Revisited" she was nastier still as Marion, the woman Charlie Wales must petition to get his daughter back. Unfortunately, Marion/Rosalind blamed Charlie/Scott for her sister's death/insanity. She "had built up all her fear of life into one wall and faced it toward him," Scott wrote. The sad part of "Babylon Revisited"—the part that made Lester Cowan cry—was the climactic moment when it seemed Charlie was going to get his daughter back, but the past caught up with him in the form of two hilarious drunks, old friends, who burst in at the wrong moment just as Marion was about to relent. Now it appeared Charlie would wander the earth forever trying to live down his past, hoping that his sister-in-law one day would judge that he had finally paid sufficient penance for his youth.

This was the story Lester Cowan wanted Scott to turn into a movie, casting Cary Grant as the father and Shirley Temple as the little girl—not a trash assignment at all, but what Fitzgerald had come to Hollywood to do. Suddenly he was excited all over again about writing for the movies. Sheilah had not seen him like this since he had begun *Madame Curie*. But there was a catch. Despite Cowan's watershed of tears, he knew a bargain when he saw it; "Babylon Revisited" was like finding a Rembrandt in your attic. Fitzgerald was worth nothing on the open market and the producer proposed to buy the story and Scott's services as a screenwriter dirt cheap. The project was to be done mostly on spec, with very little money up front.

Scott wrote to Scottie on April 11:

> I go to cinema work tomorrow on a sort of half-pay, half-"spec" (speculation) business of my own story "Babylon Revisited." Which is to say Columbia advances me living money while I work and if it goes over in installments with the producer, the company, the releasing people, I get an increasing sum. At bottom we eat—at the top the deal is very promising.

Lester did his best to squeeze whatever he could from Scott for free; before the deal was signed, he invited Scott for lunches at darkened restaurants and then to the racetrack, hoping the author would give away his ideas for the screenplay. Scott accepted the lunches but he kept his mouth shut. The deal was finally concluded by Scott's new agent, Phil Berg. Cowan agreed to pay $1,000 for all film rights, plus $400 a week to Scott for ten weeks to write the screenplay. This was a decided comedown from the $1,250 a week Scott had received at MGM, but the money was still a godsend—and best of all, the story was his own.

Lester renamed the picture *Cosmopolitan*, fearing perhaps that "Babylon Revisited" might summon too sinful an image for the Catholic censor, Joseph Breen. Scott set to work in an optimistic mood. He dictated the screenplay to Frances, pacing back and forth in his bedroom, acting out the various parts; Frances did her frantic best to jot down the dialogue in shorthand as it came flowing from her employer's mouth. Unfortunately, Cowan interrupted the work with constant phone calls. He was the sort of movie producer who loved telephones, whose life revolved around the miracle of pitching ideas back and forth upon the wires. He could talk for hours at a time. He always wanted Scott to read the latest scene to him, and when Scott read it, it was all so sad that he sobbed and sobbed over the phone. Scott often got carried away with his own performance and he cried as well—both of them, writer and producer, crying so hard about their movie they could barely get through to the end of the scene. Then Scott hung up the telephone with a devilish grin on his face, wiped away his tears, and told Frances what a delight it was to make a producer cry who was underpaying him. But the delight wore thin when Cowan continued to call several times a day, keeping Scott on the phone for hours. At the end of each tearful conversation, he felt sucked dry of energy, used up, and often he needed to lie down. Scott began to dread the sound of his ringing telephone.

Despite the ceaseless phone calls, Scott liked Lester Cowan; he found the producer unexpectedly sweet and unpretentious. But he was not pleased with the casting of Shirley Temple as the little girl. The child star at the moment was on the verge of adolescence—a tragedy all the money in Hollywood could not prevent—and Scott believed she was simply too old for the part. He was afraid a teenage daughter in the script would transform the bitter tragedy of his story into a sappy melodrama. Scott wrote to Garson Kanin, who was being considered as the director: "I want what happens in this picture to be felt in the stomach first, felt out of great conviction about the tragedy of father and child—and *not* felt in the throat to make a fat woman's holiday between chocolate creams." Meanwhile, the child actress was getting older every day; Shirley Temple's mother, a shrewd businesswoman, was balking at the details of the contract and Scott was afraid the little girl would be grown up before the movie was ever made.

Scott met Shirley Temple at least once to discuss the script. He found her intelligent for a child star and was impressed that she read *Time* magazine. Years later the actress remembered Fitzgerald "as a kindly. . . pale man, who was recovering from an illness. The thing that impressed me the most as an eleven or twelve year old was that he drank six or eight Coca-Colas during his visit. As a young girl, I thought this to be a stunning accomplishment—in fact, I still do."

But Scott could have spared himself his assorted hopes and frustrations and visits to prepubescent stars. After a number of weeks—without warning and despite his telephone tears—Lester Cowan simply took Scott off the picture and hired an experienced screenwriting team, the Epstein brothers, to take over. By this time, Scott had had enough experience with Hollywood so that he was not greatly surprised. With mixed feelings of disappointment and relief, he returned to his novel.

As for Lester Cowan, he eventually made an enormous profit on his brief bargain-basement association with Fitzgerald: He sold Scott's screenplay to MGM for one hundred thousand dollars and the movie was made with the inappropriate title, *The Last Time I Saw Paris,* starring Van Johnson as the father and Elizabeth Taylor as the miscast "little girl." Everyone made money except Scott, who needed it most.

It was hard to find just the right place to live in Los Angeles. Malibu was too cold in the winter, but the valley was too hot in the summer—unbearably hot. After the summer of 1939, Scott was inspired to plan a heat-wave scene for his new novel which he hoped would rival the one in *Gatsby.* There would be heat so heavy on the California land that decent people could barely crawl from their swimming pools. Such weather made good atmospherics for a book, but not for real life.

In May 1940, dreading the approach of another summer, Scott turned to his favorite real estate agent and asked her to find him a new residence. Sheilah set herself in motion. This time she came up with a more modest solution than her earlier attempts: a small inexpensive apartment on Laurel Avenue in Hollywood just off Sunset Boulevard, only one block from Sheilah's own apartment on Hayworth. It was almost Scott's fantasy of having two houses side by side with a discreet connecting tunnel underneath; they would be so close to each other that they could share a maid. (Poverty in Hollywood, of course, did not mean going without a maid.) Scott would no longer have the long drive from the valley into town when there was work at the studios; he would be a block from Schwab's and The Garden of Allah, right in the thick of things again. Sheilah did not worry that the proximity to The Garden of Allah would cause Scott to drink again; after four months of living up to his promise, she trusted him completely.

Before he left Belly Acres, Scott decided to throw a small luncheon party to celebrate his pending escape. He and Sheilah had been living a reclusive life and this was something of an event. On May 13 he wrote gaily to Sid and Laura Perelman—misspelling, as was his habit, Sid's name:

Dear Syd and Laura:

This is a love missive so do not be alarmed. I am not giving a tea for the Princess Razzarascal or Twoticker Forsite. *But* I am leaving this Elysian haunt in two weeks (the 29th to be exact) and sometime before that nonce I wish you two would dine or lunch. . . .

We could either dine *à quatre* or add the Wests and some other couple. . . and afterwards play with my model parachute troops. At any event, side arms will not be *de rigueur.* Sheilah will be with me, just as merry as can be, to greet you on the porch with a julep. I have just reread *Crime and Punishment* and the chapters on gang labor in *Capitalist Production* and am meek as a liberal bourgeois lamb.

The Wests—Nathanael West and his wife Eileen—were the sister and brother-in-law of Sid Perelman. Scott was fond of Nat West and the previous summer had read and very much admired his surrealistic novel on Hollywood, *The Day of the Locust.* Nat West, in fact, was a writer after Fitzgerald's heart, an artist of integrity such as Scott had not often encountered in Hollywood. After reading *The Day of the Locust,* Scott wrote an impromptu review to Perelman:

The book, though it puts Gogol's *The Lower Depth* in the class with *The Tale of Benjamin Bunny,* certainly has scenes of extraordinary power—if that phrase is still in use. Especially I was impressed by the pathological crowd at the premiere, the character and handling of the aspirant actress, and the uncanny almost medieval feeling of some of his Hollywood background, set off by those vividly drawn grotesques.

Scott did not mention in this capsule review his enormous relief that *The Day of the Locust* was in no way similar to his own novel-in-progress about Hollywood. Unfortunately, it seemed that Hollywood novels were in the air. Even young Budd Schulberg was writing one, something he called *What Makes*

Sammy Run. In the summer of 1940, Budd proudly sent Scott a copy of his first novel, unaware that this would cause Fitzgerald anxiety. But when Scott read the book, he soon relaxed. *What Makes Sammy Run* was only a certain type of popular novel, not "literature," Scott believed; Budd had captured only a very blatant view of the movie world. Scott wished the young writer well, but not in this particular field. He told Sheilah happily, "The book about Hollywood still has to be written." His book, of course.

The guest list for the final party at Belly Acres was composed of Sid and Laura, Nat and his wife, Eileen, and Eddie Mayer. Erleen and her husband Gaylord served the meal and everyone seemed pleasantly surprised to find such a sober Scott Fitzgerald quietly discussing art and politics. As for the guests: "Sid Perelman is effete—new style," Scott observed later. "Sheilah noted his strange grace doing his interpretation of 'Slythy' in the Charade the other night. I like his brother-in-law West. I wonder if he's long winded as a defense mechanism. . . [his] way of saying, 'Don't like me—I want to go back into my dreams.' I know Nat through his books which are morbid as hell, doomed to the underworld of literature."

Nat's wife, Eileen, was another story—the young woman had been the subject of Sid Perelman's play, *My Sister, Eileen,* and she seemed to have a very high opinion of herself. Eileen was stridently left-wing and though Scott was determined to be as "meek as a liberal bourgeois lamb," the party soon ran into a political storm because of her. It appeared side arms might become de rigueur after all. The trouble began after lunch when the Perelmans and Eddie took a walk around the elaborate grounds of Edward Everett Horton's estate, leaving Scott and Sheilah alone in the house to entertain Nat and Eileen. Scott brought out his scrapbooks—the same scrapbooks he had mentioned to Zelda as all he had left that the IRS might annex for back taxes. They were precious to Scott, a memory of people and places he had loved, and many years of success and failure. But Eileen looked through the pages with scorn. She ridiculed the blond and brunette locks Scott had kept as mementos of his first adolescent girlfriends in St. Paul, each lock tied carefully with a pink ribbon. There were other entirely bourgeois mementos of a politically incorrect youth—dance cards from long-ago debutante balls complete with small pink pencils, even the lace handkerchief of a girl Scott had never forgotten.

Eileen West could not contain herself at the sight of these sentimental objects; as far as she was concerned they proved conclusively that Scott Fitzgerald was an enemy of the masses. She accused Scott of only caring for the rich; she unleashed the old arguments which had been used against Scott before, all the labels and stereotypes that had carried Fitzgerald out of style. Scott accepted the tongue-lashing with a sad smile but Sheilah was up in arms. "How dare she belittle him!" she thought furiously. She had liked Eileen previously but now she could barely keep from physically assaulting the woman. Sheilah's eyes blazed with anger; she banged plates and glasses meaningfully as she cleared the table. Her hostility became so blatant that Eileen made a defensive retreat; she took her husband and left, and the party was ruined.

Scott was frustrated at being forever misunderstood. Not long after this ruined luncheon, he and Sheilah went to a small dinner gathering at Budd Schulberg's house. Eager to debate politics, Scott took Budd and Ring Lardner Jr., both members of the Communist Party, into a separate room to thrash out the issue once and for all. Scott liked Budd Schulberg very much; Ring Lardner Sr. had been one of his best friends, and the model for the character Abe North in *Tender Is the Night*. But when Scott returned to Sheilah, he could only shake his head and say, "Nothing original. They are content to follow the party line." At home later he made a scornful entry into his notebook: "Mesdames Lardner and Schulberg are kitchen fodder."

And yet he was the one who was out of style. It was discouraging, but as always he returned to his book. In his novel all these issues would be resolved—capitalism, communism, the great and the not-so-great, and whether F. Scott Fitzgerald still had any clout as a writer. He only had to find the strength and money to keep on writing. "I want to be extravagantly admired again," Scott had written once long ago to an old friend, shortly before *The Great Gatsby* was published. But by the spring of 1940

there was no applause and no extravagance anywhere in sight—
just hard, lonely work. Scott had always had a schoolboy longing
to be a hero, the sort who took bows in the footlights, and ran
across ecstatic goal lines to the cheers of the crowd. Yet it was
only now after giving up such childhood illusions that he
embarked at last upon a true heroic journey. Fiction and fact had
finally merged; Scott Fitzgerald was inseparable from his creation, Monroe Stahr.

He wrote for himself a forlorn prophecy: "I am the last of the
novelists for a long time now." It was a bleak perception, and fortunately not true. But this is what it felt like for Scott in 1940 in
Los Angeles, living his obscure existence, about to move his few
belongings from the San Fernando Valley to a small apartment
off Sunset Boulevard. He refused to give up his sense of a romantic destiny. He had Frances keep a carbon copy of every letter he
wrote, every scrap, every note; for deep in his heart he maintained a steadfast belief that future generations would be interested in his tale. And he worked hard though all the odds were
against him, certain that if he really was the last novelist, then he
had better put on a damn good show.

19

LAUREL AVENUE

I am not a great man, but sometimes I think the impersonal and objective quality of my talent and the sacrifices of it, in pieces, to preserve its essential value has some sort of epic grandeur.

F. Scott Fitzgerald, in a 1939 letter to his daughter

SCOTT MOVED INTO HIS NEW HOME, 1403 N. Laurel Avenue, at the end of May 1940. It was a modest tree-lined street which hinted at a not-too-distant Midwestern past. Small houses with porches and swings and pretty beds of flowers sat on narrow plots of ground, alternating with more recently built stucco apartment buildings. Scott was in an L-shaped apartment complex, three stories high, a building which the landlady, Mrs. Neuville, described optimistically as a "garden court." The garden, such as it was, consisted of a narrow patch of grass nestled in the L, and a few evergreen shrubs and a line of decorative cypress trees facing the street. From a block away there came a drone of traffic from Sunset Boulevard night and day, sounds of commerce and ambition, waves of motion to and fro.

Scott's apartment was on the third floor. He had a small living room, dining room, kitchen, and bedroom, all furnished in a heavy pseudo-English style. Scott hated the furniture. His living room was dominated by an absurd couch whose color he described cheerfully as "vomit green," but he had neither the time, money, nor interest to shop for anything better. He was here to work. The unaccustomed noise of his new surroundings bothered him more than the furnishings. The apartment building catered to those who subsisted on the edges of the movie industry and there were often loud parties late into the night. There was a large actress, Grace Hayle, who lived down the hall; her specialty was blood-curdling screams and laugh er for movie soundtracks. Unfortunately, she practiced her skill at odd times of the day and night. Scott noted: "Has a wide repertoire ranging from 'when a woman sees a mouse' to 'when a woman sees a murder.'" He hoped to find a spot for her in his book. Another neighbor had an annoying habit of walking her dogs on the roof above his head. Scott complained to the landlady:

Dear Mrs. Neuville:

I thought the other day that a large rat had managed to insert itself into the plaster above my bedroom and workroom. I was, however, surprised that it apparently slept at night and worked in the day, causing its greatest din around high noon.

However yesterday, much to my surprise, I deduced from the sounds it emitted that it was a dog, or rather several dogs, and evidently training for a race, for they ran round and round the tin roof. Now I don't know how these greyhounds climbed up the wall but I know dog-racing is against the law of California—so I thought you'd like to know. Beneath the arena where these races occur an old and harassed literary man is gradually going mad.

The greyhounds continued their race and a few weeks later Scott complained to his landlady once more, assuring her that "it is impossible to work or sleep while the riot is in progress." But despite the noise, Scott liked being in town again and having Sheilah only a block away. She often came by in the late afternoons after she finished her column to stretch out on the vomit-

green sofa and study her College of One curriculum while Scott
wrote in bed and Frances typed on the dining room table. On
Laurel Avenue they continued their life of domestic calm which
had begun in January in Encino. When Scott wasn't writing, his
main interests were football and following the progress of the
war in Europe. He kept a map of Europe on his study wall and
he spent hours drawing up diagrams, working out his own
plans for distant battles. He was certain he could defeat the
Nazis quickly if only someone would please put him in charge.
Meanwhile Poland had fallen the previous September and by the
late spring of 1940 it looked as if Holland, Belgium, and even
France might be next to go. In the drowsy peace of California,
the tense dramas of the world seemed very far away.

Scott and Sheilah's shared maid cooked their evening meal,
alternating each night between his apartment and hers. But
whether they ate on Hayworth Avenue or Laurel Avenue, the
dinner was always the same: a thin T-bone steak, baked potato,
peas, and grapefruit Jell-O. Night after night it never varied.
Scott and Sheilah made bets sometimes to see if the menu would
ever change and then giggled and became quite hysterical when
the inevitable dinner was set down once again on the table. After
dinner they generally stayed at home to read, or they made the
two-minute walk around the corner to Schwab's, to spend an
hour browsing through the magazines on the rack, saying hello
to passing friends, and sitting at the counter with a malted milk.
"Imagine," Sheilah said to Scott one evening, "here we are, supposedly sophisticated people, and the highlight of our day is a
chocolate malt at Schwab's!" Scott smiled wistfully. Sometimes
he seemed quite old to her, and she so very young. She still
secretly craved excitement and things to do. It seemed ironic to
her that Scott Fitzgerald was famous for his wild ways, tearing
up Paris and New York, the life of the party; now his old friends
would barely recognize the quiet and mature person he had
become. Sheilah did not miss the old melodramas. . . and yet she
could not help but feel a touch of regret at how calm her life had
become. She saw her youth slipping by.

There was a small open terrace off Scott's living room where
they often sat together on summer evenings, watching the com-

ings and goings of young couples from the front door below, listening as they said their loud good nights. Scott and Sheilah, hidden in the shadows of their third-floor balcony, made a game of trying to imagine these young lives, what they were like and what the future might hold for them. They spied upon one couple in particular: an aspiring young redheaded actress who lived down the hall, Lucille Ball, who was dating an unknown Cuban musician named Desi Arnaz. It appeared to be a love affair that was having trouble getting off the ground. Lucy was always trying to detain him, using her wiles to invite him upstairs, but Desi lingered indecisively by the front door and generally begged off. Scott and Sheilah made bets with each other as to how it would turn out; Sheilah, the sentimentalist, rooted for Lucy to get her man. She was glad that the drama of courtship was still going on someplace—though not for her. It seemed strange after all her adventures to be relegated to a balcony seat rather than center stage.

Scott knew very well that Sheilah was restless. He had little money or energy to amuse her, but he arranged a few weekend trips out of town. One weekend they drove south across the Mexican border to Tijuana, where a street photographer took a photograph of them together wearing large sombreros: Sheilah sat on a burro smiling radiantly while Scott stood at her side, posing with a serape over one shoulder and looking very wry and humorous as a caballero. They took a less successful vacation to San Francisco in the early summer to see the World's Fair. Scott began the nearly five-hundred-mile trip driving his car at a torturously slow speed, becoming more grouchy with every mile though he stoutly refused to let Sheilah take the wheel. Not far outside of Los Angeles, he decided that driving had been a mistake; they abandoned his car and took the train the rest of the way north.

On the train Scott's mood was grim until they heard over someone's small radio the news of Britain's successful evacuation from Dunkirk. It was a heroic moment as English boats of every description, large and small, crossed the channel to rescue their army. Scott was dancing in the aisles, crying out his joy. Up until this moment, he had professed little faith in the British, insisting they were doomed to lose the war. It was a subject guaranteed to cause a hot argument with Sheilah; like every other British exile in Hollywood, her patriotism and all-around Britishness had increased with her years of absence.

"Scott, you don't know the British!" she would tell him angrily.

"Oh, Sheilah, they can't possibly win," he had always told her with a patronizing smile. But now Scott was thrilled to be wrong. "You're going to win!" he cried. "You've saved your soldiers to fight another day!"

In San Francisco they ran into a gloomy Humphrey Bogart and his wife, Mayo Methot. Bogart complained about the small roles he had been doing recently at Warner Brothers, mostly villains. This was very discouraging after his promising success in *The Petrified Forest*; his career appeared to have reached a dead end and he worried he was going to be a bit player forever. When Scott and Sheilah returned to Los Angeles, they were greeted with the news of the fall of France and the Nazi occupation of Paris. This caused Scott to plunge into a new depression. He had lived in France; he loved Paris and the image of the Nazis marching their bully goose step in triumph up the Champs-Élysées was almost too terrible to bear.

Scott wrote to his daughter in a depressed mood: "I went to San Francisco with some friends for one day, and found it much too long to see that singularly second-rate and uninspired Fair." He still could not admit to Scottie that he was traveling with a woman rather than "some friends," though his daughter certainly was not fooled. Later in the summer he and Sheilah attempted another long weekend away, this time a car trip to Monterey on the northern California coast. It was nearly as long a drive as to San Francisco. Scott was so exhausted by the time they arrived that he could do little for the rest of the weekend but sleep. Sheilah sat by herself in a lawn chair in the sun, depressed to find herself burdened with a sick old man—she who was magnificently healthy and loved to swim and play tennis and be outdoors. It seemed that as long as she had known Scott, there had been something wrong with his health, real or imaginary. Sheilah tried not to think these things, but she couldn't help it.

She understood, of course, how difficult it was for Scott to be sober. Gin was only part of it; he missed even more the great rushes of inspiration. Maturity came hard—to accept that euphoria, like youth, was not the final human condition. Acquaintances still occasionally saw the old Scott Fitzgerald. One afternoon in Hollywood, Scott showed up unexpectedly at Budd Schulberg's house declaiming with undergraduate fervor about the genius of Spengler, talking about *The Decline of the West* as though it were a brand-new book that had just pushed its way onto the bestseller list. Budd was amazed at such enthusiasm, but at home these days Scott was often more subdued. He had less patience than before and he took out his petty irritations against the person closest at hand—Sheilah.

There were countless small eruptions. Scott was annoyed once to walk into Sheilah's apartment and find her reading Mortimer Adler's *How to Read a Book*. He grabbed the silly thing out of her hands. "But this will make you hate reading," he raged. For someone who had once hobnobbed with the best minds of his generation—Edmund Wilson, Ernest Hemingway, John Dos Passos, Thomas Wolfe, and many others—it was often frustrating to put up with such an appalling lack of sophistication. Another time Sheilah came back from the set of *Doctor Kildare* and told Scott with much wide-eyed enthusiasm that the actor Lew Ayres was diligently making his way through "The 100 Great Books" as defined and photographed recently on three shelves by *Life* magazine. Scott ridiculed such an absurd idea—"The 100 Great Books" indeed! It was positively crass. "He won't learn a thing from them," he assured Sheilah with scorn. But he was a man who took lists seriously and later he secretly compared his own College of One curriculum against the one hundred books considered important by the editors of *Life*. He noted carefully that from his own selections, he discovered in the magazine photograph: "5 in the first row, 6 in the second, 10 in the third—a total of 21 books."

Once a week, Sheilah brought flowers to his apartment, as she had done at Malibu in the summer of 1938, filling his rooms with living fragrance and color. She thought they would cheer him up. But finally, one afternoon in the fall, when her arms were full of flowers, Scott turned on her.

"Take those flowers away!" he said sharply. When Sheilah stared at him dumbly, he added, "I hate cut flowers!"

"But at the beach. . . ."

"I couldn't stand them there, either."

Sheilah was very hurt and had to leave the room so that he wouldn't see her cry. She could not understand why if Scott hated cut flowers he had not said something about it years ago, rather than let her continue to make a fool of herself. Sheilah suffered from these small squabbles, but it seemed to her the price she must pay for Scott's new sobriety. She too was forced to grow up and accept that a long-term relationship was often like this, once you got past the early days of courtship. Like Scott, she had to give up many romantic illusions. She told herself that this was almost like marriage. When she looked at it that way, she saw she had almost gotten what she wanted—and really, she was almost very happy.

Sheilah turned down a chance to do a second lecture tour; it would have meant a few thousand dollars, but also a great deal of stress. Most of all, she didn't think she should leave Scott. However, in the early fall of 1940 she accepted an invitation to travel to Dallas to attend the premiere of Gary Cooper's new movie, *The Westerner*. It would take her away from Scott for two days.

Sheilah had always had something of a crush on Gary Cooper; it was almost impossible not to. "Coop" was the second movie star she interviewed after coming to Hollywood on Christmas Day of 1935. She had been so nervous to meet him that she crashed her car on the way to the studio. But when she arrived at Paramount, shaken and worse for wear, he looked at her warmly with his shy blue eyes and was so gentle and charming that she was soon at ease. Years later, she described Gary Cooper as "a Yep and Nope man"—he was definitely the strong silent type. But how magnificently he said Yep, giving it so many shades of meaning! There was no doubt about it, Gary Cooper was one of the few movie stars who was as exciting offscreen as on. Even Frances found him irresistible: One day she happened to walk

behind the movie star on a studio lot and she became mesmer-
ized by the sight of his rear end. Women could barely control
themselves around him. "Gary Cooper's appeal is just that he
can't act," Scott observed with jealousy. "But they [women, that
is] think from his unwilling expression—I bet when he takes
those silly clothes off he'd be twice as exciting as those silly
actors." As Fitzgerald's remarks went, this one was not particularly incisive, but the point was clear—Coop was the sort of guy
who simply should not be allowed.

The premiere of *The Westerner* was going to be a Hollywood
extravaganza of the first degree. There would be two airplanes
carrying the press and the stars from Los Angeles to Dallas and
back, deluxe accommodations for all, and parties galore. Sheilah
phoned Mack Millar, the publicity agent in charge of the junket,
to ask that he make certain she was put on the same plane as
Gary Cooper. She wanted an interview, of course, but she admitted to herself an indefinable yearning. She felt quite guilty about
it, really, and was afraid Scott would read her mind; he always
seemed to know what she was thinking. Scott drove her to the
airport and as they stood together in the waiting room, Mack
Millar came over and said in a loud voice, "I did as you asked. I
have put you in the same plane as Gary." Sheilah glanced at Scott
nervously, afraid of his reaction. But he only smiled blandly; he
seemed like a new man. Sheilah was so relieved that she
promised herself she would behave in Texas so she could
account for her time with a clear conscience.

But it was not easy. In Dallas there was a party in a hotel suite
after the showing of the movie. Sheilah arrived first and made
her way through a bedroom to use the bathroom there before
anyone else arrived. When she came back out into the bedroom,
Coop was standing tall and handsome as he could be alone by
the bed. He had followed her. He took her hands into his own
and peered down meaningfully into her eyes from his towering
height. His lips formed an intimate smile, his eyes a question
mark—Would it be Yep, or would it be Nope? Sheilah was
awfully tempted. She felt weak in the knees. But she forced herself to remember Scott and she pulled away with a nervous gig-
gle before it could go too far.

Coop sensed her resolve was not so strong and he continued his mooning courtship throughout the weekend. There was a parade with the movie star leading the way on horseback down the main street of Dallas. Sheilah rode behind him on a splendid horse, wearing a brown felt cowboy hat which had been especially made for her by Rex, the best hatmaker in Beverly Hills. She felt glamorous and important. Every now and then she felt Coop's blue eyes upon her, watching her with an ironic twinkle, a special understanding. On the overnight flight back to Los Angeles, he was always by her side, like a big friendly dog—not her dog, unfortunately, but one she was tempted to bring home. He made her go all fluttery in her stomach. She told him she was feeling air sick and he picked her up and lifted her gallantly into her top berth so she could lie down. Then he offered to rub her stomach; he said it might make her feel a whole lot better, but Sheilah told him no, for this would be a disaster.

In the morning, Coop stepped off the plane by her side and they walked together into the terminal to find Scott. Sheilah introduced the two men but it was an awkward moment. Coop was even more sheepish than usual as he shook hands with Scott. They were both of the same generation; Gary Cooper had portrayed Fitzgerald in the biographical film about Scott and Zelda, *The Wedding Night*, written by Edwin Knopf, the man who had brought Scott to MGM in July 1937. Scott and the actor sized each other up with knowing glances, and then Coop—always the gentleman—made a polite departure.

Sheilah was anxious as she drove alone with Scott from the airport back into West Hollywood. She spoke nervously about the gala dinners and lunches she had attended, and the parade where she rode on a horse; she spoke nonstop to cover up all that she left unsaid, how tempted she had been to take just a brief ride with Gary Cooper into his cowboy sunset. She was certain Scott could see through her; she waited for the storm of his jealousy to break down upon her. But Scott was unexpectedly mild. He smiled his wan smile; he looked deathly tired. "I missed you," he said. "You must never go away again."

And indeed she never would.

*   *   *

Sheilah did not for a moment suspect the truth—that Fitzgerald had his own secrets he was all too happy to hide. While Sheilah was in Dallas, he invited Frances one night along with her young brother Morton to dinner at Victor's Restaurant on Sunset Boulevard, just a short walk from his apartment. Morton Kroll was an aspiring writer and had sent Scott several of his short stories for criticism. There was nothing Fitzgerald liked better than to pontificate and help a young person along. After reading Morton's work, Scott took the time to write a long letter cautioning him to be true to what he had seen and experienced, rather than dredge up faked "literary" feelings:

> A young writer is tempted. . . to be guided by the known, the admired, and the currently accepted as he hears a voice whisper within him, "Nobody would be interested in this feeling I have, this unimportant action. . . ." But if the man's gift is deep or luck is with him. . . some other voice. . . makes him write down those apparently exceptional and unimportant things and that and nothing else is his style, his personality—eventually his whole self as an artist. What he has thought to throw away or, only too often, what he *has* thrown away, was the saving grace vouchsafed him. Gertrude Stein was trying to express a similar thought when—speaking of life rather than letters—she said that we struggle against most of our exceptional qualities until we're about forty and then, too late, find out that they compose the real *us*. They were the most intimate self which we should have cherished and nourished.

The letter went on in this fashion for several pages. It was vintage Fitzgerald to be so generous with himself, to use his energy and talent to set down his thoughts about writing to an apparently unimportant person, his secretary's younger brother. Then at Victor's Restaurant—to Frances's great alarm—Scott ordered a bottle of wine and proceeded to drink most of it himself, since Morton was underage and Frances not much of a drinker. The wine gave Scott a pleasant glow. He continued now in a very good mood to hold forth throughout dinner. For Morton's benefit, he chatted about his friendship with Ernest Hemingway. Ernest, he said was a "poseur trying to prove his manliness by going off to Spain and Africa in pursuit of adventure." Frances hated to see Scott drinking again and was afraid this was the start of a binge. As the wine took its effect, Fitzgerald grew irritated about Hemingway; he said Ernest was all used up as a writer; he was going off on absurd adventures, to the Spanish Civil War and such, only from a desperate need to find new literary material. It was pathetic, really. Scott spoke faster as the level of the bottle went down. He began to ramble, growing sentimental about Princeton; he warmly declared his alma mater "a blend of the best of both sides of the Mason-Dixon line—northern learning and southern chivalry."

Scott at the moment was feeling himself both learned and very chivalrous. After dinner, he invited Frances and Morton back to his apartment, where he brought out a bottle of gin to lubricate further conversation. The young people declined the offer of a drink, hoping not to encourage him. But Scott was not discouraged and with the gin on his tongue he waxed ever more enthusiastically about writers he had known, old friends and past places. He seemed determined to dazzle Morton with his intelligence, blast him with the furnace of his charm. Frances was very worried now about Sheilah, imagining how angry she would be to return from Texas to find Scott had broken his great promise to her. Eventually, Frances took her brother home, hoping the evening was not her fault. She feared the worst. But Scott slept it off, and by the time Sheilah returned he was sober once again, and more than willing to excuse a variety of small human failures, both her flirting and his brief fall from the wagon.

Scott continued to drink secretly, but in moderation. In fact, although he lied about it, he had found the maturity for the first time in his life to drink in a more-or-less responsible manner, to stop when he had enough and not continue into one of his infamous binges. After the evening at Victor's, Frances never again saw Fitzgerald with a drink in his hand, but she saw the evidence he left behind—the bottles. It was no longer her job to get rid of these dead soldiers in Sepulveda Canyon since there was regular garbage service in West Hollywood. Scott only had to put his empties in an ordinary bag outside the apartment house on certain mornings and the truth would be whisked away by a conveniently passing truck. There was a bad moment when

Sheilah accidentally kicked one of these bags while walking with Scott to his car parked at the curb. The bag made a telltale sound, the unmistakable rattle of glass, but Sheilah thought nothing of it. She trusted him completely.

Scott thought this quite a joke. He told Frances about Sheilah's near miss, chuckling at the anecdote. He said he would have liked to let Sheilah in on the joke as well, but of course this was not possible.

Earlier in the year, in March, Dr. Robert Carroll had surprised Scott by suggesting that Zelda was well enough to leave Highland Hospital. This was "the Montgomery point of view" Scott had always resisted, but now Dr. Carroll convinced him that his wife's condition had improved and she might live more comfortably with her mother in Alabama. So on April 6, after four years at Highland and a decade in mental institutions, Zelda packed her old-fashioned clothes and her Bible and returned to her childhood home in Montgomery. The Sayres were delighted. This was their vindication that Zelda was a normal young woman who had only had the misfortune to marry badly. Dr. Carroll did his best to warn them at the time of her discharge that Zelda was actually far from well:

> Mrs. Fitzgerald's history shows a definite cyclic tendency and we must look forward with apprehension to her inability to meet emotional situations, to face infections, or to indulge in alcohol, tobacco or drugs, without a rapid return to her maniacal irresponsibility. Let it be known that Mrs. Fitzgerald is capable of being absolutely irresponsible and intensely suicidal. Her present condition, however, is only of gentleness, reasonable capacity for cooperation and yet with definitely reduced judgement maturity.

Scott wrote his daughter that she must make a visit to Alabama to see her mother in June before starting summer school; it was a journey Scott refused to make himself. "She is. . . like a fish out of water," Scottie reported to her father afterward. "Her ideas are too elaborately worded to be even faintly comprehensible to anyone in the town, and yet too basically wrong to be of real interest to people who really know something." Scott gave his wife an allowance of thirty dollars a week; he knew it wasn't much, but he insisted it was all he could do for her. He continued to write warm and loving letters at least once a week, though he did not invite her to California after all. When Scott moved to Laurel Avenue only a block from Sheilah, he gave Zelda a mailing address care of Phil Berg, his latest Hollywood agent. Zelda knew nothing of Sheilah but she sensed something was being kept from her. "What is your actual address?" she insisted. "S'pose I wanted to phone you—or do something unprecedented like that?"

But this was the problem. Zelda's new access to telephones was awkward for Scott. What if she called one night when Sheilah was there? The thought of such a collision between the past and present was a nightmare for Scott. But fortunately Zelda did not call, and Scott was relieved to save the enormous expense of her hospital bills. Now he only had to worry about Scottie's tuition at Vassar, back taxes to the IRS, back payments to Dr. Carroll—and seemingly hundreds of other expenses as well. At the end of May, money worries caused Scott to once again write to Max Perkins, hoping to persuade Scribner's to put his books back in print again:

> I wish I was in print. It will be odd a year or so from now when Scottie assures her friends I was an author and finds that no book is procurable. It is certainly no fault of yours. . . . Professionally, I know the next move must come from me. Would the 25-cent press keep *Gatsby* in the public eyes—or *is the book unpopular?* Has it had its chance? Would a popular reissue. . . with a preface *not* by me but by one of its admirers—I can maybe pick one—make it a favorite with classrooms, profs, lovers of English prose—anybody? But to die, so completely and unjustly after having given so much! Even now there is little published in American fiction that doesn't slightly bear my stamp—in a *small* way I was an original.

Scott was baffled that the public had rejected him so thoroughly. After all, the Depression was over and in 1940 the memory of the decadent twenties did not cause quite the same repulsive shudder it had only a few years before. He began to suspect that the very name F. Scott Fitzgerald was jinxed, so thoroughly associated in the public mind with cast-off styles and failure that no one would ever give him a chance again. Earlier in the year, in February, Scott began an extended correspondence with Arnold Gingrich at *Esquire*, suggesting the possibility that he might do much better writing under the alias of "John Darcy." "I'm awfully tired of being Scott Fitzgerald anyhow," Scott said, "as there doesn't seem to be so much money in it, and I'd like to find out if people read me just because I am Scott Fitzgerald, or what is more likely, don't read me for the same reason. In other words it would fascinate me to have one of my stories stand on its own merits completely and see if there is a response.... If the idea interests you I might invent a fictitious personality for Mr. Darcy. My ambition would be to get a fan letter from my own daughter."

Gingrich did not respond, hoping this was only a passing whim on Scott's part. But Scott was serious. Four months later, on June 25, he wrote again, trying to sell the idea of a pseudonym, this time suggesting the name "John Blue." Gingrich was not thrilled: *Esquire* still valued the name Scott Fitzgerald, which was recognizable to its readers if only for its museum quality. He wrote Scott back that both John Darcy and John Blue sounded too phony to him; he hoped to discourage the idea entirely. But Scott replied on July 13: "My name is Paul Elgin and Paul will presently send you some contributions." Later in the fall, on October 3, Paul Elgin did indeed submit a story, "On an Ocean Wave," but it was published posthumously when the name F. Scott Fitzgerald was once more on the rise. And so Scott never did get to try his experiment after all.

Scott changed the name of his California novel from *Stahr* to *The Last Tycoon*. He still thought he might give it an ironic subtitle, "A Western," just as he had called *Tender is the Night* "A Romance." "I expect it to sell at least a thousand copies," he wrote with wry humor to Arnold Gingrich, though in his heart he hoped for much more. He refused to be daunted and he gave the book his best.

Scottie did not come to California during her summer break of 1940; she went to summer school at Harvard instead so that Scott might continue his work uninterrupted. Sheilah was relieved; she had come to dread the turmoil of the visits, and probably it was a relief to the father and daughter as well. Scottie had managed to get off academic probation at Vassar, and her long-distance relationship with her father had much improved. There seemed no sense in straining matters with an extended visit.

Scott stopped work on his novel from August 26 to October 15 to accept a screenwriting assignment and earn a welcome one thousand dollars a week from Darryl Zanuck at 20th Century-Fox. Each day Scott packed his briefcase full of Coca-Cola and met Frances at the Writer's Building on the Fox lot, a group of pseudo-English cottages which encircled a small garden. The movie was called *The Light of Heart*, based on a London play by Emlyn Williams. The story was about an alcoholic actor, a famous matinee idol whose life and career become unraveled by drink: Darryl Zanuck seemed to think Fitzgerald might do well with such a plot.

Scott was told to stick to the play as much as possible, but he could not resist an occasional urge to be creative. He came up with a new beginning, a Christmas scene in which twelve Santas in red suits and white beards are introduced in a London department store, then marshaled by the store manager out into the streets to do their job. All the Santas appear to be identical, except for one—the ex-matinee idol, whose career has sunk to this level. He is staggering drunk, steadying himself on a garbage can for support. Before long, the drunk actor comes to believe he is the real Santa Claus and he loses his job for giving away toys to children for free; fortunately, he is saved in the end by a woman who idolized him when he was a star.

As always, Scott began the project with a fair amount of optimism. It was scheduled as a B movie, but Zanuck was considering upgrading it into an A. This seemed to Scott a promising sign. But eventually his script was considered too "down-beat" and Zanuck let him go. For the life of him, Fitzgerald could not give the story of drunkenness and failure the required comic touch. He was replaced on the picture by Nunnally Johnson— the writer Scott had tried to order out of Hollywood at the disastrous Malibu party in the summer of 1938.

*   *   *

Fate had dealt quite a different hand to Scott's old friend Ernest Hemingway. In the fall, Ernest sent Scott a copy of his new massive bestseller, *For Whom the Bell Tolls*, inscribed simply, "To Scott with affection and esteem." It was a nice gesture but Fitzgerald didn't like the novel very much. "It's not up to his standards. He wrote it for the movies," he assured Sheilah. "Hemingway has become a pompous bore." Scott wrote later to Zelda that the book did not have the "tensity or the freshness" of *A Farewell to Arms*, "but the point is, he is making a fortune out of it—has sold it to the movies for over a hundred thousand dollars and as it's the Book-of-the-Month selection he will make $50,000 from it in that form. Rather a long cry from his poor rooms over the saw mill in Paris."

Ernest's success was a constant reminder to Scott of his own great failure, incomprehensible when he knew in his heart that he was every bit as good a writer. Though it was painful, he managed to steel himself to thank Ernest for the book, and offer a few gracious lies:

> Dear Ernest:
>
> It's a fine novel, better than anybody else writing could do. Thanks for thinking of me and for your dedication. I read it with intense interest, participating in a lot of the writing problems as they came along and often quite unable to discover how you brought off some of the effects, but you always did. . . .
> Congratulations too on your new book's great success. I envy you like hell and there is no irony in this. . . . I envy you the time it will give you to do what you want.
>
> With old affection,
> Scott

Time to do what you want; this was what success was all about. Time was everything, better than gold, and Scott regretted every hour lost to his novel when he must dash off a Pat Hobby story, or spend a month on an ill-fated screenplay. And yet he never lamented the hours he spent on Sheilah's education. By November 1940, the F. Scott Fitzgerald College of One was going stronger than ever. It was now a full year since their great fight and he had bought Sheilah so many new books that one day he appeared at her apartment with a tape measure to order a huge bookcase that would take up an entire wall. When the bookcase came, he stopped everything for several days to organize the collection by subject and author and place each book in soothing order on the shelf.

At the moment they were doing art and music. Scott bought Sheilah a small second-hand phonograph of blond wood which matched her new bookshelves, and more 78-rpm records than he could afford—they were expensive at one or two dollars apiece. Tchaikovsky's *Nutcracker Suite*, conducted by Stokowski, in a set with the Violin Concerto in D Major played by Heifetz was $14.50 alone, but he somehow always found the money. Scott admitted that he knew little about music and he generally managed to misspell the names of the composers—such wild renderings as "Bethoven," "Menddilshun," and "Litz."

But spelling was for small minds; after all, this was a progressive education. Scott taught Mozart by dancing with Sheilah to the minuets, bowing and curtsying extravagantly in the privacy of her living room. This was more fun than such dry matters as sonata form and key modulations, which Scott knew nothing about anyway. The thing for a novelist was to get into the mood of the music. Visualize the gilded salons of Vienna, and Mozart with his laughter and his wig dying so tragically young, to be buried in a pauper's grave. When it came to studying painting, Scott and Sheilah spent hours trying to typecast each of their friends according to the style of a different artist. Sheilah decided that Dorothy Parker was a Renoir, Robert Benchley a Frans Hals, and Scott an Albrecht Dürer. As for Sheilah, Scott called her a Botticelli—he assured her that she was Venus on the half-shell.

On Saturdays, Scott drove Sheilah to the different art museums and galleries about town, particularly the Huntington Library in Pasadena which had a decent collection of such English painters as Gainsborough, Reynolds, Constable, and Turner. Scott and Sheilah stood patiently before each painting and earnestly discussed what it was precisely that the artist was trying to achieve; at home afterward they compared their interpretations against the books of art criticism Frances managed to find in the second-hand stalls on Sixth Street.

It was an odd education for two, a world of their own. One Saturday in the Huntington Library, Sheilah asked Scott in a teasing way, "How well has the best and worst student in the Fitzgerald College of One done so far?"

"Very well, Sheilo. I'm quite proud of you," he said. "You've worked hard."

"Do you think I'll be ready to graduate soon?"

He thought seriously about this, adding up the remaining curriculum in his mind, and answered that she would be ready to graduate on schedule, in June 1941. Of course she would have to pass a lengthy written examination. It would not be easy.

"And you'll really give me a diploma?"

"In your cap and gown," he said. "I promise."

20

A WINTER SOLSTICE

Show me a hero, and I'll write you a tragedy.

—F. Scott Fitzgerald, notes for *The Last Tycoon*

THE SKY WAS LOW AND OPPRESSIVE, a cold gray Thursday afternoon in November 1940, a cozy day to be indoors. Sheilah lay stretched out on the secondhand sofa in her living room with a book on music history propped up on her lap and a Bach cantata, "Singet dem Herrn," playing on the portable phonograph. Scott was reading nearby in a green leather armchair by the fireplace.

Sheilah's Hayworth Avenue apartment had a look of cheerful impermanence; she had been here now for more than a year and a half but had accumulated little to transform it into a real home. Her nesting urge had always been with Scott; her small apartment was never meant to be more than a place to write her column and hide out when they were fighting. Scott had helped her buy the furniture on a one-day shopping spree at Barker's

Bargain Basement and it varied from utilitarian to downright shabby. They still ate dinner on a wobbly folding card table she had always meant to replace. The bookcase he had built for her against an entire wall in the living room was the only solid piece of furniture in the house.

After a while Scott stood up from his armchair. "I'm going to Schwab's for cigarettes," he told her. He dressed for heavy weather in his dark topcoat and scarf, put on his battered gray homburg, and disappeared into the overcast day. He would have created an odd impression on a gray afternoon like this as he made his way along the sidewalk toward Sunset Boulevard. With his ghostly complexion and wintry city clothes, he looked like something from an old black-and-white photograph. After nearly three and a half years in Hollywood, he was still entirely foreign to Southern California. Frances recently had caught sight of him on the street and he looked to her momentarily like death.

Twenty minutes later Scott returned just as the final chorale of the Bach cantata was filling the apartment with polyphonic voices. Scott trembled as he stood by the door; his face was ashen, even more pale than usual. He lowered himself carefully into the green armchair and fumbled with a fresh pack of cigarettes.

Sheilah turned down the music. "Is anything the matter, Scott?"

He didn't answer at once. He took his time bringing a cigarette to his lips, lighting a match, inhaling, then blowing out smoke with weary satisfaction. In all her life Sheilah had never seen a person light a cigarette in quite such a melodramatic way, and it caused her a moment of irritation.

"I almost fainted at Schwab's," he said at last. "Everything started to fade." Then he warmed to the subject—it was one of his favorite subjects, his health—and he described in detail the strange slow-motion sensation of the world starting to go dim on him. He told Sheilah he had never felt anything quite like it. He thought he had better see the doctor this morning.

"Scott, I wish you would," she told him, careful to keep the irritation from her voice. Scott and his hypochondria were a test of anyone's patience. When she failed to respond with enough sympathy he accused her of being uncaring, but when she did make a fuss his dignity was ruffled and he resented her concern. Later in the morning Scott drove to Dr. Nelson's office downtown and when he returned his face was very solemn. He told Sheilah—a bit too pleased with himself, she thought—that he had suffered "a cardiac spasm."

"Is that a heart attack?" she asked.

Scott was vague. As far as Sheilah could tell, it was almost a heart attack, but not quite. "Did he say you must stay in bed?" she asked, trying to pin him down.

"No, but I must take it easy. Stairs are out."

Sheilah had read somewhere that if you had a heart attack, doctors always told you to get to bed and stay flat on your back. So this was reassuring. Whatever it was Scott had suffered, it was apparently something not quite so serious. Sheilah took charge of the situation in an efficient manner; if Scott could not climb stairs, then he must no longer remain at his third-floor apartment on Laurel Avenue. Sheilah's apartment was on the ground floor and she suggested he move into her spare bedroom. Meanwhile she and Frances would be on the lookout to find him a suitable place without stairs somewhere in the neighborhood.

Sheilah and Frances packed up Scott's papers, his bed-desk, and books, and brought the invalid and his belongings one block over from Laurel to Hayworth. Scott and Sheilah were now actually and entirely living together for the first time. Sheilah was aware that they had crossed an invisible line, flouting the current hypocrisy of Hollywood mores with their "irregular situation"; the irony was that sex had become completely out of the question.

Scott was a difficult patient. He forbade Sheilah to discuss his case with the doctor when he was not present. "I don't want him telling you anything he wouldn't tell me," he insisted. He watched suspiciously when the doctor came over to make certain she did not take him aside to whisper in corners. As a result, she could only guess at the state of his health and this was frustrating for her. Once she overheard the doctor tell Scott that the attack had damaged his heart. "How much?" Sheilah asked, speaking up quickly before Scott could stop her. "Twenty-five percent," the doctor replied. To Sheilah this seemed a frightening percent and she could not understand why Scott was not in the hospital. But of course, all she could go on were the few things Scott told her, and what she managed to overhear when the doctor came to call. She did what she could. Scott said he was not to climb stairs, and Sheilah clung to this specific fact with a nearly fanatical resolve, arranging matters so that no flight of stairs might ever cross his path.

One evening toward the end of November, Scott drove Sheilah to the screening of a new movie at MGM. As Scott parked in the narrow studio alleyway, she saw with horror that the projection room was on the second floor at the top of a long flight of metal steps. To Sheilah these stairs clinging to the outside of the building appeared a deathtrap, a vision of hell. The problem was that if she simply reminded Scott of the doctor's orders, he might do anything—run up the stairs like a teenager just to thumb his nose at her and prove he would enjoy his hypochondria on no other terms than his own. Sheilah, as so often in the past, resorted to cunning. She pretended to trip as she stepped from the car, crying out loudly with a great show of pain. She grasped her ankle, she groaned and grimaced and told Scott she was afraid she had sprained it. It gave him a chance to be very chivalrous. He supported her arm as she hobbled slowly up the stairs, one step at a time, resting on each landing.

It took five minutes in this way to reach the projection room on the second floor. If Scott knew she was only pretending, he did not let on. He was just as glad to accept the fiction that Sheilah was the weak one.

Scott set up residence in bed with his bed-desk in Sheilah's spare room. Leaning back comfortably on his pillows, he fired off a steady stream of letters to friends and family back east, complaining about Hollywood and describing every last detail of his health. Hollywood was a dump, he said; his great dreams about the place were shattered; it was such a slack, soft place, a hideous town full of the insulting gardens of its rich—and meantime his temperature was 99.2 or 99.8 or in some dangerous limbo in between.

"Except for the stage-struck young girls people come here for negative reasons—all gold rushes are essentially negative—and the young girls soon join the vicious circle," he assured Gerald Murphy. "There is no group, however small, interesting as such. Everywhere there is, after a moment, either corruption or indifference." Dottie Parker, Dash Hammett, Ben Hecht, Nunnally Johnson—these were just a few examples he readily offered of spoiled, lazy writers who had been corrupted by the movies. But not Scott Fitzgerald. What he left out, of course, was his greatest complaint of all—that he had been horribly eager to sell himself to this corrupt city and no one was willing to buy.

In Scott's novel he was taking a very different approach to Hollywood, describing a complex industry that was entirely misunderstood by haughty East Coast intellectuals. This was a town where dreams came to life; there were heroes and villains on every street corner, romance and tragedy, and all of it was extraordinarily interesting. Nevertheless, Scott was restless and believed he had lingered in this city of dreams too long. He was ready to get on the road again. In December he told Sheilah, "If I ever get out of this mess you and I will leave Hollywood and travel." They must wait until his book was finished, of course, then they would leave and never come back. Or perhaps they might return just long enough to sell his novel to the screen for some fabulous amount of money.

It was fun to imagine these things. First they would go to Europe so Scott could write about the war. Maybe he would work as a newspaper correspondent before he settled down to a great war novel. John Wheeler had hired Hemingway in 1937 to cover the war in Spain for NANA, and Ernest had not even done a very good job of it; certainly Wheeler would hire Scott to send back dispatches from the front line. When the war was over—in 1943, Scott predicted confidently—they would settle down in France or maybe make their way back to the States, to New England, where they might buy a big old house and read poetry together and take long walks up country roads. Sheilah enjoyed listening to these fantasies as much as Scott liked telling them.

Later in December, Scott broke the news to Frances that he

and Sheilah were planning to leave California and she should begin to consider another job. He was very fond of his secretary and worried that she would find it difficult to survive without him. But the wide world was calling and they must go. It would be soon now; he was certain of it.

Throughout the fall, Scott continued to write dutifully one letter a week to Zelda in Montgomery, always describing the progress of his novel. On October 19:

> I am trying desperately to finish my novel by the middle of December and it's a little like working on *Tender is the Night* at the end—I think of nothing else. . . My room is covered with charts like it used to be for *Tender is the Night,* telling the different movements of the characters and their histories. However, this one is to be short, as I originally planned it two years ago, and more on the order of *Gatsby.*

A week later:

> I am deep in the novel, living in it, and it makes me happy. It is a *constructed* novel like *Gatsby,* with passages of poetic prose when it fits the actions, but no ruminations or side-shows like *Tender.* Everything must contribute to the dramatic movement.

And again a week after that:

> The novel is hard as pulling teeth but that is because it is in its early character-planting phase. I feel people so less intently than I did once that this is harder. It means welding together hundreds of stray impressions and incidents to form the fabric of entire personalities.

Scott was obsessed with his book. On November 23, he told Zelda he was digging it out of himself "like uranium—one ounce to the cubic ton of rejected ideas." And on December 6: "Everything is my novel now—it has become of absorbing interest. I hope I'll be able to finish it by February." As far as his health went, Scott was feeling considerably better; he believed himself lucky to have caught the problem with his heart in time.

On December 13, in his weekly letter to Zelda:

The novel is about three-quarters through and I think I can go on till January 12 without doing any stories or going back to the studio. I couldn't go back to the studio anyhow in my present condition as I have to spend most of the time in bed where I write on a wooden desk that I had made a year and a half ago. The cardiogram shows that my heart is repairing itself. It is odd that the heart is one of the organs that does repair itself.

Sheilah had never seen Scott so content. She enjoyed having him at her apartment working so happily on his book. Being an invalid suited Scott very well; he had always acted like one anyway, preferring to write in bed, and now this seemed a logical progression from fantasy to fact. His bed had become a small sovereign state and Fitzgerald the emperor of the pillows. Sheilah sometimes noticed a satisfied expression on his face, as if to say, "And you thought I was only pretending."

She knew her apartment was too busy and noisy for him; her secretary Pat Duff came five days a week, and her phone was always ringing with people feeding her gossip about the stars. She and Frances kept searching the neighborhood for a suitable apartment of his own. Sheilah found something she thought he might like; it was on the ground floor, but there were four steps to the front door. Scott examined it from the curb but would not go inside; he implied with a hurt expression that perhaps she wished to kill him. Sheilah was exasperated; the steps in fact were not very daunting, less of a climb than her own path from the sidewalk on Hayworth to her front door.

Sometimes she hoped the writing of *The Last Tycoon* would go on forever. She was afraid he might start drinking again if the book was not a success. Money, as always, was the deciding factor as to whether Scott might continue his novel or need to stop for studio work. Sheilah was afraid to ask him the exact state of his finances, so she went secretly to Frances instead. Frances kept Scott's checkbook and knew everything. She told Sheilah that Scott would need to find a studio job again very soon.

Sheilah had one of her crafty ideas about how she might help out. She still had the two thousand dollars Scott had given her after their big fight in the spring of 1939. She had kept the money in a separate account, not quite certain what to do with it, but not prepared to return it to him outright. After all, it had been a great insult that he thought he might pay her off as if she were a prostitute, and she had her pride too. But Sheilah now came up with a complicated plan to give the money to Max Perkins at Scribner's, hoping to convince him to add three thousand dollars, making a total of five thousand dollars to give to Scott as an advance on *The Last Tycoon*. Scott would believe Scribner's was behind him, and he could finish his novel without interruption. It was an elaborate deception and Sheilah was afraid that if Scott ever found out he would feel the need to challenge someone to a duel. She made a draft of the main points she wanted to get across to Perkins:

> Scott never to know, even if book brings back millions. He would never forgive me. If book a success, naturally I'll be happy to get the money back; if not, that is all right, too. Important thing is for him to finish this book. No mention ever to be made of this correspondence—he'd be too humiliated, and might take to drink again, just to prove something. No drinking since last December—more than 12 months now. Been working steadily on book for five months, in addition to what done last year. It would be criminal for him to be forced to go back to a studio which destroys his confidence and may mean he'll never finish book. But all money must come from you. Query: Is it best to wait until Scott asks you for an advance? Or offer it before, in case he doesn't ask? Some tactful way of giving him $1,000 a month for five months. This is better than a lump sum. Use my $2,000 first, so if anything goes wrong, I inform you and you needn't send the rest. At worst I lose two, you lose three. At best, a good novel, Scott reclaims his position as writer and person, and we get our money back. My honest conviction this will be best of all his writing.

Meanwhile, as Scott continued to write and Sheilah in the background plotted her secret strategies to help out, Christmas was coming fast. Scott had little money to spare and no idea what to give his daughter. To Scott's astonishment, Sheilah volunteered her infamous silver-fox jacket, the very fur which had been the source of such joy and misery between them. Frances's father was a furrier and agreed to restyle the coat free of charge so that it might look more suitable for a college girl rather than a paramour. Sheilah had loved this jacket above all her possessions, but now she found it strangely easy to give away. The gift somehow resolved a number of old problems, and Sheilah always enjoyed being generous to Scottie. Earlier in the fall, she had secretly sent Scottie the money to buy a dress for her coming-out party in Baltimore, knowing that Scott did not approve of the party and did not himself have the money to spare.

So the much-traveled silver-fox was mailed east a second time, disguised beyond recognition. A few days before Christmas, Scott wrote to his daughter:

> Dearest Scottie:
>
> There has reached you by this time, I hope, a little coat. It was an almost never-worn coat of Sheilah's that she wanted to send you. It seemed very nice to me—it may fill out your rather thin wardrobe. Frances Kroll's father is a furrier and he remade it *without charge*!
> So you must *at once please* write the following letters:
>
> 1. To Sheilah, not stressing Mr. Kroll's contribution.
>
> 2. To Frances, praising the style.
>
> 3. To me (in the course of things) in such a way that I can show the letter to *Sheilah* who will certainly ask me if you liked the coat.
> You make things easier for me if you write these letters promptly. A giver gets no pleasure in a letter acknowledging a gift three weeks' late even though it crawls with apologies—you will have stolen pleasure from one who has tried to give it to you.
> (Ecclesiastes Fitzgerald)

Perhaps no father ever wrote as many letters to a daughter as did Scott Fitzgerald. Over the years he rained down upon her many thousands of words of bullying, desperate love, advice, and admonitions. But Scottie would have to make her own judgments from now on; for this lecture about Sheilah's silver-fox jacket was the last he would ever give her.

On Thursday night, December 19, Scott slept badly. Sheilah woke sometime before dawn to hear him roaming about the apartment like a restless ghost, rambling from his bedroom to the kitchen, through the darkened living room and back to his bedroom again. She could picture him pacing back and forth as he often did when he was deep in thought.

On Friday morning, he was irritable and tired. "It's the chapter," he told her. "I can't make it hang together." Scott was struggling with a difficult scene in Chapter Six between his hero, Monroe Stahr, and Brimmer, a Communist agitator whom Stahr summons to his office to thrash out the dialectics of capitalism versus Marxism, much as Scott did when he sequestered himself in a room with Budd Schulberg and Ring Lardner Jr. Scott wanted to portray Monroe Stahr as the best and (as it looked in 1940) probably the last example of capitalism—the last tycoon, in fact, an individual who swims against the stream of the new collective. Stahr, with his vision of making beautiful things, is not in tune with the modern world. This was to be the tragedy of the novel, and very hard to pull off. The problem was to humanize the confrontation so that Stahr and Brimmer remained believable three-dimensional characters rather than stereotypes. Scott was not certain he would ever get it right.

He had a breakfast of orange juice and coffee, nothing solid. Sheilah saw he was in a bad mood and tried to cheer him up. She found a mention of his name in the morning trade paper, *The Hollywood Reporter*, which quoted Erich Pommer's definition of a Hollywood intellectual as "a fugitive from the F. Scott Fitzgerald era." "You see, you are an era," Sheilah teased. Scott nodded thoughtfully, but found little comfort in seeing himself held up as the embodiment of a bygone era—the precise tragedy of his hero, Monroe Stahr. After breakfast, Scott returned to bed with a dozen Cokes within easy reach to do renewed battle with Chapter Six. He set up his bed-desk on his lap and then called irritably to Sheilah in the next room. "Where's Frances?"

"She's not coming till noon—she told you she had an appointment with her dentist," Sheilah reminded him.

Scott found his secretary's dental appointment a new cause for exasperation. Sheilah was on her way out the door to interview Spencer Tracy at MGM. Just before she left she poked her head into Scott's bedroom. "Look," she said, "why don't you try to sleep and when you wake up I'm sure Frances will be here." He grumbled that Frances was never there when he needed her, but he let Sheilah take away his bed-desk, pencils, and papers and close the venetian blinds. Then he lay back in the bed with a heavy sigh.

Sheilah had her own worries and drove to MGM fearing the worst. The problem was Spencer Tracy, a man who could be very difficult with the press. When he was in a bad mood, he had a way of looking at Sheilah as though daring her to ask one more stupid question. Sheilah knew it was absurd to be sensitive about these things, for a gossip columnist was supposed to be tough as nails. But when someone imposing like Spencer Tracy looked at her the wrong way she simply wanted to break down and cry. Today she was lucky; Tracy was in a good mood, almost charming in his own brusque way. She had a surprisingly good interview and then returned to Hayworth Avenue to find that Frances had arrived and was working with Scott. Sheilah disappeared into her office to do her column and the apartment became busy with the clickety-clack of typewriters: Sheilah writing the latest Hollywood gossip, and Scott and Frances struggling with the great political and moral issues of the times. When Frances left later in the afternoon, Scott wandered into the living room to find Sheilah. He was smiling, an entirely different man than the one grumping about the apartment in the morning. "I've been able to fix it," he told Sheilah happily. "Baby, this book will be good. It might even make enough money for us both to leave Hollywood."

Scott had decided to make his Communist, Brimmer, "a nice-looking man. . . a little on the order of Spencer Tracy, but with a stronger face and a wider range of reactions written up in it." Incidents from Scott and Sheilah's life had a disconcerting way of popping up in the novel. In the scene Scott had been working on today, Stahr invited the Communist to dinner at the Trocadero where "Gary Cooper came in and sat down in a corner with a bunch of men who breathed whenever he did and looked as if they lived off him and weren't budging."

It was a good scene, funny and not at all didactic. Scott felt momentarily on top of the world and he wanted to celebrate. He invited Sheilah out to dinner at Lyman's, a restaurant-deli-catessen on Hollywood Boulevard near the Pantages Theater, where they had tickets that night to a press preview of a new comedy, *This Thing Called Love,* starring Rosalind Russell and Melvyn Douglas. Just as he was leaving the house, Scott stopped in front of a mirror to give a last adjustment to his bow tie; he smiled and told Sheilah he had always wanted to be a dandy. She had not seen him in such a good mood for weeks. At the deli-catessen he laughed trying to pronounce the names of Jewish foods on the menu—knishes, knadlich, latkas. Sheilah adored the food of her childhood and hoped her craving would not give away dark ancestral secrets to others in the restaurant.

Scott was very quiet throughout the showing of the movie, which was not like him—usually he whispered funny little asides into her ear. Sheilah thought he must be studying the plot, as he often did with movies, still hoping to master what he often called "the strange medium of the flicks." When the movie was over, Scott stood up to let Sheilah walk past him into the aisle. She turned just in time to see Scott stagger, as if a sudden blow had thrown him off balance. He held onto the armrest of the chair for support and he was breathing hard. Sheilah took his arm.

"I feel awful," he said. "Everything started to go as it did in Schwab's. I suppose people will think I'm drunk."

"Scott, nobody saw it," she told him. She supported his arm as discreetly as possible as they made their way slowly up the aisle into the lobby. The knowing looks of acquaintances was a bitter irony; of course they thought he was drunk—why else would a man with his reputation need a helping hand out of a theater? Sheilah expected Scott to push her hand away, but when he did not, it worried her even more. This was the clearest sign to her yet of how badly he must feel. Outside the theater, Scott stood for a while breathing deeply. The fresh air seemed to revive him.

"Shall I get the doctor tonight?" she asked anxiously.

"No, he's coming tomorrow. Don't worry, Sheilo, I feel much better."

At home Scott took his usual number of sleeping pills and

went to bed immediately. But Sheilah could not sleep. She tiptoed occasionally into his room to see how he was. Scott woke at
one point in the darkened room and kissed her sleepily. "Go to
bed," he told her softly. "I'm all right."

Frances Kroll remembers the Saturday before Christmas,
December 21, 1940, as a cool overcast day—not as cold as people
on the East Coast would have it this time of year, but damp and
gloomy. Sheilah recalled the day quite differently. In her memory
it remained sharp and clear with a winter sun casting long shadows and giving little warmth; many years later she remembered
the slant of yellow sunlight coming through the venetian blinds
of her living room window making patterns on the floor. It was
the Winter Solstice, the shortest day of the year. The longest
night. Scott slept late and spent the morning in bed making further notes for Chapter Six. He was feeling very cheerful. Frances
came by briefly to drop off the mail from his Laurel Avenue
apartment; there were a few bills and the current issue of *The
Princeton Alumni Weekly*. Around noon Scott rose from bed and
dressed in slacks and a sweater. Dr. Clarence Nelson was due
after lunch with a portable cardiograph to check on his heart, but
Scott told Sheilah he felt fine now and expected a good report.
   Sheilah was trying to decide how best to give Scottie an
expensive dress for Christmas without offending her; it was a
long black velvet evening gown with short puff sleeves and a
heart-shaped neckline which she had bought for the premiere of
The Westerner. With all the dances and parties at Vassar, Sheilah
was certain Scottie could use the gown more than she could; it
would go well with the silver-fox jacket that had already been
mailed. "I don't want her to think I'm patronizing her or sending
cast-off clothes," she said to Scott. "Will you tell me just what to
write?"
   Scott, of course, was more than happy to tell her what to
write; social strategies had always been his forte. He sat Sheilah
at her typewriter and stood above her dictating a letter, supposedly from Sheilah, which would take care of any embarrassment
such expensive gifts might cause:

December 21, 1940

Dear Scottie:

I bought this dress to go to Dallas for *The Westerner*. The winter
is slipping away and because of natural unpopularity, I find no reason to use it. So there it sat in my closet, losing style week after
week. I mentioned this to your father and he told me that you
burned up dresses at the rate of one a month and suggested that
instead of selling it down the river, I contribute it to the conflagra-
tion. The coat also seems to have been waiting in my closet for the
victory celebration and I don't think now we will win before 1943.
By that time it will be unusual for English people to wear furs.

Why don't you send your father a picture of how you look
now, or he won't be able to recognize you when you meet again. I
hope you have a very happy Christmas and everything you want in
the New Year.

                          Yours,
                          Sheilah

Sheilah was about to unroll the page from her typewriter
when Scott decided upon a brief postscript. He dictated two last
sentences, neither of which, as it turned out later, happened to be
true:

P.S. Your father has not been well, but he's getting better now.
He hasn't had a drink for over a year.

Sheilah walked to Greenblatt's, a delicatessen on the corner of
Sunset and Hayworth, to buy sandwiches for lunch and a
Hershey bar to hide in the drawer of her bedside table; with
Scott's sweet tooth, she sometimes had to put chocolate bars out
of sight if she wanted any for herself. After lunch she settled into
the sofa with a biography of Beethoven and asked Scott if he
would mind if she put the Third Symphony, *Eroica*, on the
phonograph. Scott once told her he was saving Beethoven for her
old age, but Sheilah loved the Beethoven symphonies and surprised him with her appreciation of classical music.

The thunder of *Eroica* filled the living room; Sheilah had
always been attracted to things that were heroic and grand. It

was about two o'clock in the afternoon; sunlight, Sheilah remembers, streamed into the room. Scott made himself comfortable in the green leather armchair by the fireplace and opened his new copy of the *Princeton Alumni Weekly*, studying the prospects for the 1941 football season. Princeton continued to fascinate him. Less than a month earlier, on November 28, Scott had replied to the class secretary of 1917 with the fib that he had "just finished a novel," and had made a pointed reference to his daughter being at Vassar; he could not bear for his old classmates to think him a failure.

Scott read an article entitled, "Plus and Minus—An Analytical, Long Range View of the 1940 Football Team; the Outlook for Next Year," by Gilbert Lea, '36. He circled a paragraph about tackling and began to jot down some of his own ideas about next year's team, a possible lineup to beat their arch-rival, Yale. After a while Scott stood up. "I want something sweet," he said. "I'm going to Schwab's for some ice cream."

"But the doctor is coming soon," Sheilah reminded him. "I'm sure he'll have good news about your heart. Will a Hershey bar do?"

Sheilah went to her bedroom drawer and sacrificed the Hershey bar she had hidden there so that Scott would not miss Dr. Nelson. Scott ate the chocolate slowly as he continued to study the all-important question of the team lineup. Sheilah arranged herself back on the couch with her book. A few minutes later, Scott and Sheilah looked up from their separate reading at the same time and smiled at each other; Sheilah felt a great warmth and satisfaction. Scott licked the last of the chocolate lovingly from his fingers, and to Sheilah he looked as content as she had ever seen him, like a cat purring in the sun.

And then Scott let his attention return one final moment to football, his game of games. . . the cheer of the crowd, the Saturday afternoon glory, running down the green field forever. It was a fitting image to fill the mind of Scott Fitzgerald at this last millisecond of time. Then an irresistible force struck his chest and propelled him upward out of his chair. The *Eroica* symphony was rising to a climax when Sheilah, out of the corner of her eye, saw Scott jerk to his feet and clutch hold of the mantelpiece. It seemed to her that he had just had an awfully good idea; she had seen him stand up from a chair like this before, full of excitement. But now he stumbled and began to fall. Before she could reach him, he collapsed heavily onto the floor.

She was at his side in a moment. "Scott—Scott—" she cried. She was certain he had fainted. He lay on his back and there was a choking, gasping sound coming from deep in his throat. Sheilah had no idea what to do. Should she call the doctor? But the doctor was already on his way. Perhaps she should get some brandy; she had a small bottle in the kitchen. But this might start Scott drinking again and that would be a shame. Yet after the faint went on for an awfully long time, she went for the brandy anyway. She poured a stiff drink into a glass, then ran back to Scott on the floor. She tried to raise his head toward the glass but his teeth were clenched and the liquor dribbled down his chin, spilling over his neck and shirt. Sheilah was embarrassed for him; it seemed terrible to spill brandy over Scott when he wasn't able to wipe it off himself. He would be angry at her when he came out of this dreadful faint. She used her hand to try and wipe his chin, but it was hopeless.

She thought now she had better telephone someone for help. Anyone at all. She found Dr. Nelson's number, but there was no answer. She called another doctor at random, running down the list of doctors in her book. "Someone's very ill," she said to the first person who answered. "He's unconscious—can you come right over?"

She ran out of her apartment and up a flight of stairs to pound on the door of the manager, Harry Culver. "Come quickly," she cried. "Mr. Fitzgerald has fainted and it's lasted so long, I'm getting frightened." The manager trotted down the stairs after Sheilah to her apartment. Scott had not moved; he lay on his back with the sunlight through the slats of the venetian blinds making lines of light and shadow across his face. Mr. Culver knelt on the floor and put his fingers to Scott's pulse. Then he stood up and looked at Sheilah in a funny way. "He's dead," he said.

Sheilah had an idea. *Oxygen! That's what he needs—oxygen.* She was dumbfounded she had not thought of this very simple thing before. She phoned the fire department. "Someone has fainted and can't wake up," she told the man who answered. They promised to be right there with oxygen. Then she called the police to make the same urgent request. She was still on the telephone making wild calls to everyone she could think of calling when the living room filled up with people. Pat Duff had arrived, and firemen and policemen as well, people she did not know. Frances had come too. Sheilah was aware of them all as a vague murmur of distant voices saying incomprehensible things. The firemen put an oxygen mask on Scott's face. "Hurry up, please," she told them. "Hurry up, please save him." Then the mask was taken away.

Buff Cobb appeared and held Sheilah very closely; Sheilah had no idea where Buff had come from. Then a man put a white sheet over Scott's body, over his face, and she screamed at them, "Take that away, he won't be able to breathe, he'll suffocate, please, please!"

Buff led her into the kitchen away from Scott and held onto her so she could not rush back to the living room where she wanted to go. "You'll stay with us tonight," Buff said several times in a quiet voice. "We'll take care of everything. . . . " Sheilah broke free violently and ran back to Scott. But the living room was empty; the place on the floor where he had fallen was bare now. Sheilah was stunned by the silence. Scott was gone and all the people had gone away with him.

She ran out the front door into the bright winter day to follow him. But the street was empty, and there was no one anywhere. Sheilah was entirely and unexpectedly alone.

EPILOGUE

OUTSIDE THE GATE

Even Scott had left me. I had been quite angry about that. It had been cruel of him to die after teaching me how to love without reservation, without thought of tomorrow. He had been so fiercely possessive, greedy for my every thought, my every possibility as a human being. And when he died, he took it all with him, leaving me utterly destitute.

—Sheilah, writing in 1964

THE FIRST NIGHT AFTER SCOTT'S DEATH, Sheilah slept at Buff Cobb's house in Santa Monica. She barely understood any of the many kind things that were said to her and in the morning she returned home to her apartment. Her friends were surprised; they thought it morbid for her to remain in the place where Scott had died. She should go someplace, they told her—anyplace at all. But for Sheilah, Hayworth Avenue was where Scott was. His memory was in every chair and ashtray; it was almost as if he

443

had stepped out to buy cigarettes at Schwab's. She expected him back at any moment.

She refused to cry. She remained defiant and willful, as dry-eyed as when her mother had died when she was seventeen. She was angry that Scott would never finish the novel of which she was the heroine; angry that she would never graduate in cap and gown from the F. Scott Fitzgerald College of One; angry that he had left her at so inconclusive a moment, without a closing thought or saying good-bye; incredulous that she must inhabit a universe where a person might be eating a Hershey bar one moment and be forever gone the next.

Now she must fend for herself and make plans for the future. A man had died in her apartment, a man who was not her husband, and she feared there would be a scandal. A single woman had to be careful; it could damage her career to be on the wrong end of gossip. Sheilah told herself, Wasn't it a good thing Scott had died in the afternoon rather than the evening! Sometimes, as she thought of these practical matters, her shoulders heaved and she made a dry hacking sound, like a cough. But she did not allow tears to blur her vision. She was a survivor, after all.

On Sunday, the day after Scott's death, Scottie telephoned to ask how it had happened. Sheilah managed to talk calmly, she thought, almost as if she were not personally involved, reciting what would become a familiar litany of details—Scott reading the *Princeton Alumni Weekly* in the green leather armchair, the final Hershey bar, the last smile, *Eroica*, the jolt from the armchair, the fall on the floor. "Poor Sheilah," Scottie said. "How awful for you!"

But this was not the entire reason Scottie had called. Her voice, unsteady at first, now seemed very grown up. She thanked Sheilah for making her father's last years happy; she said that Sheilah should find some lasting solace in this fact. Then Scottie arrived at the delicate part of the conversation. Zelda was planning to come to the funeral, which made for an awkward situation. Scottie brought it up as if by accident: "By the way, Sheilah—we're going to bury Daddy in Baltimore. I don't think it would be advisable for you to come to the funeral, do you?"

Sheilah managed to get off the phone with a few choked

words: "No, of course not—good-by." Then in the empty silence of her apartment, the tears came at last. She cried for herself who was abandoned, as well as for Scott who had gone. She had nothing of him left. Zelda was the wife, the bereaved widow; as for Sheilah, she was still only a secret that must be kept from view. Despite their years together, she had had no status in his life, no legitimacy; she could not even go to his funeral.

He had gone from her life like an airplane streaming across the sky, leaving no tracks behind. Such was the ending Scott had envisioned for *The Last Tycoon*; after Stahr's death, the reader was to have a final glimpse of Kathleen standing alone outside the gate of his movie studio, forever excluded from the empire he had built. It was a good ending and true, but the tragedies of real life are not so easily concluded with flawless prose. Scott had consigned her to a peculiar fate, to be an unfinished heroine in only a fragment of a book.

Several days after Scott's death, Sheilah had an experience that was to affect the manner of her mourning. She had gone to his old apartment on Laurel Avenue to sort through his belongings. This was not an easy task in itself; common items such as socks, shoes, and shaving cream took on an aspect of monstrous finality in the absence of their owner. Each box and drawer had become a thing of almost sickening sorrow. Then she saw a photograph of herself in a frame on a dresser bureau. It made her smile—here was a reminder that Scott had loved her. She decided to pack the frame with his other things to send back east, but not the photograph—God forbid, Zelda might discover her existence! And wouldn't that be a shame?

With a wry smile, Sheilah removed the image of herself from Scott's frame. It was at this moment that she noticed there were words on the back of the photograph, in Scott's handwriting. The words said, "Portrait of a Prostitute." It took a moment for Sheilah's eyes to focus and her brain to take in this terrible message. She read the phrase again and again. *Portrait of a Prostitute.* It was as if the floor had disappeared from beneath her feet.

Could this really be what he thought of her? Surely these unkind words had been written in anger after one of their great fights—most likely the big fight in November 1939 when he had stolen her fur jacket and had acted such a madman. Obviously he had been drunk at the time. This could not be his final judgment of her. And yet to find this posthumous insult written on the back of her photograph was a rejection from the grave so final that it turned the memory of their love into quicksand.

She could understand Scott being angry enough to write such a remark; what she could not understand was why during their last year together he had not destroyed it. His health had been bad; she was certain he had a premonition he was going to die. Why then had he not had the simple kindness to get rid of this photograph that would prove so distressful after his death? Scott was normally most careful about his gestures. How could he have been so careless in this instance and with four words break her heart?

It seemed to Sheilah that he had truly left her with nothing. After the discovery of the photograph, she lived out the role in which Scott had cast her. It was easy enough. Men came to her sensing she was vulnerable. Grief had made her more attractive than she had ever been before, giving her a glow of almost terrible beauty. The legend of F. Scott Fitzgerald was slowly taking hold; there was a mystique to Sheilah now as Scott's last girl. The Hollywood writers in particular were drawn to her as a tangible prize, the booty a great man had left behind. John O'Hara, Irwin Shaw, Eddie Mayer—they all wanted her, as if to have Scott's girl was in some way to claim a small portion of his talent. Men who were once Scott's friends invited Sheilah to intimate dinners, they put out their arms to comfort her and then guided her skillfully into bed. With every man, Sheilah thought to herself, perhaps he will be like Scott. But none of them were. They were only smart cynical men who were successful at their trade. They did not understand her, or even particularly try.

She was drowning in sorrow, spinning out of control. At last in despair she telephoned Scott's doctor and begged him, "Please help me."

The doctor was disapproving. "You know Scott would not like this."

"I know," she cried. "I will stop, Scott would hate me like this."

Then she had an idea. To save herself, Sheilah decided she would do what Scott had planned for himself—she would go to war. In the early spring of 1941, she took the train to New York to convince John Wheeler to hire her as a roving war correspondent for NANA. Wheeler was reluctant; in his own brusque way he was fond of her. He told her she was a fool to go, she would get herself killed over there. But she worked on him and eventually he agreed to send her to England to write the human interest side of war. Before she left, Sheilah made out a new will leaving her few belongings to Scottie in the case of her death. Then she flew in a seaplane from New York to Lisbon, a city of intrigue and spies. At last she boarded another plane which took off secretly at night, the windows blacked out with heavy cloth, and she returned to the England of her birth.

She was not the first person, or the last, eager to forget her personal problems in the great adventure of war. She arrived in London at night to find a dreamscape of darkened streets and artillery guns thundering from Hyde Park. Tethered balloons hovered over the city, traps for low-flying German planes; cars with no lights glided like phantoms through the streets; from doorways came the sound of soldiers' laughter; on the sidewalks near Picadilly the prostitutes pointed dim flashlights at their faces for the men who were walking by. To Sheilah it seemed a city under a spell. She had a sense that if she left London even for a moment she might never find it again.

Death rained down each night from the sky; she never knew if she would wake up in her bed or never wake up at all. It was strong medicine against the past. She had a recurring dream of Adolf Hitler flying a fighter plane, diving out of the clouds to chase her along the darkened streets. She could not fool Hitler— he knew a Jew when he saw one, and she ran from him in her sleep as she had been running from danger all her life. In the morning when she woke, London was full of smoky rubble. And then with death everywhere around her, Sheilah discovered one day that a miracle had taken place in her body: she was pregnant. This startling development was the result of a short romance with a dashing British philosopher, A. J. Ayer. Sheilah had been drawn to the well-known intellectual by his vast learning, hoping as always that she might find someone who was like Scott. Freddie Ayer, like Scott, had established his reputation very young in a brilliant book that had made him famous—his subject was logical positivism—and then he never quite achieved the same success again. He was a very charming man, and women adored him—but he was not offering marriage.

This left Sheilah in a predicament. She desperately wanted to have a child, with the conscious hope that it would be a son and look like Scott. But she was not quite willing in 1941 to do what is more acceptable today and defy respectability by going it alone. The problem was solved by a man named Trevor Westbrook, who began to pay court to her at this auspicious time. Trevor appeared the most rock-solid sort of British citizen, a man who proudly proclaimed that he had never had time to read a single novel in his life. Sheilah found this strangely refreshing after the many literary men she had endured. Trevor had quit school at the age of fourteen and had worked hard to overcome a humble middle-class background, starting as a clerk in a large aircraft factory, until at the outbreak of war he was put in charge of the industrial effort which produced all of Britain's fighter planes and bombers. Sheilah found this admirable. He was a plodding man, certainly, but in his own plodding way, Trevor Westbrook was busy saving England from the Nazis.

On the negative side, he was narrow-minded, snobbish in a maddening way peculiar to the British middle class, and stoutly anti-Semitic. He blamed all his problems on "Jew-boys," never suspecting that the glamorous woman whom he hoped to marry was in fact a Jew. This gave Sheilah pause, naturally, though she believed herself equal to any charade. In the end, she was won by his total lack of imagination. One evening as they were driving in his car during an air raid, a bomb exploded directly behind them on Battersea Bridge, only seconds after they had crossed. Sheilah was crouching on the floor of the automobile when Trevor came to an unexpected stop. She screamed at him, demanding to know why he had stopped when there were bombs exploding everywhere. Trevor explained calmly that there was a red light. Sheilah was impressed; it seemed to her that a man who stopped for traffic signals during an air raid would provide absolute security for the child growing in her womb.

And so, less than a year after Scott's death, Sheilah committed perhaps her greatest lie. She told Trevor Westbrook that she was pregnant with his child. "I suppose we had better get married," he said waggishly. And Sheilah supposed so too; in fact, the sooner the better. She knew that it was wrong to lie to Trevor about such a grave matter, to entrap this foolish man, an anti-Semite, with a secretly Jewish wife who was pregnant with another man's child. Scott would absolutely not have approved; but Scott was not around to take care of her. And so she made a conscious decision. She decided she was willing to do anything, tell any lie to bring her child safely into the world.

Sheilah refused to have her child in wartime England. She returned to New York to give birth to a girl whom she named Wendy Frances. Wendy because she had always loved the story of *Peter Pan*, and Frances after Scottie, who was proud to act as godmother. Sheilah then took her infant to California and left her with a rich friend, a woman she knew. Only then did she return to London alone to be with Trevor. After a second trip to California to visit Wendy, Sheilah became pregnant again. As before, she had her second child in New York, at Lenox Hill Hospital, leaving Trevor in England. She called her son Robert Trevor—a middle name she hoped would please her absent husband. But Trevor was not pleased. He had become suspicious at last and strongly believed that the actor Robert Taylor was the real father of Sheilah's son—thus the first name, Robert, which appeared to him a certain giveaway—and he began divorce proceedings while she was still in the hospital.

Sheilah was not bothered in the least by the prospect of divorce. She had gotten what she wanted out of Trevor Westbrook. By illegitimate means, yes, and through a great lie. But she was alone no longer; she had what not even Scott Fitzgerald had been willing to give her, a family of her own at last.

As for Scott, he began his afterlife journey in an inexpensive coffin in the William Wordsworth Room at the Pierce Brothers Mortuary in Los Angeles. He would have appreciated the room; he always said he wished he were a poet. In the next room to his

at the mortuary lay the body of his long-winded friend
Nathanael West. Nat and his wife, Eileen, had been killed only a
few hours after Scott in a car accident on the freeway. Nat was
thirty-seven years old when he died; Scott an old man at forty-
four.

The embalmer worked on Fitzgerald's face to restore his lost
youth. Each line and gray hair was artfully concealed; his cheeks
were rouged so that in death Scott Fitzgerald at last had the sun-
tan Sheilah had so ardently wished to see at Malibu. He
appeared untouched by suffering and his difficult life—only his
hands seemed old. Not many people came to view the body.
Dorothy Parker arrived in a state of rare sobriety with her husband, Alan. She stood silently over the rouged mannequin in the
coffin for a very long time. At last she uttered one of her clever
remarks, quoting the words of "Owl-eyes" as he stood in the rain
by the coffin of the once-great Gatsby: "The poor son-of-a-bitch!"
She said it just loudly enough for those around her to hear.

Beyond a small circle of friends, the world did not much notice
the passing of F. Scott Fitzgerald. The newspaper obituaries were
quick to dismiss him as an author of minor importance who had
once written pleasantly dated stories of young love. A few felt
the need to criticize Fitzgerald's lifestyle and the youth culture of
the 1920s to which he had given voice. The most scathing
remarks came from the journalist Westbrook Pegler in *The New
York World-Telegram* on the day after Christmas:

> The death of Scott Fitzgerald recalls memories of a queer brand of
> undisciplined and self-indulgent brats who were determined not to
> pull their weight in the boat and wanted the world to drop every-
> thing and sit down and bawl with them. A kick in the pants and a
> clout of the scalp were more like their needing. . . .

Even the *New York Times* made factual errors in its obituary,
calling Scott's second book *The Beautiful and the Damned* (one *the*
too many), and referring to it as a short story rather than a novel.
Among the pundits only a few voices were raised to suggest that
Fitzgerald might have a secure place in American literature. In a
"Salute and Farewell to F. Scott Fitzgerald" for *Esquire*, the ever-
loyal Arnold Gingrich wrote the minority opinion: "*The Great*

Gatsby will undoubtedly be read and studied a century hence, when *Gone With the Wind* has long since lived up to its title." Scott would have liked this, particularly the breezy dispatch of Margaret Mitchell, but it was not a view shared by many.

At the time of his death, Scott was worth a grand total of $706.00. The casket and funeral arrangements cost $613.25, which left a balance of $92.75 for his heirs—not much, but in fact Scott's cash balance had sometimes been less when he was alive. He also left behind a life insurance policy. This was originally valued at $250,000, but he had been forced to borrow against it heavily so that there remained only $44,184. The money would go to support Zelda.

Sheilah and Frances catalogued the rest of Fitzgerald's worldly goods:

> 1 trunkful of clothes
> 4 crates of books
> 1 carton of scrapbooks and photographs
> 1 small trunk with some personal effects—the Christmas presents sent him, personal jewelry (watch, cuff links), several scrapbooks and photographs
> 2 wooden work tables, lamp, radio

It did not seem to Sheilah much to leave behind after a lifetime, a few cartons and clothes. She telephoned Harold Ober on the day after Scott's death to discuss funeral arrangements and other final matters. Ober noted during the phone call: "S. doesn't think he would like to be buried in California because he really hated California. She thinks he would like to be buried where his father is buried because he admired him." It was attempted therefore to bury Scott alongside his ancestors at St. Mary's Catholic Cemetery in Rockville outside of Baltimore, but the bishop of Baltimore unexpectedly refused to permit Scott's body to be lowered into consecrated ground. There were apparently a number of reasons for the refusal: Fitzgerald was not a practicing Catholic at the time of his death, he had not received the last rites, and his books were considered immoral by the Church.

So Scott was rejected one final time. He was buried instead in the nonsectarian Rockville Union Cemetery nearby, an outsider, separated from his people by the prodigal life he had led. The ceremony was a sad and dreary affair held in the rain on December 27 with less than thirty relatives and friends present: Gerald and Sara Murphy, Max Perkins and his wife, the Obers, Zelda's brother-in-law Newman Smith, Scottie, and a few of her young friends. Zelda did not come; in the end she did not feel well enough to make the trip from Alabama.

It seemed an inauspicious end to Scott's ambitions. And yet history has its small surprises. There was present in the group of mourners an intense young man by the name of Andrew Turnbull, the son of a family from whom Scott and Zelda had once rented a house in 1932. Scott had always been good with young people, except perhaps his own daughter. He had been particularly charming to Andrew Turnbull, writing the young man several letters of advice and encouragement, just as he had done at a later time with Frances's younger brother, Morton Kroll. With Andrew this small expenditure of attention would lead to unexpected results. The young man adored Scott Fitzgerald; he was shattered by Scott's death and greatly depressed by the unsatisfying funeral in the rain with so few mourners and a Protestant clergyman who droned on with empty clichés. "It was as if nothing were being said *of* him or *to* him that the heart could hear," Turnbull later complained.

But he would fix that when he was grown-up. Twenty-two years later, in 1962, Andrew Turnbull wrote what remains today probably the best, and certainly the most sympathetic, of the biographies about Scott Fitzgerald. In 1963, a year after the publication of his biography, Turnbull edited a six-hundred-page volume of Fitzgerald's letters to add fuel to the growing legend. And so in the terrible obscurity of Scott's funeral, there was a seed of all the future fame that was to come: a young man watching.

Zelda meanwhile was sometimes seen in Montgomery walking the streets with an open Bible in her hand, a wraithlike figure in a black dress, her face shrouded beneath a wide black hat. Often she rode the streetcar from one end of town to the other simply for something to do. She wandered about in a mist of religious mysticism and strange thoughts, slipping back and forth from lucidity into madness. In the fall of 1947 Zelda returned to

Highland Hospital in Asheville, unable to manage any longer in the outside world. At midnight on March 10, 1948, a fire broke out in the kitchen of the main building of the hospital; Zelda was trapped on an upper floor where she burned to death with six other patients. She was buried in the Union Cemetery next to Scott; they were together again at last.

But it was not to be a final rest. Starting in the late 1940s, the public began to take a second look at Scott Fitzgerald and saw now what it had failed to see before, that the man had been an astonishingly good writer. Styles had changed once again; after the war, the "socially conscious" novels of the 1930s fell from favor; there was time and leisure now to be interested in such matters as a boy kissing a girl, the romance and agony of youth, and the Jazz Age itself, when America seemed as young as the century. The legend and literary reputation of F. Scott Fitzgerald began to swell, helped by Arthur Mizener's 1949 biography, *The Far Side of Paradise*, as well as Scribner's republication of Scott's entire work—including the unfinished novel, *The Last Tycoon*, edited by Edmund Wilson.

Scott himself inspired as much interest as his books, for there was something about him, a quality of grace, pain, and boyish enthusiasm, that struck a common nerve. Scott and Zelda: It was an American tragedy, complete with Technicolor scenes set in the south of France in the 1920s, a period considered glamorous once again. Eventually even the Church reconsidered its initial harsh judgment of Scott Fitzgerald. In 1975 Scottie petitioned the bishop of Baltimore to allow the remains of her mother and father to be reinterred in the consecrated ground at St. Mary's, where Scott had wanted to be, alongside three hundred years of his ancestors. By 1975 fame had gone a long way toward making Scott a good Catholic again. Writing upon the occasion, the bishop fondly claimed the Great American Author as his own:

F. Scott Fitzgerald came out of the Maryland Catholic tradition. He was a man touched by the faith of the Catholic Church. There can be perceived in his work a Catholic consciousness of reality. He found in this faith an understanding of the human heart caught in the struggle between grace and death. His characters are involved

in this great drama, seeking God and seeking love. As an artist he
was able with lucidity and poetic imagination to portray this struggle. He also experienced in his own life the mystery of suffering
and, we hope, the power of God's grace.

When Sheilah was eighty-two years old, in May 1987, she
returned to her apartment at 1443 North Hayworth Avenue for
the first time since she had left it nearly forty-six years earlier,
several months after Scott died. During those years, she had
spent much of her time in Los Angeles, she had written books,
and talked to a steady stream of biographers and professors, but
she had passionately avoided returning to the physical location
of Scott's death. She went back now only at the request of a documentary film company that was making a television series on
great American authors. At first she said no, she could not do it.
Then she changed her mind and said yes, she would try. It was
only an apartment after all, she rather liked to be on television,
and the events that happened there were very long ago.

The film company paid Sheilah's ticket from her condominium in Palm Beach, Florida, and put her up at the Beverly
Wilshire Hotel. She had an outfit which she wore for public
appearances in her late years that never varied: a black dress
which she was convinced made her look thin, a pearl necklace, a
small black hat, and a perky blond wig to conceal her ash-white
hair. She was still doing her best to hide her age, though the
years had caught up with her at last. Her skin was old and
smooth as parchment paper and she seemed to be getting smaller
every time I saw her; I was afraid there would be nothing left of
my mother soon but the brightness of her eyes.

On the morning of the shoot, a car picked her up at the hotel
and carried her through the flats of Beverly Hills to Sunset
Boulevard, and then headed west along the Sunset Strip, past
huge billboards advertising rock bands she had never heard of.
Sunset Boulevard was almost unrecognizable from the street she
had known in 1940; it had changed even from the late sixties
when Sheilah had given up her column and sold her last
California house—a beach house north of Malibu. The Trocadero
where she and Scott had met for their second date, had become

Dino's for a time, a restaurant owned by Dean Martin, but had long since disappeared. The Mocambo had been leveled to become the parking lot for the Playboy Club, itself an anachronism. Sheilah recognized the Chateau Marmont Hotel but a half-block later she came to a modern building of brown cinderblocks, glass, and marble that gave her pause. This was the West Hollywood branch of the Great Western Bank; on this spot once stood The Garden of Allah Hotel. Today, where the bungalows had been, and the overgrown jungle and the swimming pool shaped like the Black Sea, there was an asphalt parking lot for the bank and a small strip mall dominated by a McDonald's restaurant.

Across the street, where Schwab's used to be, Sheilah saw the huge brand-new Virgin Records complex, built in a postmodern strangely Aztec style. There was a sign advertising a five-plex movie theater within—small screens to watch the reduced mythologies of a new era. Sheilah had never imagined she would live long enough to witness such change. And yet despite the new styles, and young men with ponytails and cellular telephones, she felt the unchangeable spirit of the town. The slice of Los Angeles which devotes itself to the entertainment industry was still a self-enclosed world in which the shabby and the miraculous walked hand in hand, and the American dream was not so much a metaphor as a larcenous glint in every passing eye.

When the car turned onto Hayworth Avenue, Sheilah was unprepared for the shock of finding her old apartment building exactly as she had left it forty-six years before. Nearly half a century evaporated without a trace and she felt such an onslaught of old emotions that for a moment it was difficult to breathe. Only the trees had grown taller and fuller with time; the stucco apartment building, the windows and doors, the very smell in the air, was familiar. Sheilah found that her heart was pounding and at her age this was alarming.

The film crew had arrived earlier and they were busy setting up their equipment. The producer hurried to her car to open the door for her, but Sheilah told him she had changed her mind. She could not go inside the apartment where Scott had died. Her legs were weak; she felt a terrible anxiety. The producer suggested she rest in the car and he would come back when they were set up and see how she was feeling then. She breathed deeply and told herself she was being very silly. In the end her professional instincts took over; it was bad form to keep a film crew waiting. Besides, she would have to give back the cost of her plane ticket and hotel if she failed to do her part, and this thought stirred her practical nature.

She did better once she was inside. A young agent lived in the apartment now, and he had redecorated so thoroughly with expensive antiques and crowded bric-a-brac that the place was hardly recognizable. There was a new kitchen and heavy drapes to replace the venetian blinds that once were on the windows. Over the years someone had torn down the wall where Scott's bookcase had stood, making a larger living room. In the hall Sheilah found photographs of actors and actresses, the agent's clients, and she did not recognize a face in the lot. In the entire apartment there was only a single reminder of forty-seven years ago, but for Sheilah it was not an easy one—the mantelpiece above the fireplace was just as it had been. She could not look at it without remembering too clearly how Scott had jerked to his feet, reached there as if to save himself, and then fallen upon the floor.

After all these years, she had not gotten over the death of Scott Fitzgerald. Sheilah answered the questions of the interviewer as well as she was able, and then she fled. . . still the young woman running out of the front door onto the sidewalk, hysterical with disbelief. She found she could not breathe entirely well until she was in a restaurant far away from Hayworth Avenue eating lunch.

I saw my mother a final time in the spring of 1988. She was eighty-three years old then, restlessly spending her time between a condominium in Palm Beach and a small apartment in a brownstone on East 72nd Street in New York. She had recently sold her house in London that was around the corner from Harrod's, her favorite department store, but she was no longer certain this had been a wise move. Sometimes she telephoned me

to discuss where she might settle down for her old age. Palm
Beach was sunny but boring, and she hated all the stuffy rich
people; Manhattan was too cold in the winter, too hot in the
summer; London still had an allure and she was thinking of selling the Palm Beach condo to buy another house there—only it
had become very expensive in England, and she was not entirely
certain she had the energy to move one more time across the
Atlantic.

The question of where to live kept her constantly occupied.
She felt at home nowhere. She read the real estate sections of
newspapers as some people consult the Bible or I Ching, hoping
for divine intervention. Several times a week she telephoned
realtors in key markets, sifting through the possibilities but dis-
satisfied with what she heard. Added to her indecision was the
painful fact of arthritis; she could no longer get about as easily as
she used to. A few years earlier she had gone into the Hospital
for Special Surgery in New York to replace one of her hips with a
plastic joint. This had relieved the pain somewhat, but the operation had been physically and emotionally traumatic, leaving her
unable to walk for several months, unaccustomedly helpless,
and making her feel for the first time that she was truly old.
Now her doctor was telling her she should have the other hip
replaced as well. She hated even the thought of it, but eventually
she decided she had better have it done.

I was in northern California at the time of the second hip operation and received daily reports from my sister Wendy, who
lived in Brooklyn; she was dean of Brooklyn College and taught
several courses on literature as well. At first it appeared as if the
operation had gone well. Then my phone rang early one morning, and Wendy told me that our mother had just suffered a
heart attack. It was the last thing either of us had expected.
Apparently the operation had been too stressful for her. The doctor phoned me a few minutes after my sister to say he did not
expect Sheilah to survive the day. I had better hurry to New York
if I ever wanted to see her again.

So I hurried. I was on the first plane I could get out of San
Francisco, not certain if she would be alive when I arrived on the
East Coast. The moment I was inside the terminal at La Guardia

I phoned the intensive care unit and a nurse told me my mother was still alive. It appeared her condition had stabilized. Frankly, I was not surprised. My mother's energy had always seemed monumental to me and I suspected she was immortal.

I could only get a gypsy cab from La Guardia; the enterprising driver filled his uninsured station wagon with hapless passengers like myself and drove us all at breakneck speed into the city. I found my mother in a darkened corner of the intensive care unit with a curtain closed around her; she was a tiny figure in the bed beneath a white sheet with an IV needle in a vein on the back of her hand, a plastic tube running into her nose, and many machines and green glowing screens monitoring her vital signs. She looked very old to me and fragile. Her voice was still that of a young woman when I spoke with her on the telephone, and so now it was a shock to see her without her perky blond wig or any of her usual illusions. Her hair was white and thin and wispy; her skin almost transparent. She had been dozing but she opened her eyes when I came in and smiled at me. "Rob!" she said. "You've come to see your old mother!"

I sat next to her in the eerie late-night quiet of the intensive care unit and I took her hand. In the last few years we had been getting along better, after some years of struggle. I had done many things she had found incomprehensible; after publishing my first novel at the age of twenty-three—living out very nicely her Scott Fitzgerald plans for me—I had dropped out of sight for a time, living in a redwood forest in a small cabin I had built that had no electricity or running water. We were on different sides of a generational divide. After the expensive education she had provided, I had disappointed her, working as a dishwasher, piano player in bars, cook, waiter, all sorts of things—but now I was writing again, mystery novels, and this made her very glad. It was extremely important to my mother that I was a writer, just as it was likewise important that my sister become a dean and college professor. Together we were meant to fulfill her fantasies and broken ambitions left behind by Scott.

She had always done most of the talking when I was a child, and despite her weakened condition, she did most of the talking now. She reeled off a string of anecdotes about the hospital, the terrible food, and a particular nurse she despised. She told me she had been lying in bed just before I arrived thinking of a magazine article she wanted to write about her hip operation and her experiences in this hateful hospital. She had spent a great portion of her life dreaming up salable topics for magazine and newspaper articles, ever since her first piece on Stage Door Johnnies, and she wasn't about to stop now simply because she was in an intensive care unit and had nearly died today. But eventually she became quiet and I could see that she was tired.

She closed her eyes and I sat for a while still holding her small ancient hand, looking at her. Some years earlier, in her sixties and early seventies, she had gained weight and her face had often seemed petulant to me, full of a willful anger. But as a very old woman she had become beautiful once again; all the inessentials had worn away, leaving behind only a skeletal glow of her spirit inside.

It seemed to me that she had done well with her life, better than might be expected for a daydreaming girl from a London slum. At the height of her career, in the mid-1950s, twenty million people each day had read her syndicated gossip column; she wrote a separate column for the important Hollywood trade paper, *Daily Variety*, and had a fifteen-minute live television show five mornings a week. She never did develop a taste for gossip herself, but this had not stopped her on the path to success. Together, she, Hedda Hopper, and Louella Parsons comprised what she sometimes described as the "Unholy Trinity." But it had been a lonely struggle to have come so far. Scott had left her, and her children too, as we grew up and made our own lives; even Scottie had died of cancer in 1986. My mother had never expected to outlive Scottie; she was devastated with grief. Nevertheless, she did not go to Scottie's funeral for the same reason that she had not gone to Scott's. She was an outsider to the family, and afraid her presence might prove an embarrassment.

The years carried her ever further from Scott; his posthumous fame as a great American author increased the distance, taking him to some hallowed marble place where she, a mere gossip columnist, could not follow. It would be nice to say that her three and a half years with Scott Fitzgerald had made her the legitimate person she had always wanted to be. But it hadn't quite. He had died too soon, and did not leave enough of himself behind. Yet as an old woman, there was nothing shrill about Sheilah, nor grasping, nor sour with disappointment, for Scott had left her something after all: a lingering sense of poetry. And small as this bequest might seem, it is in fact the only treasure that keeps its value as death comes near. She had loved someone, and had been loved in return, and she kept forever a sense of shimmering wonder, and bright memories of the past.

Just as I was about to leave, she told me the title she had dreamed up for the magazine article she wanted to write about her hip operation.

"Listen to this, Rob, and tell me what you think." She paused for dramatic effect. "'Hip, Hip, *Not* Hooray'!"

"Terrific," I said.

NOTES

Prologue: A Hollywood Ending

6   **"Dear Scott, . . . Only the other day"** *Beloved Infidel,* by Sheilah Graham and Gerold Frank, Henry Holt and Co., New York, 1958 (hereafter *Beloved*), p. viii, ix.

Chapter 1: A Walking Dream

13   **"I sit worrying about next week's $35.00 hotel bill!"** Scott to Harold Ober, March 23, 1937. *The Letters of F. Scott Fitzgerald,* edited by Andrew Turnbull, Charles Scribner's Sons, New York, 1963 (hereafter *Letters*), p. 404.

13   **"Oh come, my love, and join with me"** *Dorothy Parker: What Fresh Hell Is This?* by Marion Meade, Penguin Books, New York, 1989 (hereafter *Fresh Hell*), p. 277.

14   **"These Texas lands"** Scott to Corey Ford, early July 1937, *Letters*, p. 550.

14   **"Nothing is as old"** Notes for *The Last Tycoon*, Princeton University Library, Rare Books Collection (hereafter PUL).

15   **eyes that were the color of the Irish sea** *Zelda, A Biography,* by Nancy Milford, Harper & Row, New York, 1970 (hereafter Milford), p. 286. The description of Fitzgerald's eyes is attributed to Edmund Wilson.

15   **"that was aging from within"** *The Last Tycoon*, by F. Scott Fitzgerald, Charles Scribner's Sons, New York, 1941 (hereafter *Tycoon*), p. 71.

16   **"Both the first and the last time he left for Hollywood"** F.

Scott Fitzgerald. In His Own Time: A Miscellany, edited by Matthew J. Bruccoli and Jackson R. Bryer, The Kent State University Press, 1971, p. 479. The description is from Arnold Gingrich's obituary "Salute and Farewell to F. Scott Fitzgerald," *Esquire,* March 1941.

16　**"Junior writers $300"** *Some Sort of Epic Grandeur,* by Matthew J. Bruccoli, Harcourt Brace Jovanovitch, New York and London, 1981 (hereafter *Grandeur*), p. 426.

16　**"Dearest Pie: I feel a certain excitement"** Scott to Scottie, July 1937, *Letters,* p. 16.

17　**"A more irresponsible pair"** Scott to Ruth Sturtevant, March 26, 1920, ibid., p. 459.

17　**"a new generation dedicated more than the last to the fear of poverty"** *This Side of Paradise,* by F. Scott Fitzgerald, Charles Scribner's Sons, New York, 1920 (hereafter *Paradise*). Collier Books edition, p. 282.

18　**"really unbelievably handsome"** Milford, p. 124.

18　**"I have just seen the doom of youth"** *F. Scott Fitzgerald, A Biography,* by André Le Vot, Doubleday & Co., New York, 1983, translated from the French by William Bryon (hereafter Le Vot), p. 124.

19　**"There's nothing on earth to do here"** Milford, p. 128.

19　**"a tragic city of beautiful girls"** Scott to his cousin Ceci, Mrs. Richard Taylor, winter 1927, *Letters,* p. 415.

20　**"a young actress like a breakfast food"** *Grandeur,* p. 258.

20　**"almost hysterical egotism"** "Magnetism," from *The Stories of F. Scott Fitzgerald,* by F. Scott Fitzgerald, introduction by Malcolm Cowley, Charles Scribner's Sons, New York, 1951 (hereafter *Stories*), p. 231.

21　BOOTLEGGERS GONE OUT OF BUSINESS *The Far Side of Paradise,* by Arthur Mizener, Houghton Mifflin Co., Boston, 1949 (hereafter *Far Side*), p. 206.

21　**"the good gone times when we still believed in summer hotels"** *The Crack-Up,* by F. Scott Fitzgerald, edited by Edmund Wilson, New Directions Publishing Corp., New York, 1945 (hereafter *Crack-Up*), p. 53.

22　**"The second time I went was five years ago"** Scott to Scottie, July 1937, *Letters,* p. 16.

23　**"seriously began to question whether Thalberg existed"** *An Empire of Their Own,* by Neal Gabler, Crown Publishers, Inc., New York, 1988, p. 223.

23　**"was built for great emotional moments"** From "Crazy Sunday," *Stories,* p. 416.

23　**"It would be a party of the top drawer"** Ibid.

23　**"I could see at once that we had landed on our feet"** *Crazy*

Sundays, by Aaron Latham, The Viking Press, 1970 (hereafter Latham), p. 71.

23 **"I won't have anything to drink . . . the lovely girls"** From "Crazy Sunday," *Stories*, p. 416.

24 **"Why didn't you bring your horse in?"** Latham, p. 72.

24 **"his blood throbbing"** From "Crazy Sunday," *Stories*, p. 418.

24 **"their faces devoid of expression"** Latham, p. 72.

24 **"In Sunny Africa they have the elephant"** *Grandeur*, p. 136. There are two separate versions I have come across of this song "Dog! Dog! Dog!" by Edmund Wilson and Scott Fitzgerald, one quoted by Matthew Bruccoli and the other by Aaron Latham in his book *Crazy Sundays*. I have used the Bruccoli version.

25 **"the Great Lover of the screen"** From "Crazy Sunday," *Stories*, p. 419.

25 **"as he finished he had the sickening realization"** Ibid.

25 **"Just when somebody's taken him up"** *Far Side*, p. 222.

26 I THOUGHT YOU WERE ONE OF THE MOST *Grandeur*, p. 323.

26 **"If you weren't able to function in action"** *Afternoon of an Author*, by F. Scott Fitzgerald, Collier Books, Macmillian Publishing Co., New York, 1957 (hereafter *Afternoon of an Author*), p. 185. The quote comes from Fitzgerald's essay, "Author's House."

27 **he drank the portion in a single gulp** This anecdote is told by Le Vot, p. 273.

27 **"The conjuror's hat was empty"** *Crack-Up*, p. 82.

28 **"One harassed and despairing night"** Ibid., p. 80.

28 **"an over-extension of the flank"** Ibid., p. 77.

29 **"the leak through which, unknown to myself"** Ibid., p. 80.

29 **"Forget your personal tragedy"** Ernest Hemingway to Scott, May 28, 1934, PUL.

29 **"poor Scott Fitzgerald"** *Grandeur*, p. 412.

29 **"Christ, man, how do you find time in the middle of the general conflagrations"** *Fool for Love*, by Scott Donaldson, Congdon & Weed, New York, 1983 (hereafter *Fool for Love*), p. 148.

29 **The novelist John O'Hara commiserated** Ibid., p. 147.

30 **"Long ago, when he was young . . . poured himself another drink"** *F. Scott Fitzgerald—In His Own Time: A Miscellany*, edited by Matthew J. Bruccoli and Jackson R. Bryer, The Kent State University Press, 1971 (hereafter *In His Own Time*), pp. 294–296.

31 **"four grains enough to kill a horse"** *The Romantic Egoists*, edited by Matthew J. Bruccoli, Scottie Fitzgerald Smith, and Joan P. Kerr, Charles Scribner's Sons, New York, 1974, p. 212.

32 **"I want to profit by these two experiences"** Scott to Scottie, July 1937, *Letters,* p. 17.

32 **he was in debt $9,000 to Scribner's alone** These figures come from *Grandeur,* p. 423.

33 **"100 to you—commission"** Ibid., p. 423.

35 **he would celebrate when the Coke bottles completely encircled the room by going off the wagon** Latham, p. 6.

35 **"Here comes this completely crushed and frightened man"** Ibid., p. 104.

36 **"Scott had that unhealthy humility"** Ibid., p. 5.

36 **"The first time I saw Scott"** Ibid., p. 7.

36 **"We accepted [Scott] because we respected him"** Ibid., p. 9.

36 **"a sick old man. . . a sweet nature that came through"** Ibid., p. 8.

37 **"I'm riding low now"** Ibid., p. 20.

37 THE PICTURE WAS BEYOND PRAISE Ibid.

37 **"I talk with the authority of failure"** *Grandeur,* p. 435.

39 **"Smiling faintly at him from not four feet away was the face of his . . . wife"** *Tycoon,* p. 26.

39 **"Who is still there?"** *The Garden of Allah,* by Sheilah Graham, Crown Publishers, New York, 1970 (hereafter *Allah*), p. 160. As a writer, Scott Fitzgerald wasted nothing. This matter of the belt with the cut-out stars and the mistaken identity was used in a crucial scene in *Tycoon,* pp. 62, 63.

Chapter 2: The English Girl

41 **"English people don't commit suicide"** PUL.

42 **"Be sure you don't accept mink coats from directors"** *A State of Heat,* by Sheilah Graham, Grosset & Dunlap, New York, 1972 (hereafter *Heat*), p. 189.

42 **"Ninety percent of them have clap or syphilis"** Ibid., p. 190.

43 **"thrilling ecstasy. He fits perfectly"** *My Hollywood,* by Sheilah Graham, Michael Joseph Ltd., London, 1984 (hereafter *My Hollywood*), p. 16.

45 **"My name is Sheilah Graham, and I'm calling for Raoul Fleischman"** Ibid., p. 12.

47 **"Clark Gable threw back his handsome head . . . the worst dialogue and the worst direction"** Ibid., p. 15.

47 **"You are *not* Walter Winchell"** *Beloved,* p. 166.

48   **"Not even the doubtful pleasure of rubbing elbows"** Ibid., p. 167.

49   **"Take my word for it"** Ibid., p. 168.

49   **"Don't worry. . . . God takes care of drunks"** *Allah,* p. 108.

50   **"Little Sheilah, the Giant-Killer"** *Beloved,* p. 168.

50   **"until my stomach revolted"** *Allah,* p. 108.

51   **"Sometimes hearing them bounce from topic to topic"** *College of One,* by Sheilah Graham, Viking, New York, 1966 (hereafter *College*), p. 59.

54   **"Wanted: Girls with Good Teeth"** *The Late Lily Shiel,* by Sheilah Graham, Grosset & Dunlap, New York, 1978 (hereafter *Lily Shiel*), p. 120.

56   **"Here, you shouldn't be on the streets . . . you hear me?"** Ibid., p. 130.

57   **"I'm about to have dinner . . . You've had your dinner"** The dialogue between Lily and the middle-aged man at the restaurant is from *Beloved*, pp. 34–36.

59   **"By Jove . . . . if you can sell this toothbrush, you can sell anything"** *Lily Shiel,* p. 132.

60   **"Where have you been? . . . I thought I'd never find you"** Ibid., p. 133.

61   **"You're always sniffling, Lily"** *Beloved,* p. 56.

63   **"A penny for your thoughts. . . Here's to our friendship"** Ibid., p. 147.

63   **"No, we'll take *you* home first"** Ibid., p. 148.

66   **"I know this lady . . . I am prepared to forgive you if you have an explanation"** The dialogue between Lily, Johnny, and Monty Collins at the Metropole Hotel is from *Lily Shiel*, pp. 172–175.

Chapter 3: The Mysterious Mrs. Gillam

68   **"She would be a runaway all her life"** *Lily Shiel,* p. 25.

68   **"Ah, if only you were Spanish"** *Heat,* p. 21.

69   **"You're so pretty"** Ibid., p. 19.

71   **"Pragger-Wagger wanted to know who was the beautiful blonde"** *Beloved,* p. 117.

74   **"Oh, Johnny, you're wasting your time . . . Why don't *you* write it?"** Ibid., pp. 117–118.

76   **"Lord Beaverbrook says that such persistence should be rewarded"** Ibid., p. 144.

77   "Oh, Mrs. Gillam" Ibid., p. 127.

78   "You're an adventuress . . . Yes, I am" Ibid., p. 132.

79   "Of course, you've always had the advantages . . . Tell us about Hollywood, Charlie" Ibid., p. 139.

81   "Sheilah, why do you play so hard?" Ibid., p. 141.

81   "Well, I've been watching you" Ibid., p. 141.

82   "I'm in love with you, Sheilah. . . . But don't forget I asked you" Ibid., p. 143.

82   "Not what we want . . . Not bad" Ibid., p. 152. The description of how Sheilah used her sex appeal to attract John Wheeler's attention is from *Heat*, pp. 63–64; in this account, Sheilah disguised Wheeler's identity by calling him "Charles."

85   "combination of daring, brazenness and desperation" *Beloved*, p. 154.

87   "My darling Sheilah" Ibid., p. 157.

88   "It may interest you to know . . . I'll be there in two weeks" Ibid., pp. 170, 171.

89   "This will do until I have one made up in London for you" Ibid., p. 171.

89   "Bob will be our best man" Ibid.

90   "the ugliest vegetable God created" *Fresh Hell*, p. 197.

90   "Let's all go to my place" *Beloved*, p. 173.

91   "appeared to be all shades of the palest, most delicate blue" Ibid., p. 174.

91   "Who was that man?. . . No, don't bother" This dialogue is pieced together from two sources: *Allah*, p. 159, and *Beloved*, p. 174.

Chapter 4: Politics and Dancing

93   "The mood should be two people" *Tycoon* notes, PUL.

94   "You writers are being misled . . . sons of bitches, bastards and Goddamn reds" Fitzgerald Papers, PUL. These quotes are from a Screen Writers Guild, Inc., memo dated August 26, 1939, mailed to all its members, a copy of which was found in Scott Fitzgerald's papers at the time of his death.

95   "the bravest, proudest word" *Fresh Hell*, p. 278.

97   "They'll look at your hands" *The Real F. Scott Fitzgerald*, by Sheilah Graham, Grosset & Dunlap, New York, 1976 (hereafter *Real FSF*), p. 174.

98   "The white table . . . lengthened and became an altar" *Tycoon*, p. 73.

98   **"I like you"** *Allah,* p. 161.

98   **"She was shy and bold, though which quality predominated it was hard to say"** *Tycoon* notes, PUL.

99   **"She looked, for a split second like an . . . adventuress . . . wretched trollop—like a puppy, a tailless tyke washed into his backyard by a flood"** All of these unpublished descriptions from Chapter Two are from various working drafts of *Tycoon,* PUL.

99   **"Shall we dance? . . . Dottie"** *Allah,* p. 161.

100   **"He appeared to be in his forties"** *Beloved,* p. 175.

101   **"Why aren't I dancing?"** *Allah,* p. 161.

102   **"If you tell anyone, I'll ruin you"** Ibid., p. 34.

103   **"You wouldn't yield until I smacked you"** *Heat,* p. 133.

103   **"If you would only look at me"** *Allah,* p. 151.

104   **"Eddie Mayer hates women"** *Tycoon* notes, PUL.

104   **"Do you know a girl here I might like? . . . a great smile, and a great flirt"** *Heat,* p. 140.

104   **"What are you doing tonight? . . . Why don't you bring him along"** The telephone dialogue between Sheilah and Eddie Mayer is combined from the accounts in *Beloved,* p. 176, and *Allah,* p. 161.

106   **"Won't you have a drink with us?"** *Beloved,* p. 177.

106   **"I *love* dancing. . . it gave me such a feeling of freedom"** Ibid., p. 178.

107   **their own personal adjective** Fitzgerald's strategy of telling young women he had discovered their personal adjective is described in *Fool for Love,* p. 117.

107   **"How old are you? . . . How did a girl as beautiful as you come to be a columnist?"** *Beloved,* p. 178.

108   **"she was deep in it with him"** *Tycoon,* pp. 73, 74.

108   **"It is hard to put into words how Scott Fitzgerald worked this magic"** *Beloved,* p. 177.

108   **"Is it getting in your mouth? . . . A working girl didn't have a chance to be a Countess everyday"** This dialogue comes from an unpublished 1939 short story, a thinly disguised account of their meeting which Sheilah wrote as an exercise with Scott's help. She originally gave her story the florid title "Fled Is the Music," but Scott crossed this out and wrote in its place his own title, "Beloved Infidel," after a poem he had already written for her. Sheilah later used *Beloved Infidel* as the title for her 1958 book. Because the 1939 manuscript contains Scott's handwritten corrections, it now resides in the Princeton University Library in the box containing the notes for *Tycoon* (hereafter "Beloved Infidel").

109   **"We know nothing about the girl"** *Tycoon* notes, PUL.

109   **"Eddie tells me that you're engaged to a Duke. Is that higher than a Marquis"** Handwritten note in the margin of Sheilah's desk copy of *Beloved Infidel.*

109   **"[Her] weapon was her laughter"** *Tycoon* notes, PUL. This is from an early draft of Chapter Two.

109   **"We must get back to Eddie and Jonah"** *Allah,* p. 162.

111   **"Oh no, I'm leaving Hollywood for good"** *Real FSF,* p. 28.

112   **"The man's lying"** "Beloved Infidel," PUL.

113   **"Why don't I have dinner . . . All right"** *Real FSF,* p. 29.

113   **"I hope it's beautiful and a fool"** Le Vot, p. 111. Scott, as was his wont, used Zelda's words verbatim in *The Great Gatsby,* ascribing the statement to Daisy Buchanan.

113   **"That is done now"** Milford, p. 160.

114   **"I don't want you to do anything inappropriate to your age"** Scott to Scottie, July 5, 1937, *Letters,* pp. 15, 16.

114   **"put all her eggs in one bastard"** *Fresh Hell,* p. 105.

115   **"golden hair with a flame behind it"** *College,* pp. 179, 180.

115   **he was glad his daughter was overweight** *Allah,* p. 162.

115   **"Scottie, finish your meat . . . Yes, Daddy"** Ibid., p. 163.

116   **"Oh, Daddy, please"** *Beloved,* p. 181.

116   **"They make me feel old"** "Beloved Infidel," PUL.

116   **"Scottie, don't you think it's time"** *Beloved,* p. 182.

116   **"the intimacy of the car"** *Tycoon* notes, PUL.

117   *"He seduces her because she is slipping away"* Ibid.

117   **"That was the moment to go in"** *Tycoon,* pp. 85, 86.

117   **"felt inexpressibly sad that something that had been so enormously exciting"** *Beloved,* p. 182.

117   **"You look like a blue rose"** "Beloved Infidel," PUL.

117   **"Please don't go, come in"** *Beloved,* p. 182.

Chapter 5: The Brave Lie

118   **"He saw she was lying"** *Tycoon* notes, PUL.

118   BEST NEWS ON EARTH DARLING *Beloved,* p. 183.

119   **"Early August is for imprudent loves"** *Tycoon* notes, PUL.

119   **"She was very ready and it was right"** *Tycoon,* p. 152.

120   **"a gift for intimacy"** *Letters,* p. xv.

121   **"As far as I know, everyone who was really exposed to him loved him"** *Fool for Love,* p. 191. The remark comes from Margaret Egloff.

121 **"Where did that gorgeous face come from?"** *Real FSF*, p. 117.

121 **"You must have been talking to my twin brother, Irish"** *Beloved*, p. 189.

122 **"All goes beautifully here"** Scott to Max Perkins, August 1937, *Letters*, p. 274.

122 **"Wouldn't you think she was tired of seeing her own face?"** *Real FSF*, p. 77.

123 **"a languid restaurant"** *Tycoon*, p. 101.

123 **"It was so easy to fall in love"** *Real FSF*, p. 31.

124 **"No, but I must rush away . . . I'm so sorry"** The dialogue between Milton Bren, Constance Bennett, and Sheilah Graham is compiled from *Beloved*, pp. 235–236, and *My Hollywood*, p. 35.

125 **"This must be avenged"** *Beloved*, p. 237.

125 **sixty-six people who had snubbed him from 1925 to 1929** *Fool for Love*, p. 181.

126 **"It's lucky no children . . . cast as a ghost in her latest production"** *Beloved*, p. 237.

127 **"Scott, come and sit here next to me . . . I can perfectly well take care of myself"** Ibid., p. 186.

128 **the Hanging Gardens of Babylon** *Real FSF*, p. 125.

130 **"John O'Hara is in a perpetual state"** *Tycoon* notes, PUL.

130 **"Does he think I'm going to rape him or something?"** *Real FSF*, p. 90.

130 **"moral doubts about her"** *Tycoon* notes, PUL.

131 **"I don't have the right to monopolize you"** *College*, p. 60.

131 **"I didn't have the top two things"** *Fool for Love*, p. 44.

Chapter 6: Lilyanna

132 **"I was prepared to suffer any ordeal"** *Beloved*, p. 185.

132 **"Malibu: A bunch of dressing cabins"** *Tycoon* notes, PUL.

133 **"a lady whose past was booked solid with men"** *Tycoon* notes, PUL.

134 **"I've slept with six hundred and forty men"** *Tender is the Night*, by F. Scott Fitzgerald, Charles Scribner's Sons, New York, 1934 (hereafter *Tender*), p. 230 (Penguin Modern Classics edition).

135 **"This is your chance"** *Tycoon*, p. 115.

135 **"And any others? . . . It's all right, Sheilo"** The dialogue in the car is taken from *Beloved*, pp. 190, 191.

136 **"What is it, what is it?"** Ibid., p. 192.

137 **"I'm always so curious about everything"** Ibid., p. 193.

137 **"She was absorbed in herself"** *Tycoon,* p. 113.

137 **"His moralities somehow collapsed"** Ibid., p. 112.

139 **the Jews Hospital and Orphan Asylum in Norwood** I am indebted to my sister, Wendy W. Fairey, whose sleuthing uncovered the true name of the mythical orphanage our mother often mentioned. My sister wrote a vivid account of our mother's late years in her book, *One of the Family,* published by W. W. Norton & Company, New York and London, 1992.

142 **"Look what somebody did!"** *Lily Shiel,* p. 20.

143 *"What* **are you doing?"** Ibid., p. 31.

145 **"Went to battle, fought and died"** Ibid., p. 39.

145 **"Buddha made the harvest"** Ibid., p. 20.

151 **"What's going on, what do you think you're doing?"** Ibid., p. 86.

151 **"No, I won't do it, I'm tired . . . I won't"** Ibid., p. 88.

154 **"Lily . . . Lilyanna"** Ibid., p. 118.

154 **"You cannot live here by yourself"** Ibid., p. 119.

Chapter 7: Moving Pictures

157 **"More than anything in the world he wanted to make pictures"** Latham, p. 78.

158 **"For Shielah: A Beloved Infidel,"** PUL.

160 **"I'll be out of town for a week or so"** *Beloved,* p. 197.

162 **"Very few lines of mine are left"** *Grandeur,* p. 428.

162 **"Everyone is very nice to me"** Scott to Max Perkins, July 19, 1937, *Letters,* p. 274.

162 **"The work is hard as hell"** Scott to Anne Ober, July 26, 1937, Ibid., p. 553.

164 **"After almost 3 years of intermittent illness"** Scott to Margaret Turnbull, August 1937, Ibid., p. 443.

165 **"Dear Joe: This letter is only valid in case you like the script very much"** Memo from Scott to Joseph Mankiewicz, September 3, 1937, PUL.

165 **"Zelda is not better"** Scott to Beatrice Dance, November 27, 1937, Milford, p. 314.

165 DEAR SCOTT YOU MUST STOP READING ALL THOSE NASTY STORIES, PUL.

166 **"In everything I took my cue from Scott"** *Beloved,* p. 197.

167 **"Paramore's a hack"** *Real FSF,* p. 151.

167 "Out here though the bookstores were bulging" *Tycoon* notes, PUL.

168 "Have you books by F. Scott Fitzgerald? ... I'll order them from the publishers" The dialogue in the three bookstores is from *Beloved*, pp. 186, 187.

170 "Cut out all these exclamation points. . . It will be good for them" *Beloved*, p. 198.

171 "Hello, everyone, this is Sheilah Graham in Hollywood . . . You sounded a little breathless, but that was all" Ibid., p. 199.

171 "They didn't mind Cary GRA-ah-ant" *Real FSF*, p. 102.

171 "There's nothing wrong with your voice" *Beloved*, p. 199.

172 "Are you sure you can leave? ... I'll arrange it" Ibid., p. 200.

173 "[At Princeton] I used to write endless letters" Scott to Scottie, October 8, 1937, *Letters*, p. 19.

173 "Sheilah ... by the way, has broken her engagement" Ibid., p. 18.

173 "Life hasn't much to offer except youth" Scott to Mrs. Richard Taylor, June 10, 1917, Ibid., p. 414.

174 "[We] had a much better time than I had anticipated" *Far Side*, p. 275.

Chapter 8: A Bad Brownie

177 "Often people display a curious respect for a man drunk" *Tender*, p. 121.

178 "Bring me a double gin ... And when you come back, bring another one" *Beloved*, p. 200.

180 "Scott, please ... I've heard of you" Ibid., pp. 201, 202.

180 "a great lay" *Real FSF*, p. 103.

181 "It was a mistake for you to come ... Goodbye" *Beloved*, p. 202.

181 "He is a lone wolf because of his great talent" Ibid., p. 203.

182 "Oh, Scott, I thought you'd gotten off! ... needed another bottle" Ibid.

182 "Now, I've brought my script ... I never want to see you again" The dialogue between Fitzgerald, Sheilah, and Mr. Wharton is combined from accounts in *Beloved*, pp. 203 and 204, and *Real FSF*, p. 104.

185 he said what a great cunt Sheilah was Fitzgerald's conversation with the film editor of the *Chicago Daily News* is from *Real FSF*, p. 105.

186 "Now Sheilah, don't you be afraid of them... be quiet"
Beloved, p. 205.

187 "*Yeeoooohh!* ... The son of a bitch bit my finger! ... I wanted
to make him sweat a little" The dialogue between Arnold Gingrich,
Sheilah, and Fitzgerald in the Ambassador East is pieced together from
Latham, pp. 133–134, and *Beloved*, pp. 206–208.

189 "Sheilah was perfectly willing" Latham, p. 134.

190 "Doesn't she have lovely hair? ... silly bitch" *Beloved*, p. 209.

191 "Where are we?" *Allah*, p. 167.

191 "I'm going on the wagon ... As you wish, Scott" *Beloved*, p.
210.

192 "I'm not returning ... I will" The dialogue on the phone
between Scott and Sheilah is taken from *Beloved*, p. 211, and *Real FSF*, p.
105; the fact that Scott was quite right in assuming that there was a
lover waiting for Sheilah in New York was carefully omitted from
Beloved Infidel, but mentioned in her later books.

Chapter 9: Euphoria and Hangover

194 "When you once get to the point" *Tycoon* notes, PUL.

194 "Do I look like death" *Tycoon* notes, PUL.

194 "Dear Scott ... How are you?" *Tycoon* notes, PUL.

195 "through many an alcoholic mist" *Crack-Up*, p. 25.

195 the sight of his own blood brought him around *Allah*, p. 169.
Sheilah mentions Scott cutting his wrists on the broken porcelain tap
only briefly, and I never heard her talk about this incident while she
was alive. The date of Fitzgerald's quasi suicide attempt is not entirely
clear, but since it was done at The Garden of Allah it must fall within a
six-month period, sometime after he fell off the wagon in October 1937
and when he moved to Malibu the following April.

198 Dear Miss Graham before ... Dear Mr. Hutton Both the letter
from Clayton Hutton and Scott's reply are from the Sheilah Graham
file, PUL.

200 "We sat in the old commissary at Metro" *Grandeur*, p. 259.
Scott wrote down this anecdote as it appears here in 1939 as one of his
many notes for *The Last Tycoon*; he told it to Sheilah in nearly the same
words in the limousine on the way to Pasadena.

201 "No one's yet written *the* novel on Hollywood" *Beloved*, p. 215.

201 "Could I have gotten the date wrong? ... I told them they'd
done a good job" Ibid., pp. 216–217.

203 **"You don't mind, do you? . . . I must take out my poor Zelda"** Ibid., p. 225.

204 **"I cannot live in the ghost town which Zelda has become . . . happy as I shall never be again"** Scott to Dr. Robert S. Carroll, April 19, 1938, Milford, p. 319.

204 **"I wish we were astride the tops of New York taxis"** Zelda to Scott, undated, Ibid., p. 315.

205 **six thousand dollars a year plus a fifty-dollar-per-month allowance** Ibid., p. 318.

205 **"When you come out you are of course free"** PUL. This is from an undated handwritten draft of a letter to Zelda.

206 **Ernest had a good look and told Scott he was absolutely normal** Ernest Hemingway's discussion of the size of Scott's genitals is the subject of his posthumous essay "A Matter of Measurement," in *A Moveable Feast*, Macmillan Publishing Company, 1964, p. 190.

206 **"I think the pull of an afflicted person . . . somewhat paralyzing"** Scott to Scottie, March 14, 1940, *Letters*, p. 65.

206 **"Your mother was better . . . years of unhappiness"** Scott to Scottie, February 1938, Ibid., p. 22.

207 **the tension of seeing Zelda exploded into a three-day drunk** Scott made reference to this binge in a March 4, 1938, letter to Max Perkins: "My little binge lasted only three days, and I haven't had a drop since. There was one other in September, likewise three days. [Scott means the Chicago escapade, though the binge lasted at least a week and it was in fact in October.] Isn't it awful that we reformed alcoholics have to preface everything by explaining exactly how we stand on that question?" Ibid., pp. 275–276.

Chapter 10: Three Comrades

208 **"People don't seem to realize"** Scott to H. L. Mencken, May 4, 1925, *Letters*, p. 481.

209 **"What are you wearing? . . . dear, dear Sheilah"** *Beloved*, pp. 220–221.

209 **"the dancingest poem"** *College*, p. 134.

210 **"Sheilo. . . I'll slug you!"** *Beloved*, p. 220.

210 **"When Vanity Kissed Vanity"** The deceptive dedication of this poem is described in *Fool for Love*, p. 53.

211 **"Oh, well, we have never heard of her in England"** *Beloved*, p. 218.

211 **"The hell with you!"** *Allah,* p. 102.

211 **"Sit back. Let them come to you"** *Beloved,* p. 218.

212 **"George S. Kaufman bores me"** Ibid., p. 219.

212 **"You two always look as though you had a secret"** Ibid.

212 **"I'm told F. Scott Fitzgerald is in Hollywood"** Ibid., p. 217.

212 **"That young man must be mad"** *Far Side,* p. 133.

213 *"If only I could walk into your eyes"* *Beloved,* p. 220.

213 **"Why do you want to go to New York, Sheilah?. . . There's no need for you to go to New York"** Ibid., pp. 221, 222.

215 **three teaspoons of chloral and two Nembutals** These figures come from *Grandeur,* p. 426.

215 **"[Scott] has built up such immunity"** *Allah,* p. 168.

215 **"Sheilah, of course, was fascinated by you both"** Scott to Gerald Murphy, March 11, 1938, *Letters,* p. 428.

216 **"But he enjoyed painting"** *Real FSF,* p. 62.

216 **"could see a line of lights"** *Tycoon,* p. 20.

217 **"Dear Ted. We got off to a bad start. . . child without taste or judgment"** Scott to Ted Paramore, October 24, 1937, *Letters,* pp. 558–560.

218 **"seized the imagination of the multitude. . . forefinger against the sky fifty years before"** *Tycoon* notes, PUL.

219 DISAGREE VIOLENTLY WITH CERTAIN SCENES Telegram from Ted Paramore to Scott, January 25, 1938, PUL.

219 **"Joe thinks he's Shakespeare. . . he could rewrite anyone"** George Oppenheimer's and Edwin Knopf's remarks about Joe Mankiewicz are from Latham, p. 121.

220 **"Dear Joe: I read the third batch [of revisions]. . .** *monotonous* **smoothness"** Scott to Joe Mankiewicz, January 17, 1938, *Letters,* pp. 561–562.

220 **"scrawled Over. . . all shadows + rythm [sic] removed"** *F. Scott Fitzgerald's Work in the Film Studios,* by Alan Margolies, *The Princeton University Library Chronicle,* Volume XXXII, Winter 1971, p. 90.

220 **"This isn't writing"** Latham, p. 140.

220 **"Monkeybitch"** On December 29, 1938, Scott wrote to Max Perkins: "Baby am I glad to get out! I've hated the place ever since Monkeybitch rewrote 3 Comrades." *Fool for Love,* p. 207.

221 **"Joe. . . It takes an old hand to change keys"** *Tycoon* notes, PUL.

221 **"The Hollywood producers have not had the early advantages"** *Tycoon* notes, PUL.

222 **"You'll only antagonize him"** *Beloved,* p. 233.

222 **"Dear Joe: Well, I read the last part. . . but the true emotion is**

gone" Scott to Joe Mankiewicz, January 20, 1938, *Letters*, pp. 563–564.

222 **"When I rewrote Scott's dialogue. . . bite, color, rhythm"** Latham, pp. 123–124.

224 **"At least they've kept my beginning. . . doesn't he know what he's done?"** *Beloved*, pp. 233–234.

Chapter 11: Infidelity

226 **"I'm through. From now on I go nowhere"** Scott to Mrs. Harold Ober, July 26, 1937, *Letters*, p. 553.

227 **"This time I have the best producer in Hollywood"** Scott to Eben Finney, March 16, 1938, Ibid., p. 576.

227 **"I am writing a new Crawford picture"** Scott to Max Perkins, March 4, 1938, Ibid., p. 276.

228 **"My plan is to work about half the time at the studio"** PUL.

228 **"a Cooper–Gable type. . . very sweet and serious"** PUL.

228 **"In everyone's lives there are locked doors"** PUL.

229 **"I'm going to write. . . Write hard, Mr. Fitzgerald. Write hard"** *Beloved*, p. 214.

229 **"Don't like her smiling to herself. . . best expression is sadness"** Scott's observations on Joan Crawford are found in the "Movie" folder, PUL.

230 **"I am writing a picture called *Infidelity* for Joan Crawford"** Scott to Gerald Murphy, March 11, 1938, *Letters*, pp. 427–428.

230 **"We felt so desperately for Scott. . . really came to life on"** Latham, p. 152.

230 **"prowling beasts of prey"** From a manuscript draft of a short story, "The Last Kiss." *Tycoon* notes, PUL.

230 **"an emphasis as in a mining camp"** *Tycoon* notes, PUL.

231 **"The Big Academy Dinner"** *College*, pp. 130–131.

231 **"I was on fire for sex"** *Heat*, pp. 114.

232 **"quick relief"** *Real FSF*, p. 122.

232 **"Life was something you dominated"** *Crack-Up*, p. 69.

233 **"When will she be here?. . . key for her with a note"** The dialogue between Scott and Sheilah concerning Margaret Brainard comes from *Beloved*, pp. 222–223.

234 **"the chief of public morals"** *Real FSF*, p. 124.

235 **"You're not going to see him. . . He's my boss"** *Beloved*, p. 224.

235 **"So glad it went well. . . Thank God it is over and you're well again"** Ibid.

236 **"I am yours forever. . . I know you will be happy someday"**
These excerpts are from two undated letters, Zelda to Scott, Milford, p. 304.

237 **"I have, of course, my eternal hope"** Scott to Dr. Robert S. Carroll, March 4, 1938, Ibid., pp. 316–317.

238 **"not legitimate at all"** Ibid., p. 124.

239 **"would have amounted to a two day bat"** Scott to Dr. Robert S. Carroll, April 7, 1938, Ibid., p. 317.

239 US STOP THE SORT OF THING March 25, 1938, telegram from Scott to Sheilah, PUL.

241 ARRIVING MONDAY AT NOON April 3, 1938, telegram from Scott to Sheilah, PUL.

241 **"Sheilo!. . . wait for me—I'll be right over"** *Beloved*, p. 225.

241 **"Baby!. . . Don't tell anyone!"** Ibid., p. 226.

242 **"I think I've broken my shoulder. . . I know it Scott"** The dialogue between Scott and Sheilah and the nun at the emergency room is from Ibid., pp. 226–227.

243 **"Sheilo, when can I see you?"** Ibid., p. 229.

Chapter 12: Malibu

245 **"I will cure him"** *Beloved*, p. 228.

247 **"If Mr. Fitzgerald takes this place. . . Oh, yes, ma'am"** Ibid., p. 229.

247 **"If you think so, Sheilah"** Ibid.

248 **"I'm too busy"** Ibid., p. 234.

249 **"As a child I had a mysterious shyness"** *Real FSF*, p. 33.

250 **He refused to use a dictionary or thesaurus** *Beloved*, p. 232.

251 **"They're going to do it again. . . I'd do it, too, by God!"** Ibid., pp. 232–233.

251 **"Now, don't you think it was silly. . . a lettuce salad and oyster broth"** Ibid., p. 234.

251 **as many as thirty-five a day** The figure of thirty-five bottles of beer a day comes from *After the Good Gay Times*, by Tony Buttitta, Viking Press, New York, 1974 (hereafter *After the Good Gay Times*), p. 166.

252 **"Mama, I wanna walk on a floor covered with babies"** *College*, p. 133.

253 **"Don't ever use my cups or spoons. . . if I don't watch myself"** *Beloved*, p. 235.

253 "My God, slow down" Ibid.

254 "Well, it's not as good as Dickens" Ibid., p. 240.

254 "This land here cost twenty lives a foot. . . very slowly backward a few inches a day" *Tender,* p. 67.

255 "This is beautiful writing. . . It doesn't add up" *Real FSF,* p. 50.

255 "Votre femme est folle" *Beloved,* p. 242.

256 "She would never bend" Ibid., p. 244.

256 "Dear, is there anything the matter?. . . finish some work" Ibid., p. 245.

257 "But *everyone* knows that! You mustn't make fun of me" *Real FSF,* p. 192.

258 "You must not read more than ten pages" *College,* p. 61.

259 "We will have to make a mass pilgrimage to her graduation" Scott to Anne Ober, March 1938, *The Romantic Egoists,* p. 219.

260 "Scottie is the prettiest girl" Undated letter from Zelda to Scott, probably June 1938, Milford, p. 322.

260 "Dearest Scottie: I don't think I will be writing letters many more years" Scott to Scottie, July 7, 1938, *Letters,* pp. 32–34.

261 "station wagon tour of Europe" Scott to Dr. Robert S. Carroll, May 1938, PUL.

262 "waited until we were safely on the Atlantic" Scottie to Sheilah, summer 1938, *Beloved,* p. 247.

263 "Now, Scott, you stop picking on her" Ibid., p. 249.

263 "Scottie, you must have a plan" Ibid.

264 "Daddy was making fun of Errol" *Real FSF,* p. 72.

265 "Adultery, sometimes necessary plot material" Latham, p. 153.

266 "We have reached a censorship barrier" Scott to Scottie, spring 1938, *Letters,* p. 29.

267 "Aren't you kids thirsty?" Ibid., p. 254.

268 "What's the matter. . . I can't understand it" Ibid. Charlie Warren eventually had his own strange revenge for Scott's odd joke. Years later the young writer grew up to become the producer of television's most successful show, *Gunsmoke,* and in his old age told a great number of lies about Scott Fitzgerald to confuse biographers. One of the lies Charlie Warren told was that he had lived at the Malibu beach house throughout the summer of 1938 with Scott and Sheilah and Ernest Hemingway, whom he said was there secretly, hiding from ex-wives and Hollywood producers. According to Warren's account, Fitzgerald and Hemingway often read their work to him to get his

advice; Hemingway, he said, tried out on him his famous sleeping-bag scene from *For Whom the Bell Tolls*. It was a preposterous and self-serving fantasy, but at least one biographer accepted it as fact.

269   **"Listen, Nunnally, get out of Hollywood... I didn't know Scott was a Methodist... You'll die of pneumonia!"** The dialogue and account of Scott's drunken argument with Nunnally Johnson is taken from *Beloved*, pp. 255–256, and from a later interview with Nunnally Johnson, Latham, pp. 172–173.

Chapter 13: Belly Acres

272   **"Sometimes I wish I had gone along"** Scott to Scottie, November 4, 1939, *Letters*, p. 63.

274   **"How can I tell anyone I live in 'Belly Acres'?"** *Beloved*, p. 266.

274   **"And all those little pickets... We've got romance in the house"** Ibid., p. 267.

275   **"Every-body-quiet!"** Ibid., p. 310.

276   **"I have two scoring plays"** *Afternoon of an Author*, p. 128.

276   **he would use the play under one condition** *College*, p. 66.

277   **"Who wrote it?... Keats"** Ibid., p. 71.

277   **a prostitute who was working the Grove Park Inn** The incident of Scott reciting Keats to a prostitute in 1935 is recounted in *After the Good Gay Times*, p. 203.

277   **"Will you tell me what to read?"** *Beloved*, p. 261.

278   **"[Poetry] isn't something easy to get started on by yourself"** Scott to Scottie, August 3, 1940, *Letters*, p. 88.

279   **"How to learn from a Frenchman"** *Beloved*, p. 262.

279   **"He dazzled me"** Ibid., p. 258.

279   **"I'm student one in your college"** Ibid., p. 263.

279   **"We must first create a facade"** Ibid., p. 262.

280   **"How I Would Grade My Knowledge at 40"** *Tycoon* notes, PUL.

280   **one of his English teachers, Gerald Gerould** *Fool for Love*, p. 39.

281   **"an uncanny knack"** From the essay, "Princeton," *Afternoon of an Author*, p. 75.

281   **"The schools are neglecting"** *Beloved*, p. 262.

282   **"A Greek Cup They Dug Up"** *College*, pp. 101–102.

282   **"For S.G."** PUL.

282   **"Helene, je t'aime. Pierre"** *College*, p. 132.

282 **"They do this at M.G.M."** Ibid., p. 119.

283 **Lest We Forget** *Beloved*, pp. 312–314.

285 **"Each of the seven parts"** *College*, p. 63.

285 **"The Book of Lillith"** *Real FSF*, p. 18.

287 **"at charades, they always ask"** *College*, p. 132.

287 **"Sing a song for Sheilah's supper"** PUL.

288 **"Hunt's—run the gamut... proclivity for morphine"** *Tycoon* notes, PUL.

289 **"She is a member of a group... They own the earth"** Latham, p. 182.

289 **"I am intensely busy... future members of the Shriners and plain bums"** Scott to Scottie, fall 1938, *Letters*, p. 39.

290 **"I approach [*Madame Curie*] with honest reverence"** Memo dated November 7, 1938, in MGM archives. Latham, p. 203.

290 **"Bernie Hyman like Zero"** *Tycoon* notes, PUL.

290 **"I disagreed with everybody... Assistant Czar!"** Scott to his daughter, winter 1939, *Letters*, pp. 48–49.

290 **"Baby am I glad to get out!"** Scott to Max Perkins, December 29, 1938, *Fool for Love*, p. 207.

290 **He was entirely free of his debts to Max Perkins** The description of Scott's finances at this time vary slightly from biographer to biographer. Scott Donaldson in *Fool for Love* claims that Scott had trouble finding money to pay his daughter's tuition at Vassar in the fall of 1938, and unsuccessfully tried to borrow money from his brother-in-law, Newman Smith. If this is true, it is unclear how Fitzgerald finally managed the tuition. Whatever figures one accepts, it is certain that after a year and a half in Hollywood, Scott had only just managed to climb partway out of his debtor's hole and his money situation was tight as ever.

291 **"began to have that harassed and aghast feeling"** *The Pat Hobby Stories*, by F. Scott Fitzgerald, Collier Books, Macmillian Publishing Co., New York, 1962 (hereafter *Pat Hobby*), p. 151.

291 **"I read it—I mean really read it"** Scott to Scottie, winter 1939, *Letters*, pp. 49–50.

291 **"do you know in that *Gone With the Wind* job"** Scott to Max Perkins, February 25, 1939, Ibid., p. 284.

292 **"How do you bustle quaintly... They think Margaret Mitchell is Shakespeare"** *Real FSF*, p. 152.

292 **"Miss O'Hara... work it out on paper"** The dialogue between Scott and Sheilah on the staircase is from *Beloved*, p. 268.

293 **"I just couldn't make the grade as a hack"** *Grandeur*, p. 450.

Chapter 14: The Professor Goes to College

294 **"My whole theory of writing"** Scott to the Booksellers' Convention, April 1920, *Letters*, p. 459.

296 **"It's lousy... Scott Fitzgerald"** Keynote address of Budd Schulberg at the F. Scott Fitzgerald Conference, Hofstra University, September 24, 1992 (hereafter Schulberg, Conference).

296 **"My God, isn't Scott Fitzgerald dead... next office reading your script"** "Old Scott: The Mask, The Myth and the Man," by Budd Schulberg, *Esquire*, January 1961, p. 97 (hereafter, "Old Scott").

296 **"I don't think it's very good either."** Schulberg, Conference.

297 **"Scott was flattered and stimulated"** Ibid., p. 97.

297 **"I didn't think anyone your age read [my] books"** Schulberg, Conference.

298 **"Today we *have* to work on the story"** Author interview with Budd Schulberg, April 16, 1993, at Westhampton, New York (hereafter Author Interview, B.S.).

298 **"She is a freshman at Vassar"** Latham, p. 222.

298 **"My T.B.'s flared up"** *Beloved*, p. 269.

299 **"Walter, I really don't think that's necessary... Scott, I insist on it"** Schulberg, Conference.

301 **"So nice to see you... sit with Sheilah"** Author Interview, B.S.

302 **"Pal you shouldn't have left me pal"** Schulberg, Conference.

303 **"*Sieg Heil!*... I should go and apologize"** Author Interview, B.S.

303 **"How was the trip?... son of a bitch"** Author Interview, B.S.

304 **"She's a bitch... I was joking"** *The Rest of the Story*, by Sheilah Graham, Coward-McCann, Inc., New York, 1964 (hereafter *Rest of Story*), p. 284.

305 **"Budd, tell me the truth... there'll be no end to it"** Schulberg, Conference.

306 **"Where's the first set-up?"** Author Interview, B.S.

306 **"Now there's a man—that Robinson"** *Tycoon*, p. 24.

308 **"I'm going to Zelda... so damn sure of yourself"** "Old Scott."

308 **"out into the Carnival night"** "Old Scott."

308 **"You know I used to have a beautiful talent, baby"** "Old Scott."

308 **"Okay, we're ready, goddammit"** Schulberg, Conference.

309 **"He's really a wreck, isn't he?"** Author Interview, B.S.

309 **"You know, I'd love to be a professor... He knows more than any of you will ever know"** Both Scott's comment and the camera-

man's defense are from *Scott Fitzgerald,* by Andrew Turnbull, Charles Scribner's Sons, New York, 1962 (hereafter Turnbull), pp. 295–296.

310 **"Dartmouth green"** Author Interview, B.S.

311 **"I don't know what the next train is"** Schulberg, Conference.

311 **"Well, Budd, I know where I can get in"** Schulberg, Conference.

311 **"a mild to moderate upper respiratory infection"** *Grandeur,* p. 455.

311 **"I've got bad news. . . I should never have given him that champagne"** *Beloved,* p. 270.

312 **"all seem a little bit overnervous"** Scott to Robert Garis (a dejected magazine writer who had written Fitzgerald for advice), February 22, 1938, *Letters,* p. 568.

312 **"Anything Dr. Hoffmann has to say about me. . . and then go on from there"** The dialogue between Scott, Sheilah, and Dr. Richard Hoffmann is from *Beloved,* pp. 273–274.

Chapter 15: Blue Gin

314 **"When drunk I make them all pay"** Scott to Ernest Hemingway, September 9, 1929, *Letters,* p. 306.

314 **"I have come to feel somewhat neglected"** Scott to Max Perkins, December 24, 1938, Ibid., pp. 280–282.

315 **"I have asked a lot of my emotions"** *Grandeur,* p. 457.

316 **"Columbia: Story for Edward G. Robinson"** PUL.

316 **"I expect to dip in and out of the pictures"** Scott to Scottie, winter 1939, *Letters,* p. 48.

316 **"There's always some lousy condition"** *Tycoon,* p. 105.

316 **"Don't ever tell me what the sky is like"** *Real FSF,* p. 145.

317 **"The Story of an Inebriated Gentleman"** *College,* p. 67.

318 **"Which is the real you?"** *Real FSF,* p. 11.

318 **"I was never a joiner"** Ibid., p. 113.

318 **"I can only think of Lincoln's remark"** Milford, p. 272.

319 **"What's that to you?. . . through for good—then what will you do?"** *Beloved,* p. 276.

321 **"Funny, this gin is blue"** Ibid., p. 277.

322 **"I can't move my arms. . . The Good Lord tapped you on the shoulder, Scott. Let it be a warning to you"** Ibid., pp. 279–280.

323 **"Since I stopped picture work"** Scott to Scottie, July 1939, *Letters,* p. 60.

324 **"a smooth-faced bitch person"** *Fool for Love,* p. 90.

324 **a mysterious "liver ailment"** The 1933 suicide of Zelda's brother Anthony is detailed in Milford, p. 280.

325 **"Well, I don't know that Zelda is 'cured'"** undated note, PUL.

325 **"the mental laziness of the calculating girl. . . she could probably have chewed sticks"** undated note, PUL.

325 **"the Montgomery point of view"** Milford, p. 320.

326 **"Havannah is probably a substantial sort of place"** Zelda to Scott, undated, probably the end of January 1939, Ibid., p. 327.

327 **"I'm really going to sober up, Sheilo. . . I didn't pull myself out of the gutter to waste my life on a drunk like you!"** I have reconstructed the dialogue between Scott and Sheilah from the time of his telephone call to the fight over the gun from two sources: *Beloved*, pp. 280–281, and *College*, pp. 68–69.

330 **"He left for the East this morning"** *College*, p. 69.

332 **"I hated Italians once"** *After the Good Gay Times*, p. 5.

332 **"You sons of bitches"** *College*, p. 70.

333 **"It seems useless to wait any more"** Zelda to Scott, undated, Milford, pp. 327–328.

335 **"You mean he doesn't want to talk to me?. . . That gun was loaded"** The dialogue between Scott and Sheilah is from *Beloved*, pp. 282–283.

Chapter 16: Hemorrhages and Hopes

337 **"I only ask this of you"** Scott to Zelda, October 6, 1939, *Letters*, p. 110.

338 **"Dear Max"** Scott to Max Perkins, May 22, 1939, Ibid., p. 285.

339 **"I want to put your name down, Miss Kroll"** *Beloved*, p. 278.

340 **though a basic error of communication had been made** Author interview with Frances Kroll Ring, December 8, 1992 (hereafter Author Interview, F.K.R.).

341 **"He was totally lacking in energy"** *Against the Current*, by Frances Kroll Ring, Donald S. Ellis, Publisher, Creative Arts Book Co., Berkeley, 1985 (hereafter *Against the Current*), p. 32.

341 **"Dearest Zelda: Excuse this being typewritten"** Scott to Zelda, May 6, 1939, *Letters*, p. 105.

342 **"She arrived late one afternoon"** *Against the Current*, pp. 38–39.

343 TRY TO MAKE DENTIST APPOINTMENT The two telegrams are from *Against the Current*, p. 76.

344 **"May I help you?"** Ibid., p. 43.

345 **"Sickness and no money are a wretched combination"** Scott to Zelda, August 1939, *Letters*, p. 107.

345 **"Stray ideas as sending my daughter"** Scott to Max Perkins, October 16, 1936, Ibid. p. 269.

345 **"Have paid Peck & Peck"** Scott to Scottie, February 19, 1940, Ibid., p. 64.

346 **"I was short of money when your telegram came"** Harold Ober to Scott, June 21, 1939, PUL.

346 **"I have been and still am somewhat shocked"** Scott to Harold Ober, August 2, 1939, *Letters*, pp. 405–407.

347 HAVE BEEN WRITING IN BED Telegram from Scott to Max Perkins, probably July 3, 1939, *Grandeur*, p. 458.

348 STILL FLABBERGASTED AT YOUR ABRUPT CHANGE Telegram from Scott to Harold Ober, July 13, 1939, Ibid.

349 **"But Hollywood—why?"** Scott to Scottie, May 6, 1939, *Letters*, p. 56.

349 **"I am of course not drinking. . . a mockery of a home"** Scott to Scottie, July 1939, Ibid., pp. 57–58.

349 **"Perhaps I was unwise"** Scott to Zelda, August 4, 1939, Ibid. p. 108.

350 **"in the speakeasy era that followed"** *Grandeur*, p. 460.

350 **"I wish I could say the same about a recent article"** Scott to Scottie, July 1939, *Letters*, p. 59.

351 **"some sort of Hollywood starlet"** Author Interview, F.K.R.

351 **"I liked that"** *Real FSF*, p. 84.

352 **"It's because I want you to be different"** Ibid., p. 85.

352 **"I forgot to tell you that in the rain"** Scott to Scottie, April 11, 1940, *Letters*, p. 69.

352 **"Scottie is very pleasant"** Scott to Zelda, August 18, 1939, Ibid., p. 109.

353 **$360 from Gerald Murphy** These figures are from *Grandeur*, p. 470.

353 **"liked Sam Goldwyn"** PUL.

354 **"The general unacceptability of the material"** Joseph I. Breen to Samuel Goldwyn, September 6, 1939, PUL.

354 **"Dear Scott, They keep nagging me downstairs"** Arnold Gingrich to Scott, February 1, 1939, PUL.

354 **"Here's another story about Pat Hobby"** Scott to Arnold Gingrich, September 21, 1939, *Pat Hobby*, p. xi.

356 **"That's terribly exciting. . . you lose the freshness"** *Beloved*, p. 286.

356 **"Look! I have begun to write"** Scott to Scottie, October 31, 1939, *Letters*, p. 61.

356 **"Stahr is overworked and deathly tired. . . doesn't fit in with the grandeur Stahr demands of life"** *Tycoon*, pp. 139–140.

357 **Jews often named their sons after American presidents** Author Interview, F.K.R.

358 **"You don't believe this. . . I can't let you do a lecture like this"** *Beloved*, p. 286.

359 **"You can give them the gossip"** *College*, p. 155.

359 **"Stop that!. . . they want to see your face: look up now and then"** *Beloved*, p. 288.

360 **"*Gone with the Wind* had three directors. . . Hollywood's great problem"** The four excerpts from Sheilah's lecture, ascribed to Sheilah but in fact written by Scott, are from *College*, pp. 156–178.

362 **"Yes?. . . Thank you, Miss Graham"** *Beloved*, p. 288.

362 **"Lily Gillam, also known as Sheilah Graham"** The original of this October 27, 1939 will is at PUL.

362 **"interviewed several kittens"** *Rest of Story*, p. 216.

362 **"What is Loretta Young like?. . . Oh, my God!"** *Beloved*, p. 291.

363 KENNY WASHINGTON RUNNING WELL . . . VERY ANXIOUS FOR YOUR RETURN LOVE SCOTT The telegrams from Scott to Sheilah in November 1939, PUL.

364 FIRST SIX THOUSAND [WORDS] PRETTY CRYPTIC *Grandeur*, p. 470.

364 **she was afraid he might have a stroke** *Against the Current*, p. 42.

365 A BEAUTIFUL START *Grandeur*, p. 470.

365 **"Sheilah Graham got $200 for a one-night stand. . . NOT CRICKET"** *Beloved*, p. 292.

366 **"That's the most shocking thing. . . I want you to be my second"** The dialogue between Scott and Sheilah and John O'Hara is from *Beloved*, p. 293.

367 **"If you insist on going. . . doesn't get into fights, but he's a gentleman"** The telephone conversation between Scott and John O'Hara was remembered by O'Hara in *Grandeur*, p. 480.

367 **"They don't want anything by F. Scott Fitzgerald"** *Beloved*, p. 294.

Chapter 17: The Silver-Fox

368 **"[He] despised his own personality"** *Paradise*, p. 261.

369 **"My destiny is probably not worth watching over"** Scott to H. N. Swanson, November 29, 1939, PUL.

369 **He confided to Frances that Sheilah was "part Jewish"**
Author Interview, F.K.R.

369 **"Hollywood is a Jewish holiday"** *Tycoon* notes, *PUL.*

370 **"let the fish drink itself into oblivion"** *Against the Current*, p. 70.

370 **"out of generosity"** Author Interview, F.K.R. Fitzgerald told
Frances he had given Sheilah five thousand dollars though the actual
figure was two thousand dollars; after Fitzgerald's death, Scottie came
across a check stub for this amount made out to Sheilah in her father's
papers. When she asked Sheilah what it was for, Sheilah replied that "it
was a private matter."

370 **"like an exiled prince. . . Scottie in such a situation"** *Against*
the Current, p. 71.

371 **"Trained nurses on duty"** PUL.

371 **"part Indian"** *Against the Current*, p. 49.

372 **"Scott was fine until Sheilah came to visit"** Ibid., p. 45.

372 **"Meet my friends. . . That's a joke"** The dialogue with the two
tramps, Jean Steffen, through Scott and Sheilah's fight, is from *Beloved*,
pp. 295–299, and *College*, p. 143.

377 **"Get out of town, Lily Shiel. . . You'll be dead in twenty-four**
hours!" Scott's threats to Sheilah are from *Beloved*, p. 299.

377 SHEILAH GRAHAM TODAY BANNED Telegram from Scott to John
Wheeler, *Beloved*, p. 300.

378 **"We've found that a police visit. . . He'd just be falling asleep**
about that time" Ibid., p. 300.

378 **He tried to commit suicide with an overdose of sleeping pills**
College, p. 143.

378 **"Dear Sheilah, I went berserk in your presence"** Scott to
Sheilah, November 1939, PUL.

380 **"he liked women"** *Fool for Love*, p. 59.

382 **"That man!"** *Beloved*, p. 302.

382 **"Dear Miss Graham: Mr. Fitzgerald is himself again"** PUL.

383 **"When I came to myself last Tuesday"** PUL.

384 I SENT YOU THAT WIRE *Beloved*, p. 306.

384 **"It's amazing how well read you are"** Ibid.

385 **"The only way to save Scott is to get him to a hospital"** PUL.

385 **"Scott, this is *not* Princeton"** Turnbull, p. 161.

385 **"They're there, Mr. Fitzgerald. . . I've got her!"** *Beloved*, p. 304.

Chapter 18: The Last Novelist

388 **"Like all those who habitually and instinctively lie"** From
"Absolution," *The Short Stories of F. Scott Fitzgerald*, edited by Matthew

J. Bruccoli, Charles Scribner's Sons, New York, 1989 (hereafter Bruccoli, *Stories*), p. 263.

389   **"I'd very much like to see you, Sheilo"** *Beloved*, p. 307.

390   **"the fearful forties"** PUL.

390   **"Zelda and I drank with them"** *Beloved*, p. 308.

390   **"I found that with a few drinks I got expansive"** From "A New Leaf," Bruccoli, *Stories*, p. 637.

390   **"I feel that I am responsible for what happened to her. . . Don't just take my words, Sheilah. Test me"** *Beloved*, pp. 308–309.

391   **"There are no second acts in American lives"** *Tycoon*, p. 163.

392   **"Never mind, most college graduates"** *College*, p. 23.

393   **"I want to give an all-fireworks illumination"** PUL. Edmund Wilson, who edited the published version of *The Last Tycoon*, left out the names of the "railroad kings" and L. B. Mayer; I have restored the paragraph from the original manuscript.

393   **"The sentimental person"** *Paradise*, p. 229.

394   **"Rewrite from mood"** PUL.

394   **"Where will the warmth come from in this?"** *Tycoon*, p. 151.

395   **"When I'm with you, I don't breathe quite right"** Ibid., p. 74.

395   **"I was going to write my memoirs once"** Ibid., p. 3.

396   **"making herself inferior"** *Real FSF*, p. 182.

396   **"Don't be a mother"** *Tycoon*, p. 90.

397   **"Stahr. . . was due to die very soon now"** Ibid., p. 108.

397   **"All good writing is swimming under water"** Scott to Scottie, undated fragment, *Letters*, p. 101.

397   **"my cough has become a public nuisance"** Scott to Scottie, July 19, 1940, Ibid., p. 86.

397   **"aches around the elbow and shoulder"** Scott to Dr. Clarence Nelson, February 7, 1940, Ibid., p. 598.

397   **an unusual stiffness in his arms** *Against the Current*, p. 89.

397   **"At the moment I am hoping for a job at Republic Studios"** Scott to Zelda, February 6, 1940, *Letters*, p. 112.

398   **"Nothing has developed here"** Scott to Zelda, March 19, 1940, Ibid., p. 113.

398   **"I go according to the fever"** Scott to Zelda, May 4, 1940, Ibid., pp. 115–116.

399   **"had built up all her fear of life into one wall"** *Stories*, p. 407.

400   **"I go to cinema work tomorrow"** Scott to Scottie, April 11, 1940, *Letters*, p. 68.

401   **what a delight it was to make a producer cry** *Against the Current*, p. 94.

401   **"I want what happens in this picture to be felt"** Scott to Garson Kanin, September 23, 1940, Latham, p. 256.

401   **"as a kindly pale . . . man"** Ibid.

403   **"Dear Syd and Laura: This is a love missive"** Scott to Sid and Laura Perelman, May 13, 1940, PUL.

403   **"The book, though it puts Gogol's *The Lower Depth*"** Scott to S. J. Perelman, June 7, 1939, *Letters*, pp. 583–584.

404   **"The book about Hollywood still has to be written"** *Real FSF,* p. 161.

404   **"Sid Perelman is effete"** PUL.

405   **"How dare she belittle him!"** *Real FSF,* p. 205.

405   **"Nothing original"** *College,* p. 118.

405   **"Mesdames Lardner and Schulberg are kitchen fodder"** PUL.

405   **"I want to be extravagantly admired again"** Scott to John Peale Bishop, April 1925, *Letters,* p. 356.

406   **"I am the last of the novelists"** PUL.

Chapter 19: Laurel Avenue

407   **"I am not a great man"** Scott to Scottie, October 31, 1939, *Letters,* p. 62.

408   **"Has a wide repertoire"** PUL.

408   **"Dear Mrs. Neuville: I thought the other day that a large rat"** Scott to Mrs. Neuville, July 29, 1940, *Letters,* pp. 603–604.

408   **"it is impossible to work or sleep"** Scott to Mrs. Neuville, August 12, 1940, Ibid., p. 604.

409   **"Imagine, here we are, supposedly sophisticated people"** *Real FSF,* p. 201.

411   **"Scott, you don't know the British. . . another day"** *Beloved,* p. 312.

411   **"I went to San Francisco"** Scott to Scottie, June 7, 1940, *Letters,* p. 76.

412   **Scott showed up unexpectedly at Budd Schulberg's house"** Author Interview, B.S.

412   **"But this will make you hate reading"** *College,* p. 147.

412   **"He won't learn a thing from them"** Ibid., p. 147.

412   **"5 in the first row"** PUL.

413   **"Take those flowers away! . . . I couldn't stand them there, either "** *Beloved,* p. 324.

414   **"Gary Cooper's appeal"** PUL.

414 **"I did as you asked"** *Real FSF,* p. 210.

415 **"I missed you"** Ibid., p. 211.

416 **"A young writer is tempted"** Scott to Morton Kroll, July 20, 1939, *Letters,* pp. 591–592.

416 **"poseur trying to prove his manliness"** *Against the Current,* p. 97.

417 **"a blend of the best of both sides of the Mason-Dixon line"** Ibid.

418 **he would have liked to let Sheilah in on the joke** Author Interview, F.K.R. Frances told Sheilah about Scott's secret drinking in the late 1950s while she was doing research for her book *Beloved Infidel.* Sheilah and her collaborator Gerold Frank deliberately omitted this information from her autobiography since it contradicted the clean dramatic tale they wished to spin—that Scott Fitzgerald never touched another drop of alcohol after their big fight in November 1939. Nevertheless, Frances's story lingered in her mind and Sheilah mentioned it in her 1966 account, *College of One,* on p. 145.

418 **"Mrs. Fitzgerald's history"** Dr. Robert S. Carroll's memo on Zelda's release from Highland Hospital, April 6, 1940, PUL.

418 **"She is. . . like a fish out of water"** Scottie to Scott, undated, summer 1940, Milford, p. 346.

419 **"What is your actual address?"** *Fool for Love,* p. 201.

419 **"I wish I was in print"** Scott to Max Perkins, May 20, 1940, *Letters,* p. 288.

420 **"I'm awfully tired of being Scott Fitzgerald"** Scott to Arnold Gingrich, February 7, 1940, Ibid., p. 599.

420 **"My name is Paul Elgin"** Scott to Arnold Gingrich, July 13, 1940, *Pat Hobby,* p. xix.

422 **"I expect it to sell at least a thousand copies"** Scott to Arnold Gingrich, November 27, 1940, PUL.

422 **"To Scott with affection and esteem"** *Letters,* p. 312.

422 **"It's not up to his standards"** *College,* p. 151.

422 **"tensity or the freshness"** Scott to Zelda, October 26, 1940, *Letters,* pp. 128–129.

422 **"Dear Ernest: It's a fine novel"** Scott to Ernest Hemingway, November 8, 1940, Ibid., p. 312.

423 **"Bethoven," "Menddilshun," "Litz"** Fitzgerald's misspellings are from *College,* p. 121.

423 **Sheilah decided that Dorothy Parker was a Renoir** The classification of Scott and Sheilah's friends in terms of art is from *College,* p. 142.

424 "How well has the best and worst student. . . In your cap and gown. I promise" *Beloved*, pp. 316–317.

Chapter 20: A Winter Solstice

425 "Show me a hero" *Tycoon* notes, PUL.

426 "I'm going to Schwab's for cigarettes. . . stairs are out" The dialogue between Scott and Sheilah in this section is from *Beloved*, pp. 322–323.

427 "I don't want him telling you anything he wouldn't tell me" Ibid., p. 323.

427 "How much?. . . Twenty-five percent" *Real FSF*, p. 213.

429 "Except for the stage-struck young girls" Scott to Gerald Murphy, September 14, 1940, *Letters*, pp. 429–430.

429 "If I ever get out of this mess" From an unpublished manuscript Sheilah was writing at the time of her death, "One Damn Thing After Another," msp. 176.

430 "I am trying desperately to finish my novel" Scott to Zelda, October 19, 1940, *Letters*, p. 127.

430 "I am deep in the novel" Scott to Zelda, October 23, 1940, Ibid., p. 128.

430 "The novel is hard as pulling teeth" Scott to Zelda, November 2, 1940, Ibid., p. 129.

430 "like uranium" Scott to Zelda, November 23, 1940, Ibid., p. 131.

430 "Everything is my novel now" Scott to Zelda, December 6, 1940, Ibid.

431 "The novel is about three-quarters through" Scott to Zelda, December 13, 1940, Ibid., p. 132.

432 "Scott never to know, even if book brings back millions" *Beloved*, p. 325.

433 "Dearest Scottie: There has reached you by this time, I hope, a little coat" Scott to Scottie, December, 1940, *Letters*, p. 100.

434 "It's the chapter" *Real FSF*, p. 213.

434 "a fugitive from the F. Scott Fitzgerald era. . . You see, you are an era" *College*, p. 20.

434 "Where's Frances. . . when you wake up I'm sure Frances will be here" *Real FSF*, p. 213.

435 "I've been able to fix it" Ibid., p. 214.

435 "a nice-looking man. . . a little on the order of Spencer Tracy" *Tycoon*, p. 119.

435   **"Gary Cooper came in"** Ibid., p. 124.

436   **"the strange medium of the flicks"** *Real FSF*, p. 214.

436   **"I feel awful... Scott, nobody saw it"** *Beloved*, p. 327.

436   **"Shall I get the doctor tonight?... I'm all right"** *Real FSF*, p. 214.

437   **"I don't want her to think I'm patronizing her"** *Beloved*, p. 328.

438   **"Dear Scottie: I bought this dress to go to Dallas"** Sheilah to Scottie, December 21, 1940, PUL.

439   **"just finished a novel"** *Fool for Love*, p. 38.

439   **"I want something sweet... Will a Hershey bar do?"** *Real FSF*, p. 216.

440   **"Scott—Scott... We'll take care of everything"** The dialogue in the death scene is combined from two separate sources: *Beloved*, pp. 330–332, and *Real FSF*, pp. 216–217.

Epilogue: Outside the Gate

443   **"Even Scott had left me"** *Rest of Story*, p. 69.

444   **"Poor Sheilah... No, of course not—good-by"** The telephone conversation between Scottie and Sheilah is from *Beloved*, pp. 332–333.

446   **"Please help me... Scott would hate me like this"** *Heat*, p. 151.

449   **"I suppose we had better get married"** This is straight out of my family mythology, a line my mother often repeated—and I will let it stand as the only scrap of dialogue in this book for which I can give no source other than my own memory.

450   **"The poor son-of-a-bitch!"** *Fresh Hell*, p. 299.

450   **"The death of Scott Fitzgerald recalls memories"** *In His Own Time*, p. 472.

450   **"The Great Gatsby will undoubtedly be read and studied a century hence"** Ibid., p. 479.

451   **Scott was worth a grand total of $706... 2 wooden work tables, lamp, radio** This accounting of Scott's property at the time of his death is from *College*, p. 149. In other accounts the numbers vary slightly.

451   **"S. doesn't think he would like to be buried in California"** *Grandeur*, p. 490.

452   **"It was as if nothing were being said"** Turnbull, p. 322.

453   **"F. Scott Fitzgerald came out of the Maryland Catholic tradition"** Le Vot, p. 354.

INDEX